Patricia Erens teaches film at Rosary College in River Forest, Illinois. She is the author of *The Films of Shirley MacLaine* and *Akira Kurosawa: A Guide to References and Resources*. Ms. Erens has contributed to *The Feminist Art Journal, Film Comment, Jump Cut, Quarterly Review of Film Studies, Sight and Sound, Women & Film* and other film journals. In 1978 on a government grant she spent a month in Japan lecturing on women and film.

SEXUAL STRATAGEMS

The World of Women in Film

SEXUAL STRATAGEMS

The World of Women in Film

Edited by PATRICIA ERENS

HORIZON PRESS  *New York*

To my father who loved movies and
my mother who loved books

Contents

PART TWO: THE WOMEN'S CINEMA

Illustrations

Preface

This volume brings together writings revealing both the variety of images of women as they have appeared on the screen and the contribution of women as filmmakers. The book represents the thinking of men and women in the United States and Europe. As the issues raised by the portrayal and participation of women have only recently come to the attention of film critics and audiences, most of the articles were written during the Seventies. However, the relevance of these ideas dates back to the beginnings of film.

For audiences accustomed to experiencing film chiefly as entertainment, the numerous covert social implications will doubtless be challenging. For many film students and critics accustomed to stressing the traditional aspects of "film as art," the significance of sexist ramifications will be illuminating. It is naturally difficult to learn to see anew, especially with regard to films in which conventions of romance and role-playing have become an undiscriminated part of our culture, habitually accepted by millions of men and women. Seduced by the power of films to grasp the imagination, audiences seldom question repeated sexist stereotypes. One function of this book is to lay bare some of the complex factors which determine what eventually reaches the movie and television screens. Apart from questions of artistic values, several authors shed new light on the relationship between film and society.

Another problem concerns the definition of a feminist aesthetic and how it applies to women who work within the established industry and those who prefer independent production. This question has been debated with regard to film as well as literature and art. There is still much controversy concerning the nature of feminist art. Of course, women filmmakers reflect a wide range of interests and styles, and as more and more women enter the field, the issues grow.

Should traditional standards be applied to art by women or are new criteria needed? This book is designed to provide a starting point. Whether the authors advocate radical feminism or merely serious concern, all concur in the widening importance of the situation of women in film.

Before challenging the current cinema or proposing alternatives, it is necessary to look at the images of the past. Part One, "The Male-Directed Cinema," provides this overview. The opening chapters comprise a general survey of how women have been presented on the screen, followed by several chapters on specific films which show how established male directors have projected their versions of female characters.

Part Two, "The Women's Cinema," opens with a section of chapters on the possibilities of change—an alternative cinema and the criteria necessary for such an art. The following chapters on women directors deal with their contributions to the art of the cinema. Each director was chosen for her vision as an artist as well as her unique position as a filmmaker. The final group of chapters on "Films Directed by Women" applies concepts of feminist theory and criticism to specific films. These last two sections cover women from the world-renowned documentarian Leni Riefenstahl to the young filmmakers struggling without financial support and show how the small body of work produced by women in Hollywood attests not to insufficient talent, but to the discrimination rampant within the industry.

The selections are related to the availability of the films, but in a couple of cases the importance of certain filmmakers could not be overlooked despite the fact that their films have been lost or are difficult to obtain. This book will doubtless stimulate new ideas about familiar works as well as familiarize readers with an entire new body of film, some forgotten, some undiscovered, and many directed by women. (Limitations of space make it impossible to deal at necessary length with women whose influence has shaped the film in areas other than direction: screenwriters, designers, the few producers and camerawomen.)

I wish to thank Julia Lesage, Ruby Rich and Marsha Kinder for their help in the preparation of this book, and Laura Mulvey who first introduced me to the rich history of women filmmakers. I would like also to express my gratitude to Stuart Kaminsky, Paddy Whannel and Peter Wollen who encouraged my efforts in film scholarship, although they may not always have agreed with me. Lastly, I am especially grateful for the support of my editors, Ben Raeburn and Tony Outhwaite, whose enthusiasm and advice made this book possible.

*Part One
The
Male-Directed
Cinema*

In *The Hustler* (1961), Piper Laurie's lameness symbolized female weakness.

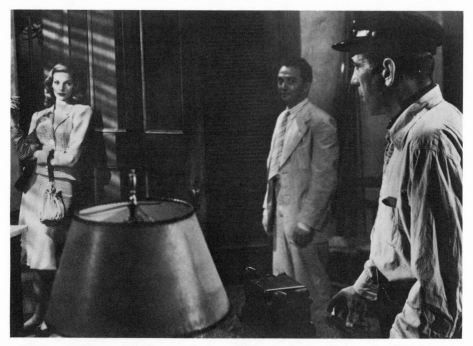

The memorable couple that signified a special relationship. Lauren Bacall and Humphrey Bogart, with Marcel Dalio, in *To Have and Have Not* (1944).

Introduction

PATRICIA ERENS

The story of women in film is primarily a history of how men have presented them. Although many women were active in developing the art of the cinema, men tended to dominate the industry as they did in most other fields. By the time movies became big business, women as filmmakers were excluded and only one or two small voices remained to represent all womankind.

The image of the screen heroine has varied over the years from idolatry to ignominy. Her fortunes have risen or fallen in relation to economic and sociological pressures; and her looks have altered according to fashion and manipulated taste. These changes have been documented in two important works: Marjorie Rosen's *Popcorn Venus: Women, Movies, and the American Dream* (1973), followed by Molly Haskell's *From Reverence to Rape: The Treatment of Women in the Movies* (1974). These books—particularly Rosen's concentration on the phenomenon of individual stars and Haskell's analysis of important directors—have stimulated much creative research. I am indebted to both for their fine contributions. Their fortunately wide availability in paperback enables me to use my space to include less accessible important material.

Marjorie Rosen's article in the present volume gives an overview of the various female stereotypes offered to film audiences. By situating specific stars and their films in a cultural context, she exposes the changing attitudes towards women through the years and the dreams which they suggest. Beginning in the 'teens with child-women like Mary Pickford and fragile virgins like Lillian Gish, Rosen moves into the Twenties with their false promise of sexual freedom embodied by the "It" girl—Clara Bow. For each era Rosen weaves together social

history and film fantasy, demonstrating how women have been di-
minished by directors and (presumably) audiences who preferred
"delectable but insubstantial" Popcorn Venuses to "true portrayals of
real women." All the ladies are there: flaming flappers, chorus cuties,
career gals, *femmes fatales*, hardboiled babes, long-legged pin-ups,
mammary goddesses, husband-chasing dames, gidgets and whores.
Rosen concludes her story in the sterile era of the Seventies, dominated by male stars and dwindling female roles—Hollywood's response to women's agitation for greater freedom.

In addition to their topical changes, the portrayals of women have
been determined by traditional formulas, the foremost being that
staple of Hollywood—the horror film. Gérard Lenne demonstrates
here how these films utilize disguised eroticism and sexuality and
how "desire becomes inseparable from fear." As victims, women
serve as sexual objects, weak and vulnerable sacrifices to a horrible
monster. As tormentors, women embody vampires, provokers,
brides of Satan. Lenne shows how these two categories satisfy
sado-masochistic fantasies of filmmakers and audiences alike.

The essays that follow on individual directors represent a cross-
section of filmmaking throughout the world and deal with the treatment of women through each director's major concerns and themes.
(In this field Joan Mellen's book *Women and Their Sexuality in the New
Film* (1973) is essential reading for anyone concerned with this subject; and is also widely available in paperback.)

In the 1930's no name was more closely identified with performing
women than Busby Berkeley. Choosing the film *Dames* for close attention, Lucy Fischer shows how Berkeley transformed females into car-
bon copy chorines and plastic abstractions. In her description of the
production numbers, Fischer reveals the ways in which the overall de-
corative design served to make literal female stereotypes which formally were only figurative. She also treats those aspects of sexuality,
fetishism and voyeurism imbedded in any Berkeley presentation.

Molly Haskell focuses on the work of Max Ophuls, especially on
his image of the romantic heroine as presented in *Madame de . . . .*
In dealing with the passionate, obsessed heroine, Haskell demonstrates how Ophuls created a truly liberated woman at odds with her
patriarchal society, how Madame de's spiritual splendor arises from
her solitary struggle, and how Ophuls' camera movement works subtly to define her character.

Jean-Luc Godard, also continually concerned with the position of
women in society, has created some highly sympathetic female protagonists. In his article on *Two or Three Things I Know About Her*,
Chuck Kleinhans reveals Godard's conscious use of anti-sexist im-

ages, shows how this film crystallizes his efforts to integrate documentary realism with fictional subjectivism, and why it is a turning point in his career—a shift from engaging dramatic characters to a confrontation with overt feminist content. The article analyzes the interrelationship between Godard's formal and stylistic innovations and his concern with prostitution on all levels. While the film focuses on one woman's life, her exploitation becomes a metaphor for the general social disorder.

Best known of contemporary European filmmakers, Ingmar Bergman has created innumerable female portraits with a few actresses, but many feminist critics have challenged his interpretations. Birgitta Steene addresses herself to this question. Recognizing Bergman's tendency to utilize female stereotypes and to objectify the role of women, she nevertheless defends his treatment of women as a subjective metaphor—an expression of his psychological and metaphysical dilemmas. Seeking to define the nature of Bergman's art, an issue often avoided by feminist critics, Steene places Bergman's women in a broad context and demonstrates how they help elucidate the major concerns of his universe from the early fifties to the present time.

In Japan, where until recently women were considered second class citizens, most directors tended to accept this attitude. Kenji Mizoguchi is an exception. Concentrating on the late works of this Oriental master, Daniel Serceau shows how the plight of women in his films reflects the rigid class structures and economic stratification of the Middle Ages, and how his dramatizations of feudal Japan has cast light on the contemporary situation of women as well. Utilizing Marxist analysis, Serceau demonstrates how prostitutes, courtesans and wives have been exploited for men's pleasure or as objects of exchange in order to maintain the economic status quo. Sympathetic to the burdens of enslavement, Mizogucni always reveals an era from the point of view of the oppressed.

The article by Anna-Marie Taylor on the Cuban film *Lucia* provides us with some insight into the place of women in the new emerging societies. The film chronicles three different periods in Cuban history as characterized by the lives and loves of an individual woman, in each case named Lucía. As such *Lucia* stands out as a rare example in film literature of a work which utilizes women as the focus of history.

This section is a revelation of our society, our values, our fantasies, our aspirations. Whether portrayed as romantic heroines, part-time prostitutes, frustrated housewives, troubled whores, feudal geishas or political activists, the image of each woman reveals much about its creator and its cultural milieu.

The essays in this section of course do not exhaust the directors who have dealt with female protagonists. In Europe Michelangelo Antonioni, Carl Dreyer and Jean Renoir have consistently built their films around the world of women. Antonioni has written, "In the first place and above all I like women. Perhaps this is because I understand them better." *La Signora Senza Camelie*, *Cronaca di un Amore*, *L'Avventura*, *The Red Desert* and *La Notte* all focused on the female sensibility. Antonioni claims to gravitate towards couples "in which the woman is more lucid than the man because the female sensibility is a much more precise filter than anyone else's and because the man, in the area of feelings, is almost always incapable of understanding reality since he tries to dominate. Male egoism assumes out of self-interest a total abstraction of woman's personality."

Like those of Antonioni, Dreyer's women often dominate his films, among them *The Passion of Joan or Arc*, *Day of Wrath*, *Ordet* and *Gertrud*, in which he develops his great themes of love and death. It is the women, through their spiritual strength and pursuit of ideal love, who break the restrictive chains and symbolize man's struggle for transcendence.

The universal humanism of a great artist like Jean Renoir has created memorable female portraits. The characters of Christine in *The Rules of the Game*, Camilla in *The Golden Coach*, Nini in *French Cancan*, as well as the women in *Boudu Saved From Drowning* and *A Day in the Country* are alive with intelligence and sensuality.

In Asia, Satyajit Ray and Susumu Hani are important for their continued interest in the representation of women. As early as 1958 Ray created a heroine of warmth and humor in *The World of Apu*. His sensitivity to the plight of women in a country not yet emerged into the twentieth century reveals itself in such films as *Devi (The Goddess)*, *Samapti (The Conclusion)*, *Mahanagar (The Big City)*, *Charulata (The Lonely Wife)* and *Distant Thunder*, which all feature heroines of self-confidence and grace.

Susumu Hani has depicted heroines with great love and respect. In a series of films which include *A Full Life*, *She and He* and *Bride of the Andes*, Hani has portrayed contemporary, middle-class women who strive for a sense of identity and worth within the confines of Japanese society. Although his heroines are not militant, their search serves as an example to millions of Oriental women not yet fully conscious of their individuality.

In Hollywood certain directors have of course devoted their career to depicting women. George Cukor, for example, has portrayed all aspects of the female world. Directing such actresses as Katharine Hepburn, Judy Holliday, Greta Garbo, and others, he has treated women's lives in *Dinner at Eight, Little Women, Camille, Holiday, The Women, The Philadelphia Story, A Life of Her Own, Adam's Rib, Pat and Mike, A Star is Born, Les Girls* and *The Chapman Report*.

In contrast, Josef von Sternberg monopolized the talents of one woman, Marlene Dietrich, to create films which explore his own obsessions and the unique aspects of Dietrich's personality.

The list of directors who have ventured into the woman's universe is of course far longer. We need to look at their works anew and reconsider their representation of women; close analysis of action films, thrillers, and comedies will yield up many unexpected insights. The following essays provide a starting point by demonstrating various approaches for clarifying the treatment of women in film.

The image of the woman is merely the trace of the exclusion of Woman. Marlene Dietrich in *Morocco* (1930).

Katharine Hepburn in a screen version of Giraudoux's *The Madwoman of Chaillot* (1968).

Bibi Andersson as Sara, the "girl of summer," and Gunnel Lindblom as Charlotta in Bergman's *Wild Strawberries* (1959).

Following the liberalized production code, Warner Brothers released *Sex and the Single Girl* (1965) with Mel Ferrer and Natalie Wood.

I.
IMAGES
AND
DISTORTIONS

Popcorn Venus or How the Movies Have Made Women Smaller Than Life

MARJORIE ROSEN

Movies have always been a form of popular culture that altered the way women looked at the world and reflected how men intended to keep it. Money, entertainment, and morality were inextricably intertwined, yet often they worked at cross-purposes, creating a Cinema Woman who has been a Popcorn Venus, a delectable but insubstantial hybrid of cultural distortions.

First came Edison's Kinetoscope, on April 23, 1896, and among his images was a prophetic one of a girl performing a hula. Within 10 years, five-minute movies had become the great escape, and sometimes even the bridge between life and death. Witness the following:

MOVED BY MOVING PICTURES
(special to *Variety*)

> Denver, Colorado; February 22, 1906: It developed at the inquest on the
> body of the woman who committed suicide on the stage of the Crystal

Theater Monday that she was moved to the act by a motion picture subject which showed the suicide of a criminal at its climax. The woman had
been in a bad mental state for some time, and was taken to the theater in
the hope that the entertainment would cheer her up. Instead, the
showing of the picture brought on acute suicidal mania and she stepped
to the stage and shot herself.

If movies at this primitive stage could have such an effect, think of the
potent fantasies that would be given shape by strong plots, sophisticated techniques and hard-sell ideas and images, images which at
first would preserve man's cherished girl-child.

Enter Mary Pickford. With her, the film industry would develop
its first real star. Known as *The Girl with the Curl*, she couldn't have
happened at a better time to stultify the growth of women's self-
image. It's no coincidence that her screen credits read like a child's
garden of verses: *In the Sultan's Garden, Little Red Riding Hood, The Little Princess.* By 1917 she made $350,000 a year; her star was still rising.

Only her age was diminishing—on screen. Mary made *Rebecca of
Sunnybrook Farm* (1917) when she was 24, *Pollyanna* at age 26, *Little
Lord Fauntleroy* at 28; she played 12-year-old Annie Rooney at 32.
Even into the Roaring Twenties, audiences clamored for her feisty
girl-children and innocent waifs. For two decades she and the public
played on each other's fears and fantasies. But her myth was an insult. In abhorring age and repressing sexuality she had created a freak
who denied—in fact made repugnant—all womanhood.

If Mary Pickford was the Eternal Child of Victorian fantasies, D.
W. Griffith was the embodiment of the male conscience that idealized
her. Griffith not only surrounded himself with nubile teenage actresses (Lillian Gish, Pickford, Blanche Sweet, Mae Marsh), but at the age
of 61 realized his fantasy by marrying Evelyn Baldwin, a woman 35
years his junior whom he'd known since she was 13. His movies continually focused on females as love objects, females as children who
had no identities other than sexual, yet who were rarely allowed to
fulfill their sexuality without negative consequences. In *The Birth of a
Nation*, the coming of age of the new medium, Lillian Gish is rescued
from near-rape, but not before the audience is on the edge of its seat
rooting for the safety of her hymen. In *Broken Blossoms* (1919) a
Chinese lusts after a 12-year-old girl, and because he hasn't the courage to act out his desires, Griffith deceptively assures us: "his love
remains a pure and holy thing—even his worst foes say this." If
Griffith's incipient nymphophilia was in tune with the nation's
Victorian conscience, it drastically clashed with the approaching
twenties' morality. The director was to falter, then fade into oblivion
as sex took a different, more nonchalant turn on the silver screen.

The 19th Amendment, ratified in January, 1919, finally granted women the right to vote. The number of workingwomen had virtually doubled since the turn of the century so that women represented more than one-fifth of the total working population. For the first time the flapper had money of her own. She could choose how and where to spend it. Films were reflecting her new situation, reinforcing the chic and high spirits of the time: *In Search of Sinners, Jazzmania, The Flappers, Our Dancing Daughters, Dancing Mothers, Wine of Youth.* But the cheeky flapper only got her man *if she deserved to.* Shopgirl Clara Bow snared her wealthy boss because she had IT (*It,* 1927), while Joan Crawford exploited the love of a millionaire and got her comeuppance by dying in an automobile wreck in *Sally, Irene, and Mary* (1925).

It is interesting, too, that flappers were always shopgirls and blue-collar workers on screen. Although more women than ever before were going to college in the twenties (the percentage earning Ph.D.'s was higher than it is today), the prevailing attitude toward education was summed up by Calvin Coolidge when he called women's colleges "hotbeds of radicalism." Movies glorified women who were young, beautiful, highly moral, and ready to drop job and glitter for a good man.

The most suitable genre to the needs of the industry was that of the chorine. Chorus Girl films—*Broadway Lady, Queen of the Chorus, Peacock Alley*—not only appealed to girlish fantasies, but also moralized endlessly. If a chorine "fell," she was disposed of during the final reel; but if, like the flapper, she overcame temptation, she was rewarded by a handsome hero's proposal. The sound of babies, not applause, would fill her ears and satisfy her ego.

As the decade closed, films held a tight rein on their "liberated" heroines. And in real life, too, women were forced to wonder about the contradictions of their partial freedom. Where would their education take them if men required them to stay home and have babies? What would a decade of working do for them if their take-home pay barely covered expenses, and employers refused to equalize it with male salaries for similar jobs?

Was liberation worth anything, after all?

Women became the sacrificial lambs of the Depression; but amid the collective pain of the nation's bellies they scarcely felt the knife. Mass despair was reflected in Tin Pan Alley's dreamy ironies like "Time on My Hands," or "Brother, Can You Spare a Dime?" In marathon dances, trials of endurance. By the end of 1930, with the worst of hard times yet to come, one-fifth of the 10 million working-women were jobless. Schools drafted regulations making women in-eligible to teach and firing single women who married during the term of employment. Professional women, whose ranks had doubled, tripled, quadrupled during the Jazz Age, were now fighting simply to maintain their status quo. But Hollywood expediently ignored reality.

The "talkies" created a new dynamic on the screen. Characters, now vocal, were also more real. Brittle edges fascinated.

Depression movies focused on women living by their wits. A curious conglomeration of detectives, spies, con artists, private secretaries, molls, and especially reporters constituted the new genre. Audiences saw the calm and elegant Myrna Loy, whose cool common sense graced *The Thin Man* (1934) and its five sequels; Bette Davis as stenographer in *Three on a Match*, political campaigner in *Dark Horse* (both 1932), copywriter in *Housewife* (1934), insurance probator in *Jimmy the Gent* (1934), and cub reporter in *Front Page Woman* (1935).

But the genre really belonged to Jean Arthur, whose best-remembered films, *Mr. Deeds Goes to Town* (1936) and *Mr. Smith Goes to Washington* (1939), cast her as a captivating but nosy go-getter who orders men's lives and smoke-screens her astuteness in a cloud of dizzy offhand conversation. She's a good deal freer than her flapper predecessors. But she's also meddlesome and manipulative, a warning from Hollywood of the dire consequences of womanpower.

In the name of escapism, such films were guilty of extravagant misrepresentations, exuding a sense of well-being to the nation in general and women in particular. Studios, purporting to ease the anguish of Depression reality, transformed movies into the politics of fantasy, the great black-and-white opiate of the masses. And along the way stars had become larger than life—and more memorable.

It was the era of Greta Garbo and Marlene Dietrich. Each casts a shadow as eerie as the mythological Circe. Each inscrutable. Each haunting in her embodiment of the yin/yang of opposites. Aloof, but inviting. Passionate, but impassive. Direct though elusive. Extravagantly beautiful—almost masculine.

Garbo and Dietrich shared the fame they gained as enigmatic incarnations of all that is mysterious to man—all that he wants to conquer, subjugate, destroy. Divinely untouchable, often unworldly, their allure lay in their denial of that humdrum destiny reserved for real-life woman. Rarely did they seek or want love, perhaps because it would be their ruin or demystification. For, once a man imposed himself on them, he consumed them.

But even though there was this sameness, they were distinctly different from each other.

Garbo excelled at conveying with exquisite precision the complexities of her emotions at the crushing devastation that would follow. She made love as if her partner were invisible; as if she were caught up on the crest of autoerotic intimacy. She was elusive, and at the same time all things to all men. "There is nothing in me, nothing of me; take me, take me as you desire me," she tells her lover in *As You Desire Me* (1932).

Dietrich was not so pliable. Much of what Garbo suggested, Dietrich carried to extremes. She could be more sultry, more seductive, more masculine. More warmhearted, more deadly. She remained from the first—with her cajoling Lola in *The Blue Angel* (1930)—the calculating serpent, ever aware of the men, their follies and weaknesses. Ever ready to spring. It evolved into a game: Who would subjugate whom? Who would crack the whip? Whose will would break first? In *Morocco* (1930), she and Gary Cooper at first evade each other, but finally, shoes in hand, she joins the women following the legionnaires into the desert.

If the Mysterious Woman was one thirties' opiate warding off the Depression's reality, another was the earthy blonde bombshell; Jean Harlow, Mae West, Carole Lombard, Joan Blondell, Ginger Rogers, Alice Faye, Marion Davies.

Of them, the most interesting of course were Jean Harlow and Mae West. Brash, brassy, and brittle, Harlow's voice echoed with worldliness and commonness simultaneously. This vocal equalizer humanized her. For men, the goddess proved fallible and not as aloof as her image threatened. For women, the voice made the image at once humorous, vulgar, and trashy enough, dumb enough to be touchingly human. Harlow, who originally scored as the tough, wisecracking gun moll of *Hell's Angels* (1930), *The Secret Six* (1931), and *The Public Enemy* (1931) under M-G-M's tutelage, finally graduated to the improbable roles of socialite (*Dinner at Eight*, 1933, *Saratoga*, 1937), smart secretary (*Suzy*, 1936), and star (*Bombshell*, 1933); the delectable heroine was often abused, misused, and misled by men, but never relinquished her feistiness.

West, on the other hand, swaggered from one artificial costume epic to another, writing her own scripts, and emanating her brand of vulgarity and ribald comedy. She made nine films between 1932 and 1943—enough to create a lasting legend. And enough to convulse the censors, the Hays Office, the Catholic Church, the Episcopalian Committee on Motion Pictures, and William Randolph Hearst himself, who accused her of being a "monster of lubricity."

It was not her physical appearance that elicited such vehemence from her detractors; actually West was a self-styled drag queen, boned and corseted and looking uncomfortably like a turn-of-the-century sausage, barely able to move because her skirt was too tight and heels too high. Nor were her hilarious one-liners like "I used to be Snow White, but I drifted" enough to anger them so. The more likely explanation is that she, as author and star, controlled plots and manipulated males with the deftness of a puppeteer. In *She Done Him Wrong* (1933), as in her other movies, she sets up harmless situations in which appointed admirers are directed to exalt her. At the end she tootles off with Cary Grant, not out of passion but convenience. It was for her boldness rather than for her innuendo that Mae West was punished.

Of the two bombshells, Harlow's impact was the happier. Without the West wit or studied style, Harlow was spontaneously willful, going after the money or man she wanted with commitment. Her desires mattered. West, although she had chutzpah, took nothing seriously. But the tart directness of Mae West and Jean Harlow were to go soft and saccharine as the Depression and the production of escapist movies wore on.

Hollywood, seeing a good thing with its explosive bombshells, converted sass to sugar and taught the blonde to dance. Joan Blondell's Depression Dollies in *Footlight Parade* (1933) and *Gold Diggers of 1933*. Ginger Rogers paired with Fred Astaire, a delicate hint of sex hovering in the air, made all the more intricate by his taut hardness flowering under her fleshy blonde femininity. Songstress Jeanette MacDonald, whose cloying courtships-over-high-C with Nelson Eddy earned them the titles of *The Iron Butterfly* and *The Singing Capon*. And Little Miss Alice Faye in *That Night in Rio* (1941) and later *The Gang's All Here* (1943), always blubberingly ernest and in love, with a strikingly adolescent ardor for so mature a woman.

Then on December 7, 1941, the Japanese bombed Pearl Harbor. Johnny got his gun. America mobilized. And social roles shifted with a speed that would have sent Wonder Woman into paroxysms of power pride. With the men at war, by 1943 more than 4 million women were employed in munitions work alone. An additional 15 million joined the labor force, doing such formerly "masculine" jobs as coal mining, operating machines, and firing and cleaning antiaircraft guns. At the beginning, nobody, not even the women themselves, imagined they might want to make it permanent.

Hollywood could therefore afford to be temporarily indulgent in the name of patriotism. So Rosie the Riveter, the lower-class working girl, queened it in forties movies. Women in combat and nurses on the front idealized female bravery and participation. But the most affecting and meaningful films were the simpler, perhaps overly sentimental and trite "woman's pictures" in which workers came to grips with their manless existence. Bitchiness and frivolity on the screen gave place to female strength; strength and love and support between mother and daughter, woman and woman. Ginger Rogers in *Tender Comrade* (1943) setting up house with three other women who later comfort her and her newborn after she receives a telegram of her husband's death. Greer Garson in *Mrs. Miniver* (1942) defending her bombed-out house from a wounded Nazi, joining forces with her teenage daughter-in-law Teresa Wright. Stoical Bette Davis watching her husband, then her sons, risk their lives for the underground in *Watch on the Rhine* (1943).

Since women workers had fallen into an abyss of obedience during the Depression, it is not surprising that at the beginning of the war, they unanimously expressed their intent to work only temporarily. By 1944, however, more than 85 percent had reconsidered and wanted to keep their jobs. Industry, though, had other ideas.

With 11 million veterans coming home, massive layoffs began. By 1947 more than 3 million women had resigned or been fired from their positions (more than during the Depression dip). Movies during the forties were no more reflective of the societal shift than those of the thirties. Movies, heretofore stressing female strength, now began to distort it.

A peculiar strain of suspense film preyed on alleged female doubts and infirmities. The most obvious method of undermining was physical. Deafness, and maniacs, plagued Dorothy McGuire in *The Spiral Staircase* (1945) and Jane Wyman in *Johnny Belinda* (1948). Plain deafness plagued Loretta Young in *And Now Tomorrow* (1944), and plain maniacs plagued Barbara Stanwyck in *The Two Mrs. Carrolls* (1944) and Teresa Wright in *Shadow of a Doubt* (1943). Then there was the mental undermining. Ingrid Bergman in *Gaslight* (1944), Olivia de Havilland in *The Snake Pit* (1947), Joan Fontaine in *Suspicion* (1941), and Ginger Rogers in *Lady in the Dark* (1941). When Rogers takes her private demons to a shrink, his diagnosis of the problem is: "You've had to prove you were superior to all men; you had to dominate them." "What's the answer?" she begs. "Perhaps some man who'll dominate you," replies the eminent doctor.

The female-victim genre emerged simultaneously with that of the Evil Woman. It may be no coincidence that at the same time women were acquiring economic and social power in real life. Hollywood simplistically interpreted this shift in the only terms it could understand: power, the quest for love or money.

By the time the Evil Woman genre had played itself out, and Hollywood had given us Mary Astor's Brigid in *The Maltese Falcon* (1941), Lana Turner in *The Postman Always Rings Twice* (1948), Bette Davis in *In This Our Life* (1942), the greedy duplicity and vicious rampage wrought by these women was inextricably intertwined with their allure. As Fred MacMurray says of murderer Barbara Stanwyck in *Double Indemnity* (1944): "How could I know that murder sometimes smells like honeysuckle?"

But honeysuckle wasn't the only peacetime blossom. The war had sanctified the idea of the pinup, and though the movies had concentrated on wholesome family entertainment (since the majority of the audiences were women), men plastered their barracks with inviting photos of film stars. Most popular of all were Rita Hayworth kneeling on an unmade bed and Betty Grable in a skintight swimsuit. The peaches-and-cream wholesome sexuality of these women in wartime musicals—Grable in *Song of the Island* (1942), Hayworth in *Cover Girl* (1944) and *You Were Never Lovelier* (1942)—soon took a back seat and with the return of the men, pure, isolated screen sex escalated like mercury on a hot summer day.

Accordingly, Hayworth, in a black strapless sheath, sang "Put the Blame on Mame" in *Gilda* (1946), and her overt sexuality pulled out all the stops that had been plugged since the demise of the Marlene Dietrich sultriness. Hayworth's sexuality was a very physical one, without mystery or pretense. The golden girl, the beautiful all-American hooker, reverberated in the public imagination, dispelling with her ripe pleasure the intense ephemeralism of the thirties' siren.

That same year marked the brief release of *The Outlaw*. A rather ordinary Western made in 1941 but held up by censors because of the film's obsession with Jane Russell's cleavage, it hit a new low in advertising and exploitation. "What are the two great reasons for Jane Russell's rise to stardom?" went an advertising slogan. Almost as tasteless were rulings such as that of a judge who complained that her breasts "hung over the picture like a thunderstorm spread out over a landscape."

Simultaneously, Esther Williams was dipping in and out of the water in *On an Island with You* (1948) and Jennifer Jones was arching her back and quivering her nostrils as the spitfire Pearl in *Duel in the Sun* (1947). Even Joan Crawford had left behind the strength of *Mildred Pierce* (1945) and *Daisy Kenyon* (1947) to be decked out as a cylindrical-breasted temptress in *Flamingo Road* (1949). And in moviemagazine back pages Frederick's of Hollywood was having a mailorder bonanza by advertising the pointy bosoms and clover behinds that every wistful housewife and movie-mad teenager was being told were truly "sexy." Hollywood, however, was not content to dictate exteriors alone. Johnny was home from the war. And by the fifties the industry was reaffirming male dominance and female subservience.

One of the few constants during that decade was the direction women were heading: backward. They married younger than at any previous time during this century; in 1951 one in three had found a husband by the age of 19. And movies reflected this with: *Women Trapping Men* in *Three Coins in the Fountain* (1954), *Gentlemen Prefer Blondes* (1953), *How To Marry a Millionaire* (1953), *Seven Brides for Seven Brothers* (1954); *Women Preparing for the Wedding* in *Father of the Bride* (1950), *High Society* (1955), *The Catered Affair* (1956); *Romancing Widows* in *The Magnificent Obsession* (1954), *Love Is a Many-Splendored Thing* (1955). *Woman alone* was portrayed as a desperate and needy neurotic—recall the *oeuvre* of Tennessee Williams, Katharine Hepburn's spinsters in *Summertime* (1955) and *The Rainmaker* (1956), or Bette Davis's Margo Channing in *All About Eve* (1950). Marriage was the be-all and end-all. Women's films divorced themselves from timely plots and controversial subjects and became "how-to's" on catching and keping a man. Veneer. Appearance. Sex Appeal.

Hollywood descended into mammary madness. Monroe, Mansfield, Bardot, Loren, Ekberg were all elevated to fame in the thrust of Russell's original largesse. Men ogled. And women emulated. While they were going off to colleges to find their man (because the G.I. Bill was sending more men to college than ever before), they were also allowing themselves to be molded and beautified.

But despite Hollywood's enthusiasm for the (highly profitable) Mammary Woman, the industry was still unable to shake off a depression. So, as early as 1950, Hollywood began thinking young; the movies intrepidly went to work on America's daughters.

Daddy's little girl would merge with Everyman's ideal, and precocious teenager Debbie Reynolds, clowning around in Dick Powell's oversized pajamas in *Susan Slept Here* (1954), froze the frame on the archetypal teenager of the decade. Reynolds led a gaggle of girls-next-door—Doris Day, Pier Angeli, Terry Moore, Janet Leigh, Natalie Wood. Pretty, amusing, and childish, they enjoyed marvelous popularity among fans who could relate to them as they never had to the haughty sophistication of Joan Crawford, Bette Davis, Lana Turner. Movie magazines boomed. Who could dislike Audrey Hepburn's fawnlike elegance in *Roman Holiday* (1953) and *Sabrina* (1954), or Leslie Caron's pouting Mademoiselle in *An American in Paris* (1951), her girl-women in *Gigi* (1958) and *Fanny* (1961)?

A good many fifties' notions about little girls and burgeoning sexuality were embodied on screen by Sandra Dee. While Dee presented the most passive fluttery pink-and-white-ribbons perfection, her ample mouth recalled the petulance of an adolescent Bardot. By scaling down this image of feline sexuality for the high school set, Dee wove the transition between the fifties' naiveté and the sixties' nymphet, exhibiting a provocative self-awareness, almost a fear of her own sexuality. She enjoyed a swift and sweeping success, giving new dimensions to such teenage fantasy films as *Gidget* (1959) and later *A Summer Place* (1959), in which even youthful motherhood and a hasty marriage couldn't upstage the fact of teenage eroticism, which had never been explored so directly.

And kids responded to it. *A Summer Place* grossed more than $1.9 million in its first two months in movie theaters. The heroine's pregnancy was almost immaterial, for the picture was tied up in such an attractively passionate package that nobody cared.

Change, however, was hovering at the edge of the sixties. By the close of the decade middleclass girls were *expected* to attend college. And while a good percentage were hunting for husbands, others picked up degrees and career ambitions. Also, as divorce rates skyrocketed, the first generation brought up on "happily ever after" Hollywood endings discovered that reality delivered something else.

The sixties' woman possessed a unique problem: she was single, and often self-supporting. Movies reduced her "problem" to one question: *Will she or won't she?* Love stories—starring Natalie Wood, Connie Stevens, and most obviously Doris Day—focused on this dilemma to the exclusion of most other plot or character conflicts. At the same time, offscreen, the Pill had happened. And off the American screen, so had *La Dolce Vita* (1961), the Beatles, LSD, glaumphing *Georgy Girl* (1966), glamorously amoral *Darling* (1965), and David Hemmings, romping on colored paper with two nude "birds" in *Blow-Up* (1966). Audiences traded in Doris Day for Julie Christie, and Sandra Dee for Twiggy. Teenagers were sexually mobilized.

Meanwhile back in Hollywood moviemakers were offering *Mary Poppins* (1964), *The Sound of Music* (1965), and *The Group* (1966); they seemed unwilling or unable to reflect the tapestry of the youth culture. Yet the English heroines, for all their freewheeling carryings-on, were at best unable to get a grip on their lives, only on their libidos. And a new kind of sex object was born—the amoral nymphet. Exemplified by Genevieve Waite in *Joanna* (1968), she was baby-faced, reed-slender; her emotional lineage may have been that of *Darling*, but physically her family tree revealed a bit of Hayley Mills's childish faun, a good deal more of *Baby Doll* (1956) and *Lolita* (1962). Most significant about this new gamine was the elevation to an ideal of her helplessness and little-boy body—an almost violent reaction to the breasts-and-buttocks fetishes of the Monroe period. *Joanna* is the sixties' sex symbol. Waite's heroine, as nonthreatening and pure as a nine-year-old, signified a futuristic trend: woman as androgyne.

Movieland sex used to go with romance, but as profits sagged and theater audiences dwindled, male moviemakers began to dissect the sex act itself—as men fantasize it.

And so we have *Deep Throat* (1972), with Linda Lovelace's shaved pubis and carefully guarded secret—how to control her gag reflexes while giving head. We have *The Killing of Sister George* (1968) and *X, Y, and Zee* (1972)—sensational exploitation of lesbianism (hasn't it always been an erotic turn-on for men, from the old stag-movie days?). We have, with Andy Warhol's films, *Trash* (1970), *Women in Revolt* (1972), and *Heat* (1972), contemptuous exploitation of femininity. We have women getting gang-banged, as in *Straw Dogs* (1971), and liking it.

And we have films that don't even need women at all: *Bullitt* (1968), *2001* (1969), *Patton* (1970), *The French Connection* (1971), *Dirty Harry* (1971), *Prime Cut* (1972), *Deliverance* (1972), *Papillon* (1973).

It is ironic that sixties' and seventies' women have seized on a more productive lifestyle than ever before, but the industry has turned its back on reflecting it in any constructive or analytical way. Is there any hope for intelligent portrayals of women as productive and emotional beings, as intriguing protagonists and heroic models? Have movies, since women have united to raise their own consciousness and society's, produced anything worthwhile for us?

A few do exist. Joanne Woodward's lonely and aching spinster in *Rachel, Rachel* (1968); Shirley MacLaine, nicely manipulating a happy husband and happy lover in *The Bliss of Mrs. Blossom* (1968); Jane Fonda's gritty and needy call girl Bree in *Klute* (1971); Ellen Burstyn and Cloris Leachman in *The Last Picture Show* (1971). And perhaps the most gloriously intelligent film of the past few years, *Sunday Bloody Sunday* (1971), in which Glenda Jackson emerges from an unsatisfactory affair, alone, but with her integrity intact. "I used to believe anything was better than nothing," she tells her lover. "Now I know that sometimes nothing is better."

Think, too, of the dignity black women are finally gaining on screen—Diana Ross's lovely and agonizing portrait of Billie Holiday in *Lady Sings the Blues* (1972), and Cicely Tyson's watchful, proud, and loving mother in *Sounder* (1972). With the exception of a few rare movies—*Porgy and Bess* (1959), for one—Hollywood's attitude toward blacks has historically been shamelessly racist. From the first pickaninnies dancing in the streets, their mouths full of watermelon, in Griffith's *The Birth of a Nation*, through Mae West's shuffling, yassum maids and King Vidor's fetching but disloyal and dumb temptress Nina Mae Kinney in *Hallelujah!* (1930), to Butterfly McQueen's lazy featherhead Prissy in *Gone with the Wind* (1939), black women have been herded into the most abominably simplistic and offensive molds.

But the Chicana has yet to appear on the screen. The closest Hollywood came to acknowledging her presence was in the Latin Spitfire, the exoticism of Dolores Del Rio in *Bird of Paradise* (1932),

Lupe Velez in *Cuban Love Song* (1932) and *Mexican Spitfire* (1939), and Maria Montez in *Gypsy Wildcat* (1944) and later Katy Jurado in *High Noon* (1952) and *One-Eyed Jacks* (1961). All were merely sultry sex objects, "wildcats" in need of taming.

Women filmmakers with a sense of their own history and a political perspective on the future must become integrated into the fabric of commerical moviemaking. Until then, it's up to us to vocalize loudly about what *we* want, to support it when it comes along, and to boycott those movies which disregard or do injustice to the image of woman. There's no excuse for the insubstantial Popcorn Venuses that have embodied and distorted our fantasies and shaped false realities. If movies unconsciously or consciously define and reflect us, we must *demand* substance as well as chimera.

Diana Ross's portrait of Billie Holiday in *Lady Sings the Blues* (1972) created dignity for black women on the screen.

Monster and Victim:

WOMEN IN THE HORROR FILM

GÉRARD LENNE

Translated by Elayne Donenberg and Thomas Agabiti

Woman is, in essence, a dual being. Can such an assertion be contested? If I assert that she has such duality, would I then be sanctioning, even in appearance, the sexist myth of feminine duplicity? I shall nevertheless repeat that woman is a dual being, and I shall add, moreover, that, because of this essential duality, she belongs, of her very nature, to that world of ghosts and vampires and demons and monsters and automatons and lunatics and evil geniuses that we call the realm of the fantastic. Now I must ask if this essential duality is true only for woman, or if it applies as well to all humanity. But is not the female sex in some way more *human* than the male? Can we not see the concept of the double, which is the true key to the whole genre of the fantastic, etched to perfection in woman's appearance and behavior?

To explore these questions, let us begin our search in the futuristic and apocalyptic darkness which engulfs Lang's subterranean *Metropolis.* Who is it that we meet there? Whom do we see heading up a regiment of the oppressed and, at the same time, leading the wanton orgies of the oppressors? We see woman, the same woman—Maria! The same woman in appearance, of course, because she has the same face; but whereas one Maria is a woman of flesh and blood who preaches peace and reconciliation, the other Maria is a robot without a soul who incites hatred and violence. Let us take her as a symbol: the

31

centering point of an obvious parable, the link between two disparate
worlds, the same character played by the same actress, embodying
two opposing forces.

At the risk of getting lost in commonplaces, let us make the pre-
fatory declaration that the horror film, a popular and immediate form
of the fantastic, is the chosen domain of eroticism and sexuality. Particularly was this the case in that period of time when the cinema was
forced to disguise eroticism and sexuality. Fear in such films is inseparable from sexual desire: the shriekings of an exquisite victim—
such as Fay Wray in *King Kong*—convey ecstasy as much as terror, in
the same way that convulsions and spasms, a half-open mouth, and
eyes bulging out of their sockets manifest orgasm as much as fear.

Ideally, then, if Lang's clearsightedness had been followed,
woman in the fantastic film would have continued to be both torturer
and tortured, sadist and masochist, monster and victim. This revolutionary view does not, however, take into account phallocratism, or
the rule of the phallus, which prevailed in Europe as elsewhere.
Men in general, or so it was thought, did not like to acknowledge the
sexuality of their wives and daughters, and they did not like for them
to acknowledge it either. Therefore, since films were produced in
massive quantities and were intended for a mass market, they could
not afford a value system appreciably different from that of other
works having to please a mass public which permitted no prurient
thought. Consequently, the overt value system of the fantastic film
remained substantially the same as that of confessional magazines,
soap opera, and Victorian melodrama with its neutered heroines. The
effect of this requirement was to force imaginative directors working
prior to the recent evolution to search for appropriate evasions.

THE WOMAN AS OBJECT

If it is true that the fantastic has its origin in the fairy tale, which is
itself the literary expression of the wondrous, then we must conclude
that the fantastic's structures—like fossil imprints in rock—have a
kind of timelessness. In the world of the fairy tale, woman is almost
always a princess who, no matter what happens, never participates
directly in the action. She is the object of desire, ravished by a dragon
or some other kind of monster, and she is, as well, the object of reward, since, traditionally, her father the king bestows her hand in
marriage to the one who will accomplish some specific feat that has
been announced. In brief, during all the action that takes place—
during the chases, the voyages, and the duels—she is usually not

present. She is, if I dare use an expression of Hitchcock's, the Mac-Guffin, the pretext for the adventure. She plays the same role as, for example, the uranium in *Notorious*.

In countless fantastic films of the adventure type, woman is reduced to the status of a one-dimensional companion, an "extra" in the adventure, who is used by screenwriters primarily as a device for arousing our emotions—her cries of terror, her wild flights—and as a means for leaping out of the commonplace and diving into the erotic—the excitement of her clothes torn in some fortuitous mishap, the sense of sexual release in the closing image of her head resting against the shoulder of some egotistical male brute. To verify this usage, we have only to refer again to *King Kong*, a masterpiece and model of this bastardized line. Consider how often Fay Wray, in principle the object of contention, is left abandoned in a corner for the duration of each sequence in which the giant beasts engage in battle.

It is clear, then, that, in one area of the fantastic, woman is the female counterpart of the fairy tale's princess and, logically enough, appears as a supplementary item designed to satisfy a presumed public need. However, this gratuitousness of the woman's role fades in direct proportion as the woman becomes the designated or, even better, the quintessential victim of an archetypical monster. For the monster and his misdeeds cannot be truly horrifying if the victim is not truly pathetic. She must be weak and vulnerable, yes, but she must be far more than just weak and vulnerable; for that, a child would be sufficient, as we have seen in a few unconvincing films. To become pathetic, she also must be capable of arousing desire. The victim in the fantastic is always a sexual object and the aggression of the monster takes on all the characteristics of rape. Not accidentally do we associate with the fantastic those endlessly proliferating films which deal with sexual murders, like the Jack the Ripper films. Even the traditional hairiness of the monster-aggressor—beast, ape, werewolf—reinforces the sense of the rape ritual. The symbolism is rather clear. And we could not possibly list here the myriad number of concomitant symbols of this type, of which the most "striking" is without any doubt the phallic stake plunged by the *Voyeur* into his victims' throat.

The woman-object is a human sacrificial offering, in keeping with the prototypical image of a writhing Fay Wray tied and bound on a monumental primitive altar. To a greater or lesser extent, she is the prize of a combat to the death. And she is also often the shelter from that combat—as, for example, in *The Most Dangerous Game (The Hounds of Zaroff)*, where she is ritually assigned the function of respite for the hunter. But whether as reward or palliative, this woman-object never herself participates in the action.

AGGRESSIVE SEXUALITY

The connection between sexuality and action is quite different in another important area of the fantastic. This is the area of the vampire film, where sexual desire is, not the pretext for action, but the very condition on which the action depends for its existence. And the nature of sexuality has also changed, being no longer confined to simple acts of assault against an inert woman-object but, rather, presuming a complex and interrelated series of acts, involving woman's participation in seductions, proselytism, subtle transferences, and multi-faceted relationships. Vampirism is the product of a deliberate crossbreeding between the fantastic and the erotic, the symbolic expression of which is thinly disguised, albeit less and less so as time goes by. We need only recall the trembling and quivering young women dressed in low-cut negligees who, having just flung open their bedroom window, lie stretched out on their bed, waiting expectantly! We shall not dwell on the all too obvious sexual meaning of the vampiric act—biting, penetrating, sucking. Let us say only that, because of a growing permissiveness in the cinema, the vampiric act, at one time implied and disguised, is today more and more graphically depicted. Sometimes this emphasis causes superfluous effects that can be harmful to the vampire film; I am thinking of films like Freddie Francis' *Dracula Has Risen From The Grave*. But sometimes, also, such films reveal possibilities for exploration, for the creation of new parables, following the example of Geissendorffer's *Jonathan*.

What matters for our discussion here is that in the vampire film woman herself engages in action. At first merely an object of lust and desire, she does not remain passive for very long. She enters the game and takes up the torch in her turn to transmit the vampire's pleasure to someone else, an activity which the reactionary Van Helsings of the world regard, typically enough, as a disease of epidemic proportions.

Even as vampire, though, woman has remained for a long time confined to secondary roles. Dracula's companions, whether they be his brides, mistresses, or acolytes, are still submissive servants and blind followers of their Master, who himself remains the living-dead symbol of the phallus-conqueror. I believe this situation will soon change, and it is only right that it should, for once it does, the possibilities for new subject matter will increase, and this new subject matter will open up new directions for the plot. One of these new subjects is the interaction of spiritual and physical love, with vampirism representing the experience of the latter. Already, cartain modern vampire films like *Jonathan*, where the hero's still virginal

fiancée is initiated into sex by the nocturnal Count, have explored this
subject and by this exploration have produced various kinds of conflicts new to the vampire film.

Such is the place of woman in the fantastic: indispensable, but re-
legated to the rank of a minor role. Perfect as a tearful victim, what
she does best is to faint in the arms of a gorilla, or a mummy, or a
werewolf, or a Frankensteinian creature. An exquisite and pathetic
figure endlessly shrieking either from fear or from the pain of torture,
she satisfies the sado-masochistic phantasmagoria that is part and
parcel of all fantastic films, the inferior ones as well as the masterpieces.

When woman is not being either hunted or violated, she appears
only as a spoil-sport. Just look at the unhappy girlfriends of Jekyll and
Frankenstein who, if their words had not been ignored, would have
succeeded in preventing the pursuit of all those impassioned experiments. Very rarely are the keystone characters of the fantastic, the
monsters, permitted to be female, and for obvious reasons. To take
pleasure in deforming a woman's beauty would be truly misogynous.
Yet there is one kind of female monster that is permitted. The legend
of Pygmalion mythologically authorizes the choice of woman as a
created thing, as a creature, without having to make her ugly. The
robot Maria in *Metropolis* is the perfect double of the beautiful girl who
served as her model; and the bride created by Dr. Praetorius in *The
Bride of Frankenstein* is not, like the Medusa, without a certain awesome beauty. A more problematic matter is the treatment of those
half-human, half-animal hybrid female monsters who range the
gamut anywhere from Lota the panther-woman in *Island of Lost Souls*,
who is still womanly in her savagery, to the revolting, incrusted
figure in John Gilling's *The Reptile*, who is a product of the great tradition of greasepaint pyrotechnics.

BEAUTY AS INSTIGATOR

Generally, however, there are very few monstrous and disfigured
women in the fantastic, and so much the better. Is it not reasonable
that woman, who, in life, is both mother and lover, should be represented by characters that convey the feeling of a sheltering peace?
Seldom do we encounter images similar to that of the frightening old
woman in Mario Bava's *I Tre Volti della Paura* (the "Drop of Water"
episode in *Black Sabbath*). Quite naturally, woman embodies beauty.
And it is as the embodiment of beauty that she is capable of setting a
drama in motion. The mere existence of the almost supernatural
beauty of a Ligeia, a Morella, or a Rowena in the works of Edgar Allan

Poe is sufficient to give birth to the fantastic. These creatures occupy a privileged place somewhere between death and life, dream and reality. Yet, in the fantastic, there is a kind of perverse linking of beauty as a propelling force with an inverted form of redemption. Woman has always been accorded the power to provide, by her response, relief from loathsomeness. We discover one example of this redemptive principle in the legend of the werewolf whom love alone can save. The structure belongs to the fairy tale: the accursed beast or frog or whatever changes back into a handsome prince once he has received the required expiatory kiss or declaration of love. To a degree, the saving power accorded to woman confers on her a function which no longer can be considered entirely passive. And when woman's capacity for being an active redemptive force is coupled with the inciting power of her beauty, the fantastic is born. The insane, overwhelming passions that are at the source of certain really terrifying tales are propelled specifically by a fascination with the beautiful. We can never forget the consuming love of the mummy Kharis, the Egyptian highpriest from across the centuries, a tragically impressive figure who has provided material for a continuing series of films. Memorable also is Vincent Price, who has become famous for the role of the desperate lover of the beautiful: a demented Phibes, committing crimes for his embalmed beloved Victoria, and, long before Phibes, the obsessed sculptor of *House of Wax*. The character in *House of Wax*, very close to that of the "sculptor" in *Bucket of Blood*, is first and foremost an artist. What he wants is to create an image of beauty, an image of life. But in creating this image, he destroys life itself. And therein lies the aberration, the thorn, the deviation that makes him a monster. Poe's "Oval Portrait" is one of the most poetic examples of this kind of work: to the extent that the portrait takes on life, the model for the portrait, the painter's young wife, withers and dies.

Another form of this obsession is displayed by Pierre Brasseur in *Les Yeux Sans Visage* (*Eyes Without a Face*), who sacrifices other young women in order to restore the beauty of his daughter Edith Scob. Although the daughter is the beneficiary of these monstrous operations, she is not the instigator of them. But the fact of her acquiescence is already a participation. Nonetheless, her character is both frail and vulnerable in the extreme. And it is from these two disparate aspects of her personality— her willingness to participate in murder and her vulnerability, existing side by side in her—that we can call her at once both executioner and victim. It is not far from innocence to evil, from the masochism of the tortured to the sadism of the torturer. The fact that certain recent films have tried to use this profound truth, perhaps to political ends, and that they sometimes have been justifiably criticized for it, is beside the point. The fantastic has the merit of conveying to us, without equivocation and without deleterious repercussions, the meaning of the intimate relationship of good and evil.

The process of radical metamorphosis from victim into monster can be seen in its pure state in vampirism. Less symbolically expressed transformations occur in the films of Roman Polanski, one of those directors working in the border areas of the fantastic. The two heroines of *Rosemary's Baby* and *Repulsion* serve as examples. If Rosemary is the perfect victim, defenseless and ignorant of what is happening to her, she is. Insofar as she is a woman, as indispensable to the Satanic sect which has gained control of her as the Virgin Mary is indispensable to Roman Catholic dogma. And in *Repulsion* Catherine Deneuve, although a victim in the sense that she is very ill and isolated from the outside world, becomes as well, against her will, a fiendish murderess.

Obviosuly schizophrenia has all the makings to have become a favorite theme of the fantastic, which itself is based entirely on duality and on the concept of the double. The heroine of *Sisters*, whose slaughters are as savage as those of the heroine in *Repulsion*, will transfer the guilt for them to her Siamese twin sister, exactly in the way that her prototype, Anthony Perkins in *Psycho*, transfers the guilt to his mother. The parallel is even stronger if one remembers that Perkins is disguised as a woman when he commits his murders, thus making him, in a sense, his mother's "twin." We notice that, in the fantastic, schizophrenia is readily assimilated to female behavior. This should not seem astonishing; the dual nature of woman has belonged to the fantastic from its outset. For the fantastic derives most of its thematic material from the provocative writings of the Marquis de Sade, specifically, his diptych *Justine, or the Misfortunes of Virtue* and *Juliette, or the Fortunes of Vice*, which contain everything that films will later treat in their own way. And the pivotal point upon which these two novels are hinged is precisely that of a single heroine split into two characters, the sisters Justine and Juliette, who are so similar in their difference.

WOMAN AS SUBJUGATOR

Juliette, the embodiment of vice, has had fewer emulators than her sister Justine, the embodiment of virtue. Can the explanation for Juliette's infrequent appearances be found in a wish to cater to the sexism of the mass audience? Whatever the reason, it is an incontestable fact that Juliette's all too few descendants have been developed almost entirely within one ignominious domain, the pulp paperback novel, where they cavort as overbearing and vulgar figures in black leather boots and jacket. Rare is the female character of the Juliette type, the imperious woman-subjugator, who escapes from these narrow confines. When it comes to films, woman is seldom to be found among the great psychopaths, the figureheads of the fantastic. We have had more than enough male mad scientists, but not one single female mad scientist. From your own experience, just try to imagine a movie Madame Curie suddenly revealing Frankensteinian ambitions. The great monsters are all male.

Perhaps one might be inclined to place in this category the ogress personified by Shelley Winters in *Who Slew Auntie Roo*? But that would not be accurate. Because, first of all, she is an ogress only in the imagination of a hateful little kid, whereas, in actuality, she is merely a daffy old lady who likes to give treats to children. (Notice that here again we have the concept of duality.) And secondly, the film does not intend to portray a legitimate ogress but is, instead, one of those exploitative vehicles created merely to furnish a character—or is it a caricature?—role for a middle-aged screen star, an exception that proves the rule about mass cinema finding it repugnant to make a woman ugly. In this regard, *The Exorcist*, too, is a novelty.

The evolution displayed in films like *Auntie Roo* and *The Exorcist* is of very recent vintage and has been brought about by the prevailing trend for making female versions of the great myths of the fantastic. Dracula is a case in point. Here, screenwriters have taken their inspiration from a character just as legendary as the Roumanian count, namely, the famous Hungarian countess Erszbèth Bathory, who, curiously enough and perhaps as the result of cowardice, had never previously haunted the screen; she has had to wait until the seventies to make her début. Peter Sasdy has treated her historically in *Countess Dracula*: Harry Kümel has treated her in a contemporary manner in *Blut an den Lippen* (*Daughters of Darkness/Blood on Red Lips*). The same phenomenon has occurred with regard to the Jekyll myth. Dr. Jekyll has recently been transformed into a woman, and what a woman— the fascinating Martine Beswick in Roy Ward Baker's *Dr. Jekyll and Sister Hyde*. And in *Lady Frankenstein*, a film which has been misunderstood and unjustly vilified, we see the apotheosis of the Frankensteinian myth: the Baron's daughter, a medical student, throwing herself passionately into her father's experiments and picking up where he left off by creating a handsome young man who ultimately is to become her lover.

Recent, too, is the making of female versions of another traditional character—the assistant, who is, like the women, indispensable but secondary. Since the male version of the assistant has often been neglected by critics, we should take care to cite certain of the more remarkable female assistants who belong to these newer films. In *Blud an den Lippen*, Andrea Rau, playing Delphine Seyrig's lover, companion, and servant with an unforgettable eroticism, adds a new dimension to the role of the vampire count's valet. Equally outstanding is the daughter and expert collaborator of Dr. Fu Manchu, who, in a rather bad Don Sharp film, brings to the foreground a quite uncommon erotic intensity. In one scene, this beautiful Chinese woman, just before whipping a female prisoner, gently passes the lashes of the whip over her victim's naked back, as if softly caressing her. Nor should we forget the improbable Vulnavia, who aids our friend Phibes so effectively. But more interesting still is the character of Lionheart's daughter in the plagiaristic *Theatre of Blood* (*Much Ado About Murder*) who serves Lionheart as his assistant while dressed in male attire, a parodic touch that gives her a certain distinctiveness.

THE DEVIL'S BEAUTY

No matter how ravishing or exciting these women may be, they play only supporting roles. There is, however, one indisputably active role in the fantastic that is exclusively female—the role of the witch. Where witches are involved, sexual relations, symbolically implicit in vampirism, occur overtly, sometimes with phantoms and ghosts— very physically in *House of the Damned*—and sometimes even with the Devil. Brides of Satan, witches are nuns from Hell whose pact with their Master is an explicitly physical one. Just as *God Needs Men*, so Satan needs women.

The witch—a term which today makes us think of a toothless old hag riding her broomstick— is, in the realm of the fantastic, more likely to have the icy beauty of a Barbara Steele or, on the periphery of the genre, the perverse ingenuousness of an Anicee Alvina. The attractiveness of these witches should not surprise us; Christian casuistry, the off-shoot of a morality of mortification and anti-pleasure, has always likened flesh to the Devil. Does not the seductress, who is, like Matilda in Lewis' *Monk*, the perverse temptress par excellence, incarnate the Devil himself? And does not the Devil appear as well under the guise of a little girl in Mario Bava's *Operazione Paura* (*Kill, Baby, Kill* /*Curse of the Living Dead*) and again in Fellini's "Toby Dammit"/"Never Bet the Devil Your Head," an episode in *Histoires Extraordinaires* (*Spirits of the Dead*)? It is not remarkable, therefore, that He should take possession of an adolescent girl's body in *The Exorcist*, the novelty there being only in the violence of the treatment.

To conclude our exploration, let us pay homage to three women in particular, each of whose exemplary destinies has immutably shaped the contours of the fantastic. First, to Erszbèth Bathory, the red countess, whom we mention not so as to give our approbation to her reprehensible acts, but rather to bring attention to the unforgettably bizarre nature of her case. Second, to Sharon Tate, the unfortunate victim of real monsters in life after having been the victim of harmless vampires in Polanski's film. And last, to Mary Shelley, a minister's daughter and an accomplished novelist who, were she here today, would be quite surprised to see the fresco of horror which her imagination has inspired.

Alice Brady, kneeling with harassed stage director Adolphe Menjou in Busby Berkeley's *Gold Diggers of 1935.*

II.
FILMS
DIRECTED BY
MEN

The Image of Woman As Image:
The Optical Politics of Dames

LUCY FISCHER

> What do you go for?
> Go see the show for?
> Tell the truth—
> You go to see those beautiful dames.
> —Lyrics from "Dames" by
> Al Dubin and Harry Warren

I never had the intention of making eroticism or pornography. I love beautiful girls and I love to gather and show many beautiful girls with regular features and well-made bodies. It is the idea of spectacle which is expressed in "What do you go for?" What do you come to do, why do you go to a spectacle? It is not the story, it is not the stars, nor the music. What people want to see are beautiful girls.
> —Busby Berkeley[1]

In the proliferation of literature on the status of women in film the most common critical strategy has been that of distilling from the cinematic narrative an abstract "image" of women in film.

Thus, from the reverential treatment accorded to the Gish persona in the films of D.W. Griffith, writer Marjorie Rosen extracts the image of woman as posed on a Victorian pedestal. From the relationship of the Doris Day character to her male protagonists she posits a vision of woman as militant crusader for chastity. To characterize the adolescent film heroines of the 1950's she conjures the image of a Popcorn Venus.[2] Similarly, critic Molly Haskell compares the malign erotic presence of Rita Hayworth in *Lady From Shanghai* to that of a mythological siren; and reads from the machismo sexuality of contemporary cinema the image of woman as victim of rape.[3]

In approaching the production numbers of Busby Berkeley, however, we encounter cinematic texts of another order. For rather than present us with a realistic narrative from which we must decoct a feminine "image," Berkeley's plastic abstractions present us with the essence of image itself—a vision of female stereotypes in their purest, most distillate form.

Berkeley's mise-en-scène, in fact, has a comic propensity to literalize the very metaphors upon which critics like Rosen and Haskell have seized in their characterization of the portrayal of women. For while Griffith treats Lillian Gish as though she were on a pedastal, Berkeley, in *Broadway Serenade*, situates Jeanette MacDonald geographically upon a pedastal. While some directors shroud their virginal heroines in an aura of sexual impenetrability, Berkeley, in "Pettin' in the Park," shrouds Ruby Keeler in a suit of metal armour. While films of the '50's cast women metaphorically in the role of Popcorn Venus, Berkeley, in *Fashions of 1934*, cast them literally as the goddess and her galley slaves. While certain stars filled the screen with the sense of mythical sirens, Berkeley in *By a Waterfall* fills the screen with the presence of mermaids themselves. And, finally, as Molly Haskell finds the image of rape inscribed in the content of contemporary films, so one finds in the style of Berkeley's "through-the-leg tracking shots" implications of the sexual act transposed to the rhetoric of camera technique.

Thus an examination of Berkeley's production numbers provides a spectrum of images of women that range the continuum From Reverence to Rape. On this level Berkeley's oeuvre comes to constitute a definitive text upon the subject—an illustrated catalogue whose elegant pages enumerate the cinematic image of woman in all its varied embodiments and incarnations.

A privileged work in this respect is *Dames* (1934), a film whose very title seems to propose it as relevant to a discussion of women in cinema. What distinguishes *Dames* from other works in the Berkeley repertoire is the manner in which its production numbers (with their symbolic discourse on the feminine stereotype) are implanted within a narrative that deals with the same thematic issues. The dramatic episodes of the film were, of course, directed by another man—Ray Enright. But it is, nonetheless, intriguing to examine this Centaurian construction and disclose the ways in which its discrete, contrasting segments inflect upon each other and create a rather curious cinematic text. For in its hybrid totality *Dames* constitutes an eccentric treatise addressed to three interlocking aspects of the portrayal of women in cinema: (1) the nature of the image of women in film; (2) the character of the relationship between the female screen presence and the male spectator and/or director; (3) the attitude of the Hollywood industry toward the position of women in the commercial film medium.

THE FEMININE MYSTIQUE AND CINEMATIC TECHNIQUE

While conventional film narratives situate their female personae in a realistic universe, the Berkeley production numbers posit their existence in the realm of pure imagery itself. For the space in which his sequences transpire does not conform to that of the concrete external world. Rather, it is abstract, and in its fluid chain of spatial metamorphoses, essentially ambiguous. From this perspective it becomes the perfect dècor for fantasy, and often the narrative prologues explicitly locate the numbers in a character's consciousness. "I Only Have Eyes For You," for example, proposes itself as an oneiric meditation occasioned by Dick Powell's having fallen asleep on the subway.

But beyond the motivational ploys of the framing stories, it is the quality of Berkeley's cinematic technique which renders screen space as quintessentially fantastic. Often the numbers unfold in a void, black space whose dimensions are fundamentally unknowable. The mechanics of concealed cuts transport us magically from one locale to another creating a geography unnavigable by the human body. In "I Only Have Eyes For You," a cut-out face of Ruby Keeler falls away to reveal "behind" it a ferris wheel of costumed girls. In actuality, the sites are connected only by a splice and the image of spatial relation is merely an illusion. Similarly in "Dames"[4] a fabric placed over the lens in one set but removed in another gives the impression of continuity to the disjunctive locales in which the sequence transpires. Spatial paradoxes emerge as well. In "I Only Have Eyes For You," we leave Keeler on the exterior rim of the ferris wheel in one shot, only to discover her on its interior surface in another. Movement in the numbers also declares itself synthetic, as images rotate, girls fly up to the lens of the camera, or advance forward propelled by Eisensteinian jump-cuts.[5]

If the geography of the numbers is unchartable, their temporality is unmeasurable; and it is as far removed from the flow of normal time as is that ebony vacuum from the boundaries of conventional space. The constraints of causality are dissolved as well. Thus in "I

Only Have Eyes For You", the external world responds to Dick Powell's obsessional fantasies and a crowd of people can be made at will to simply "disappear from view." But having established Berkeley's mise-en-scène as the potential environment of fantasy, with what particular visions of the female image is it populated?

One approach to the question entails an examination of Berkeley's formal technique and the manner in which certain myths concerning women are inscribed in the seemingly innocent level of plastic composition. One should keep in mind the obvious fact that excepting their narrative prologues the production numbers of *Dames* exclude the presence of men and permit only women. They are, in fact, elaborate corporeo-plastic constructions of women's bodies "composed" in particular dècors. Clearly those compositions are more than just pictorial; and from their physical arrangements of the female form can be read covert assumptions about the female "norm."

We might begin with the very concept of *stereotype*, which in one sense denotes "having no individuality, as though cast from a mold." Ironically, one of the stereotypes of female screen portrayal is the depiction of woman as stereotype itself. Thus, Molly Haskell claims that the silent cinema:

> exploited the tendency of American women to conform to type, to choose hairstyles, dress, even personalities according to the models of "in-ness" . . . of any given period.[6]

And, similarly, Marjorie Rosen speaks of the disappearance of the ideal of individual attractiveness in the 1930's and its replacement by conformity to popular image.[7]

One need only to attend to the chorus-line phenomenon of the Berkeley numbers to witness the manifestation of "stereotype" in its most hyperbolic form. Part of the humor of the numbers arises from our perception that the women (whether standard blonde or occasional brunette) look remarkably alike. This notion is, of course, catapulted into another realm entirely in "I Only Have Eyes For You" where women are not merely similar but disconcertingly identical. Berkeley clearly prides himself on this stylistic penchant. He speaks, for example, in an interview of a particular day of hiring in which he auditioned 723 women to select only three. He says:

> My sixteen regular girls were sitting on the side waiting; so after I picked the three girls I put them next to my special sixteen and they *matched just like pearls*. (Italics, mine)[8]

Ultimately this conception of female as stereotype is embodied within the mise-en-scène of the Berkeley numbers, particularly "Dames".

For as though to demonstrate the precise matching of the Berkeley girls he lines them up behind one another until their multiplicity is subsumed in an image of apparent unity. Similarly, "Dames" contains a sequence which stands as emblematic of woman's alleged conformity to an external image. For in depicting a row of show girls making up before their dressing table mirrors, Berkeley deploys yet another row to represent their reflections. One thinks of Molly Haskell's statement on this issue and the way that Berkeley's iconography tends to literalize it. For in speaking of the genesis of feminine cinematic stereotypes, she refers to how the Gish persona was succeeded by "a long line of replica mirror-image virgins."[9]

Although Berkeley's relish of the chorus line takes on a transcendent quality, its presence is, afterall, a convention of musical comedy. But his mode of engaging it is not, and it is on this level of stylistic innovation that more significant attitudes toward women emerge.

For what happens in most Berkeley numbers (and quintessentially in "Dames"), is that the women lose their individuation in a more profound sense than through the similarity of their physical appearance. Rather, their identities are completely consumed in the creation of an overall abstract design. As Haskell puts it, the Hollywood bureaucracy "preferred its women malleable."[10] And what could be more malleable than female bodies which serve as fragmentary pieces of a kaleidoscopic pattern.

The configurations those patterns take can also be read for meaning. The perpetual arrangement of girls in circular format seems not without its bonds to symbols of female sexuality. And when the girls in "Dames" delineate the sentimental boundaries of a heart it is certainly not a matter of pure ornamentation.

The patterns tend, as well, to comically literalize the notion of two dimensional feminine screen portrayal. For if there is any match for the "flatness" of the Ruby Keeler character in the Enright narrative, it is clearly the chorus girls in *"Dames"* whose bodies are pressed into black and white patterns or employed interchangeably with animated graphic designs.

This reduction of the female form to biotic tiles in a patterned mosaic is not devoid of overtones of power. And as one envisions a God-like Berkeley aloft the Olympus of a crane, one thinks of the words of von Sternberg:

> It is the nature of woman to be passive, receptive, dependent on male aggression . . . In other words, she is not normally outraged at being manipulated; on the contrary, she usually enjoys it. I have plenty of evidence to assume that no woman, as opposed to male, has ever failed to

enjoy this possibly mortifying experience of *being reorganized in the course of incarnating my vision of her*. (Italics, mine)[11]

Even the narrative element of the production number, "Dames", alludes to the sexuality of power; for it portrays an all-male theatrical board of trustees which choreographs the careers of show girls from behind the scenes.

Privileged in the canon of female stereotypes is the conception of woman as decoration, a notion which has had its supreme manifestation in the history of film. As Molly Haskell writes:

> The conception of woman as idol, art object . . . visual entity, is afterall the first principle of the aesthetics of film as a visual medium.[12]

Once more, in the iconography of the Berkeley sequences we find this cliché in its rarefied form, unencumbered by the obfuscations of a plot. For the function of the women in a number like "I Only Have Eyes For You" is essentially plastic, and their status is equal to that of the dècor. They are, in fact, simply elements of the total mise-en-scène—facets of its comprehensive ornamental structure. Even the frills of their white organza costumes seem to tell us that they are, afterall, pure "fluff."

Relevant to this impression is the fact that Berkeley girls did not (and, often, *could* not) dance—a phenomenon which accentuates our perception of their role as visual embellishments. As Berkeley himself unabashedly confesses:

> I never cared whether a girl knew her right foot from her left so long as she was beautiful. I'd get her to move or dance, or do something. All my girls were beautiful and some of them could dance a little, some of them couldn't.[13]

Thus in a number like "I Only Have Eyes For You", the women's gestures (of swaying back and forth or undulating the folds of their gowns) clearly do not function as choreography. Rather they serve as kinetic designs which interact dialectically with the complex trajectories of the mobile dècor and the moving camera.

But the awesome proficiency of Berkeley's mechanical dècor tends to underscore the technical incompetence of the Berkeley Girls and concretize the image of women as essentially passive. for the sets of "I Only Have Eyes For You" are elaborate pre-programmed machines for action which transport the girls through dizzying cycles of aimless, repetitive movement.

What heightens this sense of passivity is the zombiism of the Berkeley Girls, a quality that they exude beneath the surface of their opaque dissociative grins.

In "From Reverence to Rape"? Haskell talks about the contemporary cinematic predilection for models: "bland, young, fashion plate girls with symmetrical features who can be shaped by the director or adapted to the critics fantasies."[14] The Berkeley girls, however, seem to extend passivity into ths realm of catatonia and transmute the image of female as "model" into a vision of female as Surrealist mannequin.

But like the work of the Surrealists Berkeley's creations seem informed with a sense of the marvelous. And if women in his numbers are varnished with an exterior coating of inertia, they seem nonetheless imbued with a core of interior power for the cycle of transformations and metamorphoses in which they participate seem to identify them with the force of magic. Once more Berkeley's imagery taps a female stereotype. Simone De Beauvoir, for example, in "The Second Sex," talks of the myth of women and magic and its dependence on the projection of passivity.[15] And in a work on the subject of the fear of women, Dr. Wolfgang Lederer finds the vision of woman as magical central to primeval societies and bound to the mysteries of the reproductive process:

> Woman's most exclusive and essential function . . . is best represented by means of the central symbolism of feminity, that of the magic vessel . . . deep within the unknowable darkness of the womb; unconsciously purposeful, silent as the night; women transform food and blood into new life.[16]

He then proceeds to trace the association of women and magic to its crystallization in the Indian goddess *Shakti* who stands as representative of a potent creative energy:

> and that which this energy creates is *maya*. Maya: the measuring out or creation, or display of forms; maya: any illusion, trick, artifice, deceit, jugglery, sorcery, work of witchcraft, *any phantasm or deception of the sight*. (Italics, mine)[17]

It is with this sense of *maya* that the optical marvels of Berkeley's numbers are informed. In the tradition of Méliès, it is, of course, the man who directs the magical feats. But it is the women who ultimately perform them and who seem empowered to make the journey "elsewhere."

What becomes apparent from a reading of Berkeley's mise-en-scène is the way in which he generates an image of woman as "image" itself. This portrayal proceeds on multiple levels: She is represented as image in terms of her embodiment of cultural stereotypes, as well as in her posture of conjured male projection. But the presentation of these first two conceptions depends upon the establishment of a third, and that is Berkeley's obsession with the status of woman as *film image*—as plastic, synthetic, celluloid screen object. Von Sternberg once said of Marlene Dietrich that "she was a perfect medium . . . who absorbed [his] direction and . . . responded to [his] conception of a female archetype."[18] While von Sternberg perhaps offered this figuratively, Berkeley adopted it literally. For through his articulation of woman as film image she becomes quite concretely a medium—one which in its pliancy can be molded to the configurations of the Berkeley imagination.

Significantly, all these varied senses of woman as image seem encoded within the iconography of "I Only Have Eyes For You." It is, first of all, a sequence whose feminine imagery is diegetically situated within the realm of Dick Powell's fantasies. Its references to women and advertising (the subway posters for Society Cosmetics and Willards for the Hair) furthermore invoke the cultural clichés of surface beauty and vanity. But what is most important in the sequences occurs with the magical dissolves on the advertising posters (transforming each model's face into that of Ruby Keeler) and with the fluid bridge from the final poster to the Ruby Keeler "cut-out" head adrift in a black amorphous space. For through those shot transitions we move from the domain of extra-filmic senses of the female image to the possibilities of its embodiment in cinematic imagery itself.

During the course of the number Berkeley proceeds not only to catalogue those possibilities in formal terms, but, ironically, to create a fabric of imagery that comments on his very act of creation. One thinks, for example, of a final segment of the number comprised of an elaborate chain of processed shots: Thus, we see Ruby Keeler step into a mock-up mirror frame, which becomes reduced in scale and supported by a base consisting of small Ruby Keeler figures aligned in apparent unity. Eventually the entire 'mirror" is "grasped" by the hand of a large Ruby Keeler figure who enters from off-screen left. What we have here, of course, is a pictorial allegory—one which dramatizes the employment of women through cinematic processes to present and support a falsely stereotypical image of women.

But the most evocative trope of the number comes in the form of the giant, jig-saw puzzle vision of Ruby Keeler's face. For what we see is an obedient cluster of three dimensional women proceed to cover their bodies with a two dimensional photographic representation; (a process which, significantly, is accomplished by lifting their skirts above their heads.)

What is most intriguing, however, is the form that photograph takes and the way it appears. For it comes to us in the guise of a jig-saw puzzle—a fragmented version of an image that must be sequentially assembled. In his choice of this conceit Berkeley has generated an iconography metaphoric of the portrayal of women in film. For it is a portrayal which, afterall, involves the constitution of a giant synthetic image through the assemblage of interlocking pieces which we commonly refer to as "shots."

"SWEET AND HOT"

In addition to translating certain stereotypes concerning women into the figurative discourse of cinematic imagery, Berkeley's mise-en-scène proposes a particular vision of female sexuality. In order to disclose this, however, it is necessary to locate Berkeley's production numbers within the narrative framework of Enright's *Dames*, and to situate *Dames* within the historical context of film censorship.

The Hollywood production code officially came into being in 1930; but since there were no adequate provisions of enforcement it remained an "advisory document."[19] In the early thirties, public criticism of film content mounted and, according to Richard Randall in "Censorship of the Movies," the year 1934 (the release date of *Dames*), marked "the turning point in self-regulation":

> American Catholic bishops formed the Legion of Decency to review and rate films. At the same time they threatened the industry with a general boycott by Catholic patrons if the moral tone of films did not improve. This pressure resulted in the MPPDA's [Motion Picture Producers and Distributors of America] formation of the Production Code Administration (PCA) as a quasi-independent, self-supporting body charged with enforcing and interpreting the code.[20]

Evidently the power of the MPPDA and the PCA was based on their domination by the five largest companies in the industry which, in turn, controlled 70% of the theatres for film exhibition.

From this historical perspective the plot of *Dames* seems a tendentious parody of the censorship of movies. For the Legion of Decency, we have the Ounce Foundation for the Elevation of American Morals. (Although the constant reference to the organization as the "Of for the E of Am" seems to mock the alphabetics of the MPPDA and the PCA as well). For the censorship of film is substituted the censorship of theatre. In keeping with the economic realities of film censorship Ezra Ounce (Hugh Herbert) is portrayed as a millionaire and the opening sequence of the film catalogues the name plaques of the myriad enterprises which constitute his monopolistic empire.

Typically, Ezra Ounce's specific objections to the theatre focus on the figure of the show girl. It is the flagrant display of women on the musical stage that he identifies as the source of its moral danger.

Clearly we are to regard Ezra Ounce as a blustering fool, a repressed, adolescent man who mistakes "good clean fun" for sinful prurience. Afterall, what goes on on the stage of the theatre is to be *so* innocuous as to permit the participation of the antiseptic Ruby Keeler (who plays his niece, Barbara).

But ironically what Ezra Ounce views on the stage as theatrical numbers within the diegesis of *Dames* are, in actuality, the cinematic insertions of Busby Berkeley. This stylistic dislocation is echoed by a shift in sensibility as well. For while the Enright narrative proceeds to spoof the need for censorship of female sexuality, the Berkeley numbers intercede to present it in more perverse configurations than even Ezra could have anticipated. This tonal disjunction seems epitomized in the title of the fictional musical comedy from which the numbers emerge, which is "Sweet and Hot." For the diegesis of the film would have us believe that what transpires on the stage is naively "sweet." But the realities of our viewing experience contradict this and assert that what Berkeley depicts on the screen is unremittingly "hot".

"The Girl at the Ironing Board," for example, presents us with what was called in those days a "specialty number." The epithet seems peculiarly apt since it unfolds as a comic vignette on the sexual "specialty" of fetishism. It begins with Joan Blondell voyeuristically peering through the laundry window at a loving couple in a carriage outside. She sings:

> Nobody ever has whispered to me
> The sweet things a girl loves to hear
> Nobody's arms ever twined around mine
> Still I'm not lonely for romance is near—
> A girl who works at the laundry
> Has a dream lover all of her own
> A lover, unseen, whose love she keeps clean
> With water and soap and a washing machine.

Then, as though the subject of erotic symbolism and fetishistic partialism were not sufficiently overt, she continues:

> There is something about your pajamas
> That fills me with sweet ecstacy
> And because it's part of you, I'm learning to love you
> So bring back your laundry to me.

The rest of the number dramatizes the notion of fetish as symbolic substitute for the "normal" sexual object. Thus we see animated male laundry sing and gesture to her from the clothesline; she even whisks a pair of longjohns from the pile and dances with them. At the end of the number she is "gang raped" by a mass of laundry which slides down upon her from the lines.

In keeping with the syndrome of paraphilia the number represents the fetish in the context of a series from this Blondell choses a favorite partner with "whom" she departs:

Mae West and George Raft in
Night After Night (1932).

Greta Garbo excelled at conveying with exquisite precision
the complexities of her emotions. With Erich von Stro-
heim in *As You Desire Me*
(1932).

Mary Pickford, "the Eternal Child of Victorian Fantasies," in love with Buddy Rogers, the boss's son in *My Best Girl* (1927).

Jean Harlow was spontaneously willful, going after the money or the man she wanted. With Stan Laurel and Oliver Hardy in *Double Whoopee* (1929).

Marilyn Monroe in *Some Like it Hot* (1959).

A peculiar strain of suspense films presenting "female" doubts (Ingrid Bergman with Charles Boyer, *Gaslight*, 1944, above), and infirmities (here Dorothy McGuire's deafness)—to be exploited. With Ethel Barrymore, *The Spiral Staircase* (1945).

While Sandra Dee presented passive, fluttery perfection, her ample mouth recalled the petulance of an adolescent Bardot; in *Doctor, You've Got to be Kidding* (1967).

Single, often self-supporting, the star's problem was: *Will she or won't she?* Love stories with Natalie Wood, Connie Stevens, notably Doris Day, focussed on this dilemma. Clark Gable and Doris Day in *Teacher's Pet* (1958).

High romanticism of the 1940s. Humphrey Bogart, Ingrid Bergman, and Dooley Wilson in *Casablanca* (1940).

Woman alone portrayed as a desperate, needy neurotic. Katharine Hepburn in *The Rainmaker* (1956).

> The construction of a series of love objects is exhibited in the [fetishist's] choice of a partner by first imagining a whole row of possibilities and then
> . . . picking one of them as a favorite.[21]

Significantly, the one aspect of the number that does not conform to the paraphilic syndrome is the notion of the fetishist as female. For although stereotypes of sexual behavior are currently under re-evaluation for their cultural determinants, it is nonetheless the case that as late as the Kinsey Report of 1953 fetishism was considered an overwhelmingly male syndrome:

> It has been known for some time, and our own data confirm it, that fetishism is an almost exclusively male phenomenon.[22]

Thus in "The Girl at the Ironing Board" we would seem to have a clear case of the imposition of a classically male fantasy on the behavior of a female screen persona.[23]

Finally, "The Girl at the Ironing Board" abounds in elements that seem to comment parodistically on the idea of censorship. After its eccentric portrayal of sexuality, the sequence ends on the saccharine note of a chirping bird which sings as Blondell and her laundry walk into the sunset. The Griffith-like sentimentality of this touch is comically false, as disingenuous as the stuffed bird itself which sits on an artificial prop tree.

One thinks as well of the song lyric which speaks of "keeping love clean" as one views this as a work whose implications had bypassed the process of Production Code laundering. The "moral status" of the numbers is much like that of the character of Horace Hemingway (Guy Kibbee) whose false piety Ezra Ounce suspects is "nothing but a snare and illusion."

From the reviews one reads at the time of the film's release, it seems likely that its overtones escaped the public eye. A *New York Times* film critic of August 26, 1934, for example, described it innocuously as "an original combination of comedy and song . . . which is staged very cleverly."

THE GOLD DIGGERS OR THE MEN WITH THE MOVIE CAMERAS

But certain things clearly did not escape the public eye and it is precisely to the subject of spectator vision that one must turn to complete an analysis of *Dames*.

The title number of the film confronts the issue most explicitly. It begins with an all-male theatrical board meeting at which various inventors argue about the elements wich insure commercial stage success. One says: "I tell you gentlemen, if I'm going to put money into this show I want to be sure that we get the best music possible." And another responds: "You're right! Great songs are what draw people to the theatre." Others interrupt advocating the importance of story or publicity until finally Dick Powell breaks into a song which establishes the economic base of show business on the male desire to look at women:

> Who writes the words and music for all the
> girlie shows?
> No one cares an no one knows
> Who is handsome hero some villain always frames?
> Who cares if there's a plot or not, if its got
> a lot of dames.
> What do you go for? Go see the show for?
> Tell the truth—you go to see those beautiful dames.

Then as a hoard of show girls enter the board room he expounds on this theme more thoroughly and reveals that the true gold diggers are to be found in the corporate male bureaucracy, and not in the chorus line as supposed:

> Leave your addresses, my big successes
> All depend a lot upon you beautiful dames.
> Oh dames are necessary to show business
> Dames—without you there would be no business.
> Your knees in action, that's the attraction
> What good's a show without you beautiful dames.

After this framing episode the sequence erupts into the actual production number. Significantly it emphasizes women's "knees in action" as the girls' black-stockinged legs are employed to create geometric designs against a pure white floor.

Aside from "Dames," however, the theme of vision is referred to in almost every lyric of the score. One song, for example, is entitled "Try To See It My Way;" and another (a fantasy of prenatal love) has Powell confessing that he adored Keeler when she "was a smile on her mother's lip and a twinkle in her father's eye." There is, of course, "I Only Have Eyes for You" wich alternately represents the love of a woman as optical illusion and optical obsession.

But not only is the act of looking alluded to in the song lyrics of *Dames*, it is invoked in the mode of articulating the imagery of the production numbers themselves. For what is inscribed in Berkeley's optical stylistics is a virtual discourse on voyeurism and its relation to the female screen presence: "Kino-Eye" has become that of a Peeping Tom. This notion is even brought to the literal surface of the narrative as one shot reveals an insert of a gossip column, "On the Rialto," whose byline is none other than Peeping Tom.

The implicit thesis of cinema as voyeuristic enterprise (as spectacle) is advanced on many levels in Berkeley's production numbers. One thinks immediately of his story concerning his introduction of the close-up into the vocabulary of the film musical. Evidently Sam Goldwyn came on the set of *Whoopee* and questioned Berkeley about his motivation for the technique. Berkeley responded: "Well, we've got all the beautiful girls in the picture. Why not let the public see them?"[24]

Thus just as Berkeley comprehended the difference between theatre and cinema in relation to choreographic potential he seems to have grasped intuitively their difference in terms of voyeuristic appeal. For the close-up has the power to annihilate the spatial gap which distances the theatrical spectator from the female stage presence.

The number which most clearly transposes the issue of voyeurism into stylistic terms is "Dames." Berkeley fills the screen with girls clothed in provocative Fredericks of Hollywood-type negligees and has them engaged in the visually taboo pursuits of sleeping, bathing, and dressing. As though to shame the camera for its intrusion, however, the lens is continually punished by the withdrawal of sight. A whole chain of such instances occur in the beginning of the number. In the first such shot, girls run up to the camera and obscure the lens with the fabric of their nightgowns. Then in a masked cut (with attendant change of décor) the fabric is removed to reveal a girl in a bath tub. The girl proceeds to cover the lens with a powder puff which (through another masked cut) is removed by a girl at a dressing table. Eventually that girl takes a bottle of perfume and sprays the surface of the lens. We next see the lens wiped clean, but this time our vision is identified with a particular male stagehand who is watching the show girls approach through a window that is being washed.

This dialectic of seeing and being prevented from seeing is epitomized in the number's final voyeuristic character, a "blind" man who removes his dark glasses to stare at the show girls as they pass on the street. (We should remember that as English legend has it Peeping Tom was, in fact, a Coventry tailor who went blind after peering at Lady Godiva.)

Although Berkeley plays on the notion of camera as voyeuristic tool, he nonetheless conceals its presence. Thus while mirrors figure dominantly in the imagery of the numbers (the "mirror" of women in "I Only Have Eyes for You," and the dressing-table "mirrors" in "Dames") they are most often false surfaces which refuse to reflect an image of the camera or of the man who stands behind it.

But the iconography of the Berkeley numbers seems to go beyond engaging the female screen image as source of mere voyeuristic pleasure. For in addition to the numbers whose effect depends on the presence of actual women one is struck by the existence of sequences content with their photographic image.

We might recall, for example, that on the subway in "I Only Have Eyes For You" Dick Powell conspicuously ignores the corporeal reality of Ruby Keeler to embark on a fantasy digression based on her photographic likeness. But the issue seems crystallized in the final sequence of "Dames." What we see on the screen is a shot of the Berkeley harem arranged in pyramidal fashion against a complex décor. Imperceptibly, the image of the actual women transmutes to that of a photographic representation. And in a parody of sexual entry, the number ends with Powell's head breaking through the image surface.

Thus what emerges in *Dames* is yet another sense of "the image of woman as image." For it is not so much the feminine *presence* that is glorified or clebrated in *Dames* as much as her synthetic, cinematic *image*. And ultimately the privileged status of that image and its mode of articulation propose it as a virtual substitute for woman herself. Von Sternberg had spoken of manipulating the female screen image into a "visual aphrodisiac."[25] But in *Dames* it seems, like Blondell's laundry, to have acquired the dimension of a fetish.

Once more we find ironic reverberations of the issue within the Enright narrative. In an early scene of the film, Horace Hemingway goes to visit his millionaire cousin, Ezra Ounce, and with polite duplicity remarks that his daughter, Barbara, sends her love. The following comic dialogue casually ensures, but in retrospect seems to summarize the dynamics of the portrayal of women in *Dames*:

> EZRA—Barbara sends her love to me? Why should Barbara send her love
>   to me? She's never even seen me.
> HORACE—She's seen your picture.
> EZRA—Well, then. *Maybe she's sending her love to my picture.*

[1]Busby Berkeley, "Recontre avec le grand 'Architecte du Musical'," *Cinéma*, #103 (Feb. 1966), p. 44.

[2]Marjorie Rosen, *Popcorn Venus* (New York: Avon, 1973), paraphrase of material on pages 71, 211, 300ff.

[3]Molly Haskell, *From Reverence to Rape* (New York: Penguin Books, 1974), p. 204, p. 323ff.

[4]This refers to the production number entitled "Dames" and not to the general title of the film.

[5]I am referring to the series of triadic "jump-cuts" which occur during the coronation sequence in IVAN THE TERRIBLE—PART I.

[6]Haskell, *op. cit.*, p. 48.

[7]Rosen, *op. cit.*, p. 193

[8]B. Pike & D. Martin, *The Genius of Busby Berkeley* (Reseda, Ca.: Creative Film Society), p. 64.

[9]Haskell, *op. cit.*, p. 49.

[10] *Ibid.*, p. 7.

[11]Josef von Sternberg, *Fun in a Chinese Laundry* (New York: Macmillan Co., 1965), p. 120.

[12]Haskell, *op. cit.*, p. 7

[13]Pike and Martin, *op. cit.*, pp. 51–53.

[14]Haskell, *op. cit.*, p. 18.

[15]Simone De Beauvoir, *The Second Sex* (New York: Bantam Books, 1961), p. 153.

[16]Wolfgang Lederer, *The Fear of Women* (New York: Harcourt, Brace, Jovanovich, 1968), p. 116.

[17]*Ibid.*, p. 136.

[18]Josef von Sternberg, Introduction to *The Blue Angel—Classic Film Script* (New York: Simon and Schuster, 1968) p. 12.

[19]Richard Randall, *Censorship in the Movies* (Madison: University of Wisconsin Press, 1970) p. 199.

[20]*Ibid*.

[21]Wilhelm Stekel, *Disorders of the Instincts and Emotions* (New York: Liveright, 1952) p. 33.

[22]A. Kinsey, W. Pomeroy, C. Martin, P. Gebhard, *Sexual Behavior in the Human Female* (New York: Pocket Books, 1953), p. 679.

[23]The overtones of fetishism in the iconography of *Dames* would seem to go beyond this particular number. In the Enright narrative we have the absurd character of Ezra Ounce who is depicted repeatedly toying obsessively with a series of ceramic elephants. And the image of dozens of Benda-masked Ruby Keeler likenesses in "I Only Have Eyes For You" has the distinct sense of fetishistic partialism (the necessity for the love object to display particular attributes).

[24]Tony Thomas and Jim Terry, *The Busby Berkeley Book* (New York: New York Graphic Society, 1973), p. 25.

[25]von Sternberg, Introduction to *The Blue Angel*, *op. cit., p. 12.*

Madame de: *A Musical Passage*

MOLLY HASKELL

The image of women projected by most film directors has been shaped by one of three basic attitudes: puritanical discomfort, misogyny or (the obverse of misogyny) idealization. Max Ophuls is one of the five or six great directors—Mizoguchi, Renoir, Dreyer, Sternberg, Bergman—who place women at the center of their universe and honor them with a love that neither crushes nor sanctifies. The heroines of *Madame de, Lola Montes, Letter from an Unknown Woman, Caught, The Reckless Moment* are creations of a director for whom the passionate exaltation of the eternal feminine does not preclude the dispassionate exploration of specific women, just as delirium and determinism are the the twin components of the director's style.

Like Stendhal, one of his favorite writers, Ophuls sees woman as a creature at a distinct disadvantage in a society laid out by men, but in whom the gesture toward liberation, usually in the form of a commitment to love, becomes far more daring and heroic than the deeds for which men are crowned. In "The Second Sex," Simone de Beauvoir bestows on Stendhal's women the words of praise she accords the creations of no other male writers, and they might equally well apply to Ophuls's Madame de:

> The so-called serious man is really futile, because he accepts ready-made justifications for his life; whereas a passionate and profound woman revises established values from moment to moment. She knows the constant tension of unsupported freedom; it puts her in constant danger: she can win or lose all in an instant. It is the anxious assumption of this risk that gives her story the colors of a heroic adventure. And the stakes are the highest there are: the very meaning of existence.

In the period context in which Ophuls has cast her, Madame de represents the romantic incarnation of the liberated woman, a figure whose true nobility is often clouded by the general disrepute of "women's fiction," a genre Ophuls both cherishes and transfigures. While giving special attention to this aspect of *Madame de*, I have no intention of turning the film into a Women's Lib tract (*Ms de*)! For one thing, the characters of the two men, played by Charles Boyer and Vittorio de Sica, are too important, and Boyer even draws audience sympathy away from Danielle Darrieux's Madame de. If she is the most obsessed and audacious of the three, she is not morally superior to the men (or at least to Boyer), the way Bergman's women often are to his men. Madame de does not achieve her spiritual splendor through the tarnished souls around her, but through a solitary struggle in which she surrenders the lesser part of herself for the greater part—"The woman I was made me the woman I am."

Just as Madame de progresses from self-centered society lady to saint, the film moves from soap opera to sublime art, redeeming itself and its heroine in the process. But even the most unredeemable soap opera, we should remember, has served as compensation for women who, denied the outlet of challenging work, and strung out on the interminable trivia of household chores, can feel an inverted sense of superiority in submission and self-denial. The trouble is that in pushing the ecstasies of martyrdom, soap opera has recruited more victims and reinforced rather than relieved the inequity of male-female roles.

Perhaps a key difference between soap opera and serious art on the same subject, apart from the crucial factors of intelligence and style, is that soap opera is a sedative, a kind of artistic Catholicism, which encourages passive resignation to what is seen as a general and unalterable law. Real art, on the other hand, has the opposite effect, since it shows people who dare to rebel, who break the rules, people poised on a moral precipice in which any move may be a fall but in which it is not only possible but imperative to choose the direction.

The difference between the two is the difference in *Madame de* between a tragic ending which involves the three main characters (and the death of two) and a denouement in which Madame de leaves each man one earring, or, in other words, the difference between Ophuls's film and its source, a novel by Louise de Vilmorin. The latter, an ironic, sub-Maupassant tale written and set in the thirties, was very much a "woman's story" in the pejorative sense. The circular plot (transposed by Ophuls into an aristocratic, turn-of-the-century setting) concerns the fate of a frivolous society lady who, in pawning a pair of earrings given her by her husband as a wedding present, sets up a chain of circumstances which, when she falls seriously in love, closes in and destroys her. In its skeleton form, it is a tale for which the American title, *The Earrings of Madam de*, would have been appropriate had not Ophuls transformed it into a masterpiece of visual narration in which every image, expression, line of dialogue, camera movement and dissolve has both emotional weight and structural significance.

The screenplay by Ophuls, Marcel Achard and Annette Wademant is a gem of succinct exposition and expressive dialogue, phrases reiterated but with different meanings. For example, in the magnificent ballroom scene, in which Danielle Darrieux and Vittorio de Sica waltz in one continuous motion, across the weeks and into the depths of love, the phrase "les nouvelles sont excellentes" occurs three or four times. It is uttered by Madame de, first seriously then ironically, in reply to De Sica's inquiry after her absent husband's health, and indicates both the passage of time and the growth of intimacy. The next and last time it is used, it is Boyer who reassures his wife that De Sica is well after his fall from a horse. "Je sais," she replies, using the words De Sica had used in their last exchange.

Another example of Ophuls's deepening and transfiguring of the original: the story seems to hang heavily on coincidence and chance, not just in the peregrinations of the earrings, but in the attention given fortune-telling cards, the number 13 and other signs through which luck is raised to a guiding principle. But Ophuls, while retaining the references to chance—largely as character details—emphasizes, in a beautiful observation by Boyer, the supreme naturalness of coincidence. He makes it clear that the drama lies not in the whereabouts of the earrings (except as their movement imitates an inner journey) but in their symbolic importance: the value placed on them, the lies told for them, the consequences of the lies—all the interlocking moves in a game of character, not chance, a game in which the outcome has the inevitability of tragedy.

Oscar Straus's beautifully sentimental score adjusts itself, without breaking stride, from the rapturous lilt of the waltz to the wistful and finally desolate strains of loss. It accompanies every appearance of the jewels except one: when, in a ruse to deceive her husband, Madame de lets them drop from the gloves where she has concealed them. They fall onto the table with a frightening finality, with no music to attenuate their impact at this turning point of the film. Actually, turning point is the wrong word because, although the story is full of turning points, the film itself is always turning. The movement is not only circular but spiral, so that when it comes back to the same place—as in the ballroom scene, the jewelers, the church, etc.—it has reached a deeper (or higher) level. Circles occasionally give way to straight lines, as in the movements and visual motifs of Boyer, a general, and in the single stretch in which Madame de, traveling to escape from her love, takes a long walk up the beach, trying in vain to control an emotion that is as vast and overwhelming as the ocean.

The women of Stendhal and Ophuls are not ordinary women. They are among the few who escape, who awaken fom the dream-sleep—society's lifelong anesthetic—and overcoming the taboos of both society and their own inhibitions, embark on what Simone de Beauvoir calls "the adventure of liberty."

That this is one of the greastest themes of fiction—and most beautiful in Ophuls' hands—is a notion which makes so-called serious critics uneasy. Agreeing that Ophuls is a consummate stylist, they nevertheless refuse to take him seriously, on the grounds, presumably, of his choice of subject matter and feminine orientation, and the suspicion that nothing tragic can be expressed in so nearly painless a style. To this, Jean-Luc Godard gave the answer in his remark on Hitchcock and Rossellini (cited by Andrew Sarris) when he said of Hitchcock that where there is so much form there must be content (the converse applying to Rossellini). One has but to watch and feel *Madame de* to realize that Ophuls's style is, in the words Boyer uses to describe his marriage to Darrieux, "only superficially superficial." The perpetual motion of Ophuls's camera is both circular and progressive, the representation in time and space of the human journey through eternity. Each staircase climbed and descended, each corridor traversed, takes the body one space further toward the grave, and each lilting, contrapuntal swing of the camera suggests the soul's freedom to fly. This is a more complex and ultimately more tragic vision than Louise de Vilmorin's, or even Arthur Schnitzler's, whose plays Ophuls adapted, to the horror of the literati and the glory of film history.

The dismissal, or downgrading, of Ophuls as a "woman's director," seems to rest on a cultural and (male) sexual prejudice that is as old as art itself: a belief that the life of the heart is somehow a less worthy subject of serious treatment than such "large subjects" as wars, politics, religion and social causes. Treated seriously, it is soap opera, and people are likely to overlook the fact that what in one man's hands is soap opera is, in the hands of another—say, Euripides, Racine, Stendhal, Samuel Richardson, Jane Austen, E. M. Forster, Virginia Woolf, Proust, Mozart and Ophuls—the stuff of art. And now, with the relations between the sexes at an all-time low, the concept of love is in danger of dying altogether or of being reduced, by medical authority, to a conditioned response—the saliva of sickness or need. It will be up to the French, who have always been more alert to the subject than the rest of us, to remind us that if love is an uncontrollable emotion, *to love* is a choice and therefore a moral act. Max Ophuls, German-born, a man of the world in exile, but a spiritual Frenchman, understood that the heart's engagement is lonelier and—in the eyes of the world—less glamorous than political engagement. Love takes greater risks because it gains less credit than the socially honored heroics of battle and public gesture.

This is an odd notion, and film, for young people today to appreciate, particularly if they are Americans. In a permissive society, or among a permissive generation, the idea of risk and retribution has no meaning, and the rigid, unspoken rules of a French class society are as remote to college students as kinship patterns among the Hopi tribes. This, unfortunately, indicates once again that sexual liberation actually works against true liberation: that constant, soul-defining struggle with parental authority, social restrictions and private inhibitions in which some principles are guarded, some modified and some abandoned.

So widespread is the current sense of alienation that there is no established, homogeneous majority which can represent "society." For Ophuls there was, or had to be, which is why he preferred and was most eloquent in prewar Europe as a setting. Ophuls's society, like Stendhal's, was not just an abstract idea but a system, both blessed and cursed, a collectivity of real faces ready to serve, support or censure according to the events and their role in them. And it was against such a solid ordering of human destiny that the individual flaunted his or her obsession and took the consequences.

Vittorio de Sica, Charles Boyer and Danielle Darrieux, in their incarnations as the baron, the count and Madame de are extraordinarily beautiful, radiant, rich, aristrocratic—stars in every sense of the word, yet Ophuls places them firmly within a society in which every position is clearly defined and interconnected. It is the cosmic order in miniature, its regular movements reflecting the orbit of planets, its irregular passions the trajectory óf meteors. In such a universe, it is the most natural thing imaginable for A to advance to B, and B to bump into C, and C to charm D, and D to dance with E, and E to end up sitting next to F, and F to fall into the arms of G, and so on. So on, that is, as long as they keep moving. For to stop is to cause a ripple, and in Madame de's world, a ripple is a tempest. The wealth and leisure of the aristocracy entitle them to certain freedoms denied the lower classes, but the rules are subtler and stricter, and the tiniest infraction reverberates from the orchestra to the galleries. In the marvelous and characteristically Ophulsian opera scene, the opera (Gluck this time, not Mozart) is interrupted—always a faux pas!—by Madame de's revelation that her earrings have been stolen, with the consequence that her husband is obliged to turn the opera house—and all Paris—upside down in search of them. In a stylish cacophony of hushed voices (whispers which ring out like bells), doors (inner and outer) opening and closing, rumors spreading, ushers leaping to their feet, we are given a comic vignette of a hierarchical society and the chain of command in which servants jump to their masters' bidding and masters in turn scrape before their mistresses. There is a beautifully edited sequence in which Boyer, having gone home to search for the earrings, calls the servants. In one shot, we see the entire household staff leaping at different speeds up the stairs. The next shot, with precisely the reverse motion and meaning, shows Madame de, surrounded by admiring beaux, descending the stairs of the opera with careless grace. Thus in one lyrically lighthearted episode, Ophuls gives us sociology and psychology, the world of Madame de and the disruptive influence she is to have on it.

At one point—in the jeweler's—we see Madame de gracefully swooning. At another—after De Sica's accident—she faints for four minutes instead of three, and Boyer is alarmed. This is a society which permits, even encourages, a woman to enjoy flirtations as long as she abides by the unwritten rules governing such affairs. If she falls in love—already bad form—there are even allowances for that, provided she doesn't impose her feelings on others, or compromise her husband's honor. Ophuls's complex pattern of camera movements—rapturous, lyrical pans and tracks and occasionally sudden swings, within a larger, strictly observed symmetrical system—reflects the paradox of Madame de's social situation and, on a larger scale, the mystery of free will and determinism.

Madame de, one of society's crowning jewels, rejects her "setting" (one thinks of the first time we see her, her face framed in a mirror), thus enacting the primal conflict of tragedy, the individual against society. But in one sense she, like other tragic figures, has been outside society all along. The spoiled and petted darling of the beginning of the film is no more in touch with reality than the mystically redeemed saint of the end. And when, in her passion for De Sica—loving him, then losing him—she turns her back on society, it is not just its luxuries and ornaments she rejects but its premises: her role as wife and mother. This is clear in the scene in which Boyer takes her to the country house, teeming with children of his poor relations, and forces her to make a gift of the earrings to a niece who has just given birth. Madame de tosses the earrings to her and, in a touchingly comic gesture, hastens to the crib where to hide her grief she makes a pretense of admiring the baby—a baby that arouses no more feeling in her than a harmless insect, the product of a cycle of nature in which she wants no part. If this isn't a radical gesture, I'd like to know what is!

In the beginning is the end, and in the first two and a half minutes of *Madame de*, in an extraordinary single-take sequence, we are given the particulars of her life which foreshadow her death. In one of the most graceful bits of exposition in all cinema, Ophuls introduces Madame de to us through her possessions, as she is pondering which to surrender. At first all we see is her hand as it searches with sensory pleasure among her jewels and furs and dresses, up and down, across, over and back, rejecting first one and then the other. In the course of this inventory, she drops a Bible, holds it for a second and replaces it; regrets aloud the absence of her mother who "would tell me what to do"; holds her cross fondly and at the idea of pawning it cries, "Oh no! I adore that"; and finally settles on the earrings her husband gave her, on the grounds that "I can do with them as I please."

During this sequence, Ophuls has told us Madame de's preoccupations, her character, her attitude toward and relations with her husband, with her mother and with God; in what she lacks, he has prefigured what she will come to have, and in what she possesses, what she will no longer have. The reference to her mother reveals how she has been spoiled, that she misses her mother and that it is to her mother, or her mother's memory (at the expense of her husband), that she has always turned for help. In the array of her possessions and the affection she lavishes on them, we see that they are everything to her and are no doubt compensation for a loveless marriage. In her almost sensual familiarity with the Bible (which she keeps among her furs) and the cross, she reveals a direct, childish sense of closeness to God, of whom she can ask favors and expect the indulgence of a doting parent. The decision to sell the earrings given her by her husband—not just as an ordinary present but as a wedding present—constitutes an explicit rejection of him and a repudiation of their marriage. Her comment that she can do with the earrings as she pleases is another way of saying that, having no affective value, they have no power over her (even here, at her most materialistic, she avers that the claims of love are the only binding ones); and this is in sharp contrast to her later deranged behavior toward, and possession by, the earrings when they have been given to her by the baron. Invested with the "revised value" of love, they are now as binding and inescapable as religious vows; she is at their mercy, no longer free to "do with them as (she) pleases," and thus does passion become fate.

Almost every action in the first half of the film has its double, or mirror image, in the second half, only they express the opposite relation to each other: the first images are the mirrors, the echoes, of the deeper and truer essences which will emerge.

Madame de's first visit to the church (on the way to the jeweler's), where she perfunctorily crosses herself and asks God to "make him understand and I'll never forget you," has its double in the end where she, near death herself, prays in anguished sincerity for the life of De Sica, who is about to meet Boyer in a duel. Her prayer appeals to the spiritual nature of her love: "You know we loved in thought only." And this is followed, after the duel and Madame de's death, by the third and final shot in the church in which, after a long, stately track to the altar, the camera pans from the altar to a small shrine where Madame de's earrings have been placed in memoriam, thus joining, gently, comically and reverently before God, the material and spiritual sides of Madame de, sanctifying her love and redeeming her life.

The first time we see Madame de, it is her reflected image in the mirror on her dressing table, framed by the luxuries which are an extension of her being and without which she is nothing. As the film progresses and her love grows, she dresses more severely, becomes physically wasted, and even her surroundings take on an ascetic look. She is perhaps no longer beautiful by society's standards, but she is more beautiful by the higher and more demanding ones of the spirit. In her last agonizing and comical encounter with De Sica, she has rushed to warn him about the duel, knowing he no longer loves her, but still daring to hope.

"I am not even pretty," she says sadly.

"More than ever," he replies.

"Really?" her eyes light up, with a coquetry that shows how much she is still herself. Then just as quickly, "I'm incorrigible," she confesses, with an awareness that shows just how far she has come.

One of the glories of Ophuls's conception of Madame de is that even as she is ennobled by her love, she retains some of the myopia and weakness of her former self. Thus the brutal lesson of her suffering teaches her nothing of the pain she has caused her husband, and her eyes are never opened to the mute misery he endures in loving her.

As a general in charge of an artillery unit headquartered in Paris, Boyer has the rectitude, the faith in social conventions and a certain lack of imagination characteristic of the Ophulsian military figure. At the same time, he has a stern formality that we come to realize has been forced on him and is alien to his disposition. In a heartbreaking moment late in the film, as Madame de is languishing on a chaise lounge, Boyer confesses he never had much taste for the image she had of him and for the role she made him play, but she is too far gone in her own unhappiness to hear. The brilliant subtlety of Boyer's performance, with its suggested reserves of feeling, becomes more apparent with successive viewings of the film. We begin to sense that every care lavished on Madame de—from her family, her personal servant Nanou and friends—has been love withheld from him, and that his gentleness, increasingly obvious to us, is forever hidden to her. She refuses to make the sympathetic leap, symbolized by the vast space between their beds, necessary to unleash the passion smoldering within him. Ophuls permits us to glimpse Boyer's passion, through the correlative images of fire, that is in some ways more magnificent than Madame de's for being undeclared. Unlike the simpler character of De Sica, whose love is destroyed when his honor is insulted, Boyer allows his honor to be defiled, but not his love. By not acknowledging his love or accepting his friendship, Madame de unconsciously wills his death; in order not to be turned into an object, Boyer must challenge De Sica to a duel.

The two men—one worldly, the other more innocent—react in ways perfectly justified by any normal criteria of human behavior, but they are criteria by which Madame de can no longer be judged. She has bypassed good and evil and conventional morality in the total— religious, romantic, neurotic and heroic—sublimation of her entire being into a passion which refuses to make room for anything else. The men, gentlemen and standard-bearers of the masculine code, are prevented by their straightforwardness from imagining the depths of her commitment, or from understanding the difference between her lies.

Knowing Ophuls's fondness for Stendhal and Mozart, critics have often wondered why he never used their work as the textual or musical basis for his films. He never adapted Stendhal, and he restricted his use of Mozart to the opera scenes within his films, but it is precisely by not trying to transfer classics from one medium to another that Ophuls created something comparable in his own. The whorl of *La Ronde* is closer to the sustained lyric and comic ecstacy of *Cosi fan tutte* than a film like *Sunday, Bloody Sunday*, which uses the score throughout. And *Madame de* is closer to the world of Stendhal, both in style and in its harsher view of risk and redemption, than Claude Autant-Lara's film of *The Red and the Black*. Ophuls uses objects and images the way Mozart uses music—to define character and feelings and the subtle alteration in each. Like Mozart and Stendhal, but in his own uniquely cinematic language, Ophuls conveys shifts and transitions, the crossover from playfulness to passion, without ever deviating from the elegance and grace of the original style and the world it sustains. People who are attuned to more blatant histrionics may miss the clues, expecting Wagnerian sonorities when a magic flute or a flutter of paper signals the transition. Through a conceit of cinematic metamorphosis reminiscent of Keaton's *Sherlock, Jr.*, Ophuls shows us such a transition, as the pieces of a love letter Madame de has torn and thrown from the train window metamorphose into the snow flakes of a crystallized love. To accept the fate of Madame de, you must believe that the depths of love can be rendered by a flurry of snowflakes and that the distance between death-in-life and life-in-death, symbolized by the journey of a pair of earrings, can be crossed by a moving camera. The film never stops to underline its purpose but, like a Mozart opera, is in constant motion, incorporating every moment into the highest and purest lyrical expression. Sometimes you long to catch it and hold it, to stop it in its tracks and luxuriate in an image, even as you know that its beauty is movement and that its very essence lies in the poignancy of its passing.

The situation of women in *Two or Three Things I Know About Her* (1967) was to be driven into prostitution, into being an object. Juliette (Marina Vlady) at work in Godard's film.

Two Or Three Things
I Know About Her

GODARD'S ANALYSIS OF
WOMEN IN CAPITALIST SOCIETY

CHUCK KLEINHANS

From his early films on, Jean-Luc Godard's sympathetic use of female protagonists has been remarkable. To take one preeminent example, in *Contempt* he treated Brigitte Bardot as a woman with a range of emotions, not merely a pouting sex symbol or a "dumb broad" comic actress. From *Vivre Sa Vie* (1962), which sensitively examines a woman's life, to the Godard-Gorin collaboration *Tout Va Bien* (1972) which portrays the growth and expression of feminist consciousness in the character played by Jane Fonda, and *Number Two* (1976) which concentrates on the "second" sex, Godard remains near the front rank of filmmakers presenting an anti-sexist perspective. *Two or Three Things I Know About Her* (1967) is a crucial film in Godard's development, for in taking up the theme of prostitution, Godard arrives at the limit of his earlier analysis and begins to break into the new, and more explicitly Marxist analysis that will inform his post-68 films.

Two or Three Things, although it presents a day in the life of one woman, and shows and comments on women's situation in modern Paris, cannot be satisfactorily approached only on the level of content, theme, narrative, and ideas. To obtain a fuller understanding one must also take into account the form and style Godard uses, particularly various anti-narrative and anti-sympathetic devices. In *Two or Three Things* Godard is simultaneously raising socio-political questions on the one hand and aesthetic questions on the other, and raising these questions both in form and content. When making this film he was working within the dominant Western ideology—bourgeois thought. Restless within that world view, in *Two or Three Things* Godard stretches it to its limits, both in style and ideas.

A DAY IN THE LIFE

The narrative of *Two or Three Things* portrays one day in the life of Juliette Hanson (Marina Vlady). Juliette is shown at home—washing dinner dishes, reading a magazine, and putting the two kids to bed—while her husband and his buddy listen to a short wave radio. The next morning Juliette leaves off the youngest child while she goes from her suburban apartment complex to the center of Paris. She shops for clothes, has a coke in a cafe where she talks with a woman friend and is annoyed by a pimp. Later she is seen in a hotel room with a customer, a young fellow who works in the subway. Following this encounter she goes to a beauty salon where her friend Marianne works. The pair leave to sell themselves to an American, afterwards dropping by the service station where Juliette's husband works. Juliette returns home to fix dinner, put the kids to bed, and read in bed with her husband.

However to call this sequence of events a narrative is deceiving, for Godard breaks up the sequence by inserting visual and audio asides and overlays, digressions on philosophic questions by the characters and by Godard himself (off camera). There is no effort made to present Juliette as a "character" in the usual literary or cinematic sense. The reason for a flat presentation of her is twofold, and is an example of Godard's combining formal and content concerns. First, Juliette is consistently shown as being emotionless and one-dimensional because she embodies the destructive effects of modern society on the individual. Secondly, Godard deliberately employs stylistic devices to present a very flat Juliette in order to prevent the audience from forming a close identification with her. Instead of letting us feel "with" her, Godard forces us to see Juliette in the context of her immediate and social situation, and to view both her and the situation with a certain critical distance. One short scene from Juliette's life can illustrate this duality. The scene takes place in the kitchen upon the couple's return. (*Medium shot of Juliette, followed by Robert.*)

R—Ahh . . . we've arrived!
J—Arrived where?
R—(*going off camera*) Home.

J—And after that, what are we going to do?
R—(*off*) Sleep . . . What do you mean?
J—And after that?
R—(*Off*) You get up.
J—(*unpacking the groceries*) And after that?
R—(*off*)The same. You'll begin again . . . (*J. opens a cupboard and puts in a box of macaroni*) You'll work. You'll eat.
J—And after that?
(*R. returns on camera and faces her. He lifts his glasses.*)
R—I don't know . . . (*pause, he looks at her and puts away his glasses*) Die.
J—And after that?
(*Cut to the gauges of a gasoline pump as it goes from 00.00 to 01.10 litres.*)

Here we have Robert's initial self-evident statement and the ensuing activity of unpacking the groceries juxtaposed with Juliette's basic questioning of life. In most cinema one would expect such philosophic searching to be an intense moment when it occurs, as it does here, near the end of the film. Yet it is nothing of the sort; everything is flattened out, and the kitchen routine is not a counterpoint to the dialogue, but on approximately the same level of significance. Life, questioning of life, unpacking, and digits all exist equally. Vlady, in her acting here, as throughout the film, uses little facial or body expression, and minimal inflection or intonation, which matches Juliette's condition. Juliette is unable to link the emotional and personal with the intellectual and abstract. Yet our response is, by the very flatness of the presentation, not an empathetic one with Juliette in her deepening alienation. Her questioning of life does not lead us to think she is contemplating suicide. Rather, our response at this point, and generally throughout the film, is to see Juliette's life critically and with self-awareness and thereby respond to it more intellectually. The same dialogue could be played in tear-jerker style, evoking a pathetic heroine's distress. However Godard emphatically does not attempt a sentimental portrayal of Juliette but rather a rationale of her alienated condition.

WOMEN AND SOCIETY

Bourgeois protest cinema does not extend beyond the scope of liberal analysis and liberal panaceas. It can portray the oppression of women (or any other oppressed group) under the status quo. Yet because it tends to show the plight of an individual woman and evoke an anger and possibly a pity, it also shows a basic powerlessness: what can one person do against the social order? At most it posits as remedy an individual rather than a collective solution; one woman's victory, rather than a change in the condition of all women. In portraying Juliette,

Godard tries, unsuccessfully in the end, to break through the limits of liberal thought.

While dealing most concretely with Juliette's life, he also examines the lives of other working class women, and in a larger context examines Paris, and by implication modern Western society. Juliette's situation is the most specific level of Godard's examination, and he sees her casual prostitution as a particular example of a larger social condition. As in *Vivre Sa Vie* the metaphor of prostitution expands beyond the individual. One of his sources for the film was a journalistic exposé of prostitution in large apartment complexes. Godard said that the topic expressed one of his basic ideas: "In order to live in today's Parisian society, one is forced, at whatever level one is, at whatever station one has, to prostitute oneself in one manner or another, or to live according to laws which recall those of prostitution. A factory worker prostitutes himself three-fourths of the time in this manner: he is paid to do a job which he doesn't want to do . . . In modern industrial society, prostitution is the normal condition."

In *Two or Three Things* we repeatedly see the limits placed on contemporary women: in the clothing shop employees, folding and arranging clothes and smiling at customers; in the pages of the French equivalent of *Playboy*, a garish and stylized Twiggy; in a woman trying to strike up a cafe conversation with Juliette's husband. She is rebuffed for her forwardness (he is busy "writing" and then he "starts" the conversation with her and works her into a putdown situation). Most poignantly shown in dialogue, is a cafe encounter between an older man ("Ivanov", the Nobel Prize winner, we are told) and an adolescent woman who admires him and who is then rebuffed by his deliberate professorial aloofness.

The situation of women, as portrayed in *Two or Three Things*, is to be exploited, to be driven into prostitution, into being an object. Society has turned everyone into a consumer of everyone else. Men, being on top, consume women. Juliette reads aloud a description of the wonderous effects to be gained by a new hosiery to her husband and his buddy. As the husband scorns the idiocy of the statement, Juliette responds by citing authority: "Madame *Express*", the women's page of a French newsweekly. More derision, Juliette leaves, to tend the children, and the buddy asks the husband how he paid for his new car. The husband then boasts that Juliette found the money (obviously through her prostitution) and the friend wishes he were so lucky . . . consumers all. Godard tells us that it was actually the husband who asked Juliette to sell herself, to keep up the standard of living. Money is needed for the comforts and conveniences: hot water, rent, television, auto, washing machine, vacation. Although men are portrayed unsympathetically throughout the film, Godard does not find them the source of women's situation, but focuses on the situation of women as representative of a general social disorder.

The breakdown of normal or humane society is repeatedly symbolized by the inhuman scale of the Le Corbusier-style apartment complexes, and by the repeated assault of street noise and construction sounds, which intrude into the sound track. In this kind of life, Juliette's disconnected passages of an epistemological monologue on language, reality, and so on, which match and counterpoint Godard's sound track statements on the same subjects, do not seem so discordant or curious. While a working class wife, mother of two, and part-time prostitute like Juliette cannot in normal probability be expected to articulate epistemological questions on the level that Marina Vlady playing Juliette does, her questioning functions as Godard's symbolic or metaphoric statement on Juliette's condition. In the breakdown of authentic human life, everything is called into question, including the nature of bourgeois reality and how we are to know that reality. In this sense the philosophic verbiage running through the film is not idle, but integral, for within the parameters of bourgeois ideology, phenomenologists and epistemologists have explored the effects of mass society on the individual and the nature of alienation from physical and social worlds as well as anyone else. Thus an off-camera interviewer speaks to a young boy (he is also off) in one sequence and asks, "What does your father do?" "He is in aviation." "Your mother?" "My mother . . . She doesn't work." The philosophic level intersects with the everyday . . . a mother who doesn't have a job is a form of non-being . . . there is no word for the boy to complete the phrase, "she is . . .", for housework and child care are not considered "work".

In *Two or Three Things* Godard is explicit and devastating in his portrayal of the effects of modern society. The "Her" ("Elle") in the title is not Marina Vlady or Juliette, but, as the initial title indicates, the Parisian region. The film's trailer is even more explicit about what "Elle" is: "the cruelty of neo-capitalism, prostitution, the Parisian region, the bathroom that 70% of the French don't have, the terrible law of apartment complexes, physical love, modern life, the war in Vietnam, the modern call-girl, the death of contemporary beauty, the circulation of ideas, the gestapo of structures." Yet for all of Godard's ability to show effects and to find a series of things to attack, from advanced industrial capitalism to the lack of beauty, he does not find basic causes for the conditions he describes. He has no historical context which shows why or how things evolved this way, and he presents no solution. The film ends with a lawn with various brightly colored packages of consumer products on it, and Godard as narrator telling us that he has returned to zero, and that it is necessary to start from there.

THE IMPORTANCE OF GODARD'S STYLE

The "meaning" or "message" of *Two or Three Things* is not simply the content as discussed so far, but the content as it is shaped by the form of the film. In its style, the film works within bourgeois form, yet chaffs at its restrictions. An example is the depiction of Juliette. As I pointed out, Godard does not let us form a sympathetic bond with Juliette. This is accomplished in a number of ways, such as Godard interrupting the minimal narrative of her day with film statements by and about other women, shots and sounds of Parisian construction, shots of book covers, and discourses on epistemology and cinematic art.

We are first introduced not to Juliette, but to Marina Vlady, and then a few seconds later to Marina Vlady playing the role of Juliette. The intent of this device is explicity Brechtian, for Godard is seeking to distance the audience from the screen action and to inhibit their falling into sympathy with a conventional character in a conventional narrative. We are, through this and other distancing devices, never to become too interested in what happens to or what will happen to Juliette or the other characters presented. Suspense is written off, and in its place is analysis and criticism. Despite a certain similarity in the juxtaposition of "illusion" and "reality" with the puzzle-like exploration of those two concepts in Alain Resnais's *Last Year at Marienbad*, the effect of Godard's film is not to stimulate our interest in the puzzle, but to force a more intellectual and critical viewing of the action, rather than an uncritical or emotional one. Marina Vlady's acting style in the film contributes to this effect. She does not play naturalistically, but performs an action, such as washing dishes, or shopping in a clothing store, frequently turning her full face to the camera and delivering lines with unusually long pauses between phrases. Some of the lines are delivered as responses to an off-camera interrogator (the audience does not hear the question); others are delivered by her without preparation. In this case the line was given to her by Godard, who used a small radio receiver hidden behind her ear.

The particular acting style Godard elicits from his actresses and actors has two functions. On one hand, as noted, it inhibits a sympathetic response to the character (one reason many viewers find Godard's films of this period "irritating"—a complaint he would have taken as proof he had achieved the desired effect). At the same time, Vlady's acting style symbolically stands for the fractured nature of Juliette's life, and for the complete banality of it all. For example, in the clothing store sequence, Juliette wanders in the store aimlessly looking at items, asking to try on a coat that she doesn't try on, and finally deciding on a dress in the most disinterested manner. The mechanical and unfocused nature of her other activity makes a point, that her activity is dehumanized in a consumer society.

In another sequence, Juliette enters a hotel room with a young man, but no titillating prostitute and customer scene takes place. Instead the camera treats the two as separate entities, usually showing only one at a time, with the other speaking off-camera. Neither takes any clothes off. Juliette puts on a bright red lipstick, and as she speaks in a distracted and unconnected monologue, facing the camera, the wide screen cuts her face above the chin and at the eyebrows. The wide screen lens distorts her face, forcing it out of ordinary perspective. In this sequence Godard does not intent to present the audience with a realistic portrayal of an encounter between prostitute and customer which develops the prostitute's character (as in, say *Klute*, and its establishing scenes of Bree as prostitute, where we see her distance from her "job" when she sneaks a look at her watch during intercourse). Rather, Godard uses camera framing instead of emphasizing the participants or the action to show the mechanical flatness of and alienation inherent in the transaction. Godard is not presenting the *truth*, in the sense of presenting something which we are to take as being "like real life" (and incidentally, or not-so-incidentally, titillating the audience by presenting the forbidden—with, of course, a "redeeming social value"). Godard attempts that very difficult trick of presenting us with banality, and commenting upon it. Rather than a "slice of Life" carefully sliced for sensationalism and box office, Godard shows the ordinariness of the incident. *This*, Godard is saying is the true reality of our everyday world, and beyond the appearance of the trivial there is a social structure.

Juliette's other scene as a prostitute is similar. Taken to a very exclusive hotel by her friend, Marianne, they are hired by an American, who wears a T-shirt with an American flag printed on the front and who tells us his name is John Bogus, a war correspondent on vacation from Saigon. He photographs them and has the pair undress and then parade back and forth with Pan Am and TWA flight bags over their heads (shot from the neck up). Juliette ends the scene with an epistemological monologue juxtaposed with news of Vietnam and sounds of war. The conversations are non-conversations, the encounter is a non-encounter.

MARIANNE—"Tell me, your T-shirt, it's *America uber alles?*"
AMERICAN—"Yes . . . but it's they who invented the jeep and the napalm."

MARIANNE—" . . . Yes, the city is a construction in space . . . The mobile elements of the city . . . I don't know. The inhabitants . . . Yes, the mobile elements are as important as the fixed elements . . . and even when it is banal, the spectacle of the city is able to provoke a very special pleasure . . ."

There is no logical flow to such dialogue; this is characteristic of the film, for Godard is presenting a social world in which communication hardly takes place and in which one's own thoughts hardly develop. The theme is not unusual in Godard's films; it forms the bulk of his earlier film, *Alphaville*, for example. Alphaville was a city which made no sense to the intruder and no sense to the inhabitants. Yet the city of Alphaville was controlled, there was a consciousness, however strange and deranged, at the center. The Paris of *Two or Three Things*, for all its surface familiarity, suffers an even worse illness, for there is no one in the film to articulate that this is chaos. Instead everyone is trapped in it. Even Godard, it seems, with his off-camera philosophic monologues which break in from time to time, is unable to make a statement, to conclude anything. Characters and director are trapped either in the banality and alienation of social relations, or the ethereal abstractness of philosophy.

In the beauty salon sequence, a woman under a hair dryer (shot profile, thereby lessening expressiveness) appears long enough to say, without any context as to why she says it, "I am very careful when crossing streets. I think of accidents before they happen. And if my life ended . . . unemployment . . . illness . . . old age . . . death? Never, . . . I have no plans for the future because the horizon is closed . . ." Random thoughts from an alienated life . . . that is about all one can surmise.

Repeatedly in the film, Godard comments on the situation of women, using a variety of styles. At times a fairly direct statement is made in a typical documentary style: a brief shot of a woman cashier in a supermarket, ringing items; a long lens shot of a prostitute leaning against a wall and then approached by a pimp; a woman of about forty facing the camera, in on-the-street interview style, explaining that she's too old to get a job as a secretary, though qualified, so she sells her body. Yet even in using this style, Godard deliberately breaks any residual *cinéma vérité* expectations. The woman's monologue has an unbroken soundtrack but the visual track is intercut with brief takes of a supermarket sign, an apartment complex, a furniture display, and other details of Godard's plastic Paris.

Other styles are used as well, resulting in a deliberate juxtaposition that forces attentiveness to the details of the content. In a comic passage we find an old man in his modern apartment, simultaneously running a baby-sitting service (the parents pay in commodities, underlining the critique of the consumer society), and renting the bedrooms for assignations. (When the old fellow pokes his head in one bedroom, Godard has fun with the voyeuristic expectation, by presenting a fellow in working class dress expressionlessly stroking the leg of a young woman who is equally expressionless). Juliette drops off her daughter, and the camera pans out the window, catching her on the sidewalk, and a cop dragging two arrested men along . . . the comic moment ends abruptly.

In a romantic and poetic moment, rare in Godard's films of this period, Paulette, a young Algerian woman who works in the beauty salon confesses in close-up,

> I couldn't make it as a secretary. (pause) No, I don't believe in the future. I take walks . . . I don't like to be closed in. When I'm able, I read. Yes, I like to study men's character . . . I like to walk . . . to climb . . . to ride a bicycle. Film: two or three times a month. But not in the summer . . . The theatre? I've never been. But I would like it a lot. I prefer reading. Biographies. To study the life of men . . . their character, their work . . . Travel stories, ancient history. A tree. Later, when I'll be married to Francois . . . (pause) What else would I do? A lot of ordinary things. (She smiles.)

At such a moment Godard's intended distancing of the spectator from the screen breaks down. Paulette's melancholy acceptance of her life's limit as proscribed does force an empathetic response, and in fact it is even stronger than it would have been had the body of the film constantly allowed such uncritical viewing. Here a working class woman is portrayed in a straightforward manner, and the sympathy evoked is for her sex and her class. Paulette is shown seriously and with dignity as a worthy person who deserves respect.

All of Godard's previous concerns are etched into *Two or Three Things* which is why the film is so remarkably dense. Virtually everything is commented on directly, or indirectly through image, sound and juxtaposition. Life is presented as a world of objects: the innards of a radio, high rise apartments, furniture, signs, book titles, and other physical objects. Yet the people and their social world is objectified as well. Conversations are never shot over the shoulder of one character facing another. When both are shown, both are usually on the same axis, facing the camera, or looking so that their eyes do not meet, or more typically, one person is off camera. Relationships hardly seem to exist. Juliette and the young man who works in the metro move about talking in a cheap hotel room, virtually oblivious of each other's presence, just as if they had been crowded together by accident in the subway. Thus the prostitution metaphor becomes the ultimate statement on the reification of sexuality and physical love. Indeed, people and their interactions are made to seem objects. As Marianne muses in a passage quoted above, the buildings of a city are its stationary objects, the people are its mobile objects.

From this perspective, the film is not *about* the situation of Parisian women, any more than it is *about* the Vietnam war, which is also treated. Both are taken as specific examples of a general malaise. Thus Juliette's story is universal. Such an analysis of society is an extension of Godard's view in *Vivre Sa Vie*, in which cause and effect are ignored or unknown and where motives are not clear; all we are presented with are objective situations. Yet such a mere showing or presenting is also a limit on thought, for without explanation all one can do is present or ponder a situation, but not probe why or how it came to exist, or how it could be significantly changed. At this point then, Godard is at the limit of a radical but still bourgeois critique of society, and the new element in his post-68 political films becomes the finding of causes for effects, and showing how change could take place.

Critics of the film tended to focus on the nature of cinematic art as Godard's central concern in making the film (particularly the director's commentary which accompanied an extreme close-up of a cup of coffee). Actually, I think Godard's circular examination of the nature of film within the film is unsuccessful in his own terms, and it is the realistic content, the prostitution metaphor, which remains with the audience after viewing, and which has seemed the director's central concern to me after several viewings. Yet Godard can intermittently combine the two concerns. In one of those fine moments in which Godard, at the end of the film, is able to draw on what he has taught us to that point, Juliette's 10 year old son reads his mother a school essay on "comradeship." The child likes the nice girls, the ones who are pretty and subservient, but hates the ones with glasses, the smart ones etc. His socialization is connected with his naive efforts as an essayist. Social pathology and art combine; social ideology mediates expression.

Lucía

ANNA MARIE TAYLOR

Of the more than 50 feature films which have been produced in Cuba since the revolutionary government set up the ICAIC (Instituto Cubano del Arte e Industria Cinematográficas) *Lucía* is only the second to be distributed in the United States.[1] Since its release in 1968,[2] *Lucía* has won several international awards, including the Society of Italian Producers' "Golden Globe" award, the International Film Critics' Prize, and the grand prize at the Moscow film festival.

Lucía is composed of three separate films about women named Lucía. Each lives in a distinct period of Cuban history, indictated by the dates which introduce the three parts of the film—1895, 1933, 196–. These years correspond respectively to the war of Cuban independence from Spain, the end of the dictatorship of Gerardo Machado, and the period of the post-revolutionary literacy campaign undertaken in 1961.

Solas uses different sets of actors and distinct cinematic styles for the three historical epochs. Moreover, each Lucía belongs to a different social class—landed creole aristocracy, the upper middle class of the depression years, and what would have been the rural peasant class before the Cuban revolutionary government came to power in the late fifties. Each Lucía thus lives in a period of great political and social change which inevitably and profoundly affects her private life. A love story serves as the basic plot outline for the unfolding of the three parts, and each Lucía's circumstances and choices are related to a love affair and/or marriage with one man.

According to director Solas, in an interview in the Cuban magazine *Bohemia*, the links between the three stories are:

> . . . a woman's presence, a woman's attitude during a specific period of history, and her relationship with a man. On the other hand, what is

most interesting for me is that, throughout the film, there's a theme of a particular society, though this has several levels to it. The most important level, it seems to me, concerns a certain decolonization process, which I try to reflect.

This idea of decolonization takes a different form in the three parts of the film. The first shows Cuban society in the midst of its violent rupture from Spanish colonization. In the second, Lucía breaks away from the cultural colonization implied by the US-aping bourgeoisie of her family background. The idea of decolonization can also extend to the characters' participation in the popular struggle to oust the bloody dictatorship of Gerardo Machado, and to their obscure vision of a different and better society. Solas indicates that the love story of the third part was intended to blatantly portray a relationship of submission and power. This last section of the film can thus also be seen to involve a kind of decolonization process, defined by Lucía's effort to personally liberate herself from the chauvinism and domination of her husband Tomás.

In *Lucía 1895*, the extremely stylized acting and luxurious settings reflect the nineteenth-century Romanticism which blossomed late in Latin America. The fluttery, superficial behavior of Lucía and her companions in the lavish drawing-rooms of *fin de siècle* Havana convincingly convey not only a Romantic ambience, but the latent decadence of the creole upper class which was to replace the Spanish aristocracy following Independence.

Of the three parts, *Lucía 1895* utilizes the most varied cinematic resources and places the most emphasis on symbolism.[3] The violent contrast between the space occupied by the wealthy, represented by the family of Lucía in their stately mansion, and what goes on in the streets immediately outside is the predominant technique employed to communicate the message of the first *Lucía*: the old colonial structure is crumbling and what is happening in the streets serves as a prophecy of the changes to come. One of the reasons for the more expressionistic effects of *Lucía 1895* in comparison to the forties realism of the second part and the comic social realism of the third is that the characters of the lower class portrayed in the street are at the same time allegorical figures. *Lucía 1895* is also the only part that uses surrealistic sequences, filmed in overexposure, which symbolically show the violence of Cuban life under Spanish rule.

It is in "la calle"—the central plaza between their mansions and the Church, which serves as center for the social life—that the film opens, with close-ups of lavishly dressed, parisoled daughters of the aristocracy gossiping about the latest courtships in Havana. The director spares little in the film's first scenes to show the excessive opulence, leisure, and superficiality of the Havana upper class, with its imported furniture, sculptures, photographs, and drapes. As the women sit around in Lucía's (Raquel Revuelta) drawing room making soldiers' hammocks, we learn for the first time that Cuba is in fact in the throes of a bitter war of independence against Spain. The director thus builds up to the first dramatic cut to the street scene outside— the first juxtaposition of many which make Lucía 1895 the most cinematically complex of the three sections.

In stark opposition to the previous aristocratic settings, the camera switches to a cart full of bloody, ragged bodies of soldiers making its way through the streets. For the first time the character Fernandina appears: the mad woman who plays a pivotal role in the film. Fernadina never appears anywhere but en la calle. Her figure serves to show that the Cuba of 1895 is a society in convulsion; it is as if all of the violent and brutal reality for most of Cuba bursts out like a boil on the surface in Fernandina's savage fits of public madness.

But Fernandina's "madness" has a quality of heightened lucidity. Her piercing yell, "A callarse, Cubanos" (Be still, Cubans) brings to focus the historical moment of crisis and change. "The Cubans are sleeping," she screams. Grabbing a dead man passing by in another cart, she shouts the words which will also end the film and which can be seen to represent its principal theme: "Wake up, Cubans."

From the gossiping of the young women who gather in Lucía's house, we learn of Fernandina's past. Here takes place undoubtedly the strongest visual sequence of the film: in surrealistic, overexposed shots, we witness the rape of the former nun Fernandina by Spanish soldiers. In the background of the rape sequence hang the bodies of three men on a gibbet, as nuns come to pray for the dead and dying. We watch the anguished terror of the nuns pursued and captured by rapists as music, nightmarish sighs, and silence fill the lapses in the narrations. In this dream-like allegory, the rape of Cuba by Spain is made unforgettably clear.

Although it is the film's point that the romanticized, privileged setting of life for Lucía and for the other young women of the aristocracy is about to be destroyed, it is in fact largely from their perspective that the camera views life in Havana, both in its opulence, its sordid street scenes, and its grotesque fantasies. The unfolding course of events reveals to the film viewer, and finally to Lucía, that it is in fact a world of ruthless colonization and domination to be maintained at any cost. This is the message contained in the betrayal of Lucía's love by a Spanish man of fortune, Rafael (Eduardo Moure), who convinces Lucía to go on a lovers' tryst to her family's coffee plantation, which the Spanish suspect to be a center for insurgent Cuban fighters.

The long scenes describing the vicissitudes of Lucía's affair with Rafael are perhaps the least interesting and most overdrawn parts of the film. However, the extended crescendo of their sentimental relationship heightens the sense of betrayal of subsequent events.

As Rafael dumps her in the middle of invading Spanish troops he had led to the site, Lucía realizes his betrayal. It is through her eyes that we see the subsequent battles, including the arrival of blacks on horseback who join in the fight against the Spanish—authentic reminder of the participation of the black population of Cuba in the war of independence.

According to Solas, love from Rafael's perspective is a utilitarian instrument of political and economic expediency. What interested him in filming their love affair was

> . . . how an individual at a particular time in history, in order to obtain a particular piece of military information, can reach the point of perverting and adulterating the sentiment of love . . . how bourgeois Christian morality can disorient an individual, can alienate him, inhibit him, repress him until the individual can become the victim of almost anything . . .

Despite Rafael's role as traitor in the film, he as well as Lucía is thus ultimately presented as a victim.

After Lucía's discovery of her brother's body following the Spanish raids, the film shifts to Havana and returns to the concentrated symbolism and the overexposed surrealistic shots characteristic of the earlier parts. The "mad" Fernandina again plays an integrating role in the film. Her warning from the street to Lucía, "Don't go with him," has been borne out by Rafael's betrayal, and she now returns to take part in the final drama of Rafael's murder by Lucía.

That profound cultural transformations as well as political independence from Spain take place at this period in Cuban history is a strong message of the story's ending. As Solas points out in the *Bohemia* interview, the black part of Cuban society was at that period "the purest cultural element." The music and festival activities of blacks in the background as Lucía charges through the streets suggest the important influence that the country's African heritage will have in post-independence Cuba. In the final scenes of the film, no one speaks, another of Solas' indications of deep cultural transition. According to the director, they "lose their language," "they stammer like children, as if they were being born all over again."

The ending is as extraordinary visually and symbolically as the beginning. Lucía takes to the streets in a wild nightmarish sequence in which she stabs Rafael to death before terrified onlookers. Lucía, as symbol of both colonized Cuba and exploited woman (albeit of the aristocracy) literally and symbolically kills the oppressor.

Lucía's madness at the end symbolizes further the powerful and violent nature of this cultural transformation, and lends a dramatic symmetry to the film, particularly in the culminating moment when the madness of Lucía and that of Fernandina becomes one. Fernandina reappears to observe Rafael's murder and to console Lucía as the latter is dragged away. The classes and different cultures of Cuba briefly come into climactic contact in the street in the figures of Lucía and Fernandina.

II

The second part of *Lucía* is sharply counterposed in content and style to the symbolic intensity and romanticism of the first.

The film begins as a flashback in Lucía's (Eslinda Nuñez) mind as she sits working in a grim cigar factory in Havana. The flashback starts with a shot of Lucía and her mother disembarking during one of their frequent vacation trips, while Lucía's father remains back in Havana with his mistress. Like the first part of *Lucía*, the second sets the viewer up for dramatic change by long scenes first showing the life of a privileged sector of the Cuban population, this time the well-off who enjoy a vulgar, materialistic life style embodied in Lucía's loud and dependent mother. Again, juxtapositions introduce the political theme of the film: Lucía sees the wounded Aldo (Ramón Brito) arrive clandestinely by boat after a gun battle in the streets of Havana, and eventually becomes involved with him.

One important aspect of the film which defines the differences between the three *Lucías* is not only their separation in time (each part is in fact a superb period piece) but their differences in location and in the treatment of spatial movement on the part of the characters. In *Lucía 1895*, scenes alternate between the central plaza, Lucía's house, the side streets, and one extended scene in the area of the coffee plantation. In *Lucía 1933*, after the opening scenes in the Keys, the rest of the film has frequently changing locations in and around Havana. We see much more of Cuban life—the factories and white-collar offices of Havana, the theaters, high-class brothels, government buildings, bars, beaches, working-class living quarters, etc. In contrast to the settled space of *Lucía 1895*, the next *Lucía* shows the mobile, industrialized world of Havana's middle and working class of the thirties.

Lucía, because of her relationship to Aldo, literally changes class in the film, completely abandoning her family to become a factory worker in Havana, where she helps Aldo, materially and morally, in his fight against the dictatorship of Machado. She becomes politically active herself, participating in a workers' demonstration which is violently suppressed.

As does the first Lucía, the second goes through dramatic changes brought about by personal and historical circumstances. Here too the process of changing consciousness is circumscribed by the limited possibilities of the period. For the Lucía of the independence period, disillusionment and grief lead to a nihilistic act (however symbolic its meaning within the context of the film), the murder of her lover. For the second Lucía, despite her changing awareness and participation in political struggle, all seems ultimately hopeless once Aldo is killed. The close-up on Lucía which ends the second part reveals utter despair and isolation.

That the well-intentioned and idealistic fight of Aldo and Lucía is bound to fail is exactly the point of *Lucía 1933*. Changing consciousness and political struggle lead to futility in the individualistic framework of Aldo's idealism. He and his handful of friends have no movement and no ideology, and thus are easily drawn into the materialistic and decadent rewards available to them after Machado's fall. Aldo, disillusioned by the continued injustices he sees daily, and realizing that nothing has changed, begins fighting against the next regime, only to be gunned down, leaving Lucía utterly isolated and broken.

A criticism sometimes directed at *Lucía 1933* is the difficulty of understanding what is going on politically—who they are against and why—as Aldo and his companions embark on lightning sub-machine gun raids in downtown Havana. However, it is precisely this confusion which defines many of the sporadic struggles against various repressive dictators in Cuban history. Although there were a few ideologically organized groups in the thirties, the film mirrors the general political chaos of the street fighting of the time.

If Fernandina's words "Wake up, Cubans" sum up the theme of political and cultural transition portrayed in *Lucía 1895*, the phrase "Esto es una mierda" ("This is for shit") used by Aldo and his friend toward the end of *Lucía 1933* sums up their disillusionment and the ineffectiveness of their struggle.

Several cuts to the figure of Lucía, pregnant and alone in their room outside of Havana during Aldo's long absences, dramatize the marginality of women to the events of this period. Even her political involvement at the factory can be seen as merely an adjunct to Aldo's activities. Nevertheless, the moments of solidarity among the women of the factory show more promise for the future than do Aldo's individualistic and ultimately nihilistic acts.

III

The final part of *Lucía* clearly reveals that the film is not only an account of three women named Lucía in different historical settings. It is also about the problem of revolutionary filmmaking itself and the search for new forms. One might have expected that the third part would also deal with a moment of crisis and governmental transition, perhaps 1959. Choosing to set the third part in a post-revolutionary, non-crisis situation seems to have everything to do with Solas's search for new content and for more revolutionary forms.

The story line of *Lucía 196–* is extremely simple: a sensuous young couple, Lucía (Adela Legra) and Tomás (Adolfo Llaurado) come into conflict because his *machismo* possessiveness is so strong that he refuses to allow Lucía to work once they are married, despite her will to continue working and the pressure exerted from the community. The film is comic and farcical from beginning to end; the one-dimensionality of the central problem (the couple and community seem to have only this one frustration to work out) and the simplicity of background settings are a deliberate part of this comic ambience. The background music of the popular folk-song "Guantanamera" is set to humorous and often moralistic verses which follow the ups and downs of Lucía's and Tomás's relationship. The songs, which are superbly sung by Joseito Fernández, add to the exhilarating good spirits of the story. The choice of boisterous comedy as the mood for the *Lucía* of the sixties reflects the exuberant optimism characteristic of the country-wide literacy campaign and of the tremendous efforts begun in the early sixties to develop and diversify agriculture in Cuba.

One frequently hears today from people visiting Cuba how drab and deteriorated the once thriving and lushly decadent Havana now appears. Yet as soon as one leaves the city proper, the traveler in Cuba is struck by the extraordinary amount of productive activity going on in the rural areas. Solas's shift in the third *Lucía* thus authentically reflects this real change in priorities since the advent of the revolution. The only connection to Havana evident in *Lucía 196–* is the modest presence of Lucía's literacy teacher. This change, from the violent and tragic social settings of the first two parts of the film to the sense of small, stable community which one gets in *Lucía 196–* is one of the most impressive points made by the film.

The third *Lucía* is shot in a relatively straight-on, eye-level close-up style. Long shots are so few that when they are used for the couple's chases through the salt pans where Lucía returns to work, the switch in perspective is almost startling.

The extreme localness of its rural setting in contrast to the mobile, cosmopolitan world of both of the preceding parts further promotes this sense of audience closeness to events. The close-range film-making and the limited changes in locale—the couple's modest house, the community's meeting places, the agricultural fields and salt pans, brief scenes in a bar—bring the viewer into intimate contact with the people of this small country community. The graininess of the stock used in the third part also helps lessen the distance between characters and audience through a certain "home-movie" quality. The brightness of the lighting which emanates from all of the outdoor scenes also gives some feeling for the hot, tropical climate where the characters live and work.

Yet despite Solas's consciousness of the need to find a different form of film-making to portray a revolutionary reality, the real sense of "difference" which one gets in viewing *Lucía 196-* seems to come not from its cinematic techniques but from *who* and *where* the people are in the film. The most revolutionary aspect of the third *Lucía* is the fact that its major character is a rural, illiterate woman in a multi-racial, communal society. A film with this subject matter could simply not have been made at all before the Cuban revolution. This kind of film production, both in its content and in its freedom of experimenta-tion with techniques, would have been proscribed by the capitalist, commercial nature of the Cuban film industry of pre-1959 Cuba.

Like Milos Forman's *Fireman's Ball, Lucía 196-*'s subject matter and cinematic methods successfully capture the quality of life of a whole community. Much of the good humor of the third *Lucía* comes from the fact that the characters already have patterns of collective priorities and interrelationships. In both films, a general feeling of col-lective closeness, solidarity, and human warmth gives space to indi-viduals to work out their problems whether petty thievery or male chauvinism. At the same time, both films operate as self-criticisms of real problems that persist within their societies.

Although one occasionally finds *Lucía* billed as a feminist film, it is neither told from a woman's psychological perspective (although some of the filming, particularly in *Lucía 1895* and *Lucía 1933* is done from the character Lucía's *visual* perspective), nor does it deeply explore women's oppression by patriarchal forms of society nor by individual males. Nevertheless, the film makes an important con-tribution to the image of women in film by the very length of time given to female activities together (such as the birthday party in *Lucía 1895* and the conversations in the back of the truck among the work-ers in *Lucía 196-*). In addition, the director captures the texture of the three Lucías' daily relationships to the people around them in a way rarely seen in the cinema. There is also no doubt that Solas takes seri-ously the developing political consciousness of women, recognizing both their historical importance and the imperative of their equal participation in the ongoing construction of Cuban socialism.

In the last analysis, *Lucía* reveals itself to be above all a film which magnificently shows three stages in a process of historical transition in a country which, within the space of seventy-five years, has moved from European colony through socialist revolution.

[1]Gutierrez Alea's *Memories of Underdevelopment* which was listed as one of the New York Film Critics' "Ten Best Films" of 1973 was released for general distribution in the United States previous to *Lucia*.

[2]*Lucia*, first scheduled to be shown in March, 1972, at the New York Festival of Cuban Films, was confiscated by the Treasury Department along with other films for suspected violation of the "Trading with the Enemy Act." Its first subsequent showing took place at the San Francisco International Film Festival in October, 1973. It is presently available for rental from Tricontinental Film Center, Box 4430, Berkeley, Ca. 94704.

[3]Solas has credited Visconti's *Senso* as being the major influence on the making of *Lucia 1895*. This debt is clear in the latter's impressionistic, operatic effects, and even in some similarities of plot: "Visconti (aristocrat by birth, Marxist by conviction) offers in *Senso* an extraordinary portrait of a decadent and corrupt aristocracy in which Livia's seduction and treachery and Franz's cowardice and deceit are an inevitable result of their environment." (Georges Sadoul, *Dictionary of Films*, p. 332).

Bergman's Portrait of Women: Sexism or Suggestive Metaphor?

BIRGITTA STEENE

Fairly early in his career as a film maker, Ingmar Bergman once made the statement: "The world of women is my universe."[1] Ever since, Bergman has been regarded by many movie goers as an artistic connoisseur of women, as someone who has been particularly sensitive to the subtleties of the so-called female psyche. Women, we have been told, have always liked Bergman because he has given them a larger share of his attention than he has paid to the men in his films. In her book on Ingmar Bergman, published in 1962, Swedish journalist and critic Marianne Höök summed up Bergman's status as an explorer of the world of women in the following way:

> The women in Bergman's films are for the most part more interesting than the men . . . . Bergman's subtle view of women has come as a liberation, and as far as women are concerned Bergman's films since *Waiting Women* (1952) have provided a glimpse of a genuine woman's reality, something one has been able to identify with . . . . His collaboration with women writers (such as Birgit Tengroth and Ulla Isaksson) obviously suited him, stimulated him and opened doors to a world in which he felt strangely at home.[2]

Since the publication of Höök's book, the critics' views of Bergman's portrayal of women has grown more ambivalent. Many reviewers continue of course to be fascinated by his women who are praised for their emotional depth and regarded as unsurpassed screen penetrations into the world of womanhood mystique. But in the last ten years an increasing number of writers on Bergman, several of them avowed feminists, have resented and rejected his depiction of women because they have felt that Bergman approaches women as

objects rather than subjects. Not surprisingly the feminist arguments
were first raised in Bergman's native Sweden but have more recently
been voiced in this country by such film critics as Pauline Kael in *The
New Yorker* and Joan Mellen in *Film Quarterly*.[3] But already in the
mid-1960's, in the aftermath of Bergman's film *The Silence*, Barbro
Backberger, militant Swedish feminist, wrote in her book *Det förkrympta kvinnoidealet* ("The Truncated Female Ideal"):

> In all of Ingmar Bergman's films woman is only an object, some sort of
> projective test for the man, who acts out either his nausea or his lust. In
> *The Silence* Bergman attempts to describe life from a female point of view.
> But when one of the two sisters, Gunnel Lindblom, appears in a love
> scene with a hastily caught lover, we do not get to see *his* naked
> body—which would have been the natural thing since the event is seen
> through her eyes—but *hers*. Is this the result of carelessness, prudish-
> ness or a total inability to experience woman as a subject, as a reacting
> and experiencing creature in sexual contexts?[4]

Feminist critics have continued, like Barbro Backberger, to level
scathing charges against Bergman for his exploitation of women in
their traditional stereotyped roles. From the feminist point of view
Bergman's women appear either as patient Griselda types function-
ing as catalysts for such male egomaniacs as the Knight in *The Seventh
Seal* or the artist in *Hour of the Wolf*, or else they are portrayed as hysterical and neurotic creatures in whom Angst is a camouflage for the
film maker's own hatred of women. The despair and self-disgust of
such women as Anna and Ester in *The Silence*, Elisabet Vogler in *Persona*, Anna in *The Passion*, Eva in *Shame* and Karin and Agnes in *Cries
and Whispers* are, according to Joan Mellen, a cover-up for Bergman's
"determinist misogyny."

Marianne Höök saw Bergman's curiosity about women as a positive thing: "Bergman does not possess the usual prejudices about
women. He does not despise them. And if he hates them, his hatred
is a sign of interest."[5] But Joan Mellen warns us that Bergman's supposed interest in women is not based on any genuine curiosity or
sympathy for their lot but is prompted by his deep-rooted fear of
them as sexual beings; his overriding desire therefore is not to identify with them but to get rid of them—to expose them, to hurt them
and to punish them for the insecurity or, at least, sexual ambivalence,
that they create in him. Women should no longer be fooled—so goes
the feminist argument—by an artist who, in insisting upon turning
his female characters into victims and martyrs, is in fact denying
women their full potential as aggressive and self-sustaining human
beings.

At first it seems difficult not to agree with such an analysis.
Women as man-made archetypes certainly abound in Bergman's films

from the very beginning. Many of the women figures in such early realistic films as *Waiting Women*, *Dreams*, *Illicit Interlude*, and *Brink of Life*–those very characters whom Marianne Höök admired for their self-sufficiency—must seem obsolete from today's feminist point of view, for they exist mostly within the radius of traditional womanhood and achieve identity only by playing the old-time maternal roles of women. When husbands and lovers fail them, they take refuge in church and motherhood; as one of them says in the film *Waiting Women*: "A woman's consolation lies either in Jesus or the grandchildren."

Almost all of the women in Bergman's films from the 1950's are as anxious about marriage as was any young American girl twenty years ago. But the comparison is faulty in that the American girl in the 1950's wanted to get marrried early in life because of the tremendous social pressure to do so and because of the ostracism faced by the unmarried woman of age 23 and above. Bergman, on the other hand, presents marriage as a psychological need existing outside of any social conventions. To want to get married; to belong to a man, is an axiomatic need in Bergman's films of the fifties; and, in fact, his women show no great passion or interest in anything else in life. It is true that Bergman's women of the 1950's are sometimes professional people, such as the fashion manager Susanne and her young model Doris in *Dreams* or Mari, the ballet dancer in *Illicit Interlude*; but these women are strangely indifferent to their work and Bergman's presentation of their professional milieu is negative; Susanne has to cope with the autocratic whims of her obese boss and Mari is faced with the sadistic machinations of her ballet master. Emotionally these women are not absorbed in their jobs, even though these could have been presented as having creative potential. Instead their life revolves around their erotic crises of the present and the past. Creative expressiveness and professional independence are unimportant to them and, at any rate, it cannot protect them from being more vulnerable, victimized and disillusioned than the men they love. Only their resilience can make them survive disillusionments which appear to be part of a given existential situation.

Why did these conventional presentations of women in Bergman's films from the fifties receive the acclaim of a relatively liberated woman like Marianne Höök? Perhaps because of their novel appearance within a national Swedish context. For in Swedish films of the 1940's, mostly three main types of women appeared: the *beredskapskvinna* (a kind of Swedish WAC—i.e. a woman, usually brave and self-sacrificing, who was directly or indirectly connected with the military draft during the war years), the vamp, and the country girl (the vamp inevitably dressed in black lingerie, the country girl glowing with the health of a true child of nature). The *beredskapskvinna* disappeared with the end of World War II. Eventually the vamp became a neurotic megara, and the folksy child of nature a kind of Swedish Lolita aimed for export. But when Bergman first took over the three types in his films, he transformed the *beredskapskvinna* into the brave maternal woman who can go it alone, while the vamp became a victimized slut rather than a self-destructive temptress of men; and the country girl turned into Bergman's innocent "girl of summer." The latter appears for the first time as young Mari in *Illicit Interlude*. She was to remain a favorite with Bergman and returns in many later films—as Sara in *Wild Strawberries*, Mia in *The Seventh Seal*, Karin in *The Virgin Spring*, Anne Egerman in *Smiles of a Summer Night*, young Sanna in *The Magician*. Bergman's 'girl of summer' displays some variations: carefree exuberance, coquettishness, timidity and fragility, but she always has a pure childlike view of life and refuses to accept the compromises of older women.

Bergman readily admits today that his image of female role-playing in the films of the fifties is conventional and that his women tended to be either romanticized innocents or disillusioned lovers turning into strong mothers. But in those days instead of role-playing he would have called it biological truth. He had so absorbed history's view of women in his parental Lutheran home that he believed their emotional non-intellectual approach to life, as well as their masochistic talent for survival, to be genetic facts. And, by the same token, men were by nature shiftless and unreliable—as for instance the lover of the girl Mari in *Waiting Women* and Susanne's friend Lobelius in *Dreams*—or else they appeared as unfeeling intellectuals, Bergman's arch-enemy, such as the husband of Cecilia in *Brink of Life*. If neither of these stereotypes fit the pattern, the Bergman male of the early fifties would frequently be presented as a rather innocuous and helpless creature, bound to arouse the indulgent sympathy of some maternal woman. Such is the case for instance with the husbands in *Waiting Women* and with Stina's husband in *Brink of Life*.

It is likely that the early appreciation of Bergman's female characters stands in direct relation to the uninteresting part played by many of the men in these films. With the exception of *The Naked Night* ("The Eve of Clowns"), Bergman permits the women to dominate the screen until the mid-fifties. It is only when he has found a perfect male medium for his Angst-ridden quest in the sculptured face of Max von Sydow that he shifts to male-dominated films. Now Bergman's old-fashioned male/female dichotomy—the traditional split between man and woman into intellect and body—really begins to crystallize. The men—from the questing knight Antonius Block in *The Seventh Seal* to the doubting Lutheran pastor Tomas in *Winter Light*—are almost to-

tally absorbed in their questioning of the meaning of life. The women
are practically never allowed this philosophical dimension; they appear again as Gretchen or Griselda types who protect and mother
their bungling men, as for instance Mia and the Knight's wife in *The
Seventh Seal*, or Märta, the schoolteacher (pedagogical mother substitute) in *Winter Light*. At other times they are presented as level-
headed, life-affirming housewife prototypes, like the daughter-in-law
Marianne in *Wild Strawberries*. With the exception of Märta in *Winter
Light*, these women are charming and competent in their domestic
roles; but women without depth nevertheless, without any dimension except that afforded them by Bergman as he abides by the rules
of patriarchal planning for women, promulgated as a law of nature.

* * *

When male artists have given us so-called in-depth studies of
women, the result has often been studies in hysteria: a Medea, or
Madame Bovary, or Hedda Gabler or Miss Julie. From the 19th century and on, such women have not only been neurotic but also sexually promiscuous, all the way from Dostoyevsky's Lisa to Sartre's re-
spectful whore. Bergman's portrait of women is no exception. One of
his special fortes is the hysterical, sexually disturbed woman, as wit-
nessed by a long row of films, from *Prison* and *Thirst* in the fifties to
Through a Glass Darkly, *The Silence*, and *Cries and Whispers* in the sixties
and early seventies.

Few of Bergman's emotionally disturbed women are permitted the
luxury of understanding themselves. This is, perhaps, one reason
why his portraits of women have annoyed and distressed feminist critics. The feminist screen ideal seems to be the woman who arrives at
an insight into her situation—celluloid consciousness-raising. If she
is abused or unable to cope with life, there must be some indication
on the part of her creator that he (she) condemns or regrets these circumstances and thinks they can be remedied. Bergman usually does
not, and his artistry (ability to manipulate us) is such that he seduces
us into believing in the reality he projects. Hence, someone like Joan
Mellen must dismiss a film like *Cries and Whispers* as "a suspect and
inauthentic work that stands in the way of a liberated film image of
women."

I shall now make what may seem a critical *volte face* and counter
Mellen's evaluation of Bergman's entire work by suggesting that we
ought to distinguish between those Bergman films in which women
are presented in a contemporary, realistic context—films such as *Waiting Women*, *Brink of Life*, *Scenes from a Marriage*, and to a certain extent
Face to Face—and films in which the women function within a subjec-

tive landscape of the film maker's own making, i.e. most of Bergman's films since 1960. We are more than justified in examining and exposing Bergman's often biased portrait of women who inhabit a modern everyday world—people like the three women in the maternity ward in *Brink of Life* where the milieu has a strong documentary implication. Within such a context we should, I think, challenge Bergman's traditional depiction of women as sensuous, instinctive, patiently suffering, hysterical, masochistically inclined creatures; women whose lives often seem biologically determined and whose self-image is defined in sexual and sexist terms. We should be critical of such portrayals because of the realistic mode of these films. Their presumably objective view is based on an *a priori* assumption that what we are about to witness is a matter of incontestable fact.

However, when Bergman begins to create his own subjective landscape on the screen and to project, through his women characters, his own personal *mythos*—are we really justified then in evaluating that self-imaginary world by using extrinsic criteria, such as our political convictions or contemporary feminist views? It would be a relatively simple matter to approach Bergman's entire body of films from a strict feminist viewpoint and show how Bergman deviates from our own increasing optimism about the options that may one day be open to women, once we really challenge the exponents of genetic and psychological determinism. But if we use such an approach, then we have oversimplified the complexity of artistic modes and defined a good or powerful or worthwhile film as *positive or relevant social document and contemporary realistic statement*. Before we know it, we are applying the same criteria to *Cries and Whispers* as to Pontecorvo's *Battle of Algiers* or Eisenstein's *Potemkin*.

Such an approach with its strong affinity to Marxist literary criticism, can only be justified if it also attempts, as did Lukács in his analysis of Balzac, to trace the roots of the artist's vision and examine in depth the culture and the social and political system that helped shape the artist as a human being. An understanding of the genesis of the work under analysis must precede a feminist judgment of it. But no feminist critic of Bergman has bothered to do this.

Feminist criticism in film as well as in literature should really be part of a much larger critical complex, namely our attempt to understand the *relationship* between art and empirical reality. Here our first task as critics must be an *acceptance* of ths given reality in a work of art. Acceptance here does not mean approval, but simply recognition. If we do not recognize the fictional reality as a valid existence, i.e. as in any way *meaningful*, we need not bother analyzing it.

What is *meaningful*? One might distinguish three possibilities, using Bergman's film *Cries and Whispers* as a test case:

1. Has the film anything important to say about our reality at the time of our reception of it?
2. Has the film anything important to say about ths artist a) at the time of his conception of the film and/or b) about his attitude to certain fundamental problems which appear in a whole series of works?
3. Has the film anything important to say about the time it pertains to portray, i.e. turn of the century Sweden?

If any of these questions can be answered positively, the film is worth examining and deserves our respect, i.e. our effort to understand it before we judge it. In my own view, *Cries and Whispers* is - "meaningful" in all three instances listed above, but most meaningful in terms of question 2. I shall focus my discussion on the second half (b) of that question and view *Cries and Whispers* in the context of several Bergman films, almost all of them made since 1960. I shall discuss three interrelated and complex motifs: the child/artist's need for autonomy of self; the child's search for a parent; the trauma of childhood/the fear of self.

Beginning with *Through a Glass Darkly* (1961), the first of Bergman's so-called "chamber films,"[6] an intensifed "vertical" approach to his screen characters becomes noticeable, as opposed to the earlier "horizontal" mode of presentation within an epic or conventional dramatic plot, a realistic or historical setting. The "vertical" approach implies, not intellectual probing but emotional unmasking. Philosophical questions raised but they are answered through the unfolding of psychic states. Acting out a problem is more important than discussing it. There is a strong resemblance between Bergman's emotionally distraught and hysterical women in such films as *Through a Glass Darkly*, *The Silence*, *Persona*, and *The Passion* and religious acts of exorcism. There is also a strong resemblance between the women's "primal cry"[7] and Bergman's own view of film making as "self-effusion and self-combustion."[8]

One of the changes that occur from Bergman's journey-structured films of the fifties to his inner-search, room-confined works of the sixties and seventies is a gradual shift from a predominantly male to a more emphatically female perspective. To a certain degree, the women then change from objects to subjects, a shift which is ongoing and dramatized in such a film as *The Silence*, where Bergman allows the young boy Johan to free himself from the objectively conceived, prototypal mother-whore Anna, whom we see mostly as body, and to move closer to the more subjectively portrayed[9] father substitute Ester.

Johan is aware of his mother's erotic escapades and peeved by them, but there is no indication that he has much understanding of the world of sexuality. His curiosity is aroused; he stops several times to examine a picture on the wall in the corridor, which depicts a satyr seducing a woman. But sexuality does not seem to pose a threat to him, for he does not have as yet an adult sense of self. Or to put it differently: Johan can incorporate into this world everything that he needs, and reject those aspects of reality that are not meaningful to him or that seem too enigmatic and frightening. He turns away from Ester's fumbling attempts at rapprochement and responds only when his own loneliness or hunger dictates it: he accepts an invitation to share her meal and he breaks down for a moment at her bedside when he feels miserable over Anna's neglect of him. But he has the child's ability to sweep unpleasant matters under the carpet, the way he literally disposes of the morbid photographs given him by the old waiter in the hotel. This is his privilege as a child, but as we know now from Bergman's film *Scenes from a Marriage*, where the second episode is titled "The Art of Sweeping under the Carpet," such behavior can be a disaster in an adult relationship and can lead to deceit, lies and all too fragile illusions of happiness.

The artist selecting those aspects of chaotic reality that will help him make meaningful order is in many ways like a child who still lives in a self-contained, almost autistic world, seemingly oblivious to the way others view him and irritated by, if not unaware of, their needs to approach and touch him. But an artist is also an adult who cannot deny the world of sexuality, which, however, he is unable to cope with, either because childhood traumas prevent him from doing so or because he fears its threat to his autonomy of self. Such is the dilemma of young Johan's namesake, the painter/husband in *Hour of the Wolf* (1968). When the film begins, after the wife's narrative introduction, we meet in Johan an artist who has withdrawn to a barren island, apparently in search of creativity and health. But memories and events from the past continue to haunt him and prevent him from controlling his art. The sickness that destroys him rests within himself, but there is only one conscious reference to it: a childhood trauma when he was locked in a closet as punishment and told that his toes might be chewed up by little goblins in the dark—a verbal image that recurs in several Bergman films, most recently in *Face to Face*, and that apparently is a direct reference to Bergman's own experience as a child.

But Johan dreads reliving the trauma and tries to escape it. Haunting memories overpower him, however, when threatening birds, surreal guests at a nearby castle and the specter of a former lover, Veronica Vogler, literally pursue him across the entire island. Seen from Johan's point of view, the events on the island help destroy his tor-

mented psyche. Seen from his wife's point of view, Johan is an art-
ist/husband in whom fear of otherness takes the form of fear of adult
sexuality and leads to complete withdrawal from her.

This is the double perspective we get in most of Bergman's
chamber films, and it is usually transmitted to us as viewers and may
account for our feeling of discomfort; we *enter into* the lives of
Bergman's characters but as outsiders, as Peeping Toms.

Seen in a larger thematic context, male and female characters take
turns in expressing Bergman's psychological and metaphysical dilemmas. Johan in *Hour of the Wolf* is in many ways an extension of Karin, the young schizophrenic woman in *Through a Glass Darkly*. Like
Johan, Karin is suffering from lack of parental love: she rejects her
husband's sexual advances and withdraws into an attic (which used
to be the nursery), where she is eventually destroyed by her own
haunting fantasies appearing in the shape of an imaginary rapist god
that exits from a closet to attack her. The spider-like god that feeds
upon Karin is a psychic image of her writer/father David, who
exploits her illness to sustain his own novelistic attempts.

How intimately the sexuality-childhood-artist motif; the fear of
self, of unmasking, of otherness is connected with Bergman's personal situation is perhaps best corroborated by his famous essay "The
Snakeskin," in which he describes his childhood activities, his withdrawal into an autonomous world of fantasy but also his own view of
himself as a spider who captures objects in his creative net and plays
with them for a while as long as they amuse him.[10] Even the very tone
of his essay with its mixture of self-revelation, underlying fear of reality, and coldness bears a similarity to his presentation of the screen
characters in many of his chamber films.

* * *

We know that Bergman feared for his mind while working on the
script for *Hour of the Wolf*, i.e. while attempting to perform his art of
exorcism as a film maker. We know that he had to postpone the making of the film and completed *Persona* instead. Perhaps in order to
preserve his sanity, Bergman turned to making a women-dominated
film in which he could reveal, yet camouflage his own struggle
against loss of self-control and the traumas of childhood.

It is worth noticing that not only *Persona* but also *Cries and Whispers*, in which men play only secondary roles, are among Bergman's
most controlled achievements to date. Through his choice of women
as his main characters, and through the partly symbolic mise-en-
scéne where the confines of a room can become a metaphor of self,
Bergman has found, in these two films, a new way to create the

necessary artistic and psychological distance to deeply personal feelings. Like Aman-Manda in *The Magician* (1958)—a film which could
also be titled "Portrait of an Artist"—who removes her mask in the
intimacy of the Vogler bedroom and becomes the catalyst that brings
forth Vogler's misanthropic confession, Bergman's women in such
films as *Persona* and *Cries and Whispers* are not simply objects of abuse,
but creatures through whom Bergman can express his own subjective
fears, his many frustrations and failures at preserving autonomy of
self and control of reality. At the same time, the women—and the
strange landscapes they inhabit—represent alibis against personal
immediacy and stall us in our serach for the confessional roots of the
films. Women become Bergman's personae—his alter egos and his
protective mask.

There is also a professional reason for his choice of women characters. Bergman wishes his actors and actresses to have distance to their
parts, and he has once stated that apart from Max von Sydow, whom
he describes as "robust, sound and healthy to the core," very few of
his performers, other than a number of his actresses, have the necessary detachment he seeks in the interpretation of his main characters.
"It's a question of *reflecting* despair (brustenhet), not *being* it; ex-
hibitionism is a form of acting that must disappear."[11]

Many of Bergman's women in the chamber films reject intimacy in
their lives much the same as did his male protagonists in the fifties
and thus search for some control of reality within or through the self,
beyond sex through a yearning for the spiritual or for an object—
divine or parental, but desexed. We thus get a strange paradox in
these Bergman women: an enormous self-absorption and an enormous disgust with the physicalness of their being. The fear-and-
longing to become part of an object transcending the self and the obsession with the subjective ego, is perhaps most clearly delineated in
Cries and Whispers, but can also be seen in the tension between Anna
and Ester in *The Silence* and between Elisabet Vogler and Alma in *Persona*. In the beginning of the latter film Elisabet, the actress, has
moved from a world demanding otherness—the impersonating demands of the theater and the family demands of husband and son—to
a world of isolation and muteness, a complete lack of commitment
where the only acceptable person is an attentive nurse, whose ideal is
a life of dedication to others. By the end of *Persona*, Alma, the nurse,
has been drawn into Elisabet's world and Elisabet has tried to suck
strength out of Alma's presence. Elisabet, the self-absorbed subject,
becomes from Alma's point of view a threatening object. The two of
them merge in the famous scene where Alma tells Elisabet the truth
about her motherhood. Bergman lets Alma relate the incident twice
while shifting the camera angle from Elisabet's face to Alma's until
finally the two faces fuse into one.

Alma's and Elisabet's relationship is a symbiotic one, in which Bergman shifts back and forth, between the two women, some of the central motifs we recognize from earlier films:

1. Elisabet is the ego-centered artist who rejects emotional involvement in order to preserve her integrity of self.
2. Elisabet is the artist who observes others: the parent who withholds her love in order to study the child (Alma) with bemusement.
3. Elisabet is the silent god figure who refuses to answer when the human soul (Alma) craves a sign of acknowledgement.
4. Alma is the protective parent who permits Elisabet to regress to childhood—"I rock like a foetus in the womb," she writes in her letter to her doctor.
5. Alma is the encroaching world of otherness that begins to make aggressive demands on Elisabet to respond verbally, sexually, and maternally.

The eventual obliteration of the subject-object dichotomy that occurs with the merging of Alma's and Elisabet's faces takes the verbal form of an accusation by Alma. She shows Elisabet as a failing parent but the scene ends with Alma's garbled defense of an abortion she has had earlier, prior to the actual events of the film. This failure of the mother to protect, love and respond to her child is also a central theme in *Cries and Whispers*. However, the parent/child, object/subject syndrome has really been pervasive in Bergman's production since the mid-fifties. Bergman's earlier, mostly male-oriented films might be said to examine his attitude towards his inherited father figure, camouflaged and transformed into a God figure in *The Seventh Seal*; into a withdrawn artist and family man in *Through a Glass Darkly*; and into a parson and impotent father of his flock in *Winter Light*. In all of these instances, it is the aloofness, indifference, silence and emotional limitations of the father figure that precipitates the tragedy; the child's relationship with the father is full of frustration (Antonius Block's God does not answer) or the contact is expressed in negative, parasitical terms as in Karin's discovery of her father's notebook over her illness. Tomas, the parson in *Winter Light*, is totally helpless against the despair and suicidal impulses of Jonas Person, his parishioner. All Tomas can do is talk about himself: the object that should console the seeking subject can only turn inwards upon itself.

Beginning with *The Silence* and continuing with *Persona* and *Cries and Whispers*, Bergman shifts his examination to the mother-child syndrome. The clearest expression of this is *Cries and Whispers*. In a statement made apropos of the film, Bergman has told us that *Cries and Whispers* is a portrait of his mother as he got to know her during her last illness.[12] His close contact with his dying mother, who revealed to him her own life-long frustrations, made him realize that the distant parent—an object whom he couldn't reach as a child, was herself a suffering subject, a frightened human being who could not possibly give solace and support to her children, because she herself was not always sure of her own sense of self.

All three women in *Cries and Whispers* are daughters of a beautiful but casual mother who apparently played favorites, accepting some of her daughters into her world and excluding others. One of the most important scenes in the film is where Agnes, the dying sister, remembers an incident from her childhood where she was denied her mother's affection, which instead was given to Maria, the beautiful and charming child, the mother's own image. The mother, remembered once by Agnes, as she sits in a wicker chair with an enigmatic smile on her face, is as distant and unfathomable a creature as the silent god or withdrawn artist in Bergman's earlier films. Her child Agnes hungers for her and fears her at the same time.

The British critic Isaiah Berlin once, in writing about Tolstoy, made the distinction between artists who are "foxes" and artists who are "hedgehogs". The foxes in art are quixotic, changing, outgoing. Each work is for them a new departure. The hedgehogs, on the other hand, are artists who develop slowly and who move within the narrow limits of their personal vision. The one species of artists is not superior to the other, only different.

Though Bergman once wrote a famous essay in which he maintained that "each work is my last,"—i.e. that each film is a complete and finished work,—there is strong evidence in his films that he really is a cinematic hedgehog. There is of course philosophical and psychological progression in his works and certain stylistic changes and shifts in point of view occur, especially around 1960, but to an amazing extent the issues that concerned Bergman back in 1950 are still vital to him. And so one is not really surprised to find that one of the films that *Cries and Whispers* resembles most is *The Naked Night* or "The Eve of the Clowns," made almost twenty years before and generally considered Bergman's first major work. In terms of setting one could hardly find two more dissimilar films, although the action of both takes place at about the same time, around the turn of the century. One film is set in a circus milieu, the other in an upper class mansion; one exudes earthiness, the other restraint and a certain refinement. But the film about the circus director Algot Johansson and his mistress Anne reveals, in some of its characters, the same inability as does *Cries and Whispers* to accept adulthood and a similar longing to return to the comforts of maternal protection. *The Naked*

Night ends with the clown Frost retelling a dream he has had, in which he transforms his wife Alma into a mother figure and himself into an embryo who reenters the mother's womb. Algot, the circus director, has earlier visited his former wife, a prototypal maternal woman who makes pancakes and sews buttons on his coat while her young son manages the store. Algot longs, for a moment, for the peace that his former wife seems to possess; but before leaving her to go back to the circus, he has recognized that returning to his wife's world, to the mother's world, would in fact be a form of suicide. The womb may exist in our imagination as a dream or paradise and peace, but in reality it leads to a state of complete passivity, to death.

In *Cries and Whispers*, this dream of the womb is conveyed to us in a visualized passage from Agnes' diary, read by the housekeeper Anna after Agnes' death: the three sisters are together in the garden; it is summer time and they all go to sit together in the hammock. Rocked by the mother figure Anna, as if in a cradle of nature, the sisters experience a moment of intense closeness and love. But such fleeting remembrances of being united with the mother cannot become a continuous part of the sisters' adult reality: the moment is related by Anna and exists only in the memory of a dying woman.

After Agnes' death, Anna can be dismissed by the others because she fulfills no subjective need for anyone else in the family. Only Agnes was able to accept her as a mother substitute, finding real peace and real death as Anna climbed into her bed and held her in a pietà posture. For Karin and Maria, the other two sisters, Anna is nothing but a servant whose usefulness ends with Agnes' death.

Bergman has been criticized for choosing a servant as his central mother figure, thereby making himself guilty of a double sexist prejudice: his redeemer figure is a woman in the role of passive consoler and servile subordinate, a white nanny and Aunt Jemima of the North. But seen within the context of Bergman's personal vision, Anna could not emerge from within the family; the failure of the real mother to prepare all her three daughters for adulthood is a given motif. Anna must be an outsider in the household, to whom only Agnes, the most rejected of the children, can respond. That she accepts and is comforted by Anna's love is an indictment, not only of her mother but also of her two sisters, neither of whom responds to her needs since they themselves are like self-absorbed children, trying to exert self-control against the encroachment of the men in their lives, who seem to act the part of cold scrutinizers and father figures. Beautiful Maria's lover, the doctor, leads her to a mirror and examines with vicious matter-of-factness the first aging lines in her coquettish face. Karin, the older sister, feels herself so threatened by her Vergérus-like husband[13] that she resorts to a revengeful act of self-mutilation, suggesting that sex would be the only weapon available to a woman of her situation.

There are relatively few actual children who appear in Bergman's films. But metaphorically speaking many of his main characters are like children in search of a parent, unable to accept adulthood and fearing the loss of the autonomous self. In trying to cope with the situation, the individual usually resorts to some form of escape or act of revenge, directed as much against the self as against some person threatening the self. Often the revenge expresses itself as sexual deviation, sexual excesses or sexual mutilation. Bergman sees sexuality, not just female sexuality, as a threat to the innermost self. Sexuality is a metaphor for all of that reality which cannot be subsumed under the selective scope of the child/artist's *laterna magica*. Sexuality is otherness: the taunting god, the stern or capricious parent. Its often negative treatment by Bergman is not a sign of "determinist misogyny" but rather a means of indicting the social, religious and parental world that prevents his characters from living more harmonious lives.

People's ability to fool themselves into thinking that they are actually living harmonious lives is great, however. In his last two films to date, *Scenes from a Marriage* and *Face to Face*, Bergman takes seemingly well-adjusted individuals and reveals how they, too, harbor deepseated conflicts, which are hidden beneath the facade of middle-class comfort. At first, *Scenes from a Marriage* and *Face to Face* may seem to represent a new departure for Bergman, although it is possible to see his film *The Touch* as a prelude. With their bourgeois milieus rather than remote islands, mansions and hotels, these films possess a surface realism that is deceptive to the viewer and probably was a challenge to Bergman, who proves that harrowing psychic journeys can be undertaken in the most ordinary of rooms.

Again, women stand in the center of the films. Both are professional women around 40, apparently successful. But their professions seem chosen by Bergman in order to create an ironic twist. Marianne in *Scenes from a Marriage* is a divorce lawyer who cannot perceive the impending collapse of her own marriage. Jenny in *Face to Face* is a psychiatrist who has fooled herself into believing that she is mentally strong and well adjusted. There is of course, on Bergman's part, no implication that the two women are unhappy in their jobs or that their problems arise from the fact that they pursue professional careers. But their jobs—and the kind of comfortable life style that the jobs can provide—do serve as blinders for deep-lying psychological problems. Once these problems begin to surface, the realistic frame of the films recedes into the background and we enter familiar Bergman territory. This is particularly true of *Face to Face*, where both Jenny's problem and the way it manifests itself has a familiar ring.

In *Face to Face*, Bergman juxtaposes once more the parent/child relationship and the theme of the dreaded unmasking of the self. Jenny's return to the house of her grandparents, where she is "pampered" by her grandmother, becomes the catalyst for a journey into the repressed traumas of childhood. As in *Cries and Whispers*, Bergman's technique does not follow the pattern of conventional psychoanalysis with its basically verbal reliving of the past. Rather he pursues again Arthur Janov's thesis that only a direct emotional reliving of the trauma can heal a mentally sick person. Such a view is of course in keeping with Bergman's own development as a film maker: ever since he began to explore the possibilities of the "chamber film" he has relied on the mimetic strength of his actress/medium, while using verbal expression more and more as an ironic counter-point; hence the often witty dialogue in *Scenes from a Marriage* and *Face to Face*.

Gradually Jenny's comfortable facade of a lifestyle is stripped away, and the image of a frightened child begins to emerge, a child who seeks the same protection from unreachable and unresponsive parent figures and who fears the same dark closet of isolation as so many of Bergman's earlier characters. Unable to cope with the threat of the past, which appears before her as the deadly specter of an old woman with glassy eyes, Jenny attempts suicide. Hovering in a purgatory between life and death, she fights her parents whose brief appearance suggests moralistic values that have prevented Jenny from resting secure in her adulthood: coldness of heart, repressive upbringing, excessive guilt feelings. The parents are, however, also seen as helpless victims of a *modus vivendi* that can only translate man's existential fear of death into stern self-accusation. It is embodied in the harsh stare of the old specter-woman in Jenny's nightmare, who first appears in the "realistic" part of the film as a black-veiled lady in mourning. She is a perennial figure in the Bergman canon. In looks, she is related to the black-clad, cancer-sick old woman in *Illicit Interlude*, who plays chess with the minister on young Mari's summer island and foreshadows, with her sinister appearance, the death of Mari's lover. In attitude, the morbid figure springs from the same cultural heritage as the black monk in *The Seventh Seal*, who hurls hell-and-brimstone threats at the flagellants, thus reinforcing their view that the deadly plague is a justified punishment for·sinners.

Encapsuled then in Jenny's nightmarish visions is the same harsh Lutheranism that drove the Knight in *The Seventh Seal* on his futile crusade. What was once a physical and metaphysical journey has now become an inner psychological journey, but behind both Antonius Block's 14th century search and Jenny's brushing with death lies the same Angst. Eschatological problems cannot, however, be rationalized away by the church. Nor can they be treated in the psychiatric ward. In one of her nightmares, Jenny sees herself in her profession, literally unmasking her patients to show their raw wounds; then prescribing a tranquillizer treatment. Her method is no less cruel than the monk's in *The Seventh Seal*. He provided his frightened listeners with a piece of religious rationalization; Jenny denies her patients their pain and provides them with impersonal advise and standard pharmaceutica. One method is as absent of love and compassion as the other.

Jenny survives however her own unmasking. The haunting specter, the trauma of childhood, brings her face to face with herself; but she succeeds in exorcising the deadly figure. She attempts at first to save herself through an attachment to her friend and psychiatric confessor, but he rejects her proposition of love-making. She confronts—in rather ludicrous situations unfortunately—her career husband and her teenage daughter; both are emotional light years away from her. Finally, however, she discovers healing values in the relationship between her ailing cripple of a grandfather and her strong maternal grandmother. Viewing their quiet affection for each other from behind a curtain, Jenny remains an absorbant onlooker while expressing a new affirmation of life. Unlike many earlier Bergman characters, she does not ask for parental protection: she does not demand to be taken back to the womb. She believes she has the strength to face herself as an adult, to accept her friend's earlier advice: to let a pain be a pain and a fear a fear, without trying to rationalize these feelings or cover them up. In her survival, Jenny is unique among Bergman's emotionally complex women, for she is freed from her double heritage: from her religiously rooted, punitive upbringing and from the modern, impersonal and antiseptic "treatment" of existential fear.

Face to Face is not among Bergman's best films. It often seems shot at some haste. At the end it tends to become analytical and explanatory rather than mimetic and *gestaltend*. But Bergman's depiction of his woman protagonist is important, both in the way her experience reveals the film maker's cultural syndrome and the way he suggests her liberation from it.

[1]From an interview in *Filmnytt*, No. 6 (1950), p. 13.

[2]Marianne Höök, *Ingmar Bergman*. Stockholm: Wahlström och Widstrand, 1962, p. 84. All translations from the Swedish are my own.

[3]Joan Mellen, "Bergman and Women: Cries and Whispers," *Film Quarterly*, Fall, 1973, pp. 2-11.

[4]Barbro Backberger, *Det förkrympta kvinnoidealet*. Stockholm: Bonniers, 1966, p. 13.

[5]Höök, *Ingmar Bergman*, p. 94.

[6]The term "chamber film" is an attempt on Bergman's part to transfer to the screen August Strindberg's concept and practice of the "chamber play," i.e. a dramatic work that develops according to the associative pattern of a musical composition, relying more on leitmotifs than on conventional character development. The chamber play/film usually employs a limited number of closely related (biologically or metaphorically) characters; it takes place in a confined, often symbolic space, while juxtaposing real and surreal or dreamlike situations and states of mind.

[7]The American psychoanalyst Arthur Janov has challenged Freud's approach to neurosis as being too intellectual and incomplete. Only by an actual reliving of the traumas of childhood and an acceptance of the original pain, "the primal cry", can neurotic people be helped.

[8]*Time*, March 14, 1960, p. 62. [Cover story on Ingmar Bergman].

[9]The camera is quite ambivalent in portraying Ester. On the one hand we get a much more intimate view of her than of Anna and sense her despair through a number of close-ups, while Anna's situation is always related to something in the outside world: the cafe, the crowd in the street, the cabaret incident, the view of the cooks in the kitchen during her love-making, her lover's tingling play with her bracelets. But Ester is also observed, becomes an object to ths camera, especially noticeable in the masturbation sequence. Perhaps the ambivalent view of Ester is best expressed in the episode where she performs a pantomime for the waiter, trying to make him bring her more liquor. Drunk and self-conscious at the same time, she acts out her request against a reflecting mirror.

[10]Preface to Swedish edition of *Persona*, Stockholm: Norstedt, 1966, p. iv.

[11]Björkman, Manns, Sima, *Bergman om Bergman*. Stockholm: Norstedt, 1970, p. 128.

[12]Author's interview, October, 1971.

[13]Vergérus is the critical, scrutinizing doctor in *The Magician*, who is set up as a skeptical contrast to Vogler, the artist/charlatan/psychic healer. He can be seen as Bergman's diabolic archetype.

Mizoguchi's Oppressed Women

DANIEL SERCEAU

Translated by Leah Maneaty

Those who are acquainted with Mizoguchi's films regard him as one of the most important filmmakers working during the '30s, '40s, and '50s. Most of his films concentrate on the role of women in Japanese society during different historic periods.

The majority of films examined in this article form part of the director's last period. The historical and contemporary films divide approximately in half. Two things are immediately evident: (1) Mizoguchi always took great care with historical fact, and (2) his choice of an historic subject or setting was governed largely by expediency. Censorship in Japan prevented the free expression of certain attitudes, and the problem of advancing forbidden opinions was often sidestepped by transporting them to a different time period. Transforming the past into the present, however, can be misleading and it is therefore necessary to differentiate Mizoguchi's analyses of the condition of women during the Middle Ages from that of the modern woman. However, the class character of oppression remains fundamentally the same, varying only in form and degree.

Three of Mizoguchi's films shed light on the position of women in medieval society and under the Ancient Regime. *The Life of O'Haru* (1952), *Chikamatsu Monogatari* [*The Crucified Lovers*] (1954), and *The Empress Yang Kwei Fei* (1955). *O'Haru* and *Chikamatsu Monogatari* deal with the sincere desire of men and women to love outside of marriage, unhindered by the social, moral, or ideological restrictions which serve class interests (i.e., the taboo on adultery in *Chikamatsu Monogatari*, the contempt of the ruling class for men of lower birth, and the belief in the superiority of upper class women in *O'Haru*).

O'Haru loves a young man from a lower social class. In Japan during the sixteenth century, sexual relations were strictly regulated in order to assure the unaltered continuation of the social hierarchy, and it was impossible for a man to approach a woman who was of a higher social station. With the help of a trick, however, O'Haru's lover succeeds. At first she uses the doctrine of her own class against herself and hurts him by declaring that he is unworthy to look at her. Soon, unable to withhold her feelings, she surrenders herself to him. The young man is beheaded, O'Haru and her family are ruined, exiled, condemned to poverty.

In eighteenth century Japan adultery was severly punished. Yet behind its moral facade, the taboo on adultery was frequently used to safeguard the class interests of the declining nobility. In *Chikamatsu Monogatari* the violation of the taboo allows the nobility the opportunity of seizing the wares of a merchant, thereby freeing themselves of a debt which leaves them progressively more dependent on him. Mizoguchi shows that adultery itself is of little importance to the nobility; what matters are the debts owed to the rich merchant and the fact that his wife's infidelity allows them to cancel those debts.

WOMAN AS AN OBJECT OF REPRODUCTION AND AN OBJECT OF PLEASURE

In *O'Haru* the role of the woman/mother is reduced to that of a reproductive uterus. The emperor's wife is barren, and it is necessary to mitigate her inadequacy while giving the emperor an heir whose legitimacy will not be questioned. An emissary is sent throughout the kingdom to find a new companion. The emperor scrupulously sets down each of the physical traits he desires in her, and O'Haru alone answers his stipulations. A son is born, but is hardly out of his mother's womb when he is taken away to another room and entrusted to his official educators. O'Haru's only function is biological. She must produce a body, not a child; for her son's spiritual character, moulded by his tutors, must conceal the hoax his birth represents to the throne and to the doctrine of legitimacy. It is the preservation of power by the ruling elite which is at stake here, and therefore well worth an ideological hoax and the complete denial of a woman's maternal instinct.

In a similar way (similar in the sense that she is once again an expendable tool used to further the interests of the caste in power) O'Haru exists only as a sexual object. The picture the emperor draws for his emissaries of the future mother of his son is merely the description of the erogenous body which best responds to his sexual fantasies. After the birth of her son O'Haru remains near the emperor, but their lovemaking endangers his life and the imperial counselors evict O'Haru from the palace reproaching her for not having been able to restrain the emperor's desires. She is sent back to her family and will see her son only once from a distance, twenty years later.

It is therefore O'Haru's body, both as an object of pleasure and a reproductive organ, which was used to serve the higher interests of the ruling caste, to be immediately rejected as soon as it became a threat to them. In each case, O'Haru's emotions and personality are completely denied. Never has the woman/object been more fully rendered on film, nor the cause of her subjection (i.e., the class society dominated by men in which women are servants of power and gratification) more explicitly examined.

WOMEN AS OBJECTS OF EXCHANGE

In eighth century China an emperor pines away for his deceased wife. Consequently, the affairs of the kingdom suffer and a replacement for the dead empress is sought. The heroine in *Kwei Fei*, arriving in the capital from the country, is greeted by her cousins, who in order to profit by her presence use her as a servant. Poorly dressed, without visible beauty, she is doomed to the most menial jobs. But the young girl has an astonishing likeness to the former empress and the faction out of power recognizes this as an opportunity to gain favors from the emperor by presenting her to him. Kwei Fei is then decorated, honored, beautified and magically transformed in order to make her forget her low origins. This is the same falsehood used by the caste in power in regard to O'Haru's child. The aristocracy has always justified its privileges by an alleged natural superiority. Yet the purpose of the magical practices which surround Kwei Fei's education is to convince her that there has been a veritable "transmutation" of her low birth to a noble station. She becomes the most delicate of empresses. Her cousins bring her forward in exchange for positions of power and privileges obtained from the emperor. Kwei Fei has neither the time to accept or refuse, and becomes a political pawn in the intrigues of the court. At first she shrinks from a feeling of moral prostitution and later understands that she will never be her own person. Her hanging is only the last stage in a political process over which she never had any control.

AN ILLUSIONARY HAPPINESS

Although women most often seem at odds with their situation, there exits a positive side to their role in society. At a certain point in the film, O'Haru gets married. Though she never had the opportunity of choosing a husband, O'Haru finds that by a stroke of good luck her fiancé sincerely loves her. Together they manage a fan store and are happy except for their struggle to survive. The husband spends half his nights at the store. A young couple, they already exist in a state of frustration, living in a society founded on economic competition. The impossibility of finding personal happiness in such a society is clearly shown by Mizoguchi in *Ugetsu*, where a potter, socially driven by ambition and the desire for wealth, tries to further his gains in war. This results in separation from his wife and finally death.

THE CONDITION OF JAPANESE WOMEN DURING THE '50s

Mizoguchi's modern films take place in the underworld of prostitution. The choice of this setting points to the filmmaker's concern with the exploitation and oppression of individuals in class society. Prostitution appears then as an exemplary case of how individuals are degraded to the status of merchandise, forced by necessity to submit in order to survive.

In *The Woman of Rumor* (1954), a young girl returns to her mother after completing her studies and finds that she manages a house of prostitution. The child cannot accept her mother's situation and attempts suicide several times. At first she is very antagonistic toward the prostitutes, but she slowly gets to know them and eventually crosses over to their side. At the end of the film she replaces her sick mother as head madam. However, at the outset of the film the girl is faced with a dilemma: the profits collected from the prostitutes' work provide the tuition for her education. Contrary to the dictates of morality she hates her mother and reproaches herself for these feelings. Her only alternative is to hate herself in turn and to entertain a secret desire for punishment and death. At this point the film focuses on her growing sense of guilt when faced with the necessities of daily survival which mock the values taught by her education. In reality, her education has left her egocentric, unjust, and incapable of accepting and responding to maternal love. She must overcome her prejudices in order to become friendly with the prostitutes, to make their condition her own cause, and to find a meaning in life in the struggle to end their subjugation. At the end of the film she still refuses to accept prostitution as fate, yet she is no longer inclined to fight it. She is taken by the "system" and forced to work at something she disapproves of. If the oppression suffered by this middle-class girl is not unique to the condition of women, it is characteristic of the oppression suffered by a class in which the children are sent to school to be trained to reproduce the social structure unchanged.

Dealing once again with the theme of education, *Gion Festival* (1953) examines how pedagogical institutions work to maintain society's exploitative structure. This time, however, the school itself produces the people/objects. By means of apprenticeship in dance, music, and the refinement of domestic customs, the geishas have learned the traditional Japanese art of entertaining. That is, they are taught all the ways in which to bring pleasure to their guests. This art of giving pleasure, in reality, however, conceals an aristocratic and schooled form of prostitution.

OPPRESSION IN MARRIAGE

In *Street of Shame* (1956) Micky, the daughter of a rich man, becomes a prostitute in a Kyoto whorehouse called "The Dream." One morning her father appears in her room and demands that she return home: she is hurting his business affairs and those of the eldest son who will be refused an excellent position if his sister continues to prostitute herself. Faced with such cynicism Micky ridicules her father by offering herself to him.

Micky's father proposes that she conform to the accepted feminine ideal of hostess and bearer and educator of children. Middle-class men demand that all the energies of their wives be concentrated on their maternal and domestic roles. As there is no reason to personally accept similar standards of monogamy, middle-class males need another kind of woman, more or less bound to them through prostitution, who will serve them as sexual objects. When Mickey suggests that her father sleep with her, she exposes the cause that ties the bourgeois male to prostitution. Her father becomes the victim of what he has helped produce—the prostitution of his daughter, resulting from the moral monogamy imposed on women. He is caught in the contradiction of his own values: the official condemnation of prostitution and its unabashed patronage behind the scenes.

THE EXPLOITATION AND OPPRESSION OF PROLETARIAT WOMEN

One of the residents of the "Dream" tries to escape her plight by joining her fiancé, a country laborer. Shortly thereafter, she returns to the "Dream" in tears; instead of finding a better life she encounters one still worse. From the moment she stops prostituting herself for the workman in order to become his wife, she is subject to other forces from which she cannot escape: 1)economic at first, she is forced to struggle to survive. A fundamental law in a free economy, the woman becomes a source of free labor to her husband, 2)sexual next, at the "Dream" her husband had to pay his sexual expenses at the "Dream." Now he enjoys them for free, using his wife sexually without establishing any real sexual rapport. In marriage as in prostitution, the man continues to use his partner as an object to satisfy his sexual needs. At least at the "Dream" she was paid for her labor. Now she has nothing left; everything is freely at the disposal of her husband.

PROSTITUTION: A RESULT OF WOMAN'S ECONOMIC POVERTY

Except in the case of Micky where social and psychological causes intermingle, prostitution is seen in Mizoguchi's films as the result of the social restrictions and economic hardship imposed on women. Deprived of any professional skill or training, prostitution remains for many women the only way they can provide for their own and their families' needs.

One of the prostitutes in *Street of Shame* is the mother of a family in which the consumptive husband is unable to provide economic support. In *The Woman of Rumor* a very young girl insists, throughout the entire film, on working in a house of prostitution. In *Street of Shame* the same thing happens and one of the prostitutes is trying to pay off her father's debts. As one of her colleagues states, women who sell themselves actually belong more to themselves than women in the rest of society.

In *Gion Festival* Mizoguchi shows how geishas are used as objects of commercial transactions. The seller in this film sends a geisha ahead in order to gratify his client. The client profits by taking her to bed. It is obvious that within these dealings ths geisha has no existence of her own. She is merely the coin of exchange underlying the official currency.

In *The Sisters of Gion* (1936) [remade in 1953 as *Gion Festival Music*], two geisha sisters live together. One is modern; the other tied to tradition. The modern one, conscious of her oppression, rejects her condition and decides to submit others to what she is made to suffer. Since this society is based on man's exploitation of man, the solution, she thinks, is to transform herself into an exploiter. One day she takes advantage of the love of a kimono vendor in order to obtain a beautiful kimono without paying for it. Rather than uniting against their common enemy, she uses a man of her own class, exploited and oppressed as she is. He avenges himself by throwing her under a moving vehicle, breaking both her legs. Confined to her bed, she realizes the uselessness of individual revolt.

SUMMARIZING MIZOGUCHI'S WORK

I have not tried to analyze Mizoguchi's directing techniques. Rather, my purpose has been to examine how he views the condition of Japanese women in his films. With the exception of the geisha, the condition of the Japanese woman is not unique—it is the condition of all women, regardless of social position, in societies dominated by men of power. One can now perhaps better understand why Mizoguchi attaches such importance to prostitution. It is because the differences between sexual prostitution and social prostitution are of degree and not of kind. A woman surrenders the use of her body to another person in order to survive, in the same way a worker surrenders his labor.

Those who would reproach Mizoguchi for being content to merely denounce the forms of oppression and exploitation inherent in the capitalist system must take into account the historical period during which his films were produced—the '50s. The protest movement was very small at the time, yet Mizoguchi, of all filmmakers, most clearly examined the class exploitation of the masses.

Except in the case of Micky (*Street of Shame*, 1956) where social and psychological causes intermingled, prostitution in Mizoguchi's films was the result of social restrictions and economic hardship imposed on women.

In *Gilda* (1946), Rita Hayworth sang "Put the Blame
on Mame."

Gennarino turns sadist, brutalizing the woman so that she can emerge in her "true colors." Mariangela Melato and Giancarlo Giannini in Wertmüller's *Swept Away* (1975).

If Rosemary is the perfect victim, defenseless and ignorant, she is indispensable to the satanic sect. John Cassavetes, Mia Farrow, and Ralph Bellamy in *Rosemary's Baby* (1968).

The victim in the fantastic is always a sexual object and the "monster's" aggression takes on the characteristics of rape. Evelyn Ankers and Lon Chaney, Jr. in *The Ghost of Frankenstein* (1942).

Agnes Moorehead and Bette Davis as grotesqueries in *Hush . . . Hush, Sweet Charlotte* (1965).

Maria is a woman who preaches peace and reconciliation; the other Maria is a robot without a soul who incites hatred and violence. The false Maria in Fritz Lang's *Metropolis* (1927).

Jane Fonda as the prostitute in *Klute* (1971).

The amoral model works her way up. Julie Christie in *Darling* (1965).

Boccaccio '70 (1962),
Sophia Loren.

For Howard Hawks, there is only the male and the non-male: in order to be accepted into the male universe, the woman must *become* a man; alternatively she becomes woman-as-phallus. Jane Russell and Marilyn Monroe in Hawks's *Gentlemen Prefer Blondes* (1953).

Jeanne Moreau and Orson Welles in *L'Histoire Immortelle* (1968), made by Welles for French television.

Part Two
The
Women's
Cinema

Ingrid Thulin in *Night Games* (1966), for all its sexual frills a film essentially about loneliness.

Father's "strength" is contrasted with her man's "weakness" in *Merrily We Go To Hell* (1932). Charles Coleman, Sylvia Sidney and Fredric March.

Introduction

The preceding pages have demonstrated the representation and mis-representation of women in films by directors in Hollywood and other capitals around the world. In many cases, the image of women has been limited and sexist. Now, what is to be done?

"The Women's Cinema" attempts to answer this question. First, there exists a need for criticism continuously responsive to new developments. Second, there must be ample opportunities for creating new forms of cinema. Without dismissing traditional forms, the authors here explore alternatives for a cinema in which women, by exerting control of direction, may present themselves on film.

Most of the articles which follow appeared after the significant month of June in 1972, when The First International Women's Film Festival was held in New York City. Similar events were subsequently held in Edinburgh, London, Toronto, Washington, Chicago and Paris—festivals which provided the first extensive screening of films directed by women and prompted serious new scholarship on the subject. Since then film critics, both male and female, have been questioning long accepted notions and looking at *all* films through new eyes. Old films have been given new readings; neglected works have taken on a new life; previously ignored works by women are now being screened and studied. Naturally, not all are masterpieces, but they do reveal the frustrations and aspirations of women within the specific cultural milieu and the dominant ideology of the period.

"Women's Cinema as Counter-Cinema" by Claire Johnston deals with the importance of myth as an indicator of the dominant ideology. Influenced by Marxist philosophy, linguistical and semiological studies, and Freudian analysis, Johnston emphasizes the need to decode and demystify the cinema. She shows that films seldom present woman as woman: "Within a sexist ideology and a male-dominated cinema, woman is presented as what she represents for man."

Recognizing the impossibility of escaping ideology in any artistic creation, Johnston sees women's cinema as a means of interrogating male, bourgeois cinema, and defines women's cinema as one which accepts and utilizes fantasy and which challenges the present depictions of reality. Selecting films by two women, Dorothy Arzner and Ida Lupino, she demonstrates how the former, while utilizing traditional female stereotypes, deconstructs the text and creates a self-critique, while the latter, using melodrama, juxtaposes Hollywood myths about women with a female perspective.

In "Feminist Film Criticism: Theory and Practice" Julia Lesage proceeds from an opposing philosophy. Embracing a feminist commitment to political and social reality and employing methods inherited from Umberto Eco, Bertolt Brecht, Christian Metz and Roland Barthes, she sets forth a stratagem for feminist film criticism.

According to Lesage, the purposes of feminist criticism are to re-evaluate neglected films, demythologize traditional cinematic heroes (fictional and directorial) and to aid feminist political activity. As opposed to Johnston, Lesage is anxious to approach all mechanisms in and outside of a film work, including questions of verisimilitude.

She identifies six factors which influence the finished film product: 1) the prefilmic milieu, 2) the filmmaker(s), 3) the film, 4) the audience, 5) the audience's milieu and 6) the production/distribution system—all the forces which must be treated by the feminist critic. Like Johnston, Lesage believes that the end product of film analysis is a changing consciousness which will evoke feedback from viewers and effect social change.

Lastly, my selection, "Towards a Feminist Aesthetic: Reflection-Revolution-Ritual," differs from both the preceding articles, dealing with specific films which have been produced, and, without ignoring the socio-cultural context, concentrating on the works themselves. The article attempts to analyze those elements within the feminist consciousness which motivate the form and content of individual creations.

The article sets forth three aesthetics within which women have created films: 1) the aesthetic of reflection which represents the artist's efforts to discover feelings about herself or others and to appraise relationships with society, 2) the aesthetic of revolution which generally deals with group action, posing a direct challenge to the status quo and 3) the aesthetic of ritual which addresses itself to the question of art and which by nature is androgenous. I have indicated how these aesthetics can inform films created in different eras and in various modes—experimental, documentary, and narrative fiction.

"A Feminist Perspective" serves to define the theoretical underpinnings of women's films and criticism. Obviously women will create films which reflect differences; and they will doubtless reach out into new areas to extend filmmaking beyond the parameters set forth here.

Despite the fact that recognition of them is only currently being acknowledged, women directors are not a new phenomenon. They have had a long, glorious career in cinema from the very beginnings of film history. A complete record would require a volume of its own. The following chapters touch upon the high water marks, treating those women who have made significant contributions to their fields of specialization. The last decade and a half have produced amazing talents. Of course, not all of them could be treated in depth. These selections, however, provide a cross-section of nationalities and styles of those women whose output has been significant.

The following brief history of women's place in film history is intended to place in perspective those women treated here and to provide information about those who are not. (The reader will find the filmographies listed in the back of this book and the bibliography with additional information on directors.)

The work of women in the cinema dates back to 1896 (one year after the first projected film), when Alice Guy, working for the producer, Leon Gaumont, was given the responsibility of directing the company's first fiction films. Between 1897 and 1906, proceeding along the same lines as George Méliès, she directed many films based on fairy tales, myths, Biblical stories, and original comedies. In 1907 she emigrated to America with her husband, Herbert Blanché, and continued to direct for their own production company, Solax, until 1915. A director of over 270 silent films, Guy is remembered as a prolific pioneer and enterprising executive. The article by Francis Lacassin, based on personal contact with Madame Guy-Blaché, documents her remarkable contribution.

During Hollywood's formative years, many women were employed as writers, editors and directors. From 1913 to 1927, twenty-six women worked behind the camera, directing films about everything from women's suffrage to girls-on-the-make. Most of them owed their opportunities to Universal's Carl Laemmle and Paramount's Adolph Zukor, producers who were willing to risk countering prevalent attitudes about "the place of women" and their "inability" to handle cameras and crews.

Of the women who worked in Hollywood during that early period, Lois Weber was one of the most prolific, making her first film in 1913, and by 1916 managing her own production company, leased to her by Universal Studios. She began with the controversial issue of birth control and virtually ended her career in 1927 with a series of exploitation films on loose women. Unfortunately much of the work done by her and other directors such as Ruth Ann Baldwin, Cleo Madison and Ida May Park, has been lost through neglect or remains inaccessible.

During this period several successful actresses, among them Lillian Gish, Alla Nazimova, Mabel Normand and Mary Pickford, managed to direct themselves in films, although none received screen credit. Many women were active as writers. The prodigious Anita Loos turned out over 200 scenarios for Douglas Fairbanks and D. W. Griffith, as well as her famous *Gentlemen Prefer Blondes*. June Mathis scripted several classics of the silent period, including *Blood and Sand*, *Greed* and *Ben Hur*. The British novelist, Elinor Glyn, beginning her Hollywood career at the age of fifty-six, not only wrote, but served as producer for both Paramount and MGM, exerting tremendous control over her films. Frances Marion, best known for such screenplays as *Humoresque*, *Stella Dallas*, *The Wind* and *Dinner at Eight*, began in the teens as well.

Several women in Europe were also active as directors and innovators during the silent era. Among those whose contributions were unique are Germaine Dulac in France, Lotte Reiniger in Germany, and Esther Schub in Russia. As a member of the post-war avant-garde, Dulac was one of the first artists to use film for surrealistic expression. Her masterpiece, *The Smiling Madame Beudet* (1923) and *The Seashell and the Clergyman* (1927), exploit cinema's fullest capabilities to depict the subjective reality of her female protagonists. Regina Cornwell, in her article devoted to Dulac and Maya Deren, demonstrates how Dulac's works exist both as milestones of experimental cinema and of women's contributions to film history.

In Germany Lotte Reiniger was pioneering the art of film animation, and in 1919 developed the use of animated silhouette figures which she later utilized in the first full-length animated film, *The Adventures of Prince Achmed* (1923–26). She has remained a leader in the field for more than a half-century, inspiring many women, who have found in animation an outlet for their creative talents and an alternative to feature filmmaking.

Working without the essential tools of filmmaking (camera and film stock), Esther Schub produced the first compilation film, *The Fall of the Romanov Dynasty* (1927), commemorating the tenth anniversary of the Soviet Revolution. The Russian scholar, Jay Leyda, chronicles how Schub, surmounting those limitations, created a totally new approach to film which has influenced documentary production ever since. In the same year Olga Preobrajenskaia directed her masterpiece, *Peasant Women of Ryazan*, a narrative fiction depicting the plight and servitude of women in pre-revolutionary Russia.

With the emergence of sound in America in 1927, few women could find steady employment in jobs other than screenwriting. More numerous than in any other period in Hollywood history, the ranks of women screenwriters included Frances Marion, Zöe Akins, Anita Loos, Jane Murfin and Jane Farnum, joined in the Forties by Leigh Brackett.

Some women continued as editors, and Margaret Booth eventually became one of MGM's top executives. But only one woman survived the transition to sound in the capacity of a director—Dorothy Arzner. Beginning her career as an editor, she made her first film for Paramount in 1927 and, until 1943, directed strong actresses, among them Katharine Hepburn, Rosalind Russell, Claudette Colbert, and Sylvia Sidney, in roles which presented the intelligent, independent aspects of the female personality. Pam Cook, in analyzing her work, expecially *Merrily We Go to Hell*, shows how Arzner handled traditional aspects of image and narrative so as to bring into question the forms of cinematographic representation.

The only other women of note who made commercial films during the dark period of the Thirties were Leontine Sagan and Leni Riefenstahl in Germany. Sagan's *Maedchen in Uniform* (1931) is a sensitive portrayal of life in a girls' boarding school and the tragic results of authoritarianism. The critique by Nancy Scholar focuses on the conflict between a repressive system of education and the emotional responses of the students.

Also in Germany, Riefenstahl was raising the art of the documentary to new heights. Beginning as an actress in the German "mountain films" similar to her own *The Blue Light* (1932), she emerged as an international figure with the completion of *Triumph of the Will* (1934) and *Olympia* (1936–38), proving that women were capable of marshalling large crews with great expertise. Her films have become landmarks in the history of documentary cinema. B. Ruby Rich here illuminates Riefenstahl's use of German romanticism in her mature works and her interest in the Amazon, which carries implications for all women working within a patriarchal system. Both Sagan and Riefenstahl, though philosophically opposed, ultimately became victims of German political upheavals and, after brilliant beginnings, were silenced.

By the Forties the position of women was stalemated. Only in the USSR and France did women continue to work on major projects. In Russia, Julia Solntseva worked as co-director beside her husband, Alexander Dovzhenko, while Vera Stroyeva, famous for several Soviet filmed performances, worked on shorts. In France, Jacqueline Audry, sister of Colette, became the sole woman director of narrative features.

It was at this moment that women artists in America realized the potential of film as a medium for personal expression. Shut out of the industry, they began to utilize 16mm equipment, pushing filmmaking in new directions. Beginning with the experiments of Maya Deren in the mid-Forties, filmmakers such as Marie Menken and Shirley Clarke developed the art of the independent cinema. Deren's *Meshes of the Afternoon* (1943), as well as her later dance films, were responsible for inspiring a whole generation of young filmmakers. Along with other members of the New York underground, she fought to establish adequate means of distributing and screening new works through the establishment of cooperatives, festivals and film societies. Her efforts are treated in Cornwell's article on avant-garde filmmaking.

With the emergence of independent filmmaking, women gained a small foothold in the industry. Ida Lupino began to supplement her acting career with directing. Her first film, *Not Wanted*, was released in 1949. By appearing in her own works she re-established the tradition begun by famous actresses. In England, Muriel Box moved from writing and producing to directing with *The Happy Family* (1952).

During those dry years some women did find employment in the less glamorous field of animation. Mary Ellen Bute began to work in 1934, the same year in which Claire Parker, collaborating with her husband, Alexandre Alexeieff, invented the pin-screen and produced *A Night on Bald Mountain*. In the Forties Joy Batchelor (later co-creator of *Animal Farm*) produced animated works in Britain as Evelyn Lambart did in Canada. Of course, Reiniger remained prodigious throughout, although her output in the Forties was very small.

By the Sixties women again appeared, in great numbers, as directors of independent and commercial productions. In Europe, Mai Zetterling, Agnès Varda, Larissa Shepitko, Lina Wertmüller, Nelly Kaplan, Nadine Trintignant and Marguerite Duras.

Notable films included: *Loving Couples* (1964), *Night Games* (1966), and *Doctor Glas* (1968) by Zetterling; *Cleo From 5 to 7* (1962), *Le Bonheur* (1965), and *Lions Love* (1969) by Varda; *Heat* (1963) and *Wings* (1966) by Shepitko; *The Lizards (1963)* and *Let's Talk About Men* by Wertmüller; *A Very Curious Girl* (1969) by Kaplan; *Mon Amour, Mon Amour* (1967) and *The Crime Thief* (1969) by Trintignant; and *Destroy, She Said* (1969) by Duras. An in-depth analysis of Zetterling who, like many women, began her career as a documentarian before turning to features, appears in this volume, by Derek Elley. Also included is a critique of Nelly Kaplan's *A Very Curious Girl*, written by Karyn Kay, which demonstrates how Kaplan's heroine gains revenge over her male antagonist and doesn't have to 'pay the consequences' at the end.

In Eastern Europe the lists were extended by such artists as Vera Chytilova, Marta Mészáros, Anna Sokolowska, and Judit Elek. Their films include: *Something Different* (1963), *Daisies* (1966) and *The Fruit of Paradise* (1969) by Chytilova; *The Girl* (1967) and *Binding Sentiments* (1968) by Mészáros; *Beata* (1965) by Sokolowska; and *The Lady From Constantinople* (1968) by Elek—ranging from avant-garde experiments to vehicles of popular entertainment.

In America Shirley Clarke produced harsh, penetrating black-and-white 16mm features such as *The Connection* (1960), *The Cool*

World (1963) and *Portrait of Jason* (1967) before turning to videotaping. Directors Barbara Peeters and Stephanie Rothman, who also worked on low-budget productions made exploitation films such as *Bury Me an Angel* (1971) and *The Student Nurses* (1970). Mary Ellen Bute extended her animation techniques into live-action features like *Passages From Finnegan's Wake* (1965).

Susan Sontag directed her first film, *Brother Carl* (1969) in Sweden and Sylvia Spring's low-budget *Madeleine Is* (1970) became the first Canadian feature directed by a woman since 1930. Also in Canada, Mireille Dansereau began making short biographies and Joyce Wieland produced experimental works.

At the same time women in the Orient and in third-world countries also became directors. In Hong Kong, Shu Shuen and Go Bo Se directed such historical dramas and action films as *The Cannibal* and *The Arch* (1968). In Japan the international film star Kinuyo Tanaka, who had begun directing as early as 1953 (*Love Letter*), continued working into the Sixties. Margot Benaceraf of Venezuela made her first full-length film, *Araya*, in 1958 and Sarah Maldorer made *Sambizanga* in Angola in 1972.

In the early Seventies the prospects for women were brighter than ever, although Hollywood studios had yet to entrust the direction of a major film to anyone other than Elaine May. Formerly a comedienne, May directed two commercially successful films, *The New Leaf* (1970) and *The Heartbreak Kid* (1972) and completed *Mickey and Nicky*. Other women, looking for alternative avenues, began to distribute their own works. Independently financed films by women, *Hester Street* (1975—Joan Micklin Silver) and *Antonia* (1974—Judy Collins and Jill Godmilow), found theatrical bookings and received glowing reviews. Karen Arthur's *Legacy* (1975) also found commercial outlets.

Actresses such as Jeanne Moreau, Anna Karina, Barbara Loden, and Liliane de Kermadec and the dancer, Yvonne Rainer, chose to work in *Lumiere* (1976), *Living Together* (1973), *Wanda* (1971), *Aloise* (1975) and *Film About a Woman Who . . .* (1974), among others. Camerawoman Babette Mangolte directed her own feature.

Above all loomed the figure of Lina Wertmüller, who achieved great fame as a member of the elite group of international film directors. From 1971 on, she produced such features as *The Seduction of Mimi* (1971), *Love and Anarchy* (1972), *All Screwed Up* (1974), *Swept Away* (1974), and *Seven Beauties* (1975). These works provoked hot controversies and brought increased attention to women as directors. Molly Haskell tackles the Wertmüller phenomenon in her article on *Swept Away by an Unusual Destiny in the Blue Sea of August*.

Established directors continued to produce new works, among the most important were: *Papa, les petits bateau* (1971—Kaplan), *Brother*

Carl and *Promised Lands* (1971, 1974—Sontag), *Good Riddance* and *The Adoption* (1973, 1975—Mészáros), *Defense de Savoir* and *Voyage de Noces* (1973, 1975—Trintignant), *Woman of the Ganges* and *India Song* (1973, 1974—Duras), *Visions of Eight* (1973—Zetterling) and *Daguerreotypes* (1976—Varda). Liliana Cavani who made her first feature in 1970 (*The Year of the Cannibal*), caused a sensation on both sides of the Atlantic with *The Night Porter* (1974). Later she directed *Milarepa* (1974) and *The People of Misar* (1976).

The newest, and youngest woman to join the ranks of major directors, has been Belgium filmmaker Chantal Akerman. Her feature *Jeanne Dielman* was one of the most important works to emerge in the Seventies. In her analysis of the film, Marsha Kinder demonstrates how this lengthy and intensely probing study of the life of one bourgeois housewife, filmed in Akerman's uniquely innovative style, provided a radical, feminist perspective on the lives of all women.

In America women were actively pursuing careers in all areas of production. Dede Allen and Verna Fields have gained wide reputations as film editors. Scriptwriters such as Gloria Katz, Joan Tewkesbury, Joan Didion, Carole Eastman and Gail Parent emerged next to such established writers as Eleanor Perry and Fay Kanin. In 1974, Julia Phillips became the first woman in history to receive an Oscar as a producer (*The Sting*).

Many women remained committed to political and experimental filmmaking. Important documentary features appeared: by Cinda Firestone (*Attica*, 1974), Shirley MacLaine and Claudia Weill (*The Other Half of the Sky*, 1974), Donna Deitch (*Woman to Woman*, 1975), Martha Coolidge (*Not a Pretty Picture*, 1976), Julia Reichert and Jim Klein (*Methadone*, 1974), Sandra Hochman (*Year of the Woman*, 1972), Amalie Rothschild (*It Happen to Us*, 1971), Third World Newsreel Women (*The Women's Film*, 1971), Kate Millett (*Three Lives*, 1971) and Reichert and Klein (*Growing Up Female*, 1971). These represented but a small sampling of the many documentaries by women. Many were devoted solely to feminist concerns, exploring women's lives in works such as those treated in Elisabeth Weis' article on film biographies. The list of experimental filmmakers include: Freude, Constance Beeson, Liane Brandon, Abigail Child, Nell Cox, Sally Cruikshank, Storm de Hirsch, Suzan Pitt Kraning, Gunvor Nelson, Sheila Page, Carolee Schneemann, and Chick Strand. Each year the roster will grow longer.

Many women were working in cooperative groups to produce films and videotapes: the London Women's Film Group, the San Francisco Women's Health Collective, the New York Herstory Collective and the International Women's Film Project, as well as the distribution cooperative New Day Films.

Each woman mentioned above deserves more attention. Women have been productive in all areas of film—narrative fiction, documentary, experimental, and animation. Books dealing with those women whose works could not be treated here are bound to follow. Happily and healthily the state of women and film is in constant flux. As older material surfaces in archives and from other sources and as new women artists emerge as they must, the history of cinema will be rewritten. For the present, the articles here demonstrate the breadth and profound importance of women's work during the past century, portents of an enormously fertile future.

————P.E.

Ray Walston, Eileen Brennan, and Paul Newman in *The Sting* (1974), produced by Julia Phillips, the first woman to win an Oscar as a producer.

Director Dorothy Arzner.

Director Claudia Weill.

Director Agnes Varda.

Maya Deren in her *Meshes of the Afternoon* (1943).

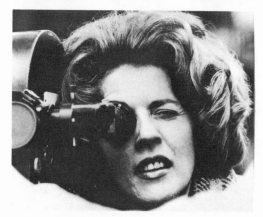

Director Nelly Kaplan.

Filmmaker Shirley Clarke.

I. A FEMINIST
PERSPECTIVE

Women's Cinema as
Counter-Cinema

CLAIRE JOHNSTON

MYTHS OF WOMEN IN THE CINEMA

. . . there arose, identifiable by standard appearance, behaviour and attributes, the well-remembered types of the Vamp and the Straight Girl
(perhaps the most convincing modern equivalents of the medieval per-
sonifications of the Vices and Virtues), the Family Man and the Villain,
the latter marked by a black moustache and walking stick. Nocturnal
scenes were printed on blue or green film. A checkered table-cloth
meant, once for all, a 'poor but honest' milieu; a happy marriage, soon to
be endangered by the shadows from the past symbolised by the young
wife's pouring of the breakfast coffee for her husband; the first kiss was
invariably announced by the lady's gently playing with her partner's
necktie and was invariably accompanied by her kicking out with her left
foot. The conduct of the characters was predetermined accordingly (Er-
win Panofsky in "Style and Medium in the Motion Pictures," 1934 and in
"Film: An Anthology," D. Talbot ed., New York, 1959).

Panofsky's detection of the primitive stereotyping which characterised the early cinema could prove useful for discerning the way
myths of women have operated in the cinema: why the image of man
underwent rapid differentiation, while the primitive stereotyping of

women remained with some modifications. Much writing on the stereotyping of women in the cinema takes as its starting point a monolithic view of the media as repressive and manipulative: in this way, Hollywood has been viewed as a dream factory producing an oppressive cultural product. This over-politicised view bears little relation to the ideas on art expressed either by Marx or Lenin, who both pointed to there being no direct connection between the development of art and the material basis of society. The idea of the intentionality of art which this view implies is extremely misleading and retrograde, and short-circuits the possibility of a critique which could prove useful for developing a strategy for women's cinema. If we accept that the developing of female stereotypes was not a conscious strategy of the Hollywood dream machine, what are we left with? Panofsky locates the origins of iconography and stereotype in the cinema in terms of practical necessity; he suggests that in the early cinema the audience had much difficulty deciphering what appeared on the screen. Fixed iconography, then, was introduced to aid understanding and provide the audience with basic facts with which to comprehend the narrative. Iconography as a specific kind of sign or cluster of signs based on certain conventions within the Hollywood genres has been partly responsible for the stereotyping of women within the commercial cinema in general, but the fact that there is a far greater differentiation of men's roles than of women's roles in the history of the cinema relates to sexist ideology itself, and the basic opposition which places man inside history, and woman as ahistoric and eternal. As the cinema developed, the stereotyping of man was increasingly interpreted as contravening the realisation of the notion of 'character'; in the case of woman, this was not the case; the dominant ideology presented her as eternal and unchanging, except for modifications in terms of fashion etc. In general, the myths governing the cinema are no different from those governing other cultural products: they relate to a standard value system informing all cultural systems in a given society. Myth uses icons, but the icon is its weakest point. Furthermore, it is possible to use icons, (ie conventional configurations) in the face of and against the mythology usually associated with them. In his magisterial work on myth ("Mythologies," Jonathan Cape, London 1971), the critic Roland Barthes examines how myth, as the signifier of an ideology, operates, by analysing a whole range of items: a national dish, a society wedding, a photograph from *Paris Match*. In his book he analyses how a sign can be emptied of its original denotative meaning and a new connotative meaning superimposed on it. What was a complete sign consisting of a signifier plus a signified, becomes merely the signifier of a new signified, which subtly usurps the place of the original denotation. In this way, the new connotation is mistaken for the natural, obvious and evident denotation: this is what makes it the signifier of the ideology of the society in which it is used.

Myth then, as a form of speech or discourse, represents the major means in which women have been used in the cinema: myth transmits and transforms the ideology of sexism and renders it invisible—when it is made visible it evaporates—and therefore natural. This process puts the question of the stereotyping of women in a somewhat different light. In the first place, such a view of the way cinema operates challenges the notion that the commercial cinema is more manipulative of the image of woman than the art cinema. It could be argued that precisely because of the iconography of Hollywood, the system offers some resistance to the unconscious workings of myth. Sexist ideology is no less present in the European art cinema because stereotyping appears less obvious; it is in the nature of myth to drain the sign (the image of woman/the function of woman in the narrative) of its meaning and superimpose another which thus appears natural: in fact, a strong argument could be made for the art film inviting a greater invasion from myth. This point assumes considerable importance when considering the emerging women's cinema. The conventional view about women working in Hollywood (Arzner, Weber, Lupino etc) is that they had little opportunity for real expression within the dominant sexist ideology; they were token women and little more. In fact, because iconography offers in some ways a greater resistance to the realist characterisations, the mythic qualities of certain stereotypes become far more easily detachable and can be used as a short-hand for referring to an ideological tradition in order to provide a critique of it. It is possible to disengage the icons from the myth and thus bring about reverberations within the sexist ideology in which the film is made. Dorothy Arzner certainly made use of such techniques and the work of Nelly Kaplan is particularly important in this respect. As a European director she understands the dangers of myth invading the sign in the art film, and deliberately makes use of Hollywood iconography to counteract this. The use of crazy comedy by some women directors (e.g. Stephanie Rothman) also derives from this insight.

In rejecting a sociological analysis of woman in the cinema we reject any view in terms of realism, for this would involve an acceptance of the apparent natural denotation of the sign and would involve a denial of the reality of myth in operation. Within a sexist ideology and a male-dominated cinema, woman is presented as what she represents for man. Laura Mulvey in her most useful essay on the pop artist Allen Jones ('You Don't Know What You're Doing Do You, Mr. Jones?', Laura Mulvey in *Spare Rib*, February 1973), points out that woman as woman is totally absent in Jones' work. The fetishistic image portrayed relates only to male narcissism: woman represents not herself, but by a process of displacement, the male phallus. It is probably true to say that despite the enormous emphasis placed on woman as spectacle in the cinema, woman as woman is largely absent. A sociological analysis based on the empirical study of recurring roles and motifs would lead to a critique in terms of an enumeration of the notion of career/home/motherhood/sexuality, an examination of women as the central figures in the narrative, etc. If we view the image of woman as sign within the sexist ideology, we see that the portrayal of woman is merely one item subject to the law of verisimilitude, a law which directors worked with or reacted against. The law of verisimilitude (that which determines the impression of realism) in the cinema is precisely responsible for the repression of the image of woman as woman and the celebration of her non-existence.

This point becomes clearer when we look at a film which revolves around a woman entirely and the idea of the female star. In their analysis of Sternberg's *Morocco*, the critics of *Cahiers du Cinema* delineate the system which is in operation: in order that the man remain within the centre of the universe in a text which focuses on the image of woman, the auteur is forced to repress the idea of woman as a social and sexual being (her Otherness) and to deny the opposition man/woman altogether. The woman as sign, then, becomes the pseudo-centre of the filmic discourse. The real opposition posed by the sign is male/non-male, which Sternberg establishes by his use of masculine clothing envelopping the image of Dietrich. This masquerade indicates the absence of man, an absence which is simultaneously negated and recuperated by man. The image of the woman becomes merely the trace of the exclusion and repression of Woman. All fetishism, as Freud has observed, is a phallic replacement, a projection of male narcissistic fantasy. The star system as a whole depended on the fetishization of woman. Much of the work done on the star system concentrates on the star as the focus for false and alienating dreams. This empirical approach is essentially concerned with the effects of the star system and audience reaction. What the fetishization of the star does indicate is the collective fantasy of phallocentrism. This is particularly interesting when we look at the persona of Mae West. Many women have read into her parody of the star system and her verbal aggression an attempt at the subversion of male domination in the cinema. If we look more closely there are many traces of phallic replacement in her persona which suggest quite the opposite. The voice itself is strongly masculine, suggesting the absence of the male, and establishes a male/non-male dichotomy. The characteristic phallic dress possesses .elements of the fetish. The female element which is introduced, the mother image, expresses male oedipal fantasy. In other words, at the unconscious level, the persona of Mae West is entirely consistent with sexist ideology; it in no way subverts existing myths, but reinforces them.

In their first editorial, the editors of *Women and Film* attack the notion of auteur theory, describing it as 'an oppressive theory making the director a superstar as if film-making were a one-man show.' This is to miss the point. Quite clearly, some developments of the auteur theory have led to a tendency to deify the personality of the (male) director, and Andrew Sarris (the major target for attack in the editorial) is one of the worst offenders in this respect. His derogatory treatment of women directors in *The American Cinema* gives a clear indication of his sexism. Nevertheless, the development of the auteur theory marked an important intervention in film criticism: its polemics challenged the entrenched view of Hollywood as monolithic, and stripped of its normative aspects the classification of films by director has proved an extremely productive way of ordering our experience of the cinema. In demonstrating that Hollywood was at least as interesting as the art cinema, it marked an important step forward. The test of any theory should be the degree to which it produces new knowledge: the auteur theory has certainly achieved this. Further elaborations of the auteur theory (cf Peter Wollen "Signs and Meanings in the Cinema," Secker & Warburg, Cinema One Series, London 1972) have stressed the use of the theory to delineate the unconscious structure of the film. As Peter Wollen says, 'the structure is associated with a single director, an individual, not because he has played the role of artist, expressing himself or his vision in the film, but it is through the force of his preoccupations that an unconscious, unintended meaning can be decoded in the film, usually to the surprise of the individual concerned.' In this way Wollen disengages both from the notion of creativity which dominates the notion of 'art', and from the idea of intentionality.

In briefly examining the myths of woman which underlie the work of two Hollywood directors, Ford and Hawks, making use of findings and insights derived from auteur analysis, it is possible to see that the image of woman assumes very different meanings within the different texts of each author's work. An analysis in terms of the presence or absence of 'positive' heroine figures within the same directors' *oeuvre* would produce a very different view. What Peter Wollen refers to as the 'force of the author's preoccupations', (including the obsessions about women) is generated by the psychoanalytic history of the author. This organised network of obsessions is outside the scope of the author's choice.

Hawks vs. Ford

Hawks' films celebrate the solidarity and validity of the exclusive all-male group, dedicated to the life of action and adventure, and a rigid professional ethic. When women intrude into their world, they represent a threat to the very existence of the group. However, women appear to possess 'positive' qualities in Hawks' films: they are often career women and show signs of independence and aggression in the face of the male, particularly in his crazy comedies. Robin Wood has pointed out quite correctly that the crazy comedies portray an inverted version of Hawks' universe. The male is often humiliated or depicted as infantile or regressed. Such films as *Bringing Up Baby, His Girl Friday* and *Gentlemen Prefer Blondes* combine, as Robin Wood has said, 'farce and horror'; they are 'disturbing'. For Hawks, there is only the male and the non-male: in order to be accepted into the male universe, the woman must *become* a man; alternatively she becomes woman-as-phallus (Marilyn Monroe in *Gentlemen Prefer Blondes*). This disturbing quality in Hawks' films relates directly to the presence of woman; she is a traumatic presence which must be negated. Ford's is a very different universe, in which women play a pivotal role: it is around their presence that the tensions between the desire for the wandering existence and the desire for settlement/the idea of the wilderness and the idea of the garden revolve. For Ford woman represents the home, and with it the possibility of culture: she becomes a cipher onto which Ford projects his profoundly ambivalent attitude to the concepts of civilisation and psychological 'wholeness.'

While the depiction of women in Hawks involves a direct confrontation with the problematic (traumatic) presence of Woman, a confrontation which results in his need to repress her, Ford's use of woman as a symbol for civilisation considerably complicates the whole question of the repression of woman in his work and leaves room for more progressive elements to emerge (eg *Seven Women* and *Cheyenne Autumn*).

TOWARDS A COUNTER-CINEMA

There is no such thing as unmanipulated writing, filming or broadcasting.

> The question is therefore not whether the media are manipulated, but who manipulates them. A revolutionary plan should not require the manipulators to disappear; on the contrary, it must make everyone a

manipulator (Hans Magnus Enzensberger in "Constituents of a Theory of Media," New Left Review No. 64).

Enzensberger suggests the major contradiction operating in the media is that between their present constitution and their revolutionary potential. Quite clearly, a strategic use of the media, and film in particular, is essential for disseminating our ideas. At the moment the possibility of feedback is low, though the potential already exists. In the light of such possibilities, it is particularly important to analyse what the nature of cinema is and what strategic use can be made of it in all its forms: the political film/the commercial entertainment film. Polemics for women's creativity are fine as long as we realize they are polemics. The notion of women's creativity *per se* is as limited as the notion of men's creativity. It is basically an idealist conception which elevates the idea of the 'artist' (involving the pitfall of elitism), and undermines any view of art as a material thing within a cultural context which forms it and is formed by it. All films or works of art are products: products of an existing system of economic relations, in the final analysis. This applies equally to experimental films, political films and commercial entertainment cinema. Film is also an ideological product—the product of bourgeois ideology. The idea that art is universal and thus potentially androgynous is basically an idealist notion: art can only be defined as a discourse within a particular conjuncture—for the purpose of women's cinema, ths bourgeois, sexist ideology of male dominated capitalism. It is important to point out that the workings of ideology do not involve a process of deception/intentionality. For Marx, ideology is a reality, it is not a lie. Such a misapprehension can prove extremely misleading; there is no way in which we can eliminate ideology as if by an effort of will. This is extremely important when it comes to discussing women's cinema. The tools and techniques of cinema themselves, as part of reality, are an expression of the prevailing ideology: they are not neutral, as many 'revolutionary' film-makers appear to believe. It is idealist mystification to believe that 'truth' can be captured by the camera or that the conditions of a film's production (eg a film made collectively by women) can *of itself* reflect the conditions of its production. This is mere utopianism: new meaning has to *be manufactured* within the text of the film. The camera was developed in order to accurately reproduce reality and safeguard the bourgeois notion of realism which was being replaced in painting. An element of sexism governing the technical development of the camera can also be discerned. In fact, the lightweight camera was developed as early as the 1930's in Nazi Germany for propaganda purposes; the reason why it was not until the 1950's that it assumed common usage remains obscure.

Much of the emerging women's cinema has taken its aesthetics from television and cinema vérité techniques (eg *Three Lives*, *Women Talking*); Shirley Clarke's *Portrait of Jason* has been cited as an important influence. These films largely depict images of women talking to camera about their experiences, with little or no intervention by the film maker. Kate Millett sums up the approach in *Three Lives* by saying, "I did not want to analyse any more, but to express and film is a very powerful way to express oneself."

Clearly, if we accept that cinema involves the production of signs, the idea of non-intervention is pure mystification. The sign is always a product. What the camera in fact grasps is the 'natural' world of the dominant ideology. Women's cinema cannot afford such idealism; the 'truth' of our oppression cannot be 'captured' on celluloid with the 'innocence' of the camera: it has to be constructed/manufactured. New meanings have to be created by disrupting the fabric of the male bourgeois cinema within the text of the film. As Peter Wollen points out, 'reality is always adaptive'. Eisenstein's method is instructive here. In his use of fragmentation as a revolutionary strategy, a concept is generated by the clash of two specific images, so that it serves as an abstract concept in the filmic discourse. This idea of fragmentation as an analytical tool is quite different from the use of fragmentation suggested by Barbara Martineau in her essay. She sees fragmentation as the juxtaposition of disparate elements (cf *Lion's Love*) to bring about emotional reverberations, but these reverberations do not provide a means of understanding within them. In the context of women's cinema such a strategy would be totally recuperable by the dominant ideology: indeed, in that it depends on emotionality and mystery, it invites the invasion of ideology. The ultimate logic of this method is automatic writing developed by the surrealists. Romanticism will not provide us with the necessary tools to construct a women's cinema: our objectification cannot be overcome simply by examining it artistically. It can only be challenged by developing the means to interrogate the male, bourgeois cinema. Furthermore, a desire for change can only come about by drawing on fantasy. The danger of developing a cinema of non-intervention is that it promotes a passive subjectivity at the expense of analysis. Any revolutionary strategy must challenge the depiction of reality; it is not enough to discuss the oppression of women within the text of the film; the language of the cinema/the depiction of reality must also be interrogated, so that a break between ideology and text is effected. In this respect, it is instructive to look at films made by women within the Hollywood system which attempted by formal means to bring about a dislocation between sexist ideology and the text of the film; such insights could provide useful guidelines for the emerging women's cinema to draw on.

Dorothy Arzner and Ida Lupino

Dorothy Arzner and Lois Weber were virtually the only women working in Hollywood during the 1920's and 30's who managed to build
up a consistent body of work in the cinema: unfortunately, very little
is known of their work, as yet. An analysis of one of Dorothy Arzner's
later films, *Dance, Girl, Dance*, made in 1940 gives some idea of her
approach to women's cinema within the sexist ideology of Hollywood. A conventional vaudeville story, *Dance, Girl, Dance* centres
on the lives of a troupe of dancing girls down on their luck. The main
characters, Bubbles and Judy are representative of the primitive
iconographic depiction of women—vamp and straight-girl—
described by Panofsky. Working from this crude stereotyping, Arzner
succeeds in generating within the text of the film, an internal criticism
of it. Bubbles manages to land a job, and Judy becomes the stooge in
her act, performing ballet for the amusement of the all-male audience.
Arzner's critique centres round the notion of woman as spectacle, as
performer within the male universe. The central figures appear in a
parody form of the performance, representing opposing poles of the
myths of femininity—sexuality vs. grace & innocence. The central
contradiction articulating their existence as performers for the pleasure of men is one with which most women would identify: the contradiction between the desire to please and self-expression: Bubbles
needs to please the male, while Judy seeks self-expression as a ballet
dancer. As the film progresses, a one-way process of the performance
is firmly established, involving the humiliation of Judy as the stooge.
Towards the end of the film Arzner brings about her tour de force,
cracking open the entire fabric of the film and exposing the workings
of ideology in the construction of the stereotype of woman. Judy, in a
fit of anger, turns on her audience and tells them *how she sees them*.
This return of scrutiny in what within the film is assumed as a one-
way process constitutes a direct assault on the audience within the
film and the audience of the film, and has the effect of directly challenging the entire notion of woman as spectacle.

Ida Lupino's approach to women's cinema is somewhat different.
As an independent producer and director working in Hollywood in
the 1950's, Lupino chose to work largely within the melodrama, a
genre which, more than any other, has presented a less reified view
of women, and as Sirk's work indicates, is adaptable for expressing
rather than embodying the idea of the oppression of women. An
analysis of *Not Wanted*, Lupino's first feature film gives some idea of
the disturbing ambiguity of her films and their relationship to the
sexist ideology. Unlike Arzner, Lupino is not concerned with employing purely formal means to obtain her objective; in fact, it is doubtful

whether she operates at a conscious level at all in subverting the sexist ideology. The film tells the story of a young girl, Sally Kelton, and is told from her subjective viewpoint and filtered through her imagination. She has an illegitimate child which is eventually adopted; unable to come to terms with losing the child, she snatches one from a pram and ends up in the hands of the authorities. Finally, she finds a substitute for the child in the person of a crippled young man, who, through a process of symbolic castration—in which he is forced to chase her until he can no longer stand, whereupon she takes him up in her arms as he performs child-like gestures,—provides the "happy ending." Though Lupino's films in no way explicitly attack or expose the workings of sexist ideology, reverberations within the narrative, produced by the convergence of two irreconcilable strands— Hollywood myths of woman *vs* the female perspective—cause a series of distortions within the very structure of the narrative; the mark of disablement puts the film under the sign of disease and frustration. An example of this process is, for instance, the inverted 'happy ending' of the film.

The intention behind pointing to the interest of Hollywood directors like Dorothy Arzner and Ida Lupino is twofold. In the first place it is a polemical attempt to restore the interest of Hollywood from attacks that have been made on it. Secondly, an analysis of the workings of myth and the possibilities of subverting it in the Hollywood system could prove of use in determining a strategy for the subversion of ideology in general.

Perhaps something should be said about the European art film; undoubtedly, it is more open to the invasion of myth than the Hollywood film. This point becomes quite clear when we scrutinise the work of Riefenstahl, Companeez, Trintignant, Varda and others. The films of Agnes Varda are a particularly good example of an *oeuvre* which celebrates bourgeois myths of women, and with it the apparent innocence of the sign. *Le Bonheur* in particular, almost invites a Barthesian analysis! Varda's portrayal of female fantasy constitutes one of the nearest approximations to the facile day-dreams perpetuated by advertising that probably exists in the cinema. Her films appear totally innocent to the workings of myth; indeed, it is the purpose of myth to fabricate an impression of innocence, in which all becomes 'natural': Varda's concern for nature is a direct expression of this retreat from history: history is transmuted into nature, involving the elimination of all questions, because all appears 'natural'. There is no doubt that Varda's work is reactionary: in her rejection of culture and her placement of women outside history her films mark a retrograde step in woman's cinema.

CONCLUSION

What kind of strategy, then, is appropriate at this particular point in time? The development of collective work is obviously a major step forward; as a means of acquiring and sharing skills it constitutes a formidable challenge to male privilege in the film industry: as an expression of sisterhood, it suggests a viable alternative to the rigid hierarchical structures of male-dominated cinema and offers real opportunities for a dialogue about the nature of women's cinema within it. At this point in time, a strategy should be developed which embraces both the notion of films as a political tool and film as entertainment. For too long these have been regarded as two opposing poles with little common ground. In order to counter our objectification in the cinema, our collective fantasies must be released: women's cinema must embody the working through of desire: such an objective demands the use of the entertainment film. Ideas derived from the entertainment film, then, should inform the political film, and political ideas should inform the entertainment cinema: a two way process. Finally, a repressive moralistic assertion that women's cinema *is* collective film-making is misleading and unnecessary: we should seek to operate at all levels: within the male-dominated cinema and outside it. This essay has attempted to demonstrate the interest of women's films made within the system. Voluntarism and utopianism must be avoided if any revolutionary strategy is to emerge. A collective film *of itself* cannot reflect the conditions of its production. What collective methods do provide is the real possibility of examining how cinema works and how we can best interrogate and demystify the workings of ideology: it will be from these insights that a genuinely revolutionary conception of counter-cinema for the women's struggle will come.

Feminist Film Criticism: Theory and Practice

JULIA LESAGE

THEORY

In order to write effectively and to give her readers, especially women readers, a way to evaluate cinema themselves, the feminist film critic must work out for herself a theoretical framework to encompass the whole range of issues related to film. Her theory governs what she says to what readership, what aspects of films she will write about, what effect she hopes to gain from her criticism. A good theory includes an explanation of the mechanisms operating *within* the film (form, content, etc.) and the mechanisms that go beyond the product that is the film (such as the film industry, distribution, audience expectation, etc.)

The following schema is a useful theoretical tool to consider film as a total process, from its inception to its reception by an audience. It allows us to account for changes due to reception in a different historical period from which the film was made. By working her way through this entire schema in criticizing any one film, the critic herself can elaborate some of the interrelations between ideological superstructure and economic base, particularly as regards the mechanisms of sexism.

One: The prefilmic milieu, in the widest sense, includes past history as well as the present situation. Milieu[1] encompasses both the economic base of the filmmaker's milieu as well as the ideological superstructure. In the schema, *milieu*[1] is placed linearly before the *maker(s)* only to indicate that this is the situation prior to and in which the film is made.

That sexism which we can find in almost all of established cinema can be found in cinematic tradition, language structures, artistic conventions (especially in the photographing of women), social conventions and specific social situations. These are all part of milieu[1], and embedded in these structures and experiences we find the maker(s) of the film at the time of making. Since the whole of milieu[1] has been and still is overwhelmingly sexist, even a self consciously feminist director will find it hard to make a film which rebuts sexism in all areas. She has many pressures on her from milieu[1], which the critic should examine, and her films reveal not only a rejection of sexist social conventions from milieu[1] but artistic ones as well.

Two: The maker in film, as opposed to many visual and literary artists, is almost always not a single individual but a collective entity. In many of the contemporary women's films, such as the San Francisco Newsreel women's *The Woman's Film*, the director is not named as the maker and we are led to think that the technical crew, the sound mix person, actors and editors worked together collectively and non-hierarchically and that all had some control over the final film. Film processors are also "makers" of a film yet are not esteemed as such. One must ask in relation to the area of technique, why so few of the new women filmmakers are concentrating on experimental films, experimental in technique and form.

Three: The completed film is the principal object of traditional film study and of psychoanalytic and semiological studies such as those of Pam Cook and Claire Johnston. Although such analysis is extremely important for our understanding of film, hopefully feminist film criticism will constantly relate film to milieu with a specific vision of how sexism can be attacked.

Four: The audience for the completed film can be considered in both individual and collective terms.

Five: The audience's milieu is always to some extent historically/temporally/spatially/socially different from the maker's milieu, and the audience brings its experience with its milieu to its judgment of a film. Feminist film criticism, in attacking sexism and promoting women's films, will hopefully have a favorable effect on milieu[2]. The minimum effect which we would hope that feminist film criticism would have would be to get people to view the films that are a part of their milieu in a new way.

Women viewing and discussing films in a women's studies course or at a women's conference may want to get together by themselves in a group to discuss the films seen since their experience of women's oppression gives them a "milieu" different from that of the male viewers or from the makers. A group of women discussing a film by themselves will usually express different reactions than in a mixed discussion of the same film.

Six: The production/distribution system is shown in the schema as affecting all other sub-systems. Involved in distribution are producers, distributors, exhibitors, critics and audiences—all of whom are influenced by the economics of the society in which they live. Although sexism in cinema is universal, we should note that production/distribution relations differ from Western capitalistic ones to Third World capitalistic ones to Russian, Eastern European, Chinese, Third World socialist ones, etc., all of which means a difference in the way opportunities are offered to women in each country to make films (and there are far fewer opportunities than those available to men—in all cases!).

Distribution and the viewing situation influences when and how any film is received. In most cases, 35mm distribution has to be arranged at ths time of financing the film. There is very little freelance distributing of feature films once they are made, which is why we see so few films from the Third World or by radical European directors here in the United States, although they would obviously like to have them shown here. Women's films have been presented in women's film festivals which have publicized both contemporary women's films not well-distributed and older films until now "lost" by neglect. The showings in these festivals are often accompanied by panel discussions. Later, because the festivals and the accompanying publicity and reviews have brought these films to our attention, we try to have these films shown in a classroom, campus or community situation, and again the films are often followed by discussion. Because of their specific use to raise consciousness, such distribution of women's films now seems more radical than standard 35mm distribution in movie theaters, so that what is being done out of necessity, opening up new 16mm circuits, may end up benefiting women more than admission of women's films into the channels of regular distribution.

With the preliminary schema in mind we can proceed to some elaboration of the relations between the sub-systems. Each of the sub-systems has structures and these structures can "transfer" from one system to another: that is, related structures can be found in each sub-system and finding one will provide information to understand similar structures in another sub-system. For example, Howard Hawks' films present an image of the fraternity of worthy men (I call it the-boys'-club-syndrome), which derives from Hawks' unconscious attitudes as well as his conscious assumptions; this image plays upon the audience's assumptions about manliness as well. Thus a consideration of *Hatari* could draw upon what we know about Hawks (found out from any statements he's made and from his other films) as well as what we know about audience psychology. We can assume that Hawks knew that certain assumptions were made about manliness in both milieu[1] and milieu[2]. In distribution, this concept might again be emphasized by advertising photos of strong men hunting animals from a jeep, with beautiful women looking on, or perhaps no women in the picture at all.

The maker of a film receives all of milieu[1] and additionally has her/his/their own individual psychology, historical situation, and creative imagination—which only some people in the filmmaking process are allowed to use. Reaction against their milieu is a driving force for women making films and shapes both the content of the films they make and their fight to establish themselves either within or on the margin of the film industry.

Feminist critics have shown particular interest in the topic, the Image of Women; that is, in the way advertising and media images of women (created by and reflecting the needs of men) shape the present image of women in feature films, the choice of actresses, female characters' behavior—and also how these images shape us. In watching a film, the audience draws on its knowledge of the convention of the Glamorous Woman, a convention they know has a history. The way a Glamorous Woman is portrayed comes from structures and institutions in milieu,[1] structures or conventional attitudes in the director's mind, structures in the form/content of the film, conventional expectations (structures) in the audience's mind, and structures and institutions in milieu.[2] Sometimes a director will consciously play with visual and verbal structures already present in milieu,[1] which is what Royanne Rosenberg did in her documentary *Roseland* where she played off her own admiration for a very fat woman against the audience's preconceived notions and uneasiness about obesity in women.

The idea of structures existing in each part of the system is a step toward freeing us from writing about only the film or only the maker-film-audience segment. For example, the structures of language are found in the structures of perception, for we use words to identify what we see and these structures are carried from milieu[1] through their actualization in some form of communication to milieu[2]. However, the specific situation of both the filmmaker and the audience plays a determining role, for the audience may not understand the creator's "style." Thus, *Roseland* confuses many women, who react out of their own structured attitude toward obesity and do not understand that the film's emphasis on Rose's size was intended to convey the director's respect for her as a monumental, almost mythical, earth-goddess figure. Since Rose is presented in cinema-vérité style the audience reacts as they always react to a fat person; there are no structures in the film to overcome the ambiguity of attraction/rejection which the image of obesity generates.

A film is made over a period of time. The work can influence the filmmaker in this process. This is particularly true of documentaries or of films connected with a specific political struggle, which may change the consciousness of the filmmakers in the course of making the film. Although there is feedback from the work to the makers at the time the film is being made, once the film is completed the makers (cast, crew, director, producer) become part of the audience and/or distribution if the director or producer retains any control over the showing of that work. Video typically offers more feedback than film because it is usually shown to small groups by the makers. With film the audience generally has only the feedback of deciding whether to buy a ticket or not.

The film-audience relation is one to study in detail, particularly historically, for the film shapes the audience's mind as well as draws on conventions already present in milieu[1]. For example, do teenage women want to fall in love because of real experience or do they want to live up to the myth? Film is one ideological product among many that has kept "selling" the myth of love. In the economy, the myth is used in advertising to sell products: it implies love is guaranteed with an object's purchase. Feminist filmmakers such as Nelly Kaplan attack the love myth in its representation in the cinema precisely because it is an oppressive myth incorporated into the super-ego of women. However, although women filmmakers and women critics attack the love myth as oppressive, few have attacked the entire dominant concept, which sees romantic love as necessary for a woman's major satisfaction in life. Couldn't we imagine women living happily together without being in a "couple" situation, or imagine them deriving their major satisfaction from areas other than intense sexual satisfaction? This is not meant as puritanical, but many films have shown male adventurers, scientists, soldiers, fliers, businessmen, etc. as getting their *primary* satisfaction from a role other than that of romantic love (or, as the other option is for women, from fatherly love!).

When writing about a feminist film, or about any political film, the critic must evaluate what effect this film hopes to have on its audience. And what effect it actually has. Does it intend to provoke specific changes in milieu[2]? How? If milieu[2] is left relatively untouched, the critic can note this and set forth her ideas on more radical uses for film. A film which is a mere social critique ends with an audience saying, "Isn't that terrible! I cried to see it." A more radical work shapes the audience's mind, leaving the viewers with structures which go beyond their consciousness prior to viewing. They then have a tool with which to reevaluate that which they had previously accepted as "natural." In a didactic radical film, such a change in consciousness should be accompanied by a picture of how things can be changed, which is a necessary precondition for the audience's acting in a new way after the film is over.

The production-distribution system, interacting directly with all five other sub-systems and technical and critical mediations, is the determinant system within the whole: it has the greatest impact of all the sub-systems on the whole. In most countries, film production has been institutionalized so that feature films are made in remarkably similar ways. And women are not predominant in the production of films. We know that Russian and Eastern European films are also generally sexist, and we may or may not be satisfied with *The Red Detachment of Women* (I am with the content, but not the form—reminiscent of *Seven Brides for Seven Brothers*—nor with Chinese restrictions on film production). It is a phenomenon that Godard noticed when he talks about Mos Films-Paramount. Even though the films are produced under a socialist economic system, the films are still oppressive and similar in form to capitalistic films.

We need to document in detail the position of women within the process of production of Hollywood films. We must also note *how* it is that women can begin to produce films more or less independently—tracing the sources of available income and distribution. The direct input of the woman consumer on the general feature film market is almost nil. Indeed, films are not constructed with an eye to the reality of social relations but rather continue to reflect male (and bourgeois male) ideals. Distributors do not ask us what kind of films we want to see, and many of today's films reflect a reaction against the women's movement.

Women are struggling to open alternate circuits of distribution because the established distribution agencies reject politically sensitive films. However, these rare alternative circuits—distributing 16mm prints, usually in colleges and schools—reach mostly the already "convinced." It would be better for women if there were a mass feminist distribution linked to political activity; at minimum, to audience education. Since the critic plays a crucial role in distribution, she should publicize and encourage the work of women's alternative distribution circuits and also describe in greater detail the radical political use of their films.

FILM ANALYSIS

Most film criticism has traditionally centered around an analysis of the artifact, the film. Although not sufficient as an exclusive approach to film, a feminist perspective should be applied to an analysis of the form and content of both traditional narrative film and women's

films. We are oriented to write criticism of the film itself rather than
the whole film process (milieu[1]—maker(s)—film—audience
—milieu[2]) because of the close relation between film and literary criticism. We bring to film criticism New Critical, psychoanalytic and
structuralist approaches already applied to literature in the academic
world. *Auteur* criticism is, for example, marked by a psychoanalytic
approach—the search for themes, archetypes, underlying psychological patterns.

Since most films are sexist in both form and content—and this includes documentaries, feature fiction films, and experimental films
that are not abstractions—the feminist critic finds herself coming to
terms with the fact that she, like most women, still enjoys these films.
We have not abandoned Hollywood nor the whole bulk of past films.
However, and here women in audiences already differ, some women
flatly reject films sexist in content but their definition of a sexist film
differs from woman to woman.

At this point the feminist critic finds herself criticizing films other
women may praise and finding reasons to like films others may reject
as sexist. I can give a few examples from my own reviewing experience. I rejected *Carnal Knowledge* as a smug film appealing voyeuristically to precisely those men "denounced" in the story of the film;
other women, reading the film on the level of content, saw the film as
an attack on sexism. Similarly, *Cries and Whispers* was generally hailed
as a "women's film" but Constance Penley denounced Bergman's
manipulation of women's experience, his mystification of that experience only to serve his Art (*Women and Film*, nos. 3–4). Again, from my
point of view, I enjoyed *A Clockwork Orange* and *Lolita*, reading Kub-
rick's satire as misanthropy rather than misogyny. I put in these personal examples to indicate that it is at this level that feminist film criticism currently engages movie goers in lively debates, and that
analyses of content from a feminist perspective are both popular and
useful.

Because of the example of some very talented women who have
given us images of strong, unconventional, rebellious women in film,
feminist critics have often emphasized the need for women directors
to give us new female role models in film. While equally enthusiastic
about seeing such strong women characters, I see a danger in raising
the strong-female role model to the level of prescription, i.e., "This is
where women's film should go." On the one hand, the whole concept
of hero (or anti-hero) in narrative film is a carry-over from nineteenth
century romantic literature, and certainly Eisenstein's example has
shown that an emphasis on a single character's fate and interior development is neither necessary nor particularly desirble. In *I am Some-*

body, Madeline Anderson shows the role of women, even concentrating on one specific woman, during a hospital strike, but she places much more emphasis on the relation between class, sexual, and racial oppression and on the need for united action than on the delineation of a character that might serve as a model on which to specifically pattern our lives.

THE POLITICS OF FORM

Most critics do not separate their discussion of form from the content of the film, this is appropriate enough if one considers form and content as finally inseparable, but it is not satisfactory if the reviewer has simply failed to reflect on how the form affects the content. At the same time, in considering a large number of films, we can see that film form and the way of photographing women in general has in the past been inherently sexist. Makeup, the selection of women with certain size breasts, halo lighting, the whole visual iconography of women characters, and so forth, can be analyzed in detail to write the story of sexism in film. But even more, in considering film form, one should analyze where women are not, what attributes they are *not* given.

In an adventure film, men find fulfillment and self-definition through direct physical action, initiated by themselves for the end of their own integrity. Women are not allotted the same range of physical action, and when they do act, their actions are usually more circumscribed. To give an example, *Evel Knievel, Two Lane Blacktop, The Last American Hero,* and *American Graffitti* show men initiating such actions to prove their identity (both social and personal identity) as drag racing, stock car racing and motorcycle stunts. The women in these films do not initiate such actions independently but relate to the actions of the men and are dependent on them. One can take a movie such as *Day of the Jackal* and note that it would be unlikely to have an equivalent female assassin or females employing that assassin or a comparable female target to be assassinated—as if any of this were desirable. Male characters are given attributes of power much more than female characters are.

Forms for conveying sensuality are almost completely male. We don't even know yet what the visual form for a female erotic movie would be. Women so far, even when making films, have found it hard to break through to making new kinds of films with new forms. Technical experimentation with the media has so far been done by male filmmakers. There are few women making experimental films, pushing the medium itself as far as they can, perhaps this is because the technical/chemical/mechanical side of film has been traditionally of more interest or more accessible to men, women being socialized to enter cinema through its aspect as art.

Godard talks about a bourgeois camera style and rejects traditional documentary or cinema vérité. These only reproduce the so-called "normal" way of seeing things; certainly the subject of a film is never reality but only the way the maker(s) sees something. There is a great temptation to film women activists or the average woman living out her life and to let the subject "speak for herself." However all cinema-vérité dates fast, and in particular the filmmaker who thinks the subject is speaking for himself/herself (as Leacock/Pennebaker in *David* or *Don't Look Back*) ends up putting the filmmaker's opinions about class, sex, race, etc. into the *form* of the film. It is better to be aware of one's own presuppositions and state them directly, either visually or verbally, so that they will be immediately subjected to a conscious critique by the audience.

THE CRITIC'S PERSONAL AND POLITICAL STANCE

In addition to and related to her theoretical framework, the critic brings to bear on films her own likes and dislikes, education, class (usually middle), and—of special concern to us—her relation to the women's movement and her social and political practice. Intellectually, the critic must be aware of her critical preferences; for example, which aspects of the above schema does she consistently deal with in writing a film review? In addition, any woman who begins to write *feminist* criticism soon notices in what ways her reviews differ from others on the same film—and this is information that can fruitfully be passed on to their readers, for by learning about what is sexist (or feminist) in reviews, readers learn more about the film process as a whole. One's own immediate impressions of a film, a vignette of how the entire audience was responding, and one's emotional reactions are details that give liveliness and immediacy to a review.

When the critic writes with her politics up front, she provokes a political response both to her review and to the film at hand. I expect a woman writer to let me know where she stands not only in relation to the women's movement, but to various aspects of that movement (e.g., liberal reformist, radical lesbian, separatist, etc.) and to socialist politics as well. Readers do not need a précis of the critics' political stance in each article she writes. Rather, a woman's articles over a period of time plus the kinds of references she makes to activities and issues in the women's movement and to political issues in general make her politics clear. More candor about one's politics in film reviews is useful in dispelling once and for all the idea that the media

just provides entertainment or that we have to take what we are offered; politics and culture are inseparable and the feminist critic has
ideas on how to fight sexism in film. When I myself say that I am a
socialist feminist, that means that I see the major forms of oppression
in our society—sexual, class, and racial oppression, in particular—as
interrelated and that women's oppression must be fought by collective action against those institutions which are built on class, racial,
and sexual oppression: namely, the institutions of capitalism. That
the critic put a label on herself as a certain kind of feminist is not so
important as her making explicit the assumptions which underlie her
analysis of film and her value judgments about films.

When a woman works out in her criticism her ideas about class,
sexual politics, love, women's goals, money, authority, etc., this
gives her criticism real political strength. When a woman wants to
write about new uses for women's films, it is particularly valuable to
bring to bear her own organizing experience in the women's movement. For by writing criticism informed by theory and political practice, a feminist critic makes a *political* critique of film and film criticism,
which in turn makes it possible for the readers to respond to her on a
number of specific levels. On the one hand, the reader can respond
with, "I don't agree with what you said about class or race in that film
or with your political analysis." Or the reader may give a contrary
political interpretation to a film: "You say the film is progressive for a
number of reasons; however, I think the major character, with whom
we identify, sold out. These are the reasons why." The point is that
the critic owes it to her readers to make her own basic assumptions
perfectly clear so that the reader's response may also be lucid.

Women who write film criticism write for a certain audience. The
militancy of an article may depend both on the type of publication
and the intended audience. Many fine women critics, a number of
whom are film scholars, write for the established press. However, it is
only recently—probably in the context of a broader public awareness
of ideas springing from the women's movement—that we can see an
anti-sexist perspective in the work of both men and women critics in
the established press. Because of their socialization, feminists often
feel more confident writing about culture for the underground press
or women's papers or newsletters since the alternate media, both staff
and readership, sympathetically receives militant film reviews. However, once on the staff of the mixed underground paper or a radical or
cultural magazine, feminists have to struggle to write as authorities in
other areas as well as about women's affairs. This means their writing
about more than just grotesquely sexist films or else explicitly feminist
films. Thus films which are in the *auteurist* pantheon, such as those of
Peckinpah, are not exempt from a feminist critique. To fight the

liberalism of having feminist articles mainly in the "safe" area of culture, women in any mixed publication have also found that they have to push for an explicitly anti-sexist stance in all the articles in the publication as a whole. All types of local women's publications need and want feminist film criticism and this is an excellent place to start because very often first articles come out of a good political discussion with other women and, once published, stimulate more discussion from readers, especially women readers, from whom the local critic can receive feedback.

FUNCTIONS OF CRITICISM

If she writes mostly about the content and form of specific films, the feminist critic faces the problem of just fitting into a slot already prepared for her—that of writing a consumers' guide to film. No viewer wants to waste the price of a ticket; economically film reviewers serve a necessary function. However, by expanding criticism to include a critique of the whole film process, by writing for periodicals open to a broader perspective on women and film, and by working to help the practical cause of women in film, we can go beyond our assigned role as consumer guide. Like a book reviewer in a magazine or Sunday supplement, the film critic traditionally has the right to make generalizations about culture and *mores*. Thus feminists can conveniently use this ready-made journalistic vehicle not only to attack sexism in a film but also to evaluate the social milieu that generates that film. Furthermore, feminist criticism aids the growing appreciation of long-neglected women's films and hopefully will provide a basis on which to evaluate and constructively criticize those films.

Already, women critics have joined forces with women's studies courses and women's film festivals. Women, ourselves as critics included, are just beginning to know the *range* of women's films. Some of these films are being shown in courses, but too often just the same few are shown over and over again. Women are pressuring the local film societies to include women's films in their programs; and hopefully, we as critics will be able to devote ourselves to a serious study of these films. The distribution of the films women are making may well be aimed at the 16mm circuit or the exchange of video tapes.

Such films deserve more than a liberal viewing, where anything made by a woman is held as equally valuable as anything else. Rather we must use our capacity as feminist critics to see what is in these films and to see how these films fit (or can fit—and we can promote them) into the film process as a whole. Already a film such as *Janie's Janie* has proven its effectiveness in women's courses because it deals with women's issues across class and race lines and considers economic issues as well as personal ones. We do not have to promote just films having a didactic function, but I would hope that it would be from feminist critics that a woman director gets her fairest reviews.

I mentioned the direct influence feminist film criticism has on women's courses. Such criticism should have an effect on other institutions as well, hopefully especially on the production and distribution of films. As a critique of the established film industry—its history, its present practice, its international perspective—feminist criticism can bring neglected films to our attention and also demythologize some of cinema's traditional heros and themes. Even more, we can and should aid feminist political activity. Many women are using the media in forms that do not have professional distribution: 8mm or video. They are often using the media specifically as a local organizing tool. The content of their work and the technical and political mechanisms of such projects must be presented in detail so that other women can benefit immediately in their own political projects, either by using some of the material that has already been prepared or by learning how to use film and video in similar ways in their own women's groups.

The feminist critic not only combats sexism in the established cinema but also helps create a new place for women in film. Since the beginnings of a magazine like *Women and Film*, feminist criticism has rapidly moved beyond a critique of the mechanisms of sexism in the content of individual films to feminist perspectives on film theory and a support for and evaluation of the work of women in film. Hopefully, we will increasingly help women filmmakers by describing their films to prospective audiences, by developing feminist aesthetic theory, and by giving them a sound political and aesthetic critique.

This article is a synthesis of a workshop on the principles of feminist criticism given by Julia Lesage and Maureen Turim in Madison in June, 1973, and a paper presented with Charles Kleinhans at the Student Conference on Film Study, April, 1973. Many of these ideas originated with Maureen and Chuck.

Towards a Feminist Aesthetic: Reflection-Revolution-Ritual

PATRICIA ERENS

Traditionally aesthetics has been defined as an approach to beauty. Used as a tool for evaluative judgments, aesthetics becomes the means of deciding what is of worth in a work of art. As opposed to theories of art which deal with questions of ontology and which are thereby more self-reflexive, aesthetics relates to issues beyond the framework of the art object.

Throughout its eighty year history, film has been intricately linked to politics. Eisenstein's great theories of "montage" were an outgrowth of Marxist dialectical determinism. Film as propaganda was the basis of the Soviet socialist realism. In the late 1940's the rise of neo-realism reflected anti-Fascist attitudes as well as the exigencies of film production in post-war Italy. There is little doubt that film history mirrors political and social history. More importantly, films exist as a part of the system itself. Thus the work of women directors affects the system as well as reflects social issues. Further analysis of the inter-relationship between art and society as well as the function of feminist criticism can be found in "Feminist Film Criticism: Theory and Practice" by Julia Lesage in this volume.

The approach of this essay will be to establish a framework within which to analyze the work of women directors. In place of treating films as isolated works of art, I shall attempt to recast the work of women directors into a socio-political context, thereby revealing their underlying aesthetics. By aesthetics I imply more than an approach to beauty or a political ideology. The term aesthetics as used in this article refers to a response to life—a way of approaching art. It deals with the relationship between art and life and becomes the perspective

156

from which an artist creates. Aesthetics therefore concerns the form of communication, as well as the explicit content. In essence aesthetics becomes the guiding principle of an artist, as well as the reasoned response of the critic.

In an essay entitled "Subjecting Her Objectification or Communism Is Not Enough,"[1] Barbara Halpern Martineau proposes a dialectical approach for analyzing women's films. She divides works into two categories: works structured on contemplative harmonies and those based on revolutionary fragmentation. Traditional Hollywood films—films based on invisible cutting, psychological realism, logical narrative development, and illusionistic space are generally contemplative. They seek to integrate all elements into one cohesive whole. Believing that social change results only as old perceptions are destroyed, Martineau favors a fragmentary, non-organic art form—the form of revolution. Such fragmentation emphasizes juxtaposition in place of balance, the process of art in place of the art product. Revolutionary art forms strive to engage the spectator to a greater degree than harmonious structures which perpetuate illusions and reinforce the status quo.

Although Martineau's work provides a useful means of gaining insights into many feminists' works, especially in coming to terms with those which are truly revolutionary as opposed to those which are only seemingly so, I would like to expand her categories further. In revamping the lines of division I seek to extend the area of study in two directions so as to account for a greater number of works than Martineau's approach allows. In so doing I hope to defend the value of non-revolutionary art forms, especially as revolutionary works often are inaccessible to the vast majority of viewers whom they are intended to influence. Hopefully my approach will accommodate early films by women directors which lack explicit feminist content, as well as recent experimental and abstract film which cannot be adequately dealt with by Martineau's method.

In place of Martineau's contemplative/revolutionary dichotomy, I propose a triparte division: reflection, revolution, and ritual. Reflective films represent the artist's efforts to discover feelings about herself or other individuals and to appraise her relationship with society. Generally these works are typified by an outpouring of strong personal feeling and a tendency towards self-expression. Such works constitute the first stage in the development of a feminist consciousness.

Revolutionary films are a direct challenge to the status quo, either substantively or formally. Politically motivated, these films are generally concerned with the position of women as a group rather than as individuals, and appear at a time of greater fluidity within the society.

Such films form a second stage of development, typified by greater confidence and solidarity.

Lastly, ritualistic films. foreground the conscious manipulation of the artist over the expression, sensation, or impression of an emotion. Maya Deren, in her work entitled "An Anagram of Ideas on Art, Form, and Film," defined the function of art as:

> the dynamic result of the relationship of three elements the reality to which a man has access . . . the crucible of his own imagination and intellect; and the art instrument by which he realizes, through skillful exercize and control, his imaginative manipulations.[2]

It was the third variable which was the major concern to Deren.

Ritualistic films represent a stage of true equality. Ideally feminist creations should strive towards a ritualistic aesthetic, an art which is truly androgynous as Virginia Woolf defines it:

> the androgynous mind is resonant and porous; that it transmits emotion without impediment . . . In fact one goes back to Shakespeare's mind as the type of the androgynous, of the man-womanly mind, though it would be impossible to say what Shakespeare thought of women.[3]

Such works of art will not appear in large numbers until there are major changes within our society; however, ritualistic works have been created in the past (by Deren herself) and continue to be created.

The preceding categories were not imposed *a priori*, but emerged naturally after lengthy viewings of a large number of films by women. Although I have established a linear progression reflecting the logical stages of the feminist struggle, a superficial knowledge of women's films will readily reveal that their history does not follow this strict pattern. The reasons for these exceptions, especially concerning the work of early Hollywood women, will be dealt with later. Secondly, it is imperative that the successive stages of the feminist aesthetic (vis-à-vis women's relationship to society) not be equated with a hierarchy of artistic merit.

Although I personally look forward to a truly androgynous art form, in no way should non-androgynous works be considered inferior. Nor are all ritualistic works necessarily superior. Great art has been produced at all times, in all cultures, and under differing political systems.

THE AESTHETICS OF REFLECTION

In reviewing the contributions of women novelists, Virginia Woolf noted the impulse towards autobiography on the part of the first writers. She also detected the repressed anger and undigested emo-

tions which crept into these early works, preventing them from qual-
ifying as lasting works of art. Although these tendencies were representative of women writers, such was not the case with regard to the
first Hollywood directors. The reasons are two-fold. Firstly the early
days of Hollywood were free-wheeling, especially during the pre-war
period. Films were short (one and two reelers), relatively inexpensive, and rapidly executed. Strict separation between writer, director,
and cameraman was not observed. In this open atmosphere, women
were treated as equals. Over 25 women worked as directors in the
pre-sound era. The utilization of female talent in early Hollywood
typifies the structure of many emerging organizations whether economic, cultural, or political. However, as movie making grew in size
and importance, the industry grew increasingly patriarchal (again a
common tendency of entrenched authority). By the sound period
Dorothy Arzner remained the only woman director to possess a Hollywood contract.

Secondly, Hollywood filmmaking was and is a collaborative venture. As scripts were written by one person, directed by another, and
acted by yet others, the opportunity of "baring one's soul" on film
was nigh impossible. Such reactions could only evolve when director
had the same intimacy with the camera as an author outside the Hollywood studio system.

Such a situation typified the experimentation in France during the
1920's. As a member of the avant-garde Germaine Dulac's primary
interests were in exploring the capabilities of the new medium to express psychological states. As a committed feminist she chose to
channel these experiments through a female psyche. Although the
film is not autobiographical, her famous work, *The Smiling Madame
Beudet*, (1923), functions as a personal outpouring of the feelings of its
protagonist. The work depicts the stultifying life of a young provincial
woman married to a boorish, insensitive merchant. Not only is
Madame Beudet the central character, but the film represents her subjective view of the world. Her loneliness and dreams are portrayed
through her imaginings, depicted in fast and slow motion, superim-
position and extreme camera angles. Equally her relationship with
her husband is objectified through the use of similar expressionistic
shots.

Though Madame Beudet's situation may have represented the
plight of millions of women throughout the world, the film remains
the story of one woman. Though such a film may lead to an awareness of feminine problems, the film offers no solutions. Despite its
revolutionary technique which furthered the development of the
avant-garde, the film is primarily rooted in the aesthetics of reflection.
Little action occurs; no outward change takes place. Unlike Ibsen's

Nora, Madame Beudet remains securely at home in Chartes. In the end it represents the first stage of feminist consciousness—awareness of the problem. As a work of art, however, Dulac's innovation techniques, sensitivity of handling, and ability to create a balanced work which possesses universality has stood the test of time. As such *Madame Beudet* ranks high in the annals of film history.

Personal expression is not limited to experimental film. In fact, more recently reflective works have tended to be documentaries. Since documentary filmmaking usually entails less elaborate production problems, it is natural that novice filmmakers (the status of most women) should turn to documentary work as a means of learning the craft. Further, new light-weight equipment especially suitable for documentary work is easily manageable and within budget limitations. Such equipment has become the modern equivalent to the pen and paper of a by-gone era. Therefore, many young filmmakers have turned to film to reflect on their inner feelings.

Two recent films are excellent examples of the personal documentary. Joyce Chopra's *Joyce at 34* (1972) and Amalie Rothchild's *Nana, Mom and Me,* (1974) both explore feelings about being a woman, being a mother, being a filmmaker and relating to other females.

Both films were conceived as explorations to be shot over a long period of time (*Joyce* begins before the birth of her first child and ends when Sarah is close to one year old: *Nana* occurs over a two year period (1972-74). Both films are explorations into the past, thus both make use of old photographs and home movies. As we watched Madame Beudet in her musing, viewing the content of her thoughts, so we review with Joyce and Amalie the content of their past lives. The rich texture of film within film provides a means of mining the past.

Both films incorporate passages of live action as well as direct interview. Generally characters appear in real situations, followed by their own analyses of what happened and how they felt. In this manner audiences are given a chance to reflect as well—to compare their own responses against those of the filmmaker.

Reflection leads to revelation. The films are full of discoveries: Joyce's awareness of how much Sarah has come to mean in her life, her realization that one child is all she can manage, her growing desire to reintegrate herself into the family unit: the facts of Nana's unexplored past, the articulation of mom's struggle for independence, and the insights gained by Amalie concerning ties and tensions with traditional values.

There are many other films which are based on the aesthetics of reflection. They take various forms, and many are not exclusively reflective. In part Jacqueline Audry's *Pit of Loneliness* (1951) a narrative based on her sister Colette's novel "Olivia," can be approached in this manner. The story concerns the experiences of a young English girl who attends a French boarding school during the latter part of the nineteenth century. Through her attachment to one of the head principals and the tragic suicide of the other, she comes to terms with her own inner feelings about being female. The film opens with Olivia's arrival and closes with her departure. Despite the serious issues of lesbianism raised with the context of the work, the film is best approached as a 'coming of age' romance. As Olivia leaves France, her outward manner reveals her inner growth. Audry's *Pit of Loneliness*, a highly personal work, focuses on inner sensations, with little attention to the greater world beyond the individual. Past action crystalizes into present reflection.

However, reflective works provide an important function. By foregrounding the need to reflect, these films awaken dormant feelings. As a vehicle for consciousness raising, they lead inevitably to the next stage of development, one grounded in a revolutionary aesthetic.

THE AESTHETICS OF REVOLUTION

For most viewers, films with strong central characters and didactic messages have come to represent the feminist aesthetic, primarily because of their relationship with the women's movement. They speak loudest and often gain the most attention.

Revolutionary aesthetics have tended to dismiss psychological realism. This is as true of Eisenstein's adoption of Meyerhold's principles as of Godard's dismissal of French naturalism. Equally, the revolutionary films generally fragment logical narrative. As revolutionary works, personal concerns are subsumed by the greater struggle. In place of individual reflection, a revolutionary aesthetic seeks to stimulate group action. Eisenstein's theories were founded on Pavlovian psychology; Godard on Brechtian tactics.

Like the films of reflection, revolutionary films often evolve as a result of women's "lockout" from the established means of production. Such films have appeared in various modes. They may be documentary, experimental, or narrative. Often the content is foregrounded so that the film becomes didactic. In many cases formal considerations are not tackled at all.

Janie's Janie by Geri Ashur is an example of a revolutionary documentary. Although the film is not structurally innovative, the message is clear. The film charts the emerging self-confidence and burgeoning militancy of Janie, a welfare mother with six children, trying to make it on her own. As opposed to the reflective manner of

Joyce or Amalie, Janie is committed to action, through female solidarity. Through Janie's association with the filmmakers, she joined the daycare center, made new friends, and became politicized. However, the actual circumstances of the production demonstrate perfectly the revolutionary potential inherent in reflection. The film was begun by Geri Ashur and a group working out of New York Newsreel, who wanted to portray the lonely life of a woman like Janie. In this manner the filmmaking process afforded Janie an opportunity to assess her situation and actually provoked changes similar to those in Jean Rouch's *Chronicle of a Summer*.

Janie's Janie not only poses a problem, but seeks to offer a solution. Another film which functions in this manner is Madelaine Anderson's, *I Am Somebody*, (1970) which documents the struggle of five hundred black, female hospital workers in Charleston during the 1969 strike.

In the area of experimental film, several works will serve to indicate how experimental techniques can lead to a growing awareness of the need to revise old perceptions. In Liane Brandon's humorous, *Anything You Want To Be* (1971), the viewer watches the ways in which women are reformed to fit pre-existing models. By jarring juxtapositions, Brandon condenses the end result of frustrated hope and dissipated potential. Through stop motion, fast motion, and freeze frame, she suggests the importance of discarding old stereotypes in favor of finding truer images. Most importantly, the film challenges society, which limits the options of choice—promising all and delivering little.

More ambiguous, but equally provoking, Gunvor Nelson's *Take Off* (1973) presents the salacious stripper Ellion Ness going through her paces. Only at the end of the film does Nelson pull out the stops and allow us to see the logical extension of our "normal vision." Through trick photography, Nelson rechannels our eyes, pushing home the need to reevaluate the meaning of stripping and the use of the female as sex object.

However, new perceptions are not limited to new frameworks. Certainly Leontine Sagan's quiet, gentle *Maedchen in Uniform* (1931) qualifies as revolutionary, as well as the more brazen *A Very Curious Girl* (1969) by Nelly Kaplan. The fact that Goebbels found it necessary to ban *Maedchen* is a testament to its powerful challenge to Fascism. Similarly, Kaplan's difficulties in distributing *A Very Curious Girl* resulted from its supposed threat to society which foster's male superiority.

Although *Maedchen* focuses on the plight of one girl—Manuela— the lines of opposition are clearly drawn between the Prussian discipline imposed by the school's head mistress and Manuela's affection for Fraulein von Bernburg. Upon a direct confrontation, one of the two forces must wither and die. The film clearly indicates who will triumph. The problem is not reaching maturity as in *Pit of Loneliness*, but rather the necessity of destroying an intolerable, repressive system. Though situated in an exclusively female world, the theme extends beyond questions of feminist freedom to problems of personal freedom in general. In this regard, it's message speaks universally. As a result of Sagan's masterful rendering, the film qualifies as a lasting work of art.

In the same way, *A Very Curious Girl* speaks for all oppressed minorities. The film reveals how economic power serves as a repressive weapon in a male-dominated society. Mary's transition from sexually abused scullery maid to successful entrepeneur of the village's only house of 'respite,' is a modern parable. Although the film does not opt for the formation of solidarity groups nor provide a ready-made solution which is easily adoptable, Mary's awakening, growing self-confidence, and ultimate use of power provides a source of inspiration for women who continue to define themselves by male standards. The fact that the witch burns the witch hunters under-cuts traditional dramatic expectations.

There are many excellent narrative features by women directors which fall into this category. Kaplan's second feature, *Papa l'es p'tits bateaux* (1971) also parodies formula films, and again shows Kaplan's disdain for women's willing acceptance of positions of weakness. The quick-witted Cookie de Palma refuses to play victim and eventually does in her would-be kidnappers. Extended to a larger panorama, the film speaks of revolution.

Shirley Clarke's features, *The Connection* (1960), *The Cool World* (1974) and the *Portrait of Jason* (1967) also possess an urgency which reflects an uneasy status quo. Rejecting purely feminist content, Clarke's films combine a concern for the plight of the oppressed with a camera style that fractures the traditional separation between subject, filmmaker, and viewer. In *The Cool World* her semi-documentary technique and agitated hand-held camera make real a world of limited possibilities and its dire results. In *Portrait of Jason* she uses the camera to provoke responses from the subject, destroying the mask which Jason wears when confronting the world.

Likewise, in *Daisies* (1966) Czech filmmaker Vera Chytilova utilizes an abundance of experimental techniques to fragment the logical narrative of two young girls out on a spree. And Cinda Firestone's film *Attica* (1974) combines film and television footage in the manner of Esther Schub (a Russian filmmaker of the twenties who made the first historical compilation film).

Lastly, Mireille Dansereau's *Dream Life* (1971) explores the fantasies of two young women. Eventually they are able to penetrate these illusions and quite literally tear them apart. Their disillusion-ment becomes an initial step towards a revolutionary change.

All of these works posit the same message—change is essential. In the best works the revolutionary content is formally integrated into the texture of the work, which is itself revolutionary. However, whether the major emphasis remains on revolutionary content or on form, the necessity of action is inherent in the work.

THE AESTHETICS OF RITUAL

Here we arrive at the last stage of a feminist aesthetic. Quite pos-sibly the implementation of these ideas will prove self-destructive, eliminating feminist aesthetics as a separate ideology.

For Maya Deren, ritualistic art meant forms which treated the human being not as a source of dramatic action, but as an imper-sonalized element in the dramatic whole. Such an approach tends towards abstraction and experimentation. Many revolutionary films incorporate the tenets of ritualistic art. However, the degree to which these works are created in the name of a political ideology limit the degree to which some can be considered true ritualist art.

Films based on the aesthetics of reflection and revolution may or may not contain artistic distance. The superior works probably do; however, in other works the fire of emotion which produces the work may also cloud the artist's objectivity. Generally such works are of only temporary importance. Ritualistic art always possesses aesthetic distance.

Thus the elimination of uncontrolled and uncensored emotions, which are often fraught with neurotic responses, prejudices, fan-tasies, guarantees an androgynous approach. As defined in this arti-cle, ritualistic art need not be abstract, anti-narrative or self-reflexive (although many works are); a ritualistic aesthetic may underlie a fic-tion feature as well as an experimental work.

It is noteworthy that the early Hollywood filmmakers—Alice Guy-Blaché, Lois Weber, and Cleo Madison—working in a nonres-trictive environment produced androgynous works of art, which is to say the male and female characters are drawn with equal ver-isimilitude. Obviously, these are not necessarily works of art. How-ever, Guy-Blaché's slapstick comedies, Weber's romances, and Madi-son's melodramas look little different from the typical works of the time. Though their women characters are developed with great sym-pathy, this is not achieved at the expense of the male players.

On the contemporary scene several women directors have emerged who consciously reject feminist aesthetics. Among the most interesting is Lina Wertmüller. Although Wertmüller did direct one feminist work, *This Time Let's Talk About Men* (1965), she feels more committed to other subjects. In addition, she states, "my position is that by working, by making films that are successful, I can be a banner for feminism."

Her first international success, *Love and Anarchy* (1974), deals with an unsuccessful attempt to assassinate Mussolini. The drama centers on the growing love between the young anarchist and a prostitute whom he meets in Rome while awaiting his moment. Through sensitive direction, attention to details, and wry humor, Wertmüller avoids stereotypical characterizations. The feminist cause becomes only tangential to her major theme—the conflict between personal values and social obligations. However, there is little doubt that her depiction of life under a repressive regime is as valid a portrait of feminine oppression as it is a document of Fascist Italy. Wertmüller's more recent films, most particularly *Swept Away by an Unusual Destiny in the Blue Sea of August* (1974) and *Seven Beauties* (1975) have presented women in a most unflattering light. However, as issues in Wertmüller films are seldom as simple as they appear on first viewing, these films demand a close analysis.

It is in the work of Maya Deren and Leni Riefenstahl that the ritualistic aesthetic has found its greatest practioners. The art critic Linda Nochlin has stated, "The problem lies not so much with the feminists' concept of what femininity in art is, but rather with the misconception of what art is: with the naive idea that art is the direct, personal expression of individual emotional experience—a translation of personal life into visual terms. Yet art is almost never that; great art certainly never. The making of art involves a self-consistent language of form, more or less dependent upon, or free from, given temporally-defined conventions, schemata, or systems of notation, which have to be learned or worked out, through study, apprenticeship, or a long period of individual experimentation."[4] In essence, a restatement of Deren's own ideas concerning art.

Although Nochlin's definition of greatness lacks clarification, there is little doubt that Deren and Riefenstahl would qualify as artists whose major concerns were formal (i.e. ritualistic).

From her earliest film, *Meshes of the Afternoon* (1943), through to her last work, *The Very Eye of Night* (1959), Deren concentrated on purely formal concerns, although the exteriorization of an inner landscape in *Meshes* is probably reflective in many respects. Predominately, her films deal with temporal and spacial variations possible through discontinuities and 'editing across the splice,' (the combining of separate actions into one continuous movement). She strove to create new filmic realities through the use of slow motion, freeze frame, negative projection, and the rotating camera.

The results of her experimentation not only extended the syntax of filmic vocabulary, but also stimulated a whole generation of younger filmmakers who formed the ranks of the new American cinema.

The films of Leni Riefenstahl also reveal her major concern for editing, camera movement, and rhythm. Her interest in the beauty of the human body as depicted primarily in *Olympia* (1938), was a natural outgrowth of her years as a dancer (an interest she shares with Shirley Clarke and Maya Deren). Riefenstahl's use of telescopic lenses, underwater cameras, and special tracks opened up new possibilities for documentary filmmaking.

Seen as a group, these women have each sought in their own sphere to create works of art and to extend the boundaries of the medium. Placing artistic concerns above personal passions and political causes, they have created with a true androgynous sensibility. In this way, works as diverse as Wertmüller's narratives, Deren's experiments, and Riefenstahl's documentaries are fine examples of a ritualistic aesthetic.

The foregoing analyses are offered as a working hypothesis. Obviously, each category must be developed further. The categories are not intended to be rigid: it is quite possible for one film to contain elements of all three aesthetics or to move from reflection to revolution. Also many films which are steeped in a specific ideology, transcend them and become ritualistic works, as in the Riefenstahl documentaries.

Many films are available. I have tended to concentrate on those films which are fairly well known and easily available. Almost all of these films possess central characters who are female. The majority of these women are active, not passive, and all of them are defined in other than sexual terms (a perpetual shortcoming of so many male directed works). However, other alternatives exist.

For example, Barbara Loden's *Wanda* (1970) chronicles the story of a totally passive woman played by Loden herself. The controversy provoked by this work can be reconciled by viewing the film as a reflective work. Likewise, many women directors have purposely chosen to use female stars as sex objects in making specific points. Both Kaplan and Wertmüller focus on prostitutes and prostitution as a central theme. As in the films of Jean-Luc Godard, woman as object carries revolutionary implications symbolizing the plight of all oppressed people. Rather than reject out-of-hand all feminine images which do not depict strong, independent women as some feminists propose, it is preferable to see all portrayals as a point on a continuum. All have some place in the development of a feminist aesthetic.

[1]*Notes on Women's Cinema,* edited by Claire Johnston. SCREEN Pamphlet 2, Society for Education in Film and Television, London, 1973.

[2]Maya Deren, *An Anagram of Ideas on Art, Form and Film* (Alicat, 1946). p. 17.

[3]Virginia Woolf, *A Room of One's Own* (A Harbinger Book, New York and Burlingame), 1929, p. 102.

[4]Linda Nochlin, *"Why Have There Been No Great Women Artists?" "Art and Sexual Politics,"* edited by Thomas B. Hess and Elizabeth C. Baker (Collier Books, New York), 1973, p. 5.

Jeanne Moreau in Orson Welles's *L'Histoire Immortelle* (1968).

II.
WOMEN
DIRECTORS

Out of Oblivion:
Alice Guy Blaché

FRANCIS LACASSIN

There are enough women filmmakers now for it to be easy to forget just how recent a phenomenon they are. Yet it was only in the Fifties, with the growth of television and the decline of the big studio monopolies, that they began to come into their own. Until 1939, there were only a dozen women directors in the world. From 1915 to 1925, you could count them on the fingers of one hand. In 1914 there were two of them. And before that there was only one: a Frenchwoman named Alice Guy.

Still very much alive—at the age of 97, she lives quietly in an American nursing-home—Alice Guy was not only the doyenne of women film-makers. She was also the only one to have been in at the birth of the cinema. Her career, which ended in 1920 in the United States, began in the 19th century in Paris, at Buttes-Chaumont, where she built the first Gaumont studio; today the site is occupied by the ORTF television studios.[1] Her work was also the most prolific: approximately two hundred reels between 20 and 680 meters long (in terms of contemporary projection speeds, between one and forty minutes) up to 1906; more than 70 two-reelers and features between 1910 and 1920. She founded and directed, or contributed to the founding in the United States, of four production companies and one distribution company. She took on the Edison Trust, by braving their ban on productions over two reels long.

But, as far as posterity is concerned, it is better to come second or third than first.

Inaugurated in the prehistoric period and over before the history of the cinema was born, Alice Guy's career on both sides of the Atlantic has been either forgotten or attributed to other people. But a meeting with her, our subsequent correspondence, and research in New York and Los Angeles, have enabled me to reconstruct her story.

Alice Guy was born in Paris on July 1 1873, in a comfortable bourgeois family which was bankrupted on three separate occasions, once as a result of an earthquake. At the age of four, she went with her family to Santiago (a long journey: there was still no Panama Canal), left Chile again at the age of six, and was later educated at a convent in Paris. On her father's death, determined to ensure her independence, she learned shorthand-typing, still a rare accomplishment. Her mother ran various charity committees and at one of them she met some of Léon Gaumont's family. Alice was hired by Gaumont as a secretary.

In 1885 the Gaumont organisation had taken over the Comptoir de Photographie. They manufactured films and cameras, and the Lumière Brothers' invention led them to take an interest in the cinema. In 1896, with the collaboration of the engineer Demeny, Gaumont launched a 60mm. camera. In 1897, with the collaboration of Decaux, he marketed a 35mm. combined camera-projector. This was followed in 1898 by an inexpensive machine designed solely for projection: the 'Gaumont Chronophotographe', mass-produced and aimed at film exhibitors. As an accessory for demonstration purposes, Gaumont had hitherto produced a few reels of factual or news footage. The success of his new machine obliged him to provide customers with fiction films along the lines of those made by Pathé. He entrusted his active secretary with the organisation of this new branch. With no resources and no qualified staff, Mademoiselle Alice decided to tackle the job herself.

In the small garden of her boss's house in the factory grounds,[2] she set up a few backdrops and with the help of a much amused friend, Yvonne Mugnier-Serand, she shot *La Fée aux Choux* (later retitled *Sage-femme de 1ère Classe*). In a picture postcard vein of humour, it tells the story of a woman who grows children in a cabbage patch. This first effort was well received, and as she'd enjoyed the experience its author decided to continue her new career. She had plenty of time for it: it was only a question of producing a total of anything from twelve to twenty very short films a year. When I spoke to her, Alice Guy claimed that she had started making films before Méliès. It seems unlikely, however, that Gaumont would have envisaged producing fiction films before they started mass-producing their projectors in 1898; or, at the very earliest, their combined camera-projector in 1897.

For her next films, Alice Guy managed to obtain a few professional performers. The only people willing to risk appearing in films and ready to work for the fees Gaumont offered were acrobats, vaudeville actors like Henri Gallet, or *chansonniers* like Roullet-Plessis. Occasionally, in exceptional circumstances, she was able to hire some of the famous clowns of the age: the O'ners in *La Voiture Cellulaire, Déménagement à la Cloche de Bois, Ballet des Signes, La Crinoline* and (1905) *Une Noce au Lac Saint-Fargeau.* She tackled every genre. Fairytales and fantasies: *Faust et Méphisto, La Fève Enchantée, Lui, La Légende de Saint-Nicolas, La Fée Printemps* (1906, in colour). Saucy comedies: *Les Fredaines de Pierrette, Charmant Froufrou, J'ai un Hanneton dans mon Pantalon!* Trick comedies: *Le Cake-walk de la Pendule, Le Fiancé Ensorcelé.* Religious subjects: *La Messe de Minuit, Le Noël de Pierrot.*

For the comedies she sometimes concentrated on a single actor. *La Première Cigarette* (60 metres, August 1904) shows in semi-close-up the reactions, as observed by his terrified sister, of a boy sneakily smoking a cigarette. (This film has been wrongly attributed to Emile Cohl who, in fact, only started at Gaumont after Alice Guy had left.) She advanced to longer and longer films with larger and larger casts. From *Les Apaches pas Veinards* (20 metres, March 1903) she went on to *L'Assassinat du Courrier de Lyon* (122 metres, April 1904) and from there to *Rapt d'Enfants par les Romanichels* (six scenes and 225 metres; October 1904). 1904 was her year for children, who provided the inspiration for *Le Baptême de la Poupée, Les Petits Peintres* and especially *Les Petits Coupeurs de Bois Vert,* a delightfully naive melodrama. Two children, whose sick mother has fallen asleep in front of the dying fire in their humble cottage, go to gather wood in a nearby forest. They are caught by the gamekeepers and brought before a magistrate. On hearing of their plight, the latter cannot hold back his tears and lets them go after slipping a coin into the hand of the older child.

Alice Guy told me that all the films produced by Gaumont up to the autumn of 1905 can be attributed to her, except for a few films made in 1904 and 1905. It was in 1904, in fact, that she was surprised to come across Ferdinand Zecca in the streets of La Villette selling soap from door to door: formerly Charles Pathé's right-hand man and the head of his production section, a sudden fall from favour had reduced him to this extremity. One detail moved Alice Guy more than all the rest: 'Zecca was wetting the soap to make it weigh more.' She immediately offered her former rival a job; and although Zecca was in fact reinstated with Pathé a few weeks later, during his short time at

Gaumont he acted as assistant and also directed a few films himself—most notably *Les Méfaits d'une Tête de Veau*, one of the big successes of the Gaumont repertoire. For a long time, this was the only film actually attributed to Alice Guy, although by her own account it was one of the few Gaumont pictures that she *didn't* make. The source of this historical error lies with the reminiscences of Etienne Arnaud, who began work at La Villette two years after this film was made.

Working with Zecca brought home to her the need for an assistant. It was difficult for her to deal single-handed with the ever-increasing demand for films. Moreover, she wanted to devote herself to longer, more elaborate pictures. *Rélubilitation*, 'a dramatic scene' made in 1904, attained the then considerable length of 250 metres. Under the title of *Esmeralda*, she was planning an adaptation of Victor Hugo's Notre Dame; and of course she had to bring out a *Life of Christ* to compete with the one Pathé had just released. These two films—both 'superproductions' in their day—were released in December 1905 and January 1906 and were respectively 290 and 680 metres long: they both involved extensive casts, particularly the second—300 extras . . . and 25 wooden sets designed by Henri Ménessier. The engineer Decaux personally helped cut them out and mount them on mobile platforms, for some decors were set up out of doors in the forest of Fontainebleau. Handling these three hundred extras, scraped from the bottom of the barrel and reluctant to be bossed around by a woman, led Alice Guy to hire a kind of production manager who would be part assistant and part director. Her choice fell on Victorin Jasset (1862–1913), producer at the Hippodrome (now the Gaumont-Palace) of popular historical reconstructions—Vercingetorix, Joan of Arc, etc. Which is how *Esmeralda* and *La Vie du Christ* came to be wrongly attributed to Jasset, who was merely the directress' assistant. In 1963, while comparing it to stills which she had kept from the film, Alice Guy showed me the collection of chromos which had provided her visual inspiration: namely, *La Vie de Notre Seigneur Jésus-Christ* by James Tissot, published in Tours by Alfred Mame.

Jasset also assisted Alice Guy on a film shot in his native district, *Descente dans les Mines à Fumay*. Finally, Alice Guy confirmed that he himself directed two or three films including the bizarre *Rêves d'un Fumeur d'Opium*. Although she was satisfied with him both as an assistant and a director, she did not keep him because Léon Gaumont thought that the interest he showed in the young female extras was more than strictly professional. He thereby deprived himself of an exceptional collaborator. Jasset later became one of the founders of the Eclair Company and remained its artistic director until his death. It was at Eclair that he created the thriller genre (later perfected by Feuillade) with his serials *Nick Carter* (1907–1910), *Zigomar* and two masterpieces, *Balaco*, based on Gaston Leroux, and *Protéa*.

In the autumn of 1905, Gaumont deposited a pile of scripts on the desk of his artistic directress. They had been sent him by Michel Coissac of La Maison de la Bonne Presse, publishers of *La Croix* and *Le Pèlerin*, and were written by one of Coissac's former colleagues: Louis Feuillade. Alice Guy liked the scripts, sent for their author and asked if he'd like to direct the films himself. But Feuillade, who had just become a father, was reluctant to give up the security of his job with the *Revue Mondiale*. He suggested that she might instead try Etienne Arnaud (1879–1955), a friend from L'Hérault with whom he had written a one-act verse play, *Le Clos*, and founded the Toro-Club of Paris. A law graduate, a former *chansonnier*, and currently out of work, Arnaud made his debut as director by shooting Feuillade's first script, *Attrapez mon Chapeau!*, which came out in January 1906. He continued working for Gaumont, with historical films his particular specialty, until 1911. Then he went to America as director of the Eclair Company's new studios at Fort Lee on the Hudson. In 1922 he published his book of reminiscences, *Le Cinéma pour Tous*.

Feuillade's energy and cheerfulness usually infected everyone who worked with him, and he got on very well with Alice Guy. Promoted to being the company screenwriter, he brought her three scenarios regularly every week until—not many months after, according to Alice Guy—he gave up journalism for film direction. His invention was so prolific that for the next year or so he continued to provide plots for most of the films made by his colleagues—in particular Roméo Bosetti, originally the actor in the *Roméo* serials and then director of the *Calino* serials (starring Mégé) until they were taken over in 1910 by Jean Durand.

With Arnaud, Feuillade, Bosetti and J. Roullet-Plessis, another actor turned director, to meet most of Gaumont's needs, Alice Guy could spend more time on her own films; and on the Company's new department. Gaumont had always believed in talking pictures. In 1905 he marketed the 'Chronophone', which combined sound recorded on a wax cylinder with the filmed image, and throughout 1906 and until the spring of 1907, Alice Guy was kept busy directing some hundred films for the Chronophone. Rarely more than a minute or two long, they mostly featured singers in performance or *tableaux* accompanied by choral singing. After *Les Ballets de l'Opéra* (with Gaillard) and *Les Sœurs Mante Danseuses Mondaines*, she recorded Rose Caron's class at the Conservatoire in *Carmen*, *Mignon*, *Manon*, *Les Dragons de Villars*, *Les Cloches de Corneville*, *Madame Angot*, *La Vivandière*, *Fanfan la Tulipe*, and Théodore Botrel's *Le Couteau*. Among those who came to perform in front of her camera and her recording machines were Mayol, Dranem and Polin.

She didn't meanwhile lose interest in the silent film. In 1906, eager to film the bullfights at Nîmes, she decided to take advantage of the trip to film adaptations from Provençal literature. Feuillade, co-opted into the party as a scriptwriter, was allowed to work on the direction of certain films (among them *Mireille*, after Frédéric Mistral) whenever the shooting involved practical difficulties for a woman. Such as? 'Climbing up into a tree, for instance,' Alice Guy explains. Although the first negative of *Mireille* was damaged, the month-long trip was both productive and agreeable. It was during this expedition that Alice Guy fell in love with the party's English cameraman, Herbert Blaché, and soon after she married him.

In 1907 Blaché was put in charge of Gaumont's New York office. Intending to accompany him, his wife gave up directing films and also had to resign from her post as artistic director for the Gaumont Company. Léon Gaumont thought he might find a replacement by enticing someone away from Pathé; specifically, he had Albert Cappellani in mind. But Alice Guy assured him that the man he needed was already working in his own company: Louis Feuillade. Gaumont took her advice, and the future director of *Les Vampires* took up his new position on April 1, 1907.

Gaumont's New York branch was on Congress Avenue, a long way from Manhattan in the suburb of Flushing. Just outside its doors there was open countryside: wild woods and lakes that seemed made for location shooting. But, unlike Pathé, Gaumont's foreign branches were not supposed to engage in production. The New York branch was set up to function as an agency and print laboratory, and Blaché's job was to show Gaumont productions to American exhibitors and to take orders for them. Paris would then send him the negatives, he would make however many copies he needed for the American market, title them in English, and return the negatives to La Villette.

After two years, during which she gave birth to a daughter and adapted to her new life, Alice Guy began to feel bored with life as a mere wife and mother. Nostalgic for her former profession, she had the idea of making for the American public films designed to its tastes and performed by American actors. Since Gaumont was unwilling to take the risks involved in foreign production, and her husband was under exclusive contract, she had to venture into business on her own. She did, in theory, have an outlet for her films: the clients her husband had contacted on Gaumont's behalf.

On September 7, 1910, the Solax Company was registered: president, Alice Blaché; business director, George A. Magie. Although the company had an office in Manhattan—147 Fourth Avenue, on the

corner of 14th Street—it actually operated from the Gaumont building in Flushing, where Alice Guy used the print lab and comman-
deered a space for shooting interiors. The countryside around Flushing provided her locations. She engaged a cameraman, John Haas,
who photographed most of her films; she got her chief designer and
former collaborator on *La Vie de Jésus*, Henri Ménessier, to come over
from Paris. From October 21, 1910 until June 1914, under its
trademark of a blazing sun, the Solax Company produced some 325
films of assorted lengths and types. At least 35 of them were directed
by the company's lady president,[3] the rest being made by Edward
Warren, the company's principal director, and by Harry Schenk.
Throughout Solax's existence, Alice Guy personally directed an average of one film a month.

Released on October 21, Solax's first production *A Child's Sacrifice*
was made by Alice Guy, who would appear to have been thinking
back to the good old days of *Les Petits Coupeurs de Bois Vert*. *A Child's
Sacrifice* is the story of an 8-year-old girl (played by Magda Foy, the
'Solax Kid'). Her father is a worker out on strike and her mother is ill,
so she tries to sell her doll to a junk-dealer. Seeing her distress, he
buys the toy and then gives it back to her as a present. The little girl
does not content herself with bringing a few pennies into the starving
household; she also intervenes to prevent bloodshed in a quarrel provoked by the strike. Another of Alice Guy's successful melodramas,
Falling Leaves, was distributed in France. It's the touching story of a
little girl who believes she can stop her big sister dying of TB by going
out into the garden at night and putting fallen leaves back on the
branches: the doctor hints that the sister will die at the end of the autumn.

The director did not forget her recordings for the Chronophone: in
1912 she filmed two operas, *Mignon* and *Fra Diavolo*, both three-
reelers with orchestral accompaniment. Nor did she lose interest in
tougher subjects. Making good use of a trip to Washington, she shot a
series of military scenes; most of which were really cowboy pictures.
The woman who had directed *Les Apaches de Paris* and *Le Crime de la
Rue du Temple* turned out for Solax such thrillers as *The Rogues of Paris*,
The Million Dollar Robbery and *The Sewer*. The script for this last film
was by her designer, Ménessier, who had no hesitation in digging
trenches and pools in the undeveloped land around Flushing. One of
the film's main attractions was an attack on the hero by genuine
sewer rats, specially trained by an expert. The directress spared no
effort or expense to achieve realism or sensational effects. To the great
surprise of critics, who were not yet used to this type of thing, in
March 1912 she set fire to a car in the studio yard ('a Darracq only
three years old') for a crime story entitled *Mickey's Pal*. This scene was
directed by Edward Warren at the express request of Herbert Blaché,

who was somewhat alarmed at the prospect of his wife filming fires and acrobatics on the struts of the Brooklyn Bridge, using wild animals and setting off explosions. He did allow her to have animals on the set in *The Beasts of the Jungle*, but he strictly forbade her to use dynamite, standing in for her as director on scenes of *The Yellow Traffic* which he considered too dangerous.

Alice Guy made two further excursions into the realm of the fantastic: *The Pit and the Pendulum* and *The Shadows of the Moulin Rouge*, both made in 1913. Looking back for the last time to the trick comedies of the heroic age of Gaumont, she introduced—with the collaboration of the indispensable Ménessier—a short animation sequence into a 1912 melodrama, *Hotel Honeymoon*, in which the moon came to life and smiled at the lovers. She may also have been the director of *In the Year 2000*, a satire in which women ruled the earth. In any case, it would have been consistent with her character and sense of humour.

From the beginning, the stars of the 'Solax Stock Company' were Blanche Cornwall and Darwin Karr, joined in 1913 by Vinnie Burns and Claire Whitney. Others in the company included Lee Beggs, Mace Greenleaf, Marion Swayne and Billy Quirk, who specialised in comedy and was the hero of the 'Billy' series.

At first Alice Guy tried not to draw attention to her unique position as the world's only woman film director: a sensible precaution in the face of a *milieu* where skill in manipulating stock clichés was more appreciated than intuition or sensitivity. But when they discovered her existence, the trade press took an attentive interest in this charming Frenchwoman whose gentleness on the set disguised such astonishing energy. Delighted by the touch of exoticism she brought to them, they published her photo: in evening dress, in her working clothes: with a megaphone in her hand, protected from the sun by an immense hood, standing on a piece of scaffolding to direct a scene from *Fra Diavolo*. They reported every word and gesture of the woman whom they called not Mrs. Blaché; but —*toujours la politesse*—Madame Blaché. When she visited Sing Sing on a reconnaissance trip, they photographed her sitting in the famous electric chair and quoted her as saying: 'French prisons are much more comfortable, particularly the one at Fresnes.' (Heavens! How did she know?) They were fond of repeating that, according to 'Madame Blaché; French children show an innate feeling for acting even before they are out of their rompers. But the Americans can catch up with them by hard work.

In point of fact, Solax was highly successful. Its films were popular and sold well. Consequently, in January 1912 she was able to announce that she had acquired a site on the other side of the Hudson, on Palisades Avenue at Fort Lee, where she was planning to build a modern studio. Along with the Pathé studio and Eclair, where

Etienne Arnaud had just arrived, Solax helped to make Fort Lee the capital of a Franco-American cinema. The new building, which contained a large studio with two-storey-high glass windows facing south, was equipped with a laboratory capable of printing 16,000 feet of positive film a day. And meanwhile on February 3, 1912, at Weber's Theatre on Broadway, Solax organised its first gala evening, attended by everyone from the New York film world.

Herbert Blaché, who was still running Gaumont's New York office, was every bit as dynamic as his wife and was a great help in marketing her films. In May 1912 he became leader of a group of independents who were determined to put up some kind of active resistance to the Edison Trust, which was uncooperative or worse in its dealings with them. He founded a distribution company, the Film Supply Company, and became its president until it was merged in 1914 with the Mutual Company (although Mutual was later to produce Chaplin's films, it was at this time still exclusively a distribution company). In addition to Solax's pictures, the Film Supply Company distributed films made by Thanhouse, Great Northern, Majestic, Comet, Reliance and the American Film Company, as well as the films of several French companies—Gaumont, Lux, Eclair, Eclair American, and Le Film d'Art.

Almost as soon as he was released from his exclusive contract to Gaumont in October 1913, Herbert Blaché founded and became president of Blaché Features Inc. (vice-president: Alice Guy). It soon replaced Solax, which ceased its bi-weekly productions on October 31. But five Solax films which were already under way were distributed under the old label at the rate of one a month. Unlike Solax, the new company made only dramas—especially adventure stories—and these were a minimum of four reels long. Alice Guy inaugurated the production side of the company on November 17 with *The Star of India*. Of the fourteen films made by Blaché Features Inc. from November 1913 until its disappearance in November 1914, nine were made by her; the others were directed by Harry Schenk or by Blaché himself.

With his indomitable passion for founding companies, Blaché set up a new one in April 1914 with a capital of $500,000. The U.S. Amusement Corporation: vice-president Alice Guy; managing director, Joseph M. Shear. The aims of the company were set out by its president in a manifesto entitled *"The Life of a Photodrama"*: the time had come to acknowledge the development of the cinema, to make it more of an art form and to produce masterpieces. One could achieve this by adapting literary classics neglected by the cinema. Or one could do it less expensively and with less risk by bringing stage adaptations to the screen. In practical terms, this meant that the company was proposing mainly to adapt plays which would be performed—

and this was the innovatory part of the project—by actors who had successfully appeared in them on the stage. This concern with quality and culture struck a new note in the materialist American cinema; the scheme also offered all the disadvantages which Feuillade had vigorously denounced as early in 1911, at the time of his attacks on 'Le Film d'Art' and 'La Société Cinématographique des Auteurs et Gens de Lettres.' Namely, the death of the original script and the takeover of the cinema by the theatre.

The company's series of 'art films,' most of which were directed by Herbert Blaché, was inaugurated in September 1914 with a production of *The Chimes*, based on Dickens. This was followed by *The Mystery of Edwin Drood*, *The Burglar and the Lady* (from a melodrama by Langdon McCormack), etc . . . Alice Guy's contribution to the activities of the U.S. Amusement Corporation was represented by three films released early in 1917: *The Adventurer* (from the novel by Upton Sinclair), *The Empress*, and *A Man and the Woman* (based on Zola's *"Nana"*). From January 1917, the former Solax studio at Fort Lee was rented by Blaché to Apollo Pictures; its subsequent tenants, before it was sold and pulled down around 1920, included Albert Cappellani.

Meanwhile from October 1914 until August 1917, Alice Guy directed some ten five-reelers and supervised the production of a dozen others for a company whose first appearance coincided with the disappearance of Blaché Features Inc. and whose aims seem to have been a carbon-copy of the U.S. Amusement Corporation. The company was called Popular Players and Plays: president, L. Lawrence Weber; managing director, Harry J. Cohen; and director of production, Herbert Blaché. All of the films which Alice Guy directed for this company were adapted from stage plays (*"The Ragged Earl," "The Tigress"*), novels (*"Michael Strogoff," "What Will People Say?"*) or, in one case, a poem (*"My Madonna,"* based on *"The Call of the Yukon"* by Robert Service). Most of them starred one of the first 'vamps,' the Russian dancer Olga Petrova.

It is curious to note that it was the Blachés who helped Metro Pictures (which, after mergers, became Metro-Goldwyn-Mayer) to get off the ground, by entrusting them from their inception in March 1915 right up until 1918 with their various productions, thereby providing them, over a two-year period, with most of their output as distributors: a humble and unintentional contribution to the birth of a giant. But the Blachés' departure from their Fort Lee studio signified the end of an era. By 1917 it was already impossible for independents to survive and the future belonged to the big companies, as the Blachés were to discover to their cost. Pathé Exchange released Alice Guy's last two films: *The Great Adventure*, with Bessie Love, in March 1918; and *Tarnished Reputation*, based on a screenplay by Léonce Perret, in June 1920. Her husband, however, obtained a reprieve. In 1920 he directed Buster Keaton's first feature, *The Saphead*, and Ethel Barrymore's first film, *The Hope*. In 1923 he joined Universal, becoming their production director in 1925 and supervising, among other things, all the Hoot Gibson Westerns. He left the cinema in 1929 with the coming of sound.

The pioneer days of the New York cinema were gone for good. And the passers-by glancing into the window of a small lampshade shop in downtown Los Angeles little suspected that its owners had been pioneers of both the French and the American cinema. The French attributed Alice Guy's films to Jasset or to Cohl. And the Americans had quite forgotten that 'refined Frenchwoman Madame Blaché'. In a recent interview about her one film as director, Lillian Gish remembered quite clearly that before her own venture there had been a Frenchman whose wife had also directed films. But the name completely escaped her.

[1]One can't help regretting that French television should have labelled its studios A, B, C, D, like different-sized saucepans, instead of calling them after the pioneers who used to work there: Alice Guy, Léon Gaumont, Feuillade, Musidora.

[2]This little house is still standing. Until a few years ago it served as the ORTF staff canteen.

[3]I have only been able to identify 35 of the films as hers, since films made before 1914 rarely carried credit titles. The total number of films made by Alice Guy for Solax was probably closer to 50.

The doyenne of women filmmakers was the only one in at the birth of the cinema. Alice Guy Blaché on the set of her film *The Beasts of the Jungle* (1912).

Esther Schub

JAY LEYDA

By 1926 Kuleshov, Eisenstein, and Pudovkin, with their followers, had applied such engineering principles to the fictional film with a success that challenged any lazier or purely intuitional approach. The Vertov group had pioneered similarly for the documentary film. It was the task of Esther Schub to bring this discipline and strength to the new problems and possibilities latent in the rapidly accumulating store of non-current newsreels.

In 1922, as the Civil War and intervention ended and as NEP began, Esther Schub entered the distribution office of Goskino, her work to be editing and titling foreign and pre-revolutionary Russian films for Soviet audiences. (1) A friend of Mayakovsky and Eisenstein in the Meyerhold group, she brought intelligence, taste and a sense of social responsibility into this generally despised employment. The first jobs given her were to adapt American serials—with Eddie Polo, Ruth Roland, Pearl White. When she discovered that the faithful Russian audiences did not need the usual swift résumés given at the start of each new chapter of a serial thriller, Schub took these discards to the cutting table she kept in her home, and evenings were spent with film friends there making film jokes with the scraps. (One of her friends was Kuleshov, who had experienced a serious variant of this pastime when he edited newsreels of the Civil War.) Sometimes she would be handed such scraps—without title, subtitles, or any indication of order—to be transformed into a film that could be released; thus Chaplin's *Carmen* landed on her table in the form of a hundred confused little rolls. It was clearly intended as a parody on Bizet's opera, so she supplied it with titles in the same spirit, and she remembered its reception (it may have been Chaplin's introduction to Russian audiences) as gratifyingly hilarious.

179

More difficult was the transformation of the two-part German thriller, *Doctor Mabuse*, with its lengthy, time-and-metre consuming titles and involved tangle of plots, into a single film that could be followed with less dependence on titles. This required a study of each shot's content and composition, a close examination of each actor's movements and expressions, unattached to the old titles. Rhythm and tempo, of each shot and in relation one to another, became vital factors that could not be ignored, as its director, Fritz Lang, had seemed to ignore them in his original cutting. Schub learned the power of scissors and cement in relation to meaning, and Eisenstein, whose assistance on this job was his first film work, learned too.

When Russian directors saw Schub's value to their own productions, she was transferred to the Third Studio of Goskino to advise and cut new films by Tarich, Ivanov-Barkov, Froelich, Roshal, Mikhin, Molchanov. The most interesting of these was Tarich's *Wings of a Serf* (1926), with Leonidov, as Ivan the Terrible, learning as much from Schub's advice as she learned from his performance. There were also two months of work with Eisenstein, at her home, on the shooting script of *Strike*.

Schub writes that it was the impression made upon her early in 1926 by *Potemkin*[1] that induced her to seek in newsreel material another film way to show the revolutionary past. She found lists of newsreels filmed in 1917, she learned that the Tsar had maintained his own court cameraman—and she felt sure that she could find enough footage to work with. But the Goskino director, Trainin, answered her every proposal and enthusiasm with 'No', and 'told me to go on editing fictional films—I might even get an opportunity to make my own film with actors'. She turned to the Sovkino Studio, where the livelier minds of Bliakhin and Shklovsky had some say in policy, and after several conferences they said 'Yes'.

> At the end of summer, 1926, I went to Leningrad. It was even tougher there. All the valuable negatives and positives of war-time and pre-revolutionary newsreels were kept in a damp cellar on Sergievsky Street. The cans were coated with rust. In many places the dampness had caused the emulsion to come away from the celluloid base. Many shots that appeared on the lists had disappeared altogether.

> Not one metre of negative or positive on the February Revolution had been preserved, and I was even shown a document that declared that no film of that event could be found in Leningrad.(2)

In spite of such assurances Schub persisted and some of that footage *did* come to light. An old newsreel worker, Khmelnitsky, who had helped her restore some of the damaged footage, brought her small cans of 'counterrevolutionary' film that turned out to be the private 'home movies' of Nikolai II that she had hoped would turn up some day. In her two months in Leningrad Schub inspected 60,000 metres of film, from which she chose 5,200 metres to take back to work in Moscow. She spent all her free time in wandering about Leningrad, a new city for her, to feel at home with its geography and appearance in the 1917 shots. Before leaving she supervised the filming of various documents, newspapers and items associated with the events she was reconstructing.

> In the montage I tried to avoid looking at the newsreel material for its own sake, and to maintain the principle of its documentary quality. All was subordinated to the theme. This gave me the possibility, in spite of the known limitations of the photographed events and facts, to link the meanings of the material so that it evoked the pre-revolutionary period and the February days.(3)

After the first private screening (where the section on 'World War' was particularly admired) the release title was decided: *The Fall of the Romanov Dynasty*. The only credit on the posters was 'Work by E. I. Schub'.

In March 1927, as her first 'work' was released, Schub began her second. *The Great Road* was to use all Soviet newsreels for the ten years since the October Revolution, beginning (hopefully) with whatever could be found of the Revolution itself. She learned that newsreels of the recent past had been kept just as carelessly, if not more so, than had the oldest Russian newsreels unearthed for her first film. Identification of place and time of shooting was an unforeseen obstacle, but the several living cameramen of the Civil War helped her here. She had more to inspect (250,000 metres) than for the older film, but after 1921–22 the material grew thinner:

> From that date newsreels were shot without much plan and quickly put aside with little comprehension of their historic value, which of course increased with each passing year. Even worse is their change of tone after the Civil War; suddenly the concentration was on parades, meetings, arrivals, departures, delegates, and such—and almost no record was kept of how we transformed the country to a new political economy—or of the resulting construction.(4)

Some precious footage had been sold abroad, without any master copies or negatives having been kept at home—too little raw film in those years to think of such niceties, or of the future. A quantity of early reels had been sent to the United States, as thanks for the work of the American Relief Association during the months of famine. This had fallen into private hands, yet Schub traced this footage and arranged through Amtorg (the Soviet trade office in the United States) for its purchase, for $6,000. (It was cannily copied before the sale, for a future interesting use *against* the Soviet Union!)

> In this lot I found material of the imperialist war, of the funeral of victims of the February Revolution, and—six completely unfamiliar shots of Lenin [filmed in 1920 by an American cameraman]. Soviet audiences saw these intimate scenes of Lenin for the first time in *The Great Road*.(5)

The new film was intended for the celebrations of the tenth anniversary of the October Revolution—in early November. But the new film form discovered and perfected by Schub was not yet on secure ground. Her right as an 'author' of these films was challenged, and it was Mayakovsky who publicly ridiculed those who tried in any way to belittle the value of this extremely important work. (6)

The Fall of the Romanov Dynasty had used newsreel material of 1912–17; *The Great Road* continued through the archives of 1917–27. In her searches Schub had found a tempting lot of Russian newsreel from 1896 through 1912, and the Tolstoy centenary to come in 1928 offered her an opportunity to employ it. Her first Tolstoy hope was to depend on the considerable footage that had been filmed of him, but she found only about 200 feet of this—a fifth as much as the footage of his funeral! She decided to place her actual Tolstoy footage in a larger frame of Russia since the turn of the century. The result was *The Russia of Nikolai II and Lev Tolstoy*:

> This montage must serve as an eloquent illustration of the fact that any available acting method for the historical film, no matter how good or talented, has only an ephemeral value in comparison with the chronicle film, which possesses a conviction that can never pale and can never age.(7)

Schub's wisdom and craft were hereafter applied chiefly to new documentary films, but on two occasions before the Second World War (when she had several such occasions) she worked again on materials photographed far from her. The first was *Today* (a 'film-feuilleton'), released in 1930. In comparing the capitalist and socialist worlds she made ingenious use of foreign newsreels collected in Berlin. Her second occasion was *Spain* (1939), to be described below.

> . . . what interests us here is not the usual narrative montage, a consequence and corollary of cutting, but expressive montage, above all ideological. It is no accident that compilations so flourish in the USSR. It is natural that the country where the first theories of montage were formulated accords a leading position to the compilation film as an ideological weapon. One should keep in mind that montage is not a simple succession of shots, nor even a sum of their contents, but produces something new, something original. It is a remarkable application of the Marx-

ist law of dialectical change from quantity to quality. Montage rests fundamentally on the interaction of the images . . . *ideological* montage aims at a precise political or moral point in putting together images which have no strictly causal or temporal relationship.(7a)

Marcel Martin's search for a definition of the compilation film recalls Eisenstein's effort in 1929 to define 'a dramaturgy of the visual filmform as regular and precise as the existing dramaturgy of the film-story', where his enumeration of potentialities ends with 'Liberation of the whole action from the definition of time and space'; in illustrating this he gave examples from *October*, from *Arsenal*, and from *The Russia of Nikolai II and Lev Tolstoy*.(7b) And it is true that Schub's work provides many examples of a power too rarely used by the compilation film.

In Schub's first three precedent-forming films her cutting ideas usually combined a forcefully simple logic with a minute study of the formal elements in the available footage;[2] the ideas were often built on contrasts that may seem obvious now—but it took imagination to dig them from her raw material. Here is an example (8), in the *Fall of the Romanov Dynasty*, of one of her direct poster juxtapositions:

> A crowd of elegant idlers are dancing [a mazurka on the awninged deck
>   of a yacht.]
> The dancing tires some of them. They drink wine.
> Title: 'It made me sweat.'
> And again they dance.
> Title: '. . . sweat.'
> A peasant, exhausted by his work, ploughs a furrow . . .

The admired war sequence in her first film used the newsreels of all combatant countries. For me its climax was another such simple contrast, using two titles: 'He who wants war', and 'He who is to be sent to war'. In *The Great Road* she showed how a newsreel-shot parade could be reconstructed for maximum irony—*without* benefit of sound.

When Schub began this work there were no rules for the physical use of old film materials—it was catch-as-catch-can, and don't worry about either the next need or the future; but Schub's orderly mind evolved its own rules: she never cut a piece of original film, positive or negative, and never employed an original piece—her first move was to make duplicate negatives of every metre she considered using. Later editors were not so scrupulous, not even with Schub's films. Usually pleading some emergency or other they took whatever they needed[1] so that there are no complete negatives today of Schub's first three films. Among other lessons to be learned from this loss is the necessity for separating documentary archives from documentary film producing studios.

[1]Which, we should remember, employed manoeuvre newsreel shots of the British Navy in its last reel.

[2]Another great woman editor, Helen Van Dongen, gives us a good piece of advice on the close study of footage:

> I cannot emphasize enough how important repeated screenings are in the process of editing. They will not only help you memorize the material but will also make you familiar with the slightest nuances in each shot. ('Three Hundred and Fifty Cans of Film,' in *The Cinema 1951*, ed. by Roger Manvell.)

This increased familiarity she considers more useful *to her* than any written catalogue—though she agrees it may not be feasible in group work.

1. These details of Schub's career are drawn from her memoirs, *Krupnym planom* (In Close Up) (Moscow, 1959), published shortly before her death.
2. Ibid., pp. 90–1.
3. Ibid., p. 92.
4. In an interview with V. Pfeffer, *Sovietski Ekran*, November 1, 1927.
5. Schub, 'Road from the Past', *Sovietskoye Kino*, November–December 1934.
6. An extract from this speech by Mayakovsky is quoted in *Kino*, pp. 229–30.
7. 'How the Film Was Made', a drafted article (dated October 1928) by Schub, found in her archives, published in *Iskusstvo Kino*, November 1960.
7a. Marcel Martin, 'Les films de montage', in *Cin*éma 63, April 1963.
7b. Eisenstein, 'A Dialectic Approach to Film Form', in *Film Form* (1949), pp. 58–9.
8. Quoted in Ilya Weisfeld's foreword to Schub's *Krupnym planom*, p. 5.

Maya Deren and Germaine Dulac:

ACTIVISTS OF THE AVANT-GARDE

REGINA CORNWELL

In "The Woman as Film-Director," Harry Alan Potamkin writes: *I have been asked a number of times, "Can a woman become a film-director?" My answer takes two forms. First, I make the obvious retort that women are in demand as players, as scenario writers, and as film editors. Then I go on to say how few women have ever created films themselves.* (American Cinematographer, XII, January, 1932, p. 10)

After a brief enumeration of women directors, Potamkin concentrates on Germaine Dulac, identified with both the commercial and the avant-garde film. If there have been few women directors in commercial cinema, proportionately there have been and still are fewer women working within the avant-garde. Along with Germaine Dulac, one can cite Maya Deren, Marie Menken, Shirley Clarke, Storm de Hirsch, Joyce Wieland and Gunvor Nelson. Dulac and Deren can be singled out for they are important in the history of film not solely for their directing but also and perhaps equally for their roles as film activists—propagandists for the film as a serious art form.

Deren, whose name is familiar, is identified with the American avant-garde of the '40's. She is acclaimed as important; yet, seldom is the real significance of her role as an activist in this avant-garde explained. Her film career began in 1943 at the age of 26 when she made her first work in conjunction with her husband, filmmaker Alexander Hammid. From 1943 until her sudden death in 1961 at the age of forty-four, Deren completed six films: *Meshes of the Afternoon* (1943), *A Study in Choreography for Camera* (1944), *At Land* (1945), *Ritual in Transfigured Time* (1946), *Meditation on Violence* (1948), and *The Very Eye of Night* (1955). If Deren was influential through her filmmaking it was only so because she began the process of establishing, almost single-handedly, a milieu for the avant-garde film in this country— ways and means by which her work could be seen, ways and means taken up in turn by other artists.

In 1943, 16mm was still considered a substandard or inferior film gauge suitable only for educational, documentary and amateur work. But Deren seized upon the notion of "amateur" and happily applied it in its original meaning to herself and her work. She wrote later in 1959, in an article entitled "Amateur Versus Professional": "The very classification 'amateur' has an apologetic ring. But that very word— from the Latin 'amateur'—'lover' means one who does something for the love of the thing rather than for economic reasons or necessity." (reprinted in *Film Culture*, No. 39, Winter, 1965, p. 45). The avant-garde in Europe and America in the '20's had, of course, worked in 35mm. There may have been in this country in the '30's, a few filmmakers who at one time or another worked in 16mm; but, Deren served to legitimatize it as a film gauge in which one could work artis-tically, analogous to the way in which Stan Brakhage, who started working with 8mm in 1964, has begun to legitimatize its artistic use. Others in the '40's, such as Sidney Peterson, Willard Maas, James Broughton and Kenneth Anger, then followed her example; and, today the American avant-garde is principally identified with 16mm.

At the time that Deren began there were no channels of distribu-tion, let alone exhibition, for *new* avant-garde work. In 1945, having completed three films, she sent out leaflets to colleges, universities, art schools and museums around the country, advertising her work.[1] She began renting her films, using her home as a distribution base. Often she would accompany her showings with a lecture. The follow-ing year Deren set up what is credited as the first showings in a public theatre in the U.S. of privately made 16mm film. These two Prov-incetown Playhouse screenings of her work even prompted reviews in major publications, including one by James Agee in *The Nation*. Thus she paved the way for Frank Stauffacher's avant-garde "Art in Cinema" series which began in 1947 at the San Francisco Museum of Art and for Amos Vogel's "Cinema 16" begun the same year, followed up three years later by his distribution center of the same name which finally provided a professional rental outlet for avant-garde work.

But Deren did not stop with showing and promoting her work. She had, in 1946, shared the distinction with the Whitney brothers of receiving the first Guggenheim Fellowships ever awarded for creative filmmaking; she had attempted a renewal of her grant the following year but was unsuccessful. In 1954, based on her years of experience with the difficulties of obtaining grants and raising money in order to pursue independent filmmaking, she established the Creative Film Foundation which continued until two years after her death. Among those awarded grants that first year were Shirley Clarke and Stan Brakhage. As a writer, Deren spoke frequently and at length of her own work, but also about the art of the independent film in general. Very much of a dogmatist and polemicist, Deren rigidly maintained her ideas about the art of the personal film, persuading many to her camp.

She had begun her career at a time when there was negligible interest in film as an art form in this country and she provided through her active dedication an example, a hope to others for the possibilties of independent filmmaking. To call Maya Deren "Mother of the Underground Film," as Sheldon Renan does in *An Introduction to the American Underground Film*, characterizes the debt which American avant-garde filmmakers since the forties continue to owe to her.

If, apart from her directing, Deren's other contributions to film seem little known, much less is known in this country of Germaine Dulac.[2] Of the twenty-five completed films credited to Dulac's direction, only two are available in the U.S.: *La Souriante Madame Beudet* (1923), adapted from a play by Denys Amiel and André Obey, and *La Coquille et le Clergyman* (1927) from a scenario by Antonin Artaud.

It is particularly significant today, with the women's movement, that of Dulac's considerable oeuvre, *La Souriante Madame Beudet* should be available, not only because it is claimed by historians as her best work and cited as a masterpiece of the French silent period, but also because it is a woman's film in theme and subject matter made by a woman who had been an active feminist before beginning her film career. One wonders whether it was her strong belief in the postulates of feminism which gave her the courage to launch her own film company in 1915.

CAREER OF GERMAINE DULAC

Born in Amiens in 1882, from her youth she had pursued studies in the arts, most especially music and later photography. Married to Albert Dulac in 1905, she began her career as a writer for *La Francaise* in 1909 and later for *La Fronde*, both feminist journals. During her tenure as drama critic for *La Francaise*, her concerns began moving more and more toward film. In 1914 she was invited to Rome to observe the shooting of *Caligula*. This experience, as Charles Ford documents it, made the radical change in her life, for it was late during the following year that she formed Delia Film in association with her first scenarist, Irene Hillel-Erlander, with Albert Dulac assuming financial management.[3]

Even while *La Souriante Madame Beudet* has been so highly acclaimed, most accounts of the period by significant historians like Georges Sadoul and Robert Brasillach, or someone such as Jacques Brunius, mention Dulac more in passing, for instance, as a member of a circle led by Louis Delluc with Marcel L'Herbier, Jean Epstein and Abel Gance, in what has come to be characterized as the period of Impressionism. Only René Jeanne and Charles Ford seem to dwell upon a serious consideration of her work. Ford, in his long essay, "Germaine Dulac," attributes to her a co-leadership with Delluc in the beginnings of this very early avant-garde; and, he and Jeanne in *Histoire Encyclopedique du Cinema* suggest that she may even have been of more importance and influence than Delluc for her ideas and the uncompromising fashion with which she set about her tasks, never the dogmatist, always optimistic, confident and encouraging about the future of the dynamic art to which she had dedicated her life and her vision.[4] In light of their claims, it does seem significant that Louis Delluc should have asked Dulac to direct his first scenario, *La Fête Espagnole*, before he undertook to realize his own scenarios himself.

Dulac's is a curious career in contrast to filmmakers like Bunuel, Clair and Renoir who began later and are associated with the second avant-garde. Unlike Bunuel whose first two films, *Un Chien Andalou* (1928) and *L'Age D'Or* (1930), were within the avant-garde, or Clair and Renoir who in the '20's made both commercial and avant-garde films and then proceeded along a commercial path, Dulac's filmmaking began commercially, took various turns from the avant-gardist ascribed *La Fête Espagnole* and *La Souriante Madame Beudet* to very popular works, the serialized *Gossette* (1923), many other theatrical and literary adaptations, and finally ended in 1929 in the domain of the second and more radical avant-garde. Then when, according to Ford, poor health forced her to give up her rigorous directing career, from 1930 to 1940 she took charge of the newsreel, "France-Actualités-Gaumont", until the Vichy government made it impossible for her to continue in that position.

But perhaps as strange or even as contradictory as the movement of her career may appear today, for Dulac there was a consistency, a growing radicalism in the direction of her thought as she continued to make films and articulate her position. Even after, as director of "France-Actualités-Gaumont" when she became concerned with the newsreel and the scientific film, these activities seem consonant with her thinking about the magical possibilities of film—always concerned with film as a new and evolving form of art.

Nils Poppe and Bibi Andersson in Bergman's *The Seventh Seal* (1958).

One of Bergman's fortes: the hysterical, sexually disturbed woman, as in *Through a Glass Darkly* (1961), with Lars Passgard and Harriet Andersson.

In *The Silence* (1963) Ingmar Bergman allows young Johan to free himself from the objectively conceived mother-whore Anna . . . to the subjectively portrayed father substitute Ester (Ingrid Thulin).

In *Scenes From a Marriage* (1974) Bergman reveals deep-seated conflicts beneath the facade of middle-class comfort. Liv Ullmann and Erland Josephson.

A sort of amazon among the Nazis, the token exceptional woman granted privilege by the patriarchy in exchange for adopting its values, Riefenstahl shooting *Olympia*.

The thirst for order led romantics to impose an artificial structure, the geometric precision of the spectacle. Leni Riefenstahl's *Olympia* (1938).

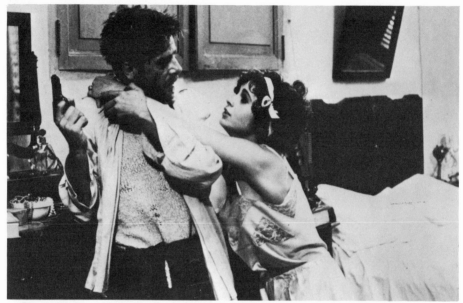

Giancarlo Giannini as Tunin and Lina Polito as Tripolina in Lina Wertmüller's *Love and Anarchy* (1974).

Chantal Akerman's *Jeanne Dielman* (1975) focusses on the average middle-class woman's banal experiences. Jan Decorte and Delphine Seyrig.

Barbara Loden in her film *Wanda* (1971), the story of a totally passive woman.

Lina Wertmuller's male chauvinism is insidious. Her women are treated as non-persons, but the man always extends as a person. Wertmüller and Giancarlo Giannini on the set of her film, *Love and Anarchy* (1974).

Manuela's sensitivity and motherlessness place her in need of emotional sustenance. Hertha Thiele and Dorothea Wieck in Leontine Sagan's *Maedchen in Uniform* (1931).

Not a Pretty Picture (1975) cuts back and forth between the true story of the rape of Martha in 1962 and the present, in which she plays herself as director of the film. Michele Manenti (left) and director Martha Coolidge.

CREATION OF A SERIOUS CINEMA

Little is said about her first four films: *Les Soeurs Ennemies* (1915) *Geo le Mysterieux*, *Venus Victrix* and *Dans L'Ouragan de la Vie* (1916), which seem to have been her apprenticeship. But with *Ames de Fous* (1917), the critics, who were preoccupied with clear and forthright articulation of plot, had already become uneasy by what they thought to be her excessive concerns with editing, lighting and the creation of atmosphere through visual means, all of which, even at that time, were becoming more important to Dulac than acting. (Ford, pp. 7–8) It was during the shooting of *Ames de Fous* that she met Louis Delluc and this introduction led to the making of *La Fête Espagnole* two years later, a film which appears to be her first really important work.

Dulac, Delluc and their associates shared strong concern about the creation of a serious cinema. America with Griffith, Ince, Chaplin and others, presented examples to the French whose cinema had lost its position of importance since World War I. This circle of energetic directors and critics aspired toward a new French cinema in repudiation of the cardboard "Film d'Art" reproductions which had taken precedence in their studios; they wished a cinema peopled by vital beings rather than puppets, one which would derive its meaning from the visuals.

Delluc went on, until his premature death at 33 in 1924, to film his own original scenarios, while Dulac continued, for the most part, to film material taken from theatre and literature, experimenting with that material by way of soft focus and special lighting, prisms and distorting mirrors, screen panels for split screen effects, and fast and slow motion as the integral technical means in her quest for a visual cinema. Harry Alan Potamkin points out, in the article cited above and elsewhere, that she was one of the first artists to use the screen panel, along with prisms, distorting mirrors and other similar effects.

While working on *La Souriante Madame Beudet*, Dulac was asked about the avant-garde quality of this film. Ford records her response:

> It is an avant-garde film, if one terms "avant-garde" a cinematographic work to which one brings a new and constant effort in the composition of the scenario, the technical realisation, and the selection of actors.

Her statement clearly articulates the position of that first avant-garde. At that time, all of the work issued from studios so that serious developments and innovations came by way of the commerical film industry. And innovations were possible. Dulac's *La Souriante Madame Beudet* stands as a remarkable testimony of this for it was made under Film d'Art. Since its successful production of *L'Assassinat du Duc de Guise* in 1909, Film d'Art had ceased to progress and had come to care only about pleasing crowds; under new management the company contracted with Dulac to make *La Souriante Madame Beudet*, which nevertheless stands as one of the few historical exceptions in the Film d'Art stable. Cinema clubs for the screening of more difficult, less popular works had already become established; but, the notion of a separate and distinct filmmaking avant-garde would only come later to Dulac and others. One must recall, as Jacques Brunius points out, that Man Ray's *Le Retour à la Raison* (1923) ". . . was the first film in France made outside normal financial channels, with no lucrative end in view," and that Francis Picabia and Rene Clair's *Entr'acte* (1924) was "the first film to be made outside the [French] film industry and yet with sufficient financial backing."[5]

Dulac's position would change, but not before making more consolidated attempts in commercial directions. Rather than pursue, as she had in *La Souriante Madame Beudet*, psychological probings through the visualization of what could not be spoken and of what Dulac explicitly did not want to convey in the conventional subtitle, she contracted to direct the serial, *Gossette*. Her conviction was that even in such a popularized work it was possible to strike a compromise without forfeiting one's principles. One could incorporate within this type of production the technical means of the avant-garde. In essence, Dulac felt that she could still work intelligently within an ostensibly commercial framework and yet achieve what she desired toward the evolution of the art of the film. While she continued to believe it possible to please both an avant-garde and a mass audience within the same work, as early as 1922 she had verbalized her interest in making three works of "integral" or "pure cinema", one of which, *L'invitation au Voyage*, she would realize in 1927. (Ford, p. 16) Her writings from at least as early as 1924 indicate her growing concern with film's relationship to music, both as visualization of and analogy to it. For Dulac music was the closest of all the arts to film. In *Cinemagazine* (Dec. 1924) she speaks of film as the "orchestration of images"; pure cinema exists in the actualization of its own intrinsic means, the "play of light", and movement of images.

LEAVING THE COMMERCIAL FILM INDUSTRY

By 1927 she finally became disillusioned with the possibilities of affecting a compromise within the realm of the commercial film, having had ample experiences with producers and distributors desirous of pleasing a mass audience and at the same time incapable of understanding her position and the manifestation of her ideas on the screen. She made one more popular commercial film in 1928, *La Princesse Mandane*, from a novel by Pierre Benoit. Dulac transformed the work into a comedy with a hero who, obsessed by the fantasies of the screen, journeys about the world in search of them and finally decides that he prefers the good life of simplicity. This work seems an appropriate finale for her retirement from the commercial film industry, while at the same time indicating something of her consciousness of the magical powers of the illusions of the popular screen which she was giving up.

At the age of 45 she joined the ranks of her much younger colleagues of the second avant-garde. *La Coquille et le Clergyman,* perhaps whose only mark of distinction is that it is considered the first surrealist film, was followed that year by *L'invitation au Voyage; Disque 927* and *Thèmes et Variations* were made in 1928, and *Etude Cinégraphique Sur une Arabesque,* in 1929—all of these last, works of "pure" or "integral cinema." She had moved from a position supporting an intelligent cinema within the domain of the French film industry to one in which she realized the impossible hiatus between the commercial and the avant-garde film. Now she felt that the avant-garde of today could only, over time, affect the commercial film of tomorrow.

DULAC AS WRITER AND EDUCATOR

Dulac the creator was inseparable from Dulac the activist-educator. For her, the notion of the evolution of the cinema was very much tied to the level of perception and sophistication an audience would bring to the screen. She had been involved in the cinema club movement from its beginnings and in 1922 became secretary general of the Cine-Club de France; by the end of the '20's she was president of the Federation des Cine-Clubs, which consisted of more than 20 active units in Paris and the provinces concerned with promoting all manner of good film from France and abroad. In 1927 or 1928, along with Louis Lumière, Dulac was instrumental in establishing L'Ecole Technique de Photographie et de Cinematographie de la Rue de Vaugirard in Paris where she also taught for a number of years. "Vaugirard" still exists today. She attempted the publication of a magazine, *Schemas,* in 1927, which met its demise after only one issue. And, as already alluded to, Dulac continued her writing, after having transferred her allegiance from theatre to film in 1915.

In "Films Visuels et Anti-Visuels" and elsewhere she speaks of the lamentable condition to which the cinema has fallen at the hands of theatre and literature. Though she had continued through most of her directorial career to use adaptations from these other arts, she makes her position on this very clear:

> "Certainly the cinema can tell a story, but one must not forget that the story is nothing. The story is a surface."

She was concerned with a cinema which was visual, one which did more than merely reproduce movement. In the same essay, she asks:

"Therefore, the cinegraphic instrument with its scientific possiblities is conceived for one goal, whereas the cinegraphic inspiration pursues another. Where is the truth? I think, in the instrument which created the seventh art."[6]

Her concern with the camera itself suggests an almost contemporary sensibility; Dulac might feel quite comfortable in the American avant-garde of today.

Her writings on the relationship of film to music were very much of her time. Others in the '20's shared this attitude. But unlike those who reacted strenuously against sound, pronouncing it the death of the cinema, Dulac was open, if reserved about its possible uses and skeptical of its abuses. In "Jouer avec les Bruits," written in 1929, she explained that she was against the talking cinema, meaning at that time, the "all-talkie," but for the sound cinema, that is the discrete use of sound which would reinforce the visuals. "Outside of all that, there is only room for silence," she wrote.[7]

One would think that Brakhage's original sound version of *Scenes From Under Childhood, pt. I,* wherein crystalline sounds punctuate the long stretches of silence, would be for Dulac an ideal manifestation of its proper aesthetic use. She herself might well have said what Brakhage writes about his film: "The visual imagery was inspired by Messiaen—Not the Sound Track, which was called-forth directly by the image-needs of the film and created by the maker to answer that necessity." (*Film-Maker's Cooperative Catalog No. 5,* N.Y., 1971, p. 40) Film remained for her an eminently visual medium; in a speech delivered two years later, she stated her position clearly: "Speech and sound may be considered as an accompaniment, a splendid projection of the image, but they have nothing to do with its essential form . . . speech and sound being indispensibly complimentary. Movement in all its truth is the scientific and artistic significance of the cinema."[8]

At that time, during the late '20's and early '30's, Dulac felt that the role of the critic was more important than that of the creator.[10] She assumed this position because of her acute consciousness of the need to cultivate and educate a serious audience so that a milieu would exist for new work. She felt that the sensitive critic could affect an audience through his challenges and thus transform the cinema theatre, wherein the screen could be viewed as the space for new ideas and new forms. But she knew also the powers of the creator; in 1917, commenting on her film *Ames de Fous,* she wrote:

"Nevertheless, I wonder if its success wasn't the result of suggestive methods which I had used to prolong the action so that the public was caught up by these methods without being able to define them." (Ford, p. 8)

Even then she seemed aware of the psychology of an audience and the magic of the cinema which made it possible for her to use the story as surface and burrow below to light, movement and form to seek her means of expression. While she concentrated on technique to achieve her goals, she struck out against the theatrical film for its abuses of technique: "Sometimes the recreational [theatrical] film is very much to blame; it prostitutes technique . . . . And why is the recreational film so rarely satisfying? Because it does not seek to raise the standards of public taste by accustoming the spectators to cinematic methods. It only flatters the public."[10] Something which Dulac herself never did.

She lectured frequently in the special cinema theatres and clubs in Paris and the provinces, in Switzerland, Belgium, Holland and elsewhere in Europe. She carried with her the ideas she had manifested in her films and writings, engaging an audience, even in their wrath, in order to promote film as a new and separate art governed by its own aesthetic.

There is virtually no information in this country concerning the last twelve years of Germaine Dulac's life, from the time that she began working for "France-Actualites-Gaumont" until her death in 1942. In 1930 she was named a Chevalier of the Legion of Honor in recognition of her contributions to the development of film as a unique art form. One knows that her activist involvements never ceased. A nebulous note from an "Hommage a Germaine Dulac" at ths Cinematheque Francaise, 1956-57, indicates that she was involved with the working of the Cinematheque during her last two years:

. . . Germaine Dulac was truly the soul of the Cinematheque, exerting herself for it in the most tragic hours, and, between 1940 and 1942, succeeding in spite of denunciations and calumny in saving the essential.[11]

If one were to compare the two film activists, Dulac and Deren, perhaps the most striking Difference between them is the focussd, single-minded direction of Deren's endeavor in contrast to Dulac's genuinely catholic tastes which brought her to so many things. For her the arena of possibilities for new film expressions was vast. She was always open to the ssrious innovation, no matter from what quarter it came. After poor health drew her out of the second avant-garde, which shortly thereafter came to its own end, one can understand her subsequent involvement with the scientific and newsreel

film during the '30's. Given the social milieu of the time and the in-
surgence of the documentary film movement, she was able to find in
these two types of film, a compliment, a continuity and a combination
amenable to her concerns for new expressions in the evolution of
film. In a paper, "The Educational and Social Value of the Newsreel,"
published by the *International Review of Educational Cinematography*,
she wrote:

> The dramatic film is an application of the cinematographic art, but not
> the expression of its inner truth, which is better illustrated by the scien-
> tific film or news-reel.

> Freed from all commercial interference, and developed in an atmosphere
> far from cinetheatrical works, having no limit to their expression of
> thought, such films have given us sincerer models than the regular
> drama with a more universally human character. (Rome, VI, August,
> 1934, p. 546)

Having faced for so many years the interferences of theatrical producers and distributors and then later the economic hardships involved
in avant-garde filmmaking, Dulac now saw these as new channels of
hope.

Two seemingly disparate attachments: her love and respect for the
Lumière brothers, and her affection for an experiment she had made
in 1928, shooting single-frame, *Germination d'un Haricot* (Growth of a
Bean Plant)—also seek to explain her interest in the newsreel and scientific film. On the one hand, for her, the Lumières, fathers of the
cinema, presented film in its innocent forms, still unadulterated by
theatre and literature; and, the subtle natural drama which the camera laid bare in *Germination* pointed to profound modes of expression
for Dulac. With this influence understood, her movements from the
avant-garde to the scientific and newsreel film merge into one. Thus,
in 1931, in talking about the importance of visual education for both
adults and children in schools and special courses, she went on to
say:

> When penetrated with the profound sense of the Cinema, they will be-
> come the public of tomorrow. The majority of artistic dramas of today
> will soon cease to be what they are, sometimes well conceived but often
> incomplete. They will be enlarged.
> And this is why the Cinema, educational or artistic, is really a single body
> with different means of expression and different applications. (*Meaning of
> Cinema*, p. 1094)

It was all one for her if it served in some way the technical advance-
ment of the film and the sensitization of the perceiver.

In the same speech, she posed what could be characterized as an autobiographic rhetorical question:

Almost everyone will judge the Cinema on its applications, not on its spirit.
And yet, has not the cinema the right to be judged in itself and for itself? (p. 1090)

Germaine Dulac was one always concerned with the cinema in and for itself.

In his 1932 article on women directors, Harry Alan Potamkin characterizes Dulac as "the outstanding and high water mark among women film makers," (p. 10) and in "Camera! Some Unsung Artists of the Cinema!" he comments: "Mme. Dulac does not end with virtuosity . . . . The camera virtuoso becomes the camera esthetician, the creative artist."[12] One can only hope that Dulac's other films will be made available in this country and that more information will be unearthed about her so that she and her work can be re-evaluated in terms of her times and her concerns as artist and activist-educator. She truly was, as Charles Ford describes her, an apostle of the cinema.

[1]Bershen, Wanda. "Departmental Paper: The Film of Maya Deren." Yale University, May, 1972. Unpublished Masters thesis. I thank Wanda Bershen for permission to use several pieces of data from her "Deren Chronology" included in her thesis on file at Anthology Film Archives. I also wish to thank P. Adams Sitney, with whom I had several long conversations about Deren, and who emphasized to me her importance in the avant-garde.

[2]Thanks to Babette Mangolte and Alicia Grant for their help in translations from the French.

[3]"Germaine Dulac," *Anthologie du Cinema*. IV, ed. Jacques Charriere. Paris, 1968, pp. 6-7. Most of the factual data on Dulac's career is taken from Ford's long essay.

[4]*: Le Cinema Francais 1895-1929*. Paris, 1947, p. 257.

[5]*Ibid.*, pp. 258-259.

[6]"Experimental Film in France," trans. Mary Kesteven, *Experiment in the Film*, ed. Roger Manvell. N.Y., 1970, pp. 86 and 89 respectively.

[7]*Le Rouge et le Noir*, Paris, July, 1928, pp. 40 and 30 respectively.

[8]*Cinea Cine Pour Tous*, August 15, 1929, in *L'Art du Cinema*, ed. Pierre Lherminier, Paris, 1960, p. 250.

[9]"Meaning of Cinema," *International Review of Educational Cinematography*, XII, Rome, Dec. 1931, pp. 1090-91.

[10]"Films Visuels et anti-Visuels," p. 31.

[11]From "Germaine Dulac" file, Museum of Modern Art Film Study Center, New York.

[12]*Theatre Guild Magazine*, VII, July, 1930. p.22.

Leni Riefenstahl:
The Deceptive Myth

B. RUBY RICH

The films of Leni Riefenstahl have never been accorded a full analysis, due both to the myths and emotionalism surrounding her best-known works (their political subject and mode of production) and to the charismatic but contradictory persona of their maker herself. Predictable passions dominate the discourse, with criticism generally concentrated in only a few areas of overworked relevance (as detailed below), skirting the very contemporary implications of Riefenstahl's films and career for cinema and more specifically feminism today. In fact, as this piece would suggest, the lesson of Riefenstahl demands a reexamination of the nature of romanticism and its entire legacy of mystic illusionism, a rethinking of the function of myth, and an analysis of the roles open to women living under a patriarchy.

There are a few firm facts in the Riefenstahl legend. She is known to have begun her career as a dancer and actor, working first with Max Reinhardt and then with Dr. Arnold Fanck, as the starring actress-athlete in the popular German genre of mountain films that he developed. Riefenstahl's own films were divided between fiction and documentary. Her first and last completed works, *The Blue Light* in 1932 and *Tiefland* in 1954, were both romantic fictions celebrating the nobility of the savage (a wild mountain girl or shepherd) over tainted civilization. The intervening films, which form the basis for claims both of her genius and her fascism, were all documentaries made under the aegis of the Third Reich: *Victory of Faith* in 1933, *Day of Freedom* in 1935, *Triumph of the Will* in 1936, and *Olympia* in 1938 (the infamous *Berchetsgaden Over Salzburg*, a 1938 home movie of Hitler's mountain retreat, is sometimes credited to her but currently disputed). Her much discussed but never realized projects were similarly divided: *Penthesilea* was to have been a film of Kleist's play about the Amazon queen, while *Black Cargo* was intended as an exposé of the African slave trade (never completed, it evolved into a book of photographs, *The Last of the Nuba*).

Riefenstahl's position in film history's pantheon has been secured by her two masterpieces *Triumph of the Will* and *Olympia*. While the latter has been wholly redeemed by aestheticians from fascist charges, it is to *Triumph* that we must look for the focus of most criticism. Two issues have been of prime importance: first, the decision as to whether *Triumph* is properly documentary or propaganda, with defenders choosing the first term and detractors the second; next, a logical extension of this, whether it is possible or correct to separate art and politics. The answers have been as various and quixotic as world events.

Just after World War II, *Triumph* was rather universally attacked and screenings well nigh impossible. Siegfried Kracauer dominated the critical forum to the extent that the Museum of Modern Art prefaced their print with a written apologia. Later, however, as the Cold War altered international alliances and history by virtue of the passage of time became depersonalized, the film's artistic brilliance began to be posited as a counterbalance to its ideology. Furthermore, with the increased publicity granted America's own racism in the early 60's, the victor's moral self-righteousness abated and the art-qua-art position gained in currency. With the late 60's, however, came an increased sophistication about cinema's inherently political functions; combined with the radicalization of filmmakers like Godard and the radical critiques of commercial cinema by Marxist critics, this attitude led the swing of the pendulum back toward condemnation. Today's emphasis on the ideology of form has led to a more far-reaching critique, as in Susan Sontag's promulgation of a Nazi aesthetic underscoring all of Riefenstahl's films and photographs. This sort of approach has the advantage of overpowering facts that previously stocked the arsenal of Riefenstahl's supporters, namely the emphasis on black athlete Jesse Owens in the allegedly fascist *Olympia*, the participation of leftist critic Béla Balázs in *The Blue Light*, the latter-day devotion to the documentation of African tribal peoples. Unfortunately, by subordinating all such facts to its formal indictment, this theory falls into the Kracauerian trap of inverting cause and effect, so that aesthetics—and not economic determinants or political strategies—become the "cause" of Naziism, a patently absurd notion.

None of the traditional critical positions have ever broken off from a reliance on the quicksand-foundation of the historical "facts" of Riefenstahl's productions: whether the Nuremberg rally was actually staged for her cameras, whether her recorded chronology was the real one, whether the Nazi party funded *Triumph* and/or *Olympia* (an admirable concern with modes of production that the same critics seldom, alas, apply to American films). Recent evidence has shown that both films were bankrolled by the Reich, as were the shorter documentaries, and that *Triumph*'s agenda wasn't true to fact. None of these investigations, though, really clinch the debate over documentary versus propaganda implied by their statistics. Riefenstahl herself has always seen the debate in these terms, basing her defense on *Triumph*'s being a mere record, ie. an apolitical historical document, and has seen a refutation of the charges of Hitler's staging the rally as key to her argument.

However, current theories of documentary ironically displace these lines of thinking. In keeping with an awareness that no camera ever captures the "truth" documentary has increased its emphasis on spirit instead. The American documentary, for instance, owes its paternity to Robert Flaherty, whose acclaimed documentaries were often faked rituals restaged for the camera by native participants who had to be Flaherty-trained in the practice of extinct customs. Parades, rallies, spectacles have traditionally been staged with an eye to public effect, a device exploited by 60's radicals whose flashy politics took full advantage of media hype, giving birth to events that had a "reality" only in the media. The act of filming, the act of editing, both manipulate and distort "reality" on-screen as well as off-frame. Camera as creator of reality is an accepted notion.

Thus Riefenstahl is well within the standards of the new documentary (or, for that matter, "new journalism") in capturing the true spirit of the Nuremberg rally regardless of chronology or staging considerations. Certainly Hitler staged the rally as the ideal mythic event to popularize his brand of Germany's mythology, but he probably would have done so without the filming, changing only his angles. And Riefenstahl photographed his event with a fidelity to this spirit, her cameras and editing reflecting its mythic stature and romantic dynamics, making *Triumph* in this sense a documentary for its communication of the truth about its subject, beliefs and ideals, all on the subject's own terms.

Since *Triumph of the Will* incorporates the best and worst aspects of Riefenstahl, and remains her most controversial film, it is the best test of any theories about her. Having surveyed these past issues and attitudes, it is possible to move beyond their cinematic and historic specificity to an issue of more immediate relevance. It is easy to identify and abhor fascism at its most extreme, but it is more important to identify its beginnings in annexing national/popular culture to its own ideology under less overt guises. An analysis of *Triumph*'s incorporation of the tenets of romanticism provides the basic training to understand the ideological nature of cinema in our society today; the following analysis is indebted to Robert Rosenblum's *Modern Painting and the Northern Romantic Tradition* for its insightful identification and interpretation of Romanticism in painting.

> "I set about, therefore, seeking a thread, a theme, a style, in the realm of legend and fantasy, something that might allow me to give free reign to my juvenile sense of romanticism and beautiful images."
>   —Leni Riefenstahl, 1965
> "Even the most horrible scenes that we must show must convey the nobility of beauty, because it is simply unadulterated nature."
>   —Leni Riefenstahl, c.1939

From its initial operatic imageless overture, *Triumph of the Will* is ingeniously filmed and edited to recapitulate the entire corpus of German legend, beauty, and history in terms of its national Romantic style. Over the leitmotif of ancient Nuremberg is imposed the reflection of a plane, bearing Hitler through the clouds for a euphoric descent into the crowds below, firmly identifying Hitler with a Faust-turned-Archangel access to a state of natural grace. Such a deification is common for Romantic portraiture, for after the breakdown of monolithic Christianity and the system of art it supported, the modes of sacred representation became secularized and applied instead to heads of state (particularly after the French Revolution which made them convincing as architects of a new cosmology) or to landscapes representing an ideal of untrammeled beauty. In landscapes, the inclusion of medieval or Gothic buildings helped to emphasize the atemporality of the scene as well as establish a material connection between the artist's idealization and its perceived concretization in a past which, though lost, was still open to revival. Riefenstahl, by picturing the beatific Fuehrer emerging from the natural universe, neatly dovetails two accepted representations into a single mythology of limitless power incarnated in Hitler. The quiet mood of Nuremberg, hushed in anticipation, has a visionary quality not unlike Friedrich's *Meadow at Greifswald*.

Like that "new Jerusalem," Nuremberg had always been considered a spiritual center (and home of Dürer, Hitler's concept of the archetypal German artist). It was for this spiritual significance, rather than any strategic importance, that Nuremberg was bombed so heavily in World War II. Riefenstahl's depiction of the opening, and hence psychologically crucial, scene incorporates the modern factories of the present as a backdrop for the ancient stone buildings, creating a world order where the past harnesses the future, a primordial order reimposed on contemporary chaos, in sum a hierarchy which Hitler—seen as outside and above it—can dominate and direct.

The thirst for order led the Romantics to "fearful symmetry," the imposition of an archaic and artificial structure onto the universe of the work, translated into *Triumph* as the massing of crowds and the geometric precision of the spectacle. The creation of such a self-contained world order was symptomatic of the Romantics' rejction of existing man-made hierarchies. In their paintings, this rejection is translated into a close-up hypnotic intensity of portraiture that removes its subject from the despised hierarchy and places that subject instead in an imagined domain removed from societal intervention. Riefenstahl adheres to this model, framing individuals in isolation, against the sky or a background thrown out of focus, so removed from any time/space continuum that might disrupt the mythic realm hereby constructed. Most noteworthy in *Triumph* is the angle of vision and lighting of the key individuals, shot from below to increase their stature, lit from behind to illuminate their other-worldly nature. Artists like Ruge had concentrated on devising images of total purity out of a desire to reconstitute the world from scratch. So did Hitler, in horrifyingly literal racist terms. So did Riefenstahl, in terms of her cinematic language. Isolating singular visual elements (the Reich eagle, heraldic standards, torches, bonfires, billowing cloth), she orchestrated these units into a single all-encompassing universe.

The absence of any middle ground in her style—where all is either the individual or the masses, close three-quarters profile or infinite panorama—is similarly prefigured in the Romantics, where that polarity underlined the struggle of the individual to decipher the cosmos. Here, the polarity functions as a distributor of power, with those singled out for representation in the halo-lit close-up the priestlike bearers of extrahuman power, and those seen only as specks in the masses the vessels made to receive this benediction and carry it toward a concrete realization.

This depiction of the crowd raises another fascinating aspect of early German Romantic painting utilized by Riefenstahl in *Triumph*. Beginning with Friedrich, there was a marked emphasis on mysterious "faceless beings" whose anonymous presence encouraged viewer empathy within the construct of the painting. Led to identify with the enigmatic personnage(s), the viewer shares the admiration for the spectacle that constitutes the painting's central subject. By means of this empathetic device, then, the viewer of the work of art is led to exchange the role of third-person audience for that of first-person participant. Hence the traditional passivity of the viewer leads to complicity in the work. A similar device motivates *Triumph*. Whereas the audience for Friedrich's painting was conceived to be the solitary viewer and so depicted within the work, the audience for cinema is quite plural and so pictured in grandiose terms as the huge crowds within the film. The angled shots that were used to magnify the stature of the speakers serve the dual function of leading the audience to identify with their ground-level point of view and therefore with the masses there listening. It's no wonder that the film entrances, for the theater audience in this way becomes its reflection, the rally crowd, swept up in the visual pageantry and urged on by Windt's brilliant orchestration of the Horst Wessel and Die Meistersinger to join in hailing Hitler with the rest.

Thus were the principles of Romanticism subjugated to the Nazi mythology by means of specifically Romantic pictorial devices. As for parallels in cinema itself, the points of relevance run from antecedents in Soviet montage or German expressionism all the way up to the present, where the practice of equating style with ideology can best be put to the test. For if the hypnotic manipulation of the audience, encouraging identification with the distorted characters within the world of the film and manipulating that identification for ideologically potent ends, is a cinema of latent fascism, then just such a cinema dominates our screens today. The conclusion is not far-fetched. There is a great deal of evidence to support the contention, as the Metz-and-Lacan-influenced critics have demonstrated. Arguing against the hypnotic seduction of a passive audience by an illusionist cinema, we may posit a new radical cinema of deconstruction, dedicated to de-mythologizing the film process and reintegrating intellectual response, so that the audience's active participation and full-awake distanciation become requisite to the viewing/understanding of a film. Admittedly, a cinema wholly given over to such a genre would displease a large potential audience; nevertheless, it is a necessary and imminent component in any development of a modern counter-cinema, and the logical conclusion reached by pursuing *Triumph's* "fascist aesthetics" to the end. The sins of Riefenstahl in the realm of aesthetics are equally the sins of Hollywood, Moscow, China, India, Egypt, Europe, of everywhere in the world where the notion of representing reality is the basis for cinema and the aim of controlling audience response its foundation of ideology.

And so Riefenstahl cannot be dismissed into history after all, but remains in the forefront of pressing cinematic concerns. In more ways than one.

> "It must be admitted that a great many women directors present no critique whatsoever of their position within society and seem to subscribe totally to the myth and rhetoric of the dominant . . . ." —festival hand-out, The Women's Event: Edinburgh International Film Festival.

So began a cycle of women's film festivals and so began the consideration of the Riefenstahl problem that continues to plague feminists. Feminism as a movement has always assumed a leftist position, whether purely Marxist (seeing women's oppression as one aspect of class struggle) or loosely anarchist (its denial of the star system and negation of hierarchical structures). Yet Riefenstahl is a woman filmmaker who is not only not a leftist, but who made films commemorating a political system notable for its fascism, rabid racism, and quintessential sexism as well. Until recently, when Lina Wertmuller arrived on the scene with her misogynist and speciously political films, Leni Riefenstahl held the position as at once the best known and most damned woman filmmaker, a thorn in the side of feminism.

Simply seen, perhaps Riefenstahl could just be condemned and ignored, an error to be expunged by revisionist histories. Or, as in the above statement, she is a woman who failed to deviate from the dominant ideology, which in her case led to tragic conclusions. But one of Riefenstahl's unrealized films, her favorite lifelong project, was *Penthesilea*, Kleist's version of the Amazon queen. Now the Amazon myth is one that has gained widely in popularity with the rise of feminist herstory, a nurturing myth to increase women's strengths though some warnings have been signalled (notably by Laura Mulvey and Peter Wollen in their film, *Penthesilea, Queen of the Amazons*, for they see the myth as a male fantasy and as such a trap that will resist feminist annexation). Riefenstahl herself was a sort of Amazon among the Nazis, the token exceptional woman who was granted "permission" by the patriarchy to be privileged to its power in exchange for adopting its values. For the Nazi values were strength, physical prowess, muscular beauty, raw power, mass force: values traditionally male in their less fascist guises. And Riefenstahl was the simultaneous incarnation of several Romantic types of women: the muse, gracing the Reich's arm with her beauty; the belle dame sans merci, as Fanck's on-screen fantasy; the Amazon, equal to the best of the men. Riefenstahl supplied female values (beauty, humanity, spirituality) with Nazi definitions (the beauty of the SS uniform, the humanity of the master race, the spirituality of Fuehrer-worship).

"Amazons would seem incredible to us if they spoke as we do today. Ridiculous, comical—women with male characteristics, without any mythical appearance. These legendary Amazons can be made humanly familiar only through the language of a great poet."

—Leni Riefenstahl, c. 1939

In *Penthesilea*, Riefenstahl seems to have sensed a way of integrating her two filmic interests (the wild mountain girl Junta destroyed by corrupt civilization and the purely male Nazi cosmology) into a self-including synthesis: a Nazi-styled militaristic culture that could admit the contradiction of women, a comprehensible reflection of her own situation. So, upon closer examination: no androgyne, Penthesilea in the vernacular becomes Leni in drag.

Riefenstahl's career thus carries a moral, not only for those who would not make the effort to critique society's dominant ideology, but also for all women who fail to challenge the assumptions of the patriarchy within which we function. Clearly the mere existence of a woman within a patriarchy's power structure does not belie its pervasive sexism. On the contrary, the complicity of the token woman, whose wholesale adoption of patriarchal standards eliminates any possibility of threat, advances the patriarchy's consolidation of power. So today, women who turned seemingly feminist expertise into corporate careers cannot be seen as "working from within." Instead of building an alternate power base from which to attack patriarchal corruption, such a defection provides the patriarchy with a female front that is, if anything, more effective for its program of unilateral imperialism.

Only by coming to terms with Riefenstahl—with the attacks on her as "Hitler's girlfriend" and the defenses of her as "Goebbel's victim," the shaping influences of Fanck and Balázs—can we understand her significance within the Nazi patriarchal pantheon and avoid repeating her mistakes in the context of our own culture.

Mai Zetterling: Free Fall

DEREK ELLEY

It should have come as no surprise, considering her BBC documentaries of the early '60s, that Mai Zetterling's episode for the Munich Olympics film *Visions of Eight* emerged (with Forman's and Pfleghar's) as the best of an uneven bunch. There was, however, prior room for doubt: her last cinema feature had been four years ago, and weightlifting (at least on the surface) seemed a curious choice of subject. Not for the first time she confounded her critics, and produced an episode which not only showed her acute grasp of integrated form but also provided the clearest statement of her interests as a director—loneliness and obsession. These twin themes had dominated her work from the very first, but had often, especially in the case of her features, been obscured by their social settings and a strong overlay of sexual neurosis. The commission for *Visions of Eight* had been unsought: producer David Wolper, obviously with an eye on the market, had phoned her one day and asked if she would like to do a segment on women in the Games. After turning down his suggestion on the grounds that it was rather too obvious a choice, she elected to direct an episode on weightlifting, because it was 'the most unobvious—the furthest thing from what I am and what I know about.' Clearly, her basic interest in the obsessive side of human nature had subconsciously dictated her preference: 'It's not a very popular sport. It's lost in the suburbs somewhere. It's so far-out and it seemed so remote that it fascinated me.' After preparatory work, 'I had two headings in my notes . . . "Isolation" and "Obsession".'

Her 13-minute segment 'The Strongest', coming immediately after Yuri Ozerov's opening 'The Beginning', is prefaced by a brief spoken introduction: 'I am not interested in sport, but I am interested in obsessions.' A clear enough explanation of her approach, but one which only half-explains the content to come. Weightlifters, by virtue of their grotesque development and sincere desire to transcend normal physical limitations, are more than open to cheap and easy humour. It is much to Zetterling's credit that she is able to explore her interest in this breed of sportsmen without resorting to either snide montage sequences or derisive visual effects. Their dedication is accepted by her as equal to that of any other top-class athlete, their size as a necessary extension of their sport. For much of the time she is concerned with the huge machinery which supports these men at the Games— the mind-boggling food statistics and frantic computerisation which have an obsessive and alienating quality of their own. Eggs mass-fried in large trays and ton after ton of meat consumed take on an unreal dimension which is hard to grasp when applying the normal comparisons of everyday life. Similarly, with the weightlifters, men who exist in the fairy-land world of the modern-day gym, men whose equipment needs four soldiers to dismantle and who dwarf those members of the public needed to judge, spectate and organise. Every sport demands concentration, but some narrow that concentration into finer channels than others: weightlifting, like gymnastics, is man versus his equipment, a sport devoid of any partnership or need of spectator co-operation. Zetterling shows her subjects at work, driving themselves deep into masochistic regions every bit as lonely as those inhabited by *Doktor Glas*, Jan in *Night Games* or Liz in *The Girls*. Beyond this, however, Zetterling shows the weightlifters' faces, and it becomes apparent that (supported by the unrealistic machinery of the Games) they are at home only in the company of their own kind— compare the actors in *The Girls*, or the society in *Night Games*—and that, as soon as the training and super-diet cease they will revert to 'ordinary' physical standards. The one part of a weightlifter which remains exposed is his face, and this Zetterling explores to pursue her particular viewpoint. There is a genuine sympathy to be found in her obvious amazement at these sportsmen which makes her episode in *Visions of Eight* so successful; allied with her definite approach and technical virtuosity (a feature of all her works, and best seen here in the visually-incisive band-playing sequence), 'The Strongest' has a depth and sense of sustained argument which escapes every other of the seven segments. The final image is a memorable example of achieving one's ends by the simplest means, and shows Zetterling (for one, satisfactorily) solving the problem of her endings: after a sustained coda showing the competitors departing (like giants to the hills) and the equipment and paraphernalia of the contest being slowly dismantled, she holds on a banner showing the weightlifting logo as, finally and inexorably, it falls into a crumpled heap on the floor.

This article is concerned only with Mai Zetterling the director, but it would be as well to note briefly the facts of her life up to the start of the last decade. Her career, whether as actress *or* director, has always been characterised by a refreshing spontaneity and single-mindedness which has been supported by sheer hard work and redeeming talent. While others have gone their own way and foundered in their basic inadequacy, Mai Zetterling has consistently vindicated her own self-belief. Born Mai Elisabet Zetterling on 24 May, 1925, in Västeras, 60 miles west of Stockholm, she spent part of her childhood abroad (sources differ as to whether South Africa or Australia), due to her father's decision to emigrate with his hat business. After financial failure, the family returned to Sweden, and at the age of 16 she made her first stage appearance in a play by Pär Lagerkvist. The same year (1941) saw her film *début* in Gunnar Olsson's *Lasse-Maja,* and in 1942 she joined the training school of the Royal Dramatic Theatre, Stockholm. Her three years there were eventful ones, climaxed in 1944 by her marriage, at the age of 19, to the dancer Tutte Lemkow and first major film role as the female lead in Alf Sjöberg's *Frenzy (Hets)*. In 1946 she left Sweden to take the title part in Basil Dearden's *Frieda* (1947), her first English-speaking role, in which she memorably evoked the problems of acceptance of a German girl in a British family. A contract with the Rank Organisation followed, and throughout the late '40's and the '50's much work, both for the theatre and cinema, in Britain, Sweden and the USA. On 26 March, 1953 she was divorced by Lemkow on the grounds of adultery and subsequent desertion, and considerable ballyhoo of the 'marriage-isn't-for-me' variety followed. A Swede resident in Britain, she provided perfect copy for eager reporters during the '50's, and on 23 April, 1958, married the writer David Hughes, who has remained the scenarist for all her own pictures up to the present day. Her acting roles showed she had an equal talent for comedy (best exhibited in the late *Only Two Can Play*), and, particularly in her feature *The Girls* (1968), she has transferred this talent to her own projects.

During the late '50's she underwent greater and greater disillusionment with acting as a sole outlet for expression. Its limitations and lack of total creative control made her hanker after direction as a means of achieving her desires, and, apparently on impulse, she proposed the idea of a film on Lapland to her husband. This idea eventually became reality, and with an advance from the BBC, she, Hughes, and a cameraman set off to film their subject. With a skeleton crew of only three, enthusiasm and improvisation were necessary ingredients, and after the best part of a year spent cutting the film, the half-hour documentary *The Polite Invasion* (1960) emerged. Showing the insidious incursions on the Laplanders' way of life, it was followed during the next few years (between acting commitments) by three other documentaries for the BBC: *Lords of Little Egypt* (1961), about the gypsies at Saintes-Maries-de-la-Mer; *The Prosperity Race* (1962), a biting piece on Swedish affluence which was not appreciated back in Stockholm; and *Do-It-Yourself Democracy* (1963), on Iceland. These documentaries show an increasing concern for technical efficiency which, as mentioned earlier, is a hallmark of her work; their concern for the standard of present-day life and the *extra*-ordinary in subject-matter gave her a new mantle to assume after being the sexual *enfant terrible* of the '50's. A full-length feature was clearly in the offing, but meanwhile there appeared *The War Game*, a 15-minute short for British Lion which attracted much praise at both the London and Leipzig 1963 Festivals. The work is a clear condemnation not only of war *per se* but also of the stupidity which can lead to war: two boys, playing on a building site, become more and more engrossed in their game, until events take a more serious turn . . . The playing by Ian Ellis and Joseph Robinson as the children is invested with a growing sense of menace which springs solely from Zetterling's choice of visuals and acute editing. The film has neither dialogue nor music as dramatic props, thus accentuating the director's underlying concern for the lack of communication which prompted such a situation. The boys' game is reduced to a purely instinctive level of behaviour, and Zetterling's interest in theatricalities as a heightened metaphor for life can be seen in *The War Game* in an embryonic form.

Her first full-length feature finally arrived in 1964. Made not in Britain, but for the Swedish company Sandrews, *Loving Couples* (Alskande par) took its title from the fifth volume of Agnes von Krusenstjerna's giant seven-volume work, 'Fröknarna von Pahlen' ('The Misses von Pahlen'). Von Krusenstjerna holds an important place in Swedish literature, and like many of the characters in her work she herself had led a somewhat unconventional life, breaking with her family to marry a (disapproved) literary critic but retaining her original name as a writer. *Loving Couples*, set in Stockholm in 1915, is necessarily a ruthlessly-compressed version of the original, telling in flashback of the various emotional experiences undergone by three women prior to their confinement in a maternity ward. The plot-line begs immediate comparisons with Bergman's *So Close to Life* (*Nära livet*, 1958), but it soon becomes clear that few parallels exist beyond the basic idea of linking the process of birth with the morality of the begetter. Bergman's film begins with a violent miscarriage, and ends pessimistically; Zetterling's is more concerned with past events *per se*, the end merely confirming the actions and desires of the three wo- men. Angela (sensitively portrayed by the delightful Gio Petleé) has a depressing background of orphanhood, adolescent lesbianism, and blighted romantic love; Agda (Harriet Andersson in flirtatious form) exists on an easy morality, accepting a marriage of convenience to a homosexual artist; and Adèle, (a marvellously saturnine Gunnel Lindblom) exists locked in a bitter marriage to an inadequate hus- band. Angela undergoes painful but successful childbirth; Agda in- consequential but successful; Adele, stillbirth. The end contains no judgement, and is the most optimistic result the women might wish for. In *Loving Couples* Zetterling laid down a groundplan for her later films from which she rarely deviated: her love of flashback and an elaborate time-structure (*Night Games, Doktor Glas*), her use of parties and gatherings to extrude emotions and climaxes, and her continual attention to the beauties of the black-and-white image—here by Sven Nykvist, but henceforth always by Rune Ericson—exploiting the dramatic possibilities of composition in depth.

Loving Couples was made for   150,000, attracted good reviews in Sweden, and managed to break even. In Britain 13 minutes were shorn from the original but the film gained the attention of the critics, many of whom latched on to the more bizarre sexual elements at a time when neurosis was considered the exclusive territory of the Swedes (Bergman's *The Silence* dates from this era). Mai Zetterling was already at work on her second feature, and even her career up to that date did little to prepare the film world for the bombshell un- veiled at Venice in 1966—the legendary *Night Games* (*Nattlek*).

Zetterling had begun to write the story in the form of a novel, and it was only when she was half-way through that she decided to switch mediums. With David Hughes she formed a 50-page synopsis from which the film was developed; only later did she sit down and finish the novel. Entitled *The Longing* during production, *Night Games* is mostly set in a 12th-century castle (Penningby Slott) near Stock- holm, a suitably baroque location in which Jan, a man in his 30's, tries to exorcise the memory of his dead mother Irene (Ingrid Thulin). The film opens simply and starkly: a hand extended against the light in an attitude of agony. Jan (played by Keve Hjelm) has brought his *fiancée* (Len Brundin) to his childhood home; soon the past (1938) and the present intermingle as he tries to expunge the memory of his suf- focating mother-love and cure the impotence which has afflicted him to the present. *Night Games*, for all its sexual frills, is essentially a film about loneliness—and the desperation which stems from that state. The young Jan is seen growing up in an atmosphere of extremes, in which normality can be abandoned as a yardstick. His mother gives birth before her party-guests to a still-born child; wild, eccentric gatherings are perpetually in motion; his relationship with his mother veers abruptly between total lack of communication and masturbation by her hand. *Night Games* is, however, something more than exotic extravaganza; the problem is to accept Zetterling's uncompromising outlook and not impose one's own sense of outraged morality. The issue is further complicated, as always, by her sense of humour—a humour which extends into region not usually inhabited by laughter. Jan as a boy is played by Jörgen Lindström, the same child actor who appeared in Bergman's *The Silence* (also with Ingrid Thulin) and the beginning of *Persona*. A line in which a character calls for music to break the silence is a direct reference to the earlier film, and throughout *Night Games* Mai Zetterling is at pains to avoid the feeling of cloying seriousness which would prove detrimental to her aims. Her concern is to show the isolation of Irene and her debauched associates from any genuine scheme of emotions; the upper-class setting is convenient to this purpose, and also gives ample scope for the baroque visual effects needed to show the orgiastic gatherings through the young Jan's eyes. Zetterling is not primarily interested in giving rational explanations or serious study of Jan's Oedipal complexes: on this account she is open to accusations of triviality. The most important point is the atmosphere of Jan's childhood, shown in extreme images which are concrete reenactions of familiar fantasies: in an earnest attempt to extract some genuine love from Irene, Jan appears in her makeup and clothing; emotionally threatened by both homosexuals and rapacious women, Jan crawls beneath his mother's dress to find shelter. *Night Games* works totally on this level, one in which the theatricalities of human behaviour are given direct visual expression.

Questioned about her frequent use of 'sex and perversion', Mai Zetterling replied: 'I use it because I believe that you can only come to a positive view of life by passing through the innumerable negative ones.' As in *Loving Couples*, the obsessive nature of the leading character's fixation is finally given optimistic release. After throwing a party for all his mother's friends, the adult Jan announces the house is to be dynamited in a few minutes: the guests pilfer as many possessions as they can carry, and as the homestead explodes there is a prolonged sequence as Jan and his *fiancée* gambol in the snow. The ending is somewhat facile, but works on the film's allegorical level: Jan's problem will never finally be solved by anyone except himself, whether his *fiancée* (who bears an uncanny resemblance to his mother) dresses in Irene's clothes or stands by him in a symbolic burial (a coffin lowered into a well). At all events, Mai Zetterling rigidly controls her depiction of Jan's indulgent childhood: for all their ripe content, the black-and-white visuals have a spartan quality which prevents the film from collapsing in a welter of self-gratification. Transitions from present to past are skilfully managed through changes of lighting and focus, and the imagery, if frequently obscure, exerts a continual fascination.

After the fuss generated by its critics-only showing at Venice, *Night Games* went on to take a key place in the development of sexual license in the cinema during the Sixties. Zetterling's third feature, *Doktor Glas*, shot during the summer of 1967 and almost shown at Cannes in 1968, created not half the fuss of its predecessor, chiefly through its lack of exploitable material. A Danish-American co-production with two Swedes and a Dane in the leading roles, *Doktor Glas* is based on the 1905 novel by Hjalmar Söderberg, which charts the obsession of a young practitioner for the wife of a *pastor*. The story is again told in flashback (a single, uninterrupted episode), and is Zetterling's harshest examination of loneliness. Dr Glas (Per Oscarsson) is shown in his large apartment, obsessed with the idea that he has wasted his life; through images of great beauty, his infatuation with Helga Gregorius (played by the Dane Lone Hertz) and the apparent waste of a beautiful young woman on an elderly lecher is given increasing weight until murder seems the only solution. The sadness of Glas' plight is that this does not gain him Helga, and he is left alone with only the memories of a single friendly kiss. Nothing could be farther from *Night Games*: here the central character is suffering from lack rather than surfeit, and the high-contrast dream sequences underline the doctor's agony. The film is the most pessimistic of Zetterling's *oeuvre*, and has been criticised for its slow pace. For most people it remains an unknown quantity in her career, and has not achieved wide release. Thematically, however, it is clearly in line with her other works.

In 1968 appeared *The Girls* (*Flickorna*), her fourth and last full-length feature to date. It is Zetterling's most successful combination of the diverse elements which characterise her films, and is, at the same time, her most wide-ranging. The story centres around three women who are touring Sweden in Aristophanes' anti-war play *Lysistrata*: Liz (Bibi Andersson) plays Lysistrata, Marianne (Harriet Andersson) plays Myrrhine, and Gunilla (Gunnel Lindblom) plays Kalonike. There is an obvious correlation between their stage roles and those in 'real' life, and the women's awareness of this grows throughout the film. *The Girls*, at first glance, *appears* to be about many things, but is, in the end, only about one. Most emphatically, it is not concerned with the emancipation of women, and the subject of war is only incidental to the main theme—lack of communication, the bugbear of all Zetterling's work. The three girls live isolated lives, cut off from their husbands by a gulf of misunderstanding and free to fantasize about themselves and their desires. The most earnest of the trio, Liz, makes a serious attempt while in a provincial town to communicate with her hosts at a dinner party: here, as also in the sequence in which she desperately harangues a disinterested audience, there is a moving despair beneath the more comical element which says much for Zetterling's ability to mix apparently disparate *genres* successfully. Marianne and Gunilla are essentially subsidiary characters to the crusading Liz (one of Bibi Andersson's best roles): despite the lack of communication not only between the sexes but also between art (the play) and the public (the theatre audience), all Liz's efforts at rousing her own sex are shown finally to be pointless. She fails because she tries to transcend the necessary boundaries (*eg* in the theatre, by expecting the audience to listen to her outside her role as an actress), and her husband's laughing 'This means war!' at the final gathering of all the characters, is Zetterling's own wary acceptance of *vive la différence*. She has, however, achieved her object of showing the consequences of such differences, taking—as in *The War Game*— events to their logical conclusions. Liz's sense of frustration climaxes in an emotionally violent striptease in front of inquisitive males, a sequence of considerable power in which she defiantly hurls her naked breasts at the eyes of her inlookers. The other women follow suit; the point has been made.

Zetterling tells her story from the viewpoint of women only; another film remains to be made for the men. Again; as in *Night Games*, her all-pervasive humour is continually in evidence, and like Aristophanes' knows no bounds of either sex or accepted morality. Fantasy blends with reality; Marianne is showered with gifts by her lover; Liz's husband contacts an endless string of mistresses in her absence; and later he arrives with two portable girls in his trunk. The technical expertise of *The Girls* is impressive even by Zetterling's established standards: 'I'd rather make films for a larger audience, not just the Academy Cinema, but it's very difficult.' Her fund of imaginative imagery is perhaps at its richest in *The Girls*: Rune Ericson's photography is a delight at all times, particularly impressive when omitting half-tones for dramatic effect. The attractive appearance and clear entertainment value of *The Girls* have led many critics to dismiss it on the grounds of glossiness. This is arrant nonsense: misunderstanding of Zetterling's objectives will naturally invite accusations of simplicity. Her concern is neither to document the cause of female emancipation nor to provide propaganda under the banner of entertainment: as in all her works, she merely shows, in a heightened and stylised form, the effects of emotional isolation and the obsessions which can develop. Above all, her films are assertions of life— perhaps glib, but always personal.

In 1968, while editing *The Girls*, she announced a nebulous plan to make a film—without script or actors—for Sandrews that summer. Photographed by Rune Ericson, it would bring a 'new dimension to the cinema'. Nothing came of the project, although clearly, with acting long since abandoned (a final courtesy part in Sven Nykvist's first feature, *The Vine Bridge*—*Lianbron*, 1965), she was looking for something new. 'I only wanted to make a very few pictures, but I want to ensure that I am completely free and independent when making them.' In 1971, with John Bulmer as the cameraman, she made *Vincent the Dutchman* in southern France. Shown on American TV in 1972, it was subsequently bought by the BBC for 'Omnibus', and has been screened twice. It deserves mention here since it is one of Zetterling's finest achievements, and prior to *Visions of Eight*, her first work in colour. Like Liz in *The Girls*, an actor (Michael Gough) slowly identifies with a character he is playing—in this case the painter Vincent van Gogh, who arrived in sunny Arles thirty months before dying at the age of thirty-five. Visually, the hour-long is particularly memorable: the fields of red poppies and chatter of crickets, the sheep noisily following Vincent as he wanders in self-absorption. 'This special torture—loneliness,' he writes to his brother Théo. 'This loneliness, this feeling of being an outcast,' he says later. Beneath the lush photography runs a despairing streak which has rarely been stronger in Zetterling's work (*Doktor Glas* is a case in point). Throughout the film one is made to share her own attempts to understand the driving force behind such a man as van Gogh. One sequence acutely summarises the deadening lethargy of the artist's early life in Arles: a girl-friend lies mute on a bed, her yellow-stockinged legs casually apart, as Vincent stands in the room. Zetterling's unique use of the sexual image to mirror the wider aspects of life has never been demonstrated more simply.

III.
FILMS
DIRECTED
BY
WOMEN

Maedchen in Uniform

NANCY SCHOLAR

In 1931, when *Maedchen in Uniform* appeared in Berlin, Paris, and London, it was praised as one of the year's best.[1] The following year, when it came to this country, after being temporarily delayed by censors,[2] it was voted the best film of the year by the New York press[3] and the National Board praised it as "one of the most human films that has been made anywhere."[4] A few years ago, Alexander Gulikhes called the work "remarkably authentic."[5] *Maedchen* remains powerful and relevant to our times. Unfortunately its withdrawal in the United States due to the poor condition of all extant prints is extremely distressing.

It is also a sad commentary that so little is known about the life of the director, Leontine Sagan. Bucher's Germany (in the SCREEN SERIES) lists her born as Leontine Schlesinger in Austria, 1889. She moved to Johannesburg where she married Dr. Victor Fleischer. Thereafter she moved to Berlin and became a student of Max Reinhardt. Later she was an actress and director in theaters in Dresden, Vienna, Frankfurt, and Berlin. In 1931 she directed *Maedchen in Uniform*. As a result of the film's success, she was invited to England by Alexander Korda to direct *Men of Tomorrow* (1932), which featured Merle Oberon. The film of young Oxford students, based on Anthony Gibbs' novel, *The Young Apollo*, did not equal her first efforts, and Sagan never made another film. She worked part-time at the Korda Studios and returned to theater. Meanwhile *The Hollywood Reporter* in 1934 wrote that Sagan was signed by David O. Selznick to direct for MGM, but that no decision had been made on a specific assignment. Nothing came of the agreement. In 1938 an article on exiled German filmmakers appeared in *The New York Times*, listing Sagan among them. In 1939 she moved back to South Africa and from 1939–1945 worked at The National Theatre in Johannesburg, which she co-founded. She died in May, 1974.

There are several remarkable aspects to Leontine Sagan's brilliant classic *Maedchen in Uniform*, the most striking of which is the absence of the customary male figures both in the direction and performance of the film. (Sagan did, however, receive the help of the male director Carl Froelich, one of the most experienced directors of the German cinema at the time.) Not only did a woman direct the film in 1931, but the script was based upon a play written by a woman (Christa Winsloe's *Gestern und Heute* or *Yesterday and Today*) and the cast is entirely composed of women. It also was the first film in Germany to have been cooperatively produced, meaning that the cast and crew formed a cooperative film company in which there were shares rather than salaries. The film becomes even more remarkable when we consider the historical context in which it appeared. By 1931, Hitler was in the ascendancy, and a wave of nationalism was spreading throughout the country; this was both reflected in and accelerated by the newreels and films, which were almost entirely nationalistic by this time. In this milieu, Sagan's film appeared, which is overtly anti-nationalistic, anti-Prussian, anti-authoritarian. Not surprisingly, a separate ending, which was pro-fascist, was shown in Germany, and eventually Goebbels had the film banned as unhealthy. Sagan and most of her cast exiled themselves from Germany after the film was released.

The setting of *Maedchen in Uniform* is a Potsdam boarding school for aristocratic girls from military families. Sagan's choice of location is an explicit indication of her intention, which is to juxtapose the Prussian values, epitomized by Potsdam and the headmistress who rules the school, against the humanitarian values of the schoolgirl Manuela and her teacher Fraulein von Bernburg. These two value systems are not simply presented in opposition. In dialectical fashion, much in the manner of Eisenstein's dialectical montage, colliding images are set up against each other in order to demonstrate their interconnection and logical progression. Thus the film opens with a montage of images suggesting the Prussian style: military statuary, the soldier-like steeple of the church, suggesting the religiosity which customarily accompanies such values, and the clock implying the relation of present time to past and future, perhaps the inevitability of the historical process, the formation of the Germany to come out of the Prussian past. From this montage of images, the camera follows the marching, regimented schoolgirls (preceded by marching soldiers, thus making the analogy between the two groups obvious) through the Gothic archways to the interior of the school, which mirrors the exterior in style and values. The Prussian headmistress who reigns within the school, with her dictates of discipline, order, hunger, is a reflection of the rising fuehrer outside; like Hitler, the headmistress shares his megalomania and its concomitant impotence, suggested by her use of the cane. The fact that it is a woman who enforced the militaristic values inherited from a patriarchal society warns against easy dichotomies between male and female values and indicates that the corruption of power knows no sexual boundaries.

Over against the headmistress and her regime, Sagan postulates Manuela, the antithesis of the Prussian values, who has suffered from the loss of her·mother and the repressive manner of an aunt before arriving at the school. Manuela's sensitivity, insecurity, and motherlessness prevent her, fortunately, from accommodating herself to her dehumanizing surroundings and place her in need of maternal and emotional sustenance. From our first glimpse of her teacher, Fraulein von Bernburg, it is apparent that von Bernburg is destined to fulfill this role. She, as well as Manuela, is photographed with a luminosity which is repeated in subsequent scenes. The most dazzling of such scenes is the one in which Fraulein von B comes to the dormitory room to give the girls their good-night kiss. They line up with rather frenzied anticipation, indicating the enormity of their emotional needs and also the erotic undertone of the school, which seems an inevitable consequence of a repressive atmosphere. This erotic ambiance is made explicit when Fraulein von B and Manuela passionately kiss. Again the photography is superlative: they are surrounded by a luminous halo, which is either a santification (reinforced by the angelic postures of the girls) of what at the time must have seemed a shocking event or a romanticization and highlighting of a love relationship in striking contrast to the headmistress' inhumanity and emotional sterility. The maternalism and religiosity of the embrace are of course ingredients of love in the western world and particularly for the Germany of that time, which equated love and patriotism with motherhood.

But the film departs quite radically from the conventional in its open presentation of the possibilities of love between two women; and *open* is the key word here, since repressed homosexuality, undeclared and unexamined, would be a matter of course, as in the Nazi movement outside. But it is the openness of Manuela's declaration in a moment of drunken hilarity, of her love for Fraulein von B which so scandalizes the headmistress. Manuela is denounced by this fuehrer, just as homosexuals were periodically denounced and purged during the Nazi era, despite the continued presence of the homosexual Captain Roehm as leader of the storm troopers. That Sagan wishes us to place the relationship between the two women in a wider context is unquestionable, since she proceeds the shot of the two women in haloed embrace with the replay of Prussian imagery: clock, military statues, garrison bugle in the background. This juxtaposition suggests both the inevitability of conflict between these values and the progression from one to the other.

To restate the film's dialectic, the collision between the headmistress' authoritarian and repressive tactics (thesis) and Manuela's emotionally and human responsiveness to another (antithesis) leads to a breakdown or breakthrough in the system (synthesis). As Wilhelm Reich has formulated: "Repression posits its own destruction, since as a result of repression instinctual energy is powerfully dammed up until it finally breaks through the repression."("Dialectical Materialism and Psychoanalysis," *Sex-Pol Essays*) The breakthrough comes not only through Manuela's open declaration of love for Fraulein von B, but also through the joining of the girls in solidarity against the headmistress, and in support of Manuela's rights. Once Manuela, who has gained the love of her schoolmates, has been ostracized by the headmistress the girls join together and seek Manuela out, in defiance of the headmistress, decree.

This last scene is enormously compelling both because of its emotional power and visual design. The same could be said for the entirety of the film. The central staircase which becomes the focal point of this last dramatic scene is used throughout the film with marvelous effect as a visual metaphor for Manuela's condition and that of all the girls, and all of society by extension. In one of the first shots of the staircase, Sagan presents us with a brilliant image of imprisonment, confinement through the striated shadow of the staircase which imprints its prison-like image on Manuela and the other girls. Later in the film, after Manuela awakens in the infirmary from her drunken declaration, she again is captured in a shadow-image of imprisonment, this time from the bars of a window. But it is primarily the staircase which is utilized as the insignia of the school's (and society's) confinement, rigid structure. Yet that same structure also contains within itself the possibility of release from that confinement:

through the stairwell. Early in the film, the stairwell is used as the setting for some playful defiance on the part of a few of the girls. This foreshadows the ending of the film, in which Manuela nearly succeeds in releasing herself from the humiliation and harsh punishment which the headmistress has inflicted upon her, through the most desperate leap of all: from the top of the stairwell. This well of dangerous space thus becomes the visual indicator of the options open to the girls) (and again, society by extension) if they choose to defy authority: freedom, release from confinement on the one hand, potential destruction, death on the other, Manuela, significantly, is saved from her demise by the other girls. She is through over the border of the staircase, back into safety, support, and warmth. Solidarity between the girls, human sympathy and concern, provide the necessary components, at least temporarily, for the dissolution of the school's effective imprisonment of their beings, and of the power of destructive forms.

Appropriately, at the top of the staircase, once Manuela has been retrieved, she and Fraulein von B are shown reunited, and their faces merge, anticipating Bergman's Persona by over 10 years. The headmistress retreats from the scene at the end, apparently defeated. Yet as she slowly descends the staircase, we hear the bugle call outside, suggesting a number of possible interpretations. On the one hand, a reflection of the political realities outside the school, and an accurate prediction of the triumph of authoritarian forces in Germany and elsewhere; on the other, it may be read as a rallying call for antiauthoritarian forces, for the forces of love and compassion represented by Manuela and Fraulein von B and the young girls who joined forces with them. Whatever interpretation we settle upon, it is clear that Sagan allows for no easy solutions, which is part of the magnificence of her achievement in this film.

[1]Mordaunt Hall, *The New York Times*, September 21, 1932, p. 26.
[2]Pauline Kael, *Kiss Kiss Bang Bang* (Boston, 1965), p. 379.
[3]Ibid.
[4]Siegfried Kracauer, *From caligari to hitler: A Psychological History of the German Film* (Princeton, 1947), p. 228.
[5]Alexander Gulikhes, "Films by women 1928–71," *Film Library Quarterly*, Winter 1972–1973, p. 47.

Approaching the Work of Dorothy Arzner

PAM COOK

The films of Dorothy Arzner provide us with an opportunity to investigate a range of film texts made within a production system already in the late 20s and early 30s highly articulated in terms of the dominant ideology of classic Hollywood cinema. There is no doubt that Arzner made complex and interesting films of great relevance to women now in our struggle for our own culture, but the point is not to claim for her a place in a pantheon of 'best Hollywood directors', since the positing of any such pantheon would ignore the complexity of the relationship between ideology and the production of film texts. In looking again at some of Arzner's films, then, we are looking at a body of work produced within the constraints of a studio system heavily determined by economic and ideological factors (*Nana*, in spite of the potential interest of the story, remains little more than a vehicle for Anna Sten, Goldwyn's protegée and hoped-for box-office answer to Dietrich and Garbo, relentlessly photographed in soft-focus by Gregg Toland). Our object will be to define some strategies for a critique of patriarchal ideology[1] in general.

To approach the films in this way is not to try to elevate them to the status of masterpieces, nor simply to regard them as objects worthy of study, but instead to see them as texts (complex products demanding an active reading in terms of the contradictions at work in them), which are produced within a system of representation which tries to fix the spectator in a specific closed relationship to the film. Thus we are attempting to take from Arzner's films some ideas which will open out the problem of the place of women within that system.

Stephen Heath in an article on Brecht remarks:

> Classic film is finally less of a question of *mise-en-scène* than of *mise-en-place*, and anything that disturbs that place, that position, the fictions of myself and my 'Reality' can only be theoretical, the theatralisation of representation in its forms: film theatre, critical cinema, a cinema of crisis and contradiction. ('Lessons from Brecht', *Screen* Vol. 15, No. 2, Summer 1974.)

In the history of classic cinema this *'mise-en-place'* has been articulated in response to the demands of patriarchal ideology, with specific consequences for the place of women in representation; for in this structure the place of woman is defined as the locus of 'lack', an empty space which must be filled in the working through of man's desire to find his own place in society.[2] The use of female stereotypes, modified only slightly to meet the demands of changing fashion, has contributed to the propagation of myths of women which relate primarily to the desires of men. The role of women in this film narrative can be seen to perform a similar function: to bring into play the desire of the male protagonists. While there is no doubt that there are progressive elements in many Hollywood films (for example, those of Sirk or Ford) which posit the idea of female desire, nevertheless ultimately these films operate a closure on the possibilities of the working through of this desire) *i.e.*, of articulating and satisfying desire through phantasy). The films of Dorothy Arzner are important in that they foreground precisely this problem of the desire of women caught in a system of representation which allows them at most the opportunity of playing on the specific demands that the system makes on them.

This concept of play permeates every level of the texts: irony operates through the dialogue, sound(s), music, through a play on image, stereotype and gesture and through complex patterns of parallels and reversals in the overall organization of the scenes. Perhaps the most exemplary film in this sense is *Dance, Girl, Dance*, which has often been acclaimed by feminist critics as a work of major importance. However, it would be a mistake to read the film in 'positive' terms as representing the progress of its heroine to 'maturity' or 'self-awareness.' The value of the film lies not in its creation of a culture-heroine with whom we can finally and fully identify, but in the ways in which it *displaces* identification with the characters and focuses our attention on the problematic position they occupy in the world. A positive reading of the film would imply a conclusion which would be a final closure of the film's contractions; but this ignores the complexity of the film's structure of reversals. When Judy O'Brien finally turns on her audience in fury and in her long speech fixes them in relation to *her* critical look at them it does indeed have the force of a 'pregnant moment'. The place of the audience *in* the film and the audience *of* the film is disturbed, creating a break between them and the ideology of woman as spectacle, object of their desire. The shock-force of the moment is emphasised by the embarassment of the audience in the film, and the silence which follows the speech. However, in another masterly reversal, the moment is upended as the enthusiastic clapping of the woman in the audience (Steve Adams' secretary, whose relationship to her boss is depicted in the film as, ironically, one of friendly but almost complete oppression of her by him) escalates into a standing ovation, thus re-locating Judy's speech *as* a performance. The cat-fight between Judy and Bubbles which follows almost immediately takes place on the stage to the accompaniment of music from the burlesque orchestra which resembles the music used for *Tom and Jerry* cartoons. This has the double force of condensing the girls' conflict of desires, and by presenting that conflict as sexually exciting for the cheering, cat-calling audience, calls into question the processes by which women's desires are presented as a spectacle for consumption. In this way our identification with Judy's inspiring words is displaced into an awareness of the continuing process of contradictions at work in the struggle with ideology.

Similarly in the court-room sequence which follows, Judy in the dock speaks with confidence and self-assurance about herself and he relationship to the other people in the film, much to the admiration of her audience and the fair-minded and liberal judge. However, we next see Judy at Steve Adams' dance academy where she finally discovers his identity and the real reason for his pursuit of her—her ability as a dancer. Even as Judy tries to assert her independence in the conversation with Steve which ends the film, the ground is pulled from under her.

> STEVE—*The judge and I decided* you were in no mood to take favours.
> JUDY—I'm still in no mood . . . .
> STEVE—Now listen to me *you silly child*. You've had *your own way* long enough—now you're going to listen to me . . .
> STEVE—(to the dancing instructor) She was born with more than any dancer we've got and she knows less. *It's our job to teach her all we know.* (My italics.)

Judy's moment of triumphant independence becomes a thing of the past as she collapses into Steve's arms *in tears*.

> JUDY—When I think how easy it might have been I could laugh.
> STEVE—Go ahead and laugh, Judy O'Brien.

In this final ironic reversal Judy 'gets what she wants' at the expense of any pretensions to 'independence' she had. Again, by displacing our expectations of identification with Judy's positive qualities into a recognition of the weakness of her position within male-dominated culture, the film's ending opens up the contradictions inherent in that position (our position) thus encouraging us as spectators to recognise the all-important problematic of the difficulties of the working through of female desire under patriarchy.

Without doubt, *Dance, Girl, Dance* provides the clearest example, by its play on stereotypes and reversals, of ironic method, especially as it foregrounds the contradiction between women's desire for self-expression and culture, and the cultural processes which articulate a place for woman as spectacle. However, further examples of Arzner's concern with playing with formal elements to conceptualise women's position in ideology can be found in another earlier film. *Merrily We Go To Hell*, made in 1932, displays the seeds of the method which is so rigorously and economically articulated in *Dance, Girl, Dance* in 1940. This is not to suggest that we can formulate a coherent and exhaustive method to apply to all Arzner films. What follows is a tentative enquiry into some of the ways in which this early post-silent comedy treats the problem of the relationship of the spectator to the forms whereby classic cinema represents the place of woman.

Merrily We Go To Hell tells the story of an insecure young heiress, Joan Prentice (Sylvia Sidney), whose stern and upright father owns a food-processing business, and who falls in love with a penniless journalist and would-be playwright, Gerry Corbett (Fredric March), who drinks heavily to forget his failure and his broken affair with a successful actress. Joan decides to marry Gerry, in spite of her father's resistance to the idea on the grounds of Gerry's unreliability. Gerry agrees to the marriage despite his fears that his continuing obsession with Claire, the actress, will prevent him from making a go of it.

Meaning is created in the film through the play of oppositions: the 'strength' of Joan's father is contrasted with Gerry's 'weakness' and inability to control his own actions. Similarly Joan's lack of confidence about her identity contrasts sharply with Claire's self-possession and ability to control her 'audience' through a highly articulated image of female sexuality. The conflict of desires between the four protagonists provides the motivation for what happens in the film, but the progress of the narrative and the final reconciliation of Joan and Gerry is complicated on several levels.

1. THE NARRATIVE

The structure of the narrative is episodic: there is no smooth flow from one scene to another, and each scene demands to be read in itself for the meanings it creates. In this way we are constantly distanced from a desire to follow the 'destiny' of the characters in any transparent or linear fashion. Rather we are led in a series of uneven 'events' to question the 'inevitable Truth'[3] of the narrative and to look at the situations in which the protagonists find themselves. By 1932 the codes of suspense were well established in Hollywood cinema. Intercutting of sequences and shots to provide an illusion of simultaneous action had been extensively used in the silent cinema not only to create comedy but also in psychological/social drama, where identification with the central character and the final *dénouement* of the story were essential to the representation of Truth. It is significant therefore that Arzner's film presents its story in a succession of tableaux, where the organisation of meanings within each scene takes precedence over the smooth forward-flow of a narrative which would give an impression of Reality. An example from the film might be the opening scene.

The film opens with an image of Fredric March (Gerry) alone in half-darkness crouched behind a barricade of whisky bottles from which position he is drunkenly and only half-aloud enacting an imaginary battle with the 'horrible people' at the 'horrible party' he is attending. The camera draws back to show us that he has withdrawn to a balcony from which he can see the party—through a brightly-lit window. A couple dancing move into view through the window and seem to begin an argument. Gerry shows an interest in the scene, and we are taken in closer to find Sylvia Sidney (Joan) struggling violently with the sexual advances of a very large, very drunk man. She breaks away and rushes out onto the balcony, unaware of Gerry's presence or the fact that he has been watching with interest and amusement.

In these first few seconds notions of watcher/watched, fear of and inability to cope with sexual demands, innocence, flight and withdrawal are quickly established. The rest of the scene takes place almost entirely on the balcony and is concerned with depicting the nature of the relationship between Gerry and Joan and Joan's place within it. Joan describes herself as 'stupid' and a 'nobody', but when she tells Gerry her name he immediately connects her with 'Prentice Products' and points out a neon advertising sign on the sky-line, thus placing *her* as a product. In the face of her self-negation he emphasises her class status (courtesy of her father), her 'niceness' (I think you're *swell*') and her need to give (the 'gingerbread and *creme-de-menthe*' song links Joan's wealth with her quality of mothering sexuality). Gerry creates Joan's 'image' for her.

Joan's escort intervenes to take her home, and in spite of her obvious pleasure in Gerry's company she leaves passively to get her coat. Gerry, after a small quarrel with Joan's friend, becomes involved in more drinking with his own friends, and when Joan comes out onto the balcony again to say goodbye we are given a subjective shot in which Gerry's vision is totally blurred—he can't see her at all, and when he asks who she is, she replies 'Oh, nobody.' From this description it can be seen that the scene is circular in structure, and that although we are given certain expectations as to what might happen next (Joan asks Gerry to tea the next day) it is rather the processes at work in the relationship between Gerry and Joan that occupy our attention, through the use of irony on the level of dialogue and image.

The next scene, showing Joan at home with her father, does not follow on easily from the first, but sets out to show a different situation: the relationship between Joan and her father in which she is depicted as child-like and over-indulged. In the first scene it is Gerry who occupies this child-like position vis-à-vis Joan. Thus by means of parallels which are also contrasts the film sets up tensions on the formal level which act as distancing mechanisms to create new meanings.

2. NARRATIVE INTERRUPTIONS

The film uses basically two forms of narrative interruption: the 'gag' and the 'pregnant moment'. Both can operate at the level of a small section of a scene, or incorporate a whole scene, but they both serve to introduce elements of discontinuity into the narrative.

Gags

An example of the short gag comes at the end of the wedding scene when Gerry places the metal corkscrew on Joan's hand instead of the ring. As she opens her hand the screw is pointing inwards, towards the soft palm of the hand. She laughs, but the vicious connotations of that image create a shock-effect on the level of their relationship and her place in it.

A long gag is used in the scene where Gerry first arrives at Joan's house, late for his tea appointment. He meets Joan's father at the door and after their initial curt encounter follows Mr Prentice into the house, practically running to keep up with the long, stern strides of the older man. Left alone, Gerry becomes interested in a picture on the far wall and has to make his way across the highly polished floor by stepping on his handkerchief so he won't lose his balance. Joan finds him there, they sit down to talk, and Gerry extends the gag as they get up to leave by expressing his insecurity again in terms of always having been used to 'places with sawdust on the floor'. The gag does nothing to further the flow of the narrative, rather it arrests it, along with any expectations we may have of the future happiness of the two protagonists.

Dance, Girl, Dance makes use of the gag as a strategy of intervention at the level of the place of the spectator in relation to the film spectacle. The burlesque show sequence plays the position of the film-audience against that of the audience *in* the film to produce a shift in meaning. We see Bubbles performing a mock striptease. From the position of the burlesque audience we watch as the wind-machine threatens to tear off all her clothes, and she hides behind a tree on the stage. The excitement of the burlesque audience is intense as Bubbles' clothes come flying onto the empty stage. The film-audience is suddenly given a privileged shot of Bubbles behind the tree, fully clothed, while the burlesque audience can still be heard whistling and shouting. In that moment our position as spectators of the spectacle is shifted, the mechanism of the phantasy structure within which Bubbles and her burlesque audience are operating is made explicit, and we are made to take a distance on our own place within the ideology of illusionism as it constructs the fictions of our Reality for us.

Pregnant moments

The force of the pregnant moment is that it works against the complex unity of the text by opening up the whole area of representation to the question of desire and its articulation. In *Merrily We Go To Hell* we see Joan at her engagement party waiting for Gerry to arrive before she announces their forthcoming marriage. The party is well under way, except for the marked absence of Gerry. Joan's father comes to the top of the stairs, the camera behind him as he dominates the party below. Cut to Joan dancing with her friend Gregg. They are chatting and move towards a large mirror on the far side of the room from the stairs and dance before it for a moment before Joan suddenly becomes aware of the 'image' of her father on the stairs, looking at her, reflected in the mirror. She stands for some seconds gazing at her own reflection in the mirror and the 'image' of her father in the background before she moves across the room to talk to him. She seems fascinated, held in a fixed relation to the 'image' in the mirror, and as *we* are faced with that image of fascination we are aware of a tension between desire and the patriarchal Law.

3. NARRATIVE REVERSALS

It has already been pointed out by Karyn Kay and Gerald Peary[4] that the narrative structure of *Dance, Girl, Dance* comprises a system of repetition and reversal, and the scenes quoted above describing the reversals which follow Judy O'Brien's speech to the burlesque audience are a good example of this method. In *Merrily We Go To Hell* we can

detect a similar structure of repetition/reversal based on the oppositions rejection/pursuit and flight/reconciliation. This form of reversal
is another way of disturbing the linear flow of the narrative: we are
pulled backwards and forwards in a play between memory and anticipation which defeats any final closure of contradictions.

In *Merrily We Go To Hell* this system is important to the central
problematic: in the absence of any code of action of her own, Joan is
forced to emulate the actions of others. This point is forcibly made in
the scene immediately following the mirror-image sequence described above. Joan's father complains irritably about Gerry's absence, because he 'can't stand for her to be humiliated'. Joan is called
outside, where she finds Gerry in a taxi lying in a foetal position, in a
drunken stupor. She becomes very upset and repeats her father's
words: 'He can't do this to me' . . . 'I can't stand the humiliation'.
She takes her car and drives wildly into the night in an attempt to
escape the intolerable pressure of contradictory demands from her
father and Gerry. As she is 'torn', so the mechanisms which attempt
to fix her place are pulled apart.

The scene of final reconciliation between Gerry and Joan is an
example of the use of ironic reversal to open up contradictions rather
than present a closure in which the destiny of the characters is sealed
and given as a fixed Truth. Joan is in the hospital after the death of her
baby. In the darkness of the hospital room she mistakes Gerry at first
for her father. Then as he kneels to put his head on her breast and
declares his love for her, she puts her arms around him and murmurs
'Gerry, my baby, my baby' as the film ends. The image of reconciliation, unity, plenitude is shot through with connotations of death, loss
and absence. The entire text of the film is cracked open as the workings of ideology in the construction of female desires is exposed.

4. PLAY WITH STEREOTYPES

The use of stereotypes in classic Hollywood cinema is generally recognised as serving a double function. As Panofsky has suggested the
use of a limited set of signs based on genre conventions in early
cinema was intended to help the audience read the narration of the
film more easily. They were given a set of fixed recognition points so
that they felt comfortable in relation to the film. However, as cinema
developed, we can see from the fact that male stereotypes changed
much more rapidly than female stereotypes that the use of
stereotypes has a specific ideological function: to represent man as inside history, and woman as eternal and unchanging, outside history.
It is this representation of myths of women as a-historical that Arz-

ner's films seek to question. By demonstrating that the fixed female stereotypes are actually a focus of contradictions for women her films cause reverberations within sexist ideology which disturb our place within it. As the myths are disengaged from ideology, the transparency of the myths is destroyed and they are recognised as constructs within representation.

Dance, Girl, Dance uses the standard stereotypes of Vamp/Straight Girl to demonstrate the operation of myth at every level of the film. Judy's position as stooge in Bubbles' act is only the logical extreme of her problem throughout the film: caught in her 'image' of a 'nice girl with class' she is also a stooge in her relationships with the rest of the girls in Madame Basilova's dancing troupe, and in her relationship with Jimmie, and finally with Steve Adams. Because the burlesque show is a logical extreme it is the point at which we can most clearly see the mechanisms of ideology at work. Bubbles controls her audience by offering them an 'image' of female sexuality which operates on the level of phantasy—an 'image' which parodies myths of women as child-like yet sexually provocative and sophisticated through the use of song and gesture. Judy's box-office value as a stooge is to stimulate the demand for Bubbles' brand of 'oomph.' The function of her performance is to increase the desire of the burlesque audience by postponing satisfaction of that desire, through her presentation of herself as spiritual, sexually innocent, dedicated to an art which transcends sexuality. By showing that both these 'images' fulfil specific demands for the burlesque audience, the film causes us to question the function of Judy's dream of dancing the 'Morning Star' ballet, which is only the other side of the coin of her burlesque performance. Judy's desires are totally compatible with the laws of sexist ideology, for as the 'Urban Ballet' sequence clearly shows (its structure is parallel, in reverse, to the burlesque show) myths of the innocence of women, whether idealised and spiritual or sexually provocative, exist at all levels of representation. By demonstrating the specific place of these myths within male-dominated culture Arzner's film denaturalises them.

Judy O'Brien's problem with her 'nice-girl image,' her contradictory desire to please others and yet fulfill her own dream, has a precedent in the form of Joan's struggle in *Merrily We Go To Hell*. This film also uses the Vamp/Straight Girl stereotypes to point up contradictions on the level of ideology, and Joan also has her 'moment of truth' when she confronts Gerry with his obsession with Claire's 'image' as she is about to leave him. The problematic of the 'nice-girl image' is presented as a problem on the level of the working through of desire. The role of the 'nice-girl' is to suppress her own desires in favour of those of the male. Yet Arzner's 'nice-girls' are shown as having desires which conflict with those of the male, at the same time as they desire to please the male. It is at this point of tension between desire and ideology in the problematic of woman as subject and object of desire that the myth breaks down, for the 'nice-girl' is impelled by her contradictory desires to explore the possibilities open to her on the level of the 'image', only to find that those possibilities are limited by factors which are outside her control.

It is on the level of 'image' that *Merrily We Go To Hell* explores this problem. When Joan describes herself as a 'nobody' to Gerry when they first meet, she is in effect offering him an empty page on which he may write his own description of her, which he proceeds to do by placing her first as her father's daughter (a child), then as a provider of loving support (the 'gingerbread and *crème-de-menthe*' song), then as a 'nice-girl' ('I think you're swell'). All aspects of this 'image' are brought into play during the film—Gerry refers to Joan more than once as 'the finest of Prentice Products', and his repetition of 'I think you're swell' continues until it is finally emptied of all significance except its ideological function (in the scene where Joan leaves him) of maintaining the image for himself after it has clearly been discarded by Joan. On the visual level Joan as a 'nice-girl' appears gift-wrapped in her wedding gown as the ideal of innocence (the place of the corkscrew gag in puncturing this image has already been noted). Joan the housewife dresses plainly and does the darning while her husband struggles creatively with his typewriter, summing up ironically his view of marriage: 'Mrs Gerry Corbett, you're Mrs Simon Legree.'[5] (As Gerry characterises himself as a slave in relation to his wife, the shot of Joan's hands darning his sock denies us the possibility of accepting his description of her as 'Mrs. Simon Legree', *i.e.*, a slave driver; by use of this irony the contradictions of the 'image' which Gerry gives Joan, contradictions which make the marriage a problem for her, are made explicit.) Again, Joan the cook is found in the kitchen dressed in a shapeless apron, apparently happy in her supportive role (the counterpart to this is Vi's bitter speech about her own failure as a wife). However, when Joan is confronted by an elegant and sophisticated Claire at the office of Gerry's agent, her own place begins to seem threatened; her 'image' becomes problematic.

Joan's problem with her place *vis-à-vis* Gerry's relationship with Claire is also formulated at the level of the 'image.' After the second meeting between Joan and Gerry when he confesses his unhappy love-affair, Gerry is shown talking to a photograph of Claire which depicts her as sexually provocative: 'I've met a girl who's just the opposite of your lovely fleshy self.' The same photograph of Claire appears later in the newspaper, which causes the fight between Gerry and the gossip-columnist over his motives for marrying Joan. In Gerry's play Claire represents a sexually experienced woman who can manipulate the demands of male ideology to make men do what she wants. Claire is public property, and it is in the tension between the place of woman as public and private property that Joan is caught. Faced with this contradiction and the prospect of losing Gerry, Joan abandons her 'nice-girl image' for that of the sophisticated and promiscuous wife, public property, a 'new identity' which is posed as problematic precisely because it is presented *as* an 'image' *articulated* in response to the demands of male ideology.

The scene which perhaps most clearly emphasises a preoccupation with the function of the image in 'holding representation at a distance' is the scene in which Gerry and Claire enact a mock love-scene in front of imaginary film cameras as Joan looks on. Gerry and Claire are framed in the doorway as they kiss, their enthusiastic audience of friends applauding. We see the 'scene' at first from behind Joan, and watch with her as the mock-kiss becomes 'real' and the mock-directors are forced to shout 'Cut!'. As Gerry and Claire become aware of Joan's presence they look towards her and in a reverse shot we now see Joan (from behind Gerry) framed in the doorway in her turn, transformed into the 'image' of an embittered, frustrated woman. This reversal, by implicating us in the pleasure/pain aspect of our voyeuristic relationship to the film, nevertheless holds off identification by reminding us that we are engaged in a process of fabricating images. This intervention prevents us from accepting the film on any level as Reality. *Merrily We Go To Hell*, by operating a process of montage of interventions, asserts the text as a process of dialectical play between image and narrative, and by implicating us in that process *as* spectators calls into question the forms of cinematographic representation through which ideology attempts to fix our place for us. From this concern in Arzner's films with the potential displacement-effect of the friction of image and diegesis[6], and the montage of interventions of ironic reversals and narrative interruptions, we can learn much about the possibility of our own intervention as feminist critics and film makers in patriarchal ideology.

---

[1]Patriarchal ideology refers to the patriarchal laws which govern our society and which produce contradictions (see Juliet Mitchell, *Psychoanalysis and Feminism*, Allen Lane, 1974).

[2]Heath bases his model of representation in the cinema on the Freudian structure of the fetish. I am suggesting that in this structure the place of woman (who is seen to be lacking the male penis, and endowed with the 'saving substitute') is fixed as the locus of the problem both of the recognition of the threat of castration, and of the disavowal of that threat

(thus she is 'the empty space which must be filled'). Heath claims that his model applies to all classic cinema. My reading of *Merrily We Go To Hell* suggests that Arzner's film offers a critique of this structure by means of a displacement of meanings which seeks to transform this 'fixed place' of the spectator. (For further discussion of this question, see 'The Place of Women in the Cinema of Raoul Walsh' by Pam Cook and Claire Johnston, op. cit.)

[3] The use of capitals is intended here and elsewhere in this article to indicate that concepts such as truth or reality are specifically constructed, not natural 'givens' with universal validity.

[4] *Dance, Girl, Dance,* by Karyn Kay and Gerald Peary, in *Velvet Light Trap* No. 10, Fall 1973, p. 26.

[5] A character from *Uncle Tom's Cabin.*

[6] The self-contained fictional world of the film.

Ava Gardner re-creates the life of a star in *The Barefoot Contessa* (1954). With her director-mentor, Humphrey Bogart.

A Very Curious Girl:

THE REVENGE OF PIRATE JENNY

KARYN KAY

A Very Curious Girl is "Dirty Mary," heroine of this acclaimed feminist work by talented French director, Nelly Kaplan. Mary rises high from local "tramp, gypsy, nobody" to town prostitute, most indispensable of local citizens. Along her furious path to the top, she exposes the sexual hypocrises of all her would-be oppressors while almost toppling the village economy.

Here is not simply another in the long line of moralistic (translation: male-conceived) prostitute pictures. *A Very Curious Girl* breaks clean of the stereotypic image of the "fallen woman" who is either killed or married off—evil punished, purity of soul rewarded. For *this* prostitute stomps on tradition, seeking revenge against all who have humiliated and degraded her; and, in the end, Mary walks off—singularly triumphant, confidently alone. As Kaplan commented about her film, "It is necessary to take revenge against one's oppressors in order to grow and continue life."

Predictably, *A Very Curious Girl* was fairly ignored by critics when first released in 1969, and much of its American run was kept to skin-flick theatres and away from art houses for "serious" foreign films. Furthermore, it was hit with an X-rating. Kaplan said in the same interview in *Women and Film*, "(M)ales . . . are strongly against the film . . . because there was no sense of sin . . . To a male dominated society a prostitute represents sex, a prostitute is full of sex and a woman with sex is something very, very dangerous and you have to punish them."[1]

Mary is an outsider. Her mysterious heritage, a past which left Mary and her mother penniless and without papers during the war, has set her apart from the more staid elements of the community; a community which used them as cheap sources of labor and sex under the guise of liberal humanitarianism (the town mayor "kindly" allowed them to sleep in his barn and work his fields without pay, when they first arrived in the village). But Mary capitalizes on her very differences. Her rebellion against past domination and servitude takes the form of prostitution—a profession marked as outside the realm of "decent" societal structures, beyond the Church, the law and family codes.

Dirty Mary is of kindred spirit to Brecht's Pirate Jenny of the *Three Penny Opera*. It is no accident that the French title of this film is *La Fiancée du Pirate* (The Pirate's Fiancee), or that Mary's song, affectionately refrained throughout the film as she conquers one after another village male, is entitled, "It's My Opera." Kaplan is inspired by the scullery maid prostitute Jenny's revenge theme, for while Jenny is "scouring the glasses/And for each one . . . making the beds," she is fantasizing a sterling revenge, the massive destruction of the town and all who have humiliated and exploited her:

> And towards noon hundreds will come on land
> And they'll walk in the shadows
> And from every doorway they will seize everyone
> And put them in chains and bring them to me
> And ask me: which one should we kill?
> And ask me: which one should we kill?
> And this noon it'll be still by the harbor
> When they ask who will have to die
> And then you'll hear me say: All of em![2]

Mary, like Pirate Jenny, is first seen working in serf-like conditions, here for the lecherous, guardian/slave-master Irene. Mary scrubs the floors, feeds Irene's ancient father, "Pops" (a grotesque refugee from a Bunuel movie), while ineffectually fighting off the sexual assaults of Julian, Irene's grubbing farmhand. But unlike Jenny whose song of revenge is mere fantasy, dependent upon pirate champions and dragon-like black freighters, Mary's revenge soon is to be carried out, and singlehandedly.

The revenge is precipitated by the sudden automobile accident death of Mary's mother (another in this line of gypsy tramps) and by the subsequent cruel treatment of the corpse by the townspeople. The village mayor, local pharmacist, grocer and priest lug the mother's body, like so much dirty garbage, home to Mary's shanty cabin. There they argue over money and religious burial proceeedings and how to dispose quickly of this dead being.

Mary ends debate with the scandalous announcement that her mother will not be buried by the church, for neither she, nor her mother, "believe in God." But having rejected a "proper" church funeral, there remains for Mary the problem of how to bury her mother. The answer to Mary's query becomes the first step in her master plan to control the village.

While prowling among her mother's sparse possessions, Mary discovers a pendant, perfume and money, material objects to be used as clever tools in her sinister revenge. She travels to the grocery store, purchases large quantities of wine with her mother's money. The townsmen, lured to Mary's house on the promise of wine and party and possibly free sex, will, when drunk, bury her mother.

Before the men arrive for this weird funeral ritual, Mary, in a darkened room, illuminated dimly by occasional candles, begins an incredible process of self-transformation. Seated before a large mirror, she applies burnt match cinders as black eye liner and crushed red berries as lip rouge. Gradually she metamorphosizes from passive, gypsy waif into painted witch-seductress. The male villagers don't have a chance.

Mary uses to good purpose the information gleaned from Mrs. Peachum and Pirate Jenny in their "Ballad of Sexual Dependency." Though men may fight involvement with the blatantly sexual female, no matter, for they ultimately will be allured by their own fevered desires:

> Many a man saw another go to pot:
> A great mind mired in a whore!
> And those who watched this, no matter what they
>   swore—
> When they rotted, who buried them? Whores.
> Whether they want to or not—they are ready.
> That's sexual dependency.
>   This one is guided by the Bible. That one gives not a hang for the
>   Civil Code.
>   This one becomes a Christian. That one an anarchist.
> At noon they force themselves to abstain . . .
> But before the night falls, they lie again on top.[3]*

Superficially, Mary's relationship with the townspeople remains constant when she turns to whoredom. She is still the sexually sub-

---

*Or, as Valerie (Wounder of Andy Warhol) Solanas tersely put it:

> Eaten up with guilt, shame, fears and insecurities and obtaining, if he's lucky, a barely perceptible physical feeling, the male is, nonetheless, obsessed with screwing; he'll swim a river of snot, wade nostril-deep through a mile of vomit, if he thinks there'll be a friendly pussy awaiting him. He'll screw a woman he despises . . . and . . . pay for the opportunity.
>
> —Valerie Solanas, SCUM Manifesto, p. 33[4]

jected "Gypsy tramp." But now the men and even Irene (who has used Mary in an an uncomfortable lesbian relationship**) must pay for what they took for free. Therefore, a most significant change has occured: the transference of power.

No one remains unscathed by Mary's newly found profession. Every male is willing to lie, cheat and steal for Mary's services, while she grows solvent on their "sexual dependency." But, as Brenda Roman explains in her excellent article on the picture in *Women and Film*, Mary's ". . .object is not so much to make money but to become independent and to humiliate her clients—first by making them pay, and then by raising her prices arbitrarily, in that way asserting the change in power relations."[5]

When Mary raises her prices and the townsmen threaten wage control, Mary publically ravishes free of charge an inveterate bum named Jesus (an appropriate name in the upside down world of Nelly Kaplan, who uses every chance to insult the powerful, propertied French Catholic Church). The townsmen watch in horror this odd coupling of Jesus and Mary realizing their total enslavement to her and her utter indifference to them.***

Mary takes her earnings to surrounding villages (never the local stores) zestfully purchasing hordes of seemingly useless material objects. She decorates the once bleak, barren walls of her one-room sanctuary with flamboyant, brightly colored piles of junk: watches, dresses, underwear, feathers, pillows, pictures (one, a WANTED poster of a man she claims to be her father), cookies L'Amour and wine. No inch of space in her cabin remains uncluttered.

She could never before afford such reckless consumerism, but now she flaunts before the villagers the objects of newly acquired power and independent means. (This is also perhaps Kaplan's way of slapping at the liberal bourgeois audience watching the film, who might wish Mary's spending to reflect some "positive" middle-class values.) Not all these good are worthless junk, however. Some objects will be used in her revenge: a record and phonograph will help seduce her victims; a tape player, which records intimate bedroom conversations, will be utilized later to humiliate the villagers.

Mary has only two friends, Andre, a roving movie projectionist (who will be discussed shortly) and a nameless goat. Like the mythical Pan who had the body of a goat and the head of a man, Mary's animal comrade has the frame of a goat and the spirit of an ideal human, for he embodies all the humane characteristics so keenly absent

---

**Here is a strange lapse in Nelly Kaplan's feminist perspective. It is an unfortunately traditional image to equate lesbianism with lechery.

***Whether she represents the Virgin Mary or Mary Magdalene seems irrelevant to this inspired blasphemy.

in the townspeople. As if to a lover, Mary croons to her goat, "Do I look nice? . . . Do you love me? You're not like those bums who kiss me at night and beat me in the morning." Mary is the inverse of this creature, part animal/part person, for while she is clearly a human being, she is treated like a beast by the villagers. While trying to lure Mary back to the farm, Irene quivers, "I fed you and kept you like a pet," to which Mary insightfully replies, "In my house, I'm no animal."

Both the goat and Mary symbolize a threat to the community. Pan, the god of the goatherds and shepherds, who romped with the woodland nymphs, is the reification of perfect natural sexuality, and the goat, like the prostitute Mary, symbolizes this unbridled sensuality—"full of sex and . . . dangerous." Because of their licentious spirits, the villagers are ripe to destroy them.[6]

Gaston, the voyeuristic, ex-militarist mailman, tries, unsuccessfully at first, to kill the goat with the very gun he toted in French/Viet Namese battles. But when Mary is accused of "stealing" Emile from his wife and five children, the whole town chases her with the ferocity of a western lynch mob. This frenzied pursuit ends with the goat lying dead of bullet wounds at the feet of the angry crowd.

Andre, the journeyman movie projectionist, is Mary's single human friend. A transient of nameless origins, he is an exotic stranger, peripheral to the community—Mary's nomadic twin of the "gypsy, tramp" spirit. While Mary wanders from man to man, Andre wanders from town to town screening films.

Mary and Andre are spiritual and financial allies against the village. Even as the priest must pay the regular price, three francs, to view Andre's films, Mary pays only two and watches the movie at Andre's side. When the villagers grumble about her presence, Andre advises them to leave with refunds.

Andre, in line with the fantasy pirate who aids Jenny in her *Three Penny Opera* song (piracy being a romantization of the nomadic existence), becomes an accomplice to Mary's revenge. He takes her to town to purchase her first "weapons," the tape, record and phonograph. And later he brings cookies and other seductive supplies to her house. Although Andre pays to sleep with Mary (just as she pays to see his movies), he is not typical of Mary's other customers, not simply another of her many victims. He suggests that she leave the village with him. To do what? "Watch movies all the time." Yet he is not hurt when she rejects his proposal, for her appreciates her need for independence and understands that Mary must avenge her past before she can create an alternative future (either with or without the movie man).**** Yet there is an inexplicable bond between them.

****It is tempting to see Andre as a fictional guise of French film genius Abel Gance, for whom Nelly Kaplan worked in close association as assistant director. But such a connection is for Nelly Kaplan to make.

When Andre leaves Mary's house for the last time, despite her urgings ("Are you sure you didn't forget anything? Are you sure you can't stay?"), Kaplan holds the camera on Mary, brooding and alone. Unlike her feelings for any other person in the film, Mary cares about him. And the striking contrast is touching.

But back to the revenge. Mary invades the local Church, filled with the now-pious hypocrites (her regular customers) and their God-fearing families. As the priest intones about her presence ("If one sheep strays, is it not the priest's duty to leave the other ninety-nine and retrieve the one?), Mary answers his condescending message by turning her tape recorder, which she has placed high on an alter, on full force. Like the voice of a blasphemous, trickster god, the tape talks itself out, repeating the actual moments when these puritan churchgoers were playing piggishly in Mary's lair.

Mary walks triumphant from the church as the infuriated villagrs smash the recorder and rip the tape to shreds. Not satisfied, they race on to Mary's house, planning to knock it also to the ground. But Mary has anticipated their Christian behavior, and burned it down herself. While the townspeople relieve their fury by stomping on the graves of Mary's mother and goat, marked reverently by abstract statues composited from the leftover junk, Mary's attention is already elsewhere.

A joyous Mary is now swinging down a country road after her ferocious exit from the choking French village. She literally has burned her bridges behind her and now throws off her shoes in an exhilirating final act of freedom. But she pauses a minute in her skipping farewell to notice a sign advertising the public screening of Andre's new film. The title is *La Fiancee du Pirate*, Mary's own story of course. The picture is playing in a nearby town, and an arrow on the poster points in the direction Mary is heading. She moves on.

A Very Curious Girl is a conscious homage by Nelly Kaplan to at least one other film Joseph Mankiewicz's 1954 *The Barefoot Contessa*, the movie which Andre shows to the villagers. The story of a woman whose sexuality led others to destroy her starred Ava Gardner as a night club dancer who rises from anonymity in the slums of Madrid to Hollywood stardom. Along the way, she has a series of brutalizing encounters with the wealthy, sychophantic men who inhabit the entertainment, night-life world. They treat her as a showpiece with little more signicance than diamond cuff-links. They display her attractions to the world, while ignoring her emotional and physical needs. When Gardner finally believes that she has found a satisfying relationship, her count husband proves incapable of sexual intercourse, having married her to provide his family line with one last beautiful contessa. And when Gardner expresses her own sexual inclinations outside of the marriage, her impotent husband kills off his object of adulation rather than share any part of her.

Gardner has one friend, her movie director and confidante, Humphrey Bogart, to whom *A Very Curious Girl*'s Andre bears striking character resemblance. Like Andre, he maintains a facade of neutrality while actually sympathetic to Gardner's unconventional behavior. He is the only person who understands that her sexual indulgences are provisions for security, and he demands nothing from her.

Dirty Mary is like the barefoot contessa in her similar objectificaton by the "respectable" villagers as a device of sexual fulfillment. And when Mary's indulgences transform into threatening subversion, the outraged citizenry attempt to destroy her. Yet she emerges victorious from her assault, and in so doing seems to avenge the Contessa Maria's murder

The final scene of *A Very Curious Girl* pays allegiance to still a second movie, borrowing freely from the famous conclusion of Sternberg's *Morocco*. Mary's barefooted departure from the French village in the general direction of Andre follows from Marlene Dietrich's Amy Jolly tromping after French legionnaire Gary Cooper into the desert, an act which necessitates her pulling off the high heeled shoes which inhibit her gait.

As with most Sternberg characters, Jolly has intentionally imprisoned herself behind masks, gestures, accoutrements which not only alienate others from herself but ultimately prove self-alienating and self-defeating. Therefore her grand exit as she strips down to a white dress and no more to trek into the desert is instantly significant as an act of purgation. Nelly Kaplan takes Jolly's action to heart by having Dirty Mary likewise burn all that she owns—veils, feathers, balloons—and walk freely, without even a suitcase, down the country road.

Andre is without knowledge that Mary might be coming to him. *Morocco*'s Gary Cooper walks so far ahead that he has no idea that Amy Jolly follows many paces behind, hidden among the Arab women, isolated in race and language from all around her. Essentially, she exists only for herself. She walks away from the safe oasis straight into a desert wasteland, an arid, asexual, unfertile clime; into the obliteration of a fierce desert storm, the wind literally sweeping off with her identity. Ultimately, Dietrich seeks something greater than Cooper: the ideal, perfect freedom, found perhaps on the other side of oblivion.

There is none of this passion marking the close of *A Very Curious Girl*, which is a scene of quiet celebration in the sun. While Amy Jolly walks into a rippling storm, Dirty Mary has emerged, perhaps forever, from the darkness.

A Very Curious Girl thus concludes as not only an answer to the song of Pirate Jenny, but as a happy alternative to the miserable conclusion of *The Barefoot Contessa* and the torment of *Morocco*. Pirate Jenny dreams a revenge which Mary carries through. While the Contessa is shot dead, Mary admirably survives her mental and physical subjugation. Though Amy Jolly discards her identity, the close of *A Very Curious Girl* is a victory of self-discovery, of an identity won.

A Very Curious Girl carries everywhere its responsibility, yet some might claim it irresponsibility. Is Nelly Kaplan's ending far too easy, a simplistic, popular conclusion, and a panacea to all exploitation of women on screen and elsewhere? Or, intrinsic to this film, does Kaplan offer any genuine solution to the complex dilemma of Mary's life? Would Mary really walk away free?

In her article on *A Very Curious Girl* in *Women and Film*, Brenda Roman articulated the basic problem. She suggests a more ironic Brechtian ending: a final verse to "It's My Opera" which would expose the reality of Mary's condition, and undercut the unbridled optimism which pervades.

> (I)n real life the townsmen would have imposed their "price control" in earnest. Mary would be reduced to servitude again, her rebellion crushed. And the villagers' humiliation would be at the price of her own. She would be unlikely to have such an ideal means of escape, since the lover . . .is an illusion, very much like the mounted messenger from the Queen in *The Three Penny Opera* who delivers a pardon at the last minute. In real life "they come far too seldom."

Ms. Roman has raised a provocative objection without easy answers, but it is tempting to dismiss it anyway—at least just this once, at this still pioneering time of women's consciousness in filmmaking. Nelly Kaplan offers a villainous female heroine who gets away with her crimes, and for women such chances to be nasty, triumphant and terribly, terribly dirty "come far too seldom."

[1]Harris, Kay, "An Interview with Nelly Kaplan," *Women and Film*, no. 2

[2]Bertolt Brecht (words), Kurt Weill (music), "Pirate Jenny or Dreams of a Kitchen Maid," "The Three Penny Opera," translated by Ray Stern.

[3]"Three Penny Opera," "The Ballad of Sexual Dependency"

[4]Solanas, Valerie, S.C.U.M. Manifesto (Society for Cutting Up Men), New York, 1968, p. 33

[5]Roman, Brenda, "Dirty Mary," *Women and Film*, no. 1.

[6]Hamilton, Edith, *Mythology*, (Boston, Mass.), 1940, p. 40.

Lina Wertmüller:

SWEPT AWAY ON A WAVE OF SEXISM

MOLLY HASKELL

Lina Wertmüller has stated that her purpose as a left-wing Italian filmmaker is to make movies with a political message that will appeal to the masses, i.e., the working classes. I don't know how her movies fare in poor Italian neighborhoods, but on New York's upper East Side, which is hardly Daily Worker territory, they seem to have found an enthusiastic audience. Is this, possibly, because Miss Wertmüller does not pursue the correct Marxist or social-realist line to its constructive conclusion, but ends with a more romantically pessimistic view wherein the individual is confounded by political realities?

In the three Lina Wertmüller films that I have seen—*Love and Anarchy*, *The Seduction of Mimi*, and now *Swept Away By an Unusual Destiny in the Blue Sea of August*—the most moving scenes are their three endings: Giancarlo Giannini as the whore-house pet and would-be assassin of Mussolini meeting his own death; Giancarlo Giannini, husband(of one woman) and lover (of another) selling out his political principles; and Giancarlo Giannini, returned to civilization, waiting in vain for this tamed capitalist shrew (Mariangela Melato) to return to their island paradise. Scenes of failure, betrayal, blinding disappointment, disillusionment. Scenes that do not stir the audience to action, but console it with the idea that political impotence is the consequence of an excess of humanity. Or rather, hu*man*-ity.

Are the scenes moving because of the stray-dog quality of Giannini himself, a wire-haired terrier with straggly hair and huge, sad eyes that, like Al Pacino's, plead for martyrdom? Or because, in the throes of an emotional convulsion, political sympathies are swept away by the drama of the individual psyche, the only drama, as Wertmüller instinctively knows, that it is truly 'popular.' The ending of *Swept Away*, with its aching sense of loss and regret, is as surefire romantic as that of *The Way We Were*, only it has much less to do with what has preceded it: a scantily-clad Marxist allegory in which Thesis and Antithesis are stranded on a deserted island. Thesis ("rich capitalist bitch") is overthrown—abused, beaten, degraded, penetrated—by Antithesis (sexy Sicilian communist male), and in the reversal of the master-slave relationship a temporary synthesis is struck. With woman's subjugation, love blossoms miraculously, in a manner closer to the Gloria Swanson movie version of *The Admirable Crichton* (retitled *Male and Female* lest small-town '20s moviegoers mistake it for a sea story!) than to James M. Barrie's witty play.

But to begin at the beginning. A private cruise ship lolls lazily in the Mediterranean, in waters just beyond human and chemical pollution, and thus just beyond human imagination. It is over 10 years since *L'Avventura*, and the ruling class has roused itself from ennui and intramural bitchery to hurl epithets across the socioeconomic divide.

Raffaella (Mariangela Melato), an imperious blonde lady, gives vent to reactionary sentiments in gusts of Italian invective, larded with the usual anti-Communist catchwords—Stalin, Siberia, etc. A fellow guest counterattacks with slogans from the male liberal catechism. But the real butt of Signora's increasingly personal vituperations is a crew member, the sad-eyed Gennarino (Giannini), who grumbles about the way upper-class men let their wives run loose. (This "minus" character trait, like Raffaella's "plus" stands on abortion and ecology, is an attempt at a more equal distribution of sympathy. But why do I feel, even so, that Wertmüller endorses Gennarino's sexism, and despises Raffaela's enlightenment? I'll get to that later.) In planting its two sexual/political antagonists in opposite corners of the ring, the film—unless I am missing something in translation—has so far exhibited all the incisiveness of a political cartoon without a punch line.

When the two find themselves adrift on the high seas, Raffaella, unconcerned, keeps up her diatribe with an inappropriateness that is apparently deliberate. I say apparently, because it is never clear precisely on what level of unreality Wertmüller is operating. The artificiality of the basic situation—these two mouthpieces of the class struggle adrift, like the owl and the pussycat, in a beautiful yellow dinghy, against a backdrop that is superbly and serenely real—sets up an incongruity that continues on the island—as metaphoric an island as ever there was, but photographed with the naturalistic eye of a travel documentary.

And what are we meant to think when the roles are reversed, and political antagonism metamorphoses into sexual desire. Gennarino turns sadist and, in the venerable tradition of man gratifying woman's sexual fantasies as envisioned by men ("understanding" her as she doesn't understand herself), he brutalizes her so that she can emerge in her true colors as the Whore She Really is Down Deep. It would be easier to interpret this as an ironic commentary, however unoriginal, if Wertmüller didn't orchestrate all that lush music, lighting, and seminude love scenes to convince us of the bliss of sexual surrender, and the genuine passion of two lovers released at last to enjoy their "natural" roles.

Wertmuller's gallery of female grotesques—the whores in *Love and Anarchy*, the huge fat woman in *The Seduction of Mimi*, and here, that arch-villainess cherished by Old Left and Macho Right alike, the frigid blonde tease—are such that she can claim to have challenged the stereotype by exaggeration, while indulging it with a relish she shares with male members of the audience. Anyone who doesn't appreciate the howling hilarity of these "parodies" is threatened with the label of humorless feminist.

Wertmüller's male chauvinism, her identification with the male sex, is insidious. All of her women are treated as nonpersons, as types—the whore, the bitch, the devouring wife—while the man— Giancarlo Giannini—is always treated as a person, a character who extends by virtue of his emotional complexity beyond the class or sexual function that defines the others. (Proof that her animus attaches to gender rather than class is that the upper-class men are not caricatures while the lower-class women are.) The reason that Raffaella's original stridency doesn't disturb us, and neither does her conversion perplex us, is that we never see her as a real woman, while Gennarino is never less than a man, and an idealized one at that. (Earlier, he has expressed the puritanical disapproval of sex and drugs typical of his class, but later, when it comes to servicing his Lady Chatterley, he is thoroughly liberated in his attitude toward certain shall we say "advanced" sexual practices.) Her virtues, such as they are, are ridiculous, while his class defects are heroic, or at least winning. His ignorance is proof of his unwarped mind; yet he is cultivated enough to wipe his mouth fastidiously with a leaf after eating.

With 11 films behind her, Wertmüller is probably the most technically accomplished, certainly the most experienced woman filmmaker working today. She is also the one who least identifies with the concerns and interests of the women's movement, from which she has repeatedly dissociated herself, proclaiming the "androgyny" of the

artists. Well, critics can be androgynes too, and I hope I'm man
enough to be able to admit to liking a film even though it might treat
men shabbily.

But aside from the fact that the humor of *Swept Away* eludes me
(wit, I realize, is too class-bound a concept to expect in proletarian
comedy), I don't buy its premise. From the notion that love is political, which I accept only in the loosest, most figurative sense, it is but one
short, false step to constructing a "love story" around political positions. Like the forced parallel between sexual and economic politics,
such formulae may strike an occasional spark of insight from the essayist, but they are poor starting points for fiction. In *The Middle of the
World*, Alain Tanner tried and failed to establish such an analogy, and
the characters owed much of the richness they achieved to the failure
of the analogy to "take." But in *Swept Away by an Unusual Destiny in
the Blue Sea of August*, scheme precedes essence. As interesting as Giannini and Melato are as actors their characters, drawn from the raw material of dialectics, are stillborn.

Viva with Jim Rado (left) and Jerome Ragni in Agnès Varda's *Lions Love* (1969).

Reflections on "Jeanne Dielman"

MARSHA KINDER

Jeanne Dielman, 23 Quai du Commerce—1080 Bruxelles (1975) is the most important film to première at this year's Filmex and the best feature that I have ever seen made by women. Starring Delphine Seyrig in the title role, the film was written, directed, and produced by Chantal Akerman (who was only 25 at the time), photographed by Babette Mangolte, and edited by Patricia Canino. Akerman belongs among that select group of filmmakers—including Welles, Bertolucci, and Fassbinder—who have created a boldly original, highly crafted masterpiece while still in their twenties.

Like many other current films focusing on women, *Jeanne Dielman* does not present a strong, positive female protagonist; Jeanne is a bourgeois widow trapped in meaningless social rituals that ultimately cause her to commit a desperate, insane act. Yet, by developing a style that is so innovative, Akerman totally transforms the material—over three and a half hours devoted to mundane gestures without any camera movement or closeups whatsoever. When I interviewed her at Filmex, she said:

> You can't tell what effect a film will have, to show the trap may bring a revolt. I don't know the alternative. The important thing is the style, the form. It shows everybody has conditioning. The attention I show to this woman's gestures is very positive, to show that someone doing the dishes can also be used for art, that is positive.

Akerman's unconventional style expresses a feminine perspective and sensibility. More than any other film-maker, she makes us realize how previous films have been almost totally restricted to a male point of view. Despite the limitations of her character Jeanne, Akerman and her female crew provide a radical feminine perspective that enriches our perception of the world. Delphine Seyrig, who also was present at Filmex, felt this contrast very intensely.

> In this role I experienced the things I've been trying to get away from all my life. What was most difficult for me was *not* to express any revolt or aggression. As I became Jeanne Dielman, I realized how easy it is to be a woman like that. Women are very malleable, they all play roles, not just actresses; they adapt more easily than men do. I felt this experience has never been shown before. No man could have made this film; it is a totally feminine film.

Unlike her heroine, Chantal Akerman has successfully rebelled against the traps laid for a Belgian bourgeoise. Born in Brussels in 1950, she developed her artistic ambitions quite young. At fifteen when she saw Godard's *Pierrot le Fou,* she decided to become a filmmaker. By seventeen she began studying directing and photography at the INSAS, a professional high school. Following the '68 riots, she went to Paris, where she attended the International University Theater. The radical influences are already strong in her first experimental shorts: *Saute Ma Ville (Blow Up My City),* 1969, and *The Loved Child,* 1971. In 1972 she lived in New York's East Village, where she was influenced by East Coast experimental film-making, which is apparent in her next group of films: *Hotel Monterrey,* 1972; *The Room 15 x 18,* 1972; and *Hanging Out in Yonkers,* 1973.

> I saw the films of Michael Snow and Jonas Mekas—they opened my mind to many things—the relationship between film and your body, time as the most important thing in film, time and energy. Seeing their films gave me courage to try something else, not just to make money. Before I went to New York, say in 1968, I thought Bergman and Fellini were the greatest film-makers. Not any more, because they are not dealing with time and space as the most important elements in film.

When she returned to Europe, she directed her first dramatic feature, *Je, Tu, Il, Elle,* 1974, a semiautobiographical film about the people she had met on three trips. Although this film did very well in Paris, none of her work has been distributed in this country.*

According to Akerman, *Jeanne Dielman* was "the result of my research, on form in the USA and on story-telling in Europe." She takes her expanded consciousness home to Brussels and concentrates it on the narrowest of subjects—a woman from her mother's generation who is trapped in the very conventions that Akerman has escaped. She admits:

> I didn't escape from my mother. This is a love film to my mother. It gives recognition to that kind of woman, it gives her "a place in the sun."

*Her latest feature *News from Home* will be shown for the first time at Cannes.

It is her first film to use a conventional plot or linear structure, yet she transforms them into a means of expressing a radical vision. Earlier she had written another script about a woman in her forties, but was dissatisfied.

> In 1973 I worked on a script with a friend of mine, but it was too explanatory—it didn't come from within myself. I got money to do it, but after awhile I realized it was not good. One night, the whole film came to me in one second. I suppose it came from my memories of all the women in my childhood, from my unconscious. I sat down and wrote it with no hesitation, no doubts. The same was true when I made the film. I did it like a bulldozer. You can feel it in the film. I knew exactly what to shoot and where to put the camera.

The film covers three days in the life an attractive widow living with her son (played by Jan Decorte). It focuses on the banalities of common experience that absorb the time and energy of the average middle-class woman—shopping for food, cooking a meal, dusting the furniture, brushing her hair, cleaning her body and her bathtub. These repetitive rituals that fill her empty life and help maintain her sanity are the same kinds of actions documented by Anna Wulf in a chapter of Doris Lessing's *Golden Notebook*. In the case of Jeanne Dielman, one of these daily habits is sleeping with a man for money; but, in the context of her life, it is no more significant than any of the other rituals. Within the repetitiveness of the pattern, she arranges for minimal variations each day of the week, she serves a different kind of meat, fixes the potatoes in a different way, and is fucked by a different man. The film explores what happens when the routine is violated. One day she gets up too early, she misbuttons her robe, she drops a spoon, she makes the coffee too strong, she leaves soap on one of her plates, she can't match a button, she leaves a pair of scissors out of place. These minor deviations are combined with too many unsettling surprises: a stamp machine is empty, she receives a disappointing birthday gift, she is rejected by a crying infant. As a result of these disruptions, she has an orgasm and commits a murder.

The film explores the relationship between identity and action. If a woman is what she does, then why is it that movies never show us the thousands of familiar moves that comprise a woman's life? Trapped in the passive roles defined by the culture, women perform actions that are considered boring and non-dramatic—except for having sex, giving birth, or going mad. In male-dominated action films, women are either passive sex objects or destructive sirens, victims or maniacs, mothers or whores. Jeanne is all of these things, yet these actions and roles do not define her adequately or completely. A more conventional film would focus on Jeanne primarily as a murderer or a prostitute, but the structure that Akerman uses prevents us from doing so. In understanding and judging her as a human being, we are forced to take into consideration all of the details that are ordinarily omitted from movies because it is precisely these banalities that explain her desperation and violence.

Time and space, the two mental constructs by which humans organize experience, are treated unconventionally. Most of the scenes are shot in real time. When Jeanne bathes before dinner, we don't see merely a few erotic glimpses of flesh in the water; rather, we witness the entire functional process as she actually scrubs every part of her body and then cleans out the tub. The graphic details destroy the eroticism and make us aware of just how unrealistic and contrived most other bath scenes really are. This use of real time forces us to see how many steps are involved in each simple task. It also accentuates the central problem of boredom: Jeanne is not terrified by "Time's winged chariot," but by the "vast deserts of eternity" that threaten to engulf her. On the morning when she awakens too early, the day stretches before her like an empty chasm; she repeatedly runs to the clock in a panic as if to make the hours pass more quickly, but these desperate motions only slow things down. Ordinarily, she copes with this problem in two ways: by dividing and patterning her time, and by trying to anticipate every move, but this makes her less capable of dealing with anything new or unpredictable. Akerman's style follows the same strategy and, as a result, it heightens the impact of every surprise.

The film is divided into three parts, like three stages in a ritual that are set off by titles ("the end of the first day," "the end of the second day"). After the first cycle, we learn the rituals and recognize the ways in which Jeanne anticipates her next move—laying a fresh towel out on the bed for her daily customer, buying wool before she runs out of it in her knitting, frugally switching lights on and off as she moves through the rooms of her apartment, saving the flour left over from breading the veal, always knowing who is at the door.

We also learn to anticipate the habits of the camera. On the second day, as she stands in her kitchen wearing her apron and hears the doorbell, we recognize that this is an exact repetition of the opening scene. She moves at the same pace; and predictably, the camera is in the same position when she reaches the door. Only the clothes have been changed: she wears a different blouse and is handed a different coat and hat. We know that we are not going to see the sex; instead, we anticipate that the next shot will be of the hallway, the lights will dim to indicate the passing of time, then she and her customer will emerge fully clothed from the bedroom, and he will say at the door, "See you next Thursday," and she will receive the same amount of money and will put it in the china dish on her dining room table. Yet she is disturbed by this encounter. We know this because she burns the potatoes and disrupts her schedule. Even the editing is affected. In later scenes, we enter at a slightly more advanced stage in the ritual; of Thursday's bath, we see only the cleaning of the tub.

Because time is so central in establishing the order, the disruptions are first experienced as a violation of sequence and a gradual acceleration of pace both in the editing and in Jeanne's movements. As the panic grows, her motions become more ragged and abrupt, her breathing quickens, she slams doors and cabinets a little too hard. When her Friday customer rings, she is not preparing dinner in her kitchen as usual but is unwrapping an ugly pink nightgown from her sister in Canada. Despite the slowness of the day, she has been caught unaware, and must stuff the garment back in the box and hide the package under the bed, lay the scissors on the dresser, and hurry to the door. We are similarly surprised by the camerawork and editing. The film cuts directly to a new subject at a new angle, something we never expected to see—the sex scene. Jeanne sits in front of the bedroom mirror, methodically removing her blouse; the sound of a cough informs us that her customer is present. Then in an overhead shot, we witness Jeanne lying on her back impassively staring at the ceiling while the man lies on top of her, breathing heavily. In slow cycles, she blinks her eyes and opens and closes her right hand. His breathing accelerates, and so does hers, as she loses control. Frantically trying to push him away, she writhes on the bed and covers her face with the quilt. Then she quiets down; a mysterious smile mixed with disgust moves across her face, and she tries to push him away. Her composure restored, she silently dresses as he watches her in the mirror. When he lies back on the bed, we continue to watch Jeanne in the mirror as she slowly finishes dressing, casually picks up the scissors on the dresser, then lunges at his throat. The murder is followed by an extremely long take of Jeanne sitting immobile at the dining room table in the dark, with bloodstains on her hands and the collar of her white blouse, her image reflected in the highly polished wood. The only movement is the reflection of outside lights flashing on the china closet and the sounds of passing traffic. In Seyrig's words, "she falls back into a lack of expression; I felt there was nothing more she could express." Gradually Jeanne begins to drop her head, then lifts it, smiles mysteriously and shuts her eyes. The film ends with this image fading to a comfortable dark blue.

The full title of the film immediately tells us that Jeanne Dielmann is defined and circumscribed by the space she occupies—"23 Quai du Commerce—1080 Bruxelles." The patterns of her life have been determined by the social-economic structures of her society. In the post office, an old woman stands patiently waiting at a window as though she has had a lifetime of training in this pastime; the department stores are full of other middle-aged women like Jeanne on quests for buttons and notions. As in the *Diaries of Anais Nin,* the consciousness and body of the female protagonist are identified with her rooms and house; all are empty spaces waiting to be entered and activated by the male visitor.

Akerman's visual treatment of space is very radical. She describes it as "essentialist and very stylized, distanced and warm." There are no close-ups; the camera never moves. The few outdoor shots are usually wide-angle; indoors, there are only medium shots. The camera relentlessly remains fixed in one spot, revealing a comfortable space that characters enter and abandon. While Bresson uses a similar technique in *Une Femme Douce,* his static camera was associated with the point of view of the husband, who entrapped his wife and drove her to suicide; here, Akerman links it to the feminine condition that has been imposed by the entire society. Yet, like Anais Nin, she also recognizes and develops the positive resources of this perspective. Not only are the colors and compositions soothing (the pastel blues and greens and pale yellows in the kitchen, the aqua tones of Jeanne's coat and the matching shutters in front of the shoemaker shop, the solidity of the cherrywood wardrobe, the symmetrical division of the screen between Jeanne knitting in the dining room and her son reading in the living room), but our long exposure to these sharply focused images allows us to appreciate their nuances.

This mode of perception expands our consciousness and leads us to a Jamesian form of realism.

> The power to guess the unseen from the seen, to trace the implication of things, to judge the whole piece by the pattern, the condition of feeling life in general so completely that you are well on your way to knowing any particular corner of it—this cluster of gifts may almost be said to constitute experience.[*]

Akerman cultivates the unseen. In her own words, "to say the most, you show the least." There are no flashbacks to the past, just a few photographs always seen at a distance. Except for a walk around the block and a few shopping expeditions, Jeanne and the camera are confined to the small apartment; the outside world must be perceived by means of flickering shadows on the walls and furniture and traffic noises that filter into her narrow life. We never see the sister in Canada though we judge her from her letter and gifts and from Jeanne's reactions. We never see the son's friend Yan, though he is fre-

*Henry James, "The Art of Fiction," *Longman's Magazine* (1884).

quently mentioned. We never see the mother who brings her infant to Jeanne, though we hear her voice (which is actually Chantal Akerman's). We must wait until the second day to see the baby; on the first day, we see only his pink booties. We must wait till the third day to see the sexual encounter.

The most important omission is the access to what is going on inside of Jeanne's mind—there are no voice-overs, no soliloquies, no subjective inserts, and minimal dialogue. We see only her external surface and, if we are to understand her behavior and her experience, we must "guess the unseen from the seen." We learn to recognize subtle signs—a stray lock of hair and the quickening of her step. When Jeanne is silent and alone, we watch her sitting in a comfortable chair, breathing faster than usual and shifting her eyes more rapidly; we know she is trying desperately to think of something to do. She pops up suddenly and goes to dust the furniture before slumping back into a dangerous lethargy. Later, as the panic worsens, she sits rigidly in a chair, her muscles tightening as we watch her in a very long take; finally, she raises a finger, as if she has thought of something to do, but then drops it as if she has rejected that idea. Immediately her breathing grows more rapid and her anxiety more intense.

Delphine Seyrig gives a brilliant performance; she is always fascinating to watch even when she is frozen and impassive. Not since Liv Ullmann in Bergman's *Persona* or Falconetti in Dreyer's *Passion of Joan of Arc* has an actress had such a difficult role that demands such a range of subtle expressiveness from her face and body. Both Seyrig and Akerman would delight Béla Balázs by the forceful way they recover and advance the language of gesture and facial expression. Seyrig goes far beyond any of her previous performances, perhaps because she is so totally committed to the film's radical vision.

> I think it's a very important film—a new step forward—not just for me, but for the history of film-making. I usually take an interest in the form or style of the films I act in; yet I realize that as an actress, I've been expressing things that are not my own, but others'. I feel a much greater involvement in this film. It's not a coincidence that Chantal asked me to do it. It's not just being an actress, but acting within a context that means something to me personally. This never happened to me before. In the past I was always able to bring something I liked to the part I was playing, something between the lines. But now I feel I don't have to hide behind a mask, I can be my own size. It changes acting into action, what it was meant to be.

The opportunity of working with a predominantly female crew also influenced her performance.

I have become aware how inhibiting it is to be watched on a set mostly by men. A woman is a foreigner in an all-male world—the film industry. I wanted to be surrounded by women in this part so that I wouldn't behave in any way other than I would as Jeanne Dielman. There is a difference in the way you walk when you are in a room full of men rather than a room full of women—you don't undress the same way, wash the same way, or brush your hair the same way. It is important that I be looked at by women while working.

The creation of Jeanne is a harmonious collaboration between Seyrig and Akerman.

Jeanne's interactions with other characters are frequently nonverbal but always highly revealing. On the third day when she tries to cuddle the baby, the infant senses her anxiety and begins to cry. Frustrated by the rejection, Jeanne takes revenge on the baby's mother by taking longer than usual to answer the door and by cutting off conversation. Later, when she goes to a restaurant for coffee, she finds another woman sitting in her usual place. While Jeanne takes the next table, the camera remains in its former position. Upset by the deviation in the routine, Jeanne asks for the usual waitress. That's the only dialogue in the scene. Yet, we learn a great deal by observing the two women—Jeanne looking vacantly and distractedly around the room and leaving abruptly, while the other woman smokes, reads, writes, and observes Jeanne critically. The other woman would be defined by her culture as more masculine both in behavior and appearance; yet she clearly has her own center and a life that is not empty like Jeanne's. We *see* that not all women in Brussels are caught in the same trap.

Akerman also cultivates the unheard; the film is practically silent. Yet, as in Japanese theater, the silence gives greater impact to the sounds that are present: the cabinets snapping open and shut, the whistling kettle, the grinding of the coffee, the sloshing of the meat as it is molded into a loaf, the crying infant, and the incessant traffic and elevator motor always audible in the background.

The dialogue is minimal. Yet at irregular intervals, there are outbursts of talk, long monologues that are highly revealing. On the first day, Jeanne reads a letter from her sister encouraging her to find a new husband and inviting her and her son to vacation in Canada. Then just before going to sleep, the son, who still longs for some romance, unexpectedly asks her how she met his father. Jeanne replies with a narrative that is full of ironic contrasts. Her sister's meeting and marrying of an American soldier in 1944 was an unexpected "miracle." She embraced the new, but Jeanne remained in the familiar pattern. She wanted children and was told that marriage was the thing to do. When her fiancé's business went bad, her aunts opposed

the match, arguing that a pretty girl like her could find a man who
would make her life easy. She did not break the engagement, but
stuck with her original plan. We surmise that she is now following her
aunt's advice with her daily customers. It makes little difference to her
whether she is a wife or a prostitute; in either role, she has been
trained to use sex for the same economic purpose. Her son cannot
understand how she could make love to a man who is ugly or whom
she didn't love. Her response is simple: "Making love is merely a detail . . . How would you know, you're not a woman."

On the second day, when the mother picks up her baby, she tells a
long comical saga about her attempts to vary her routine by copying
other women at the butcher shop. The woman can make no decisions
and cannot cope with change. While Jeanne remains practically mute
and impassive, we soon learn, when she tries to answer her sister
about the proposed trip to Canada, that she suffers precisely the same
indecisiveness. The son's second bedtime monologue is more
threatening than the first. He begins by describing his friend Yan's
sexual experience with a nurse and then reveals his own Oedipal feelings. As a child, he was disturbed by the idea of his father hurting
Jeanne, using his penis like a sword. He wanted his father to die and
then had nightmares. Jeanne cuts him off, refusing to listen; but she is
obviously disturbed and shares his negative view of sex.

On the third day, while going from store to store searching for a
missing button on her son's jacket, which was a gift from her sister
several years ago, Jeanne suddenly delivers a long complaint against
her sister, which helps to explain why the birthday gift is to upset-
ting. In fact, all of her sister's intrusions into her life are disturbing
because they are unpredictable. The shopkeeper offers a way of cop-
ing with the problem of the missing button: "Get all new buttons, it'll
look new. It's the same as going to the hairdresser." Although this
solution is superficial, it is still too threatening for Jeanne, who is incapable of handling anything new. She clings to her routine and rejects the idea of new buttons or a new husband because it would be
"too hard to get used to someone new." She has trained her son to
become just like his father; her customers "fill in" for her dead husband both sexually and financially. In fact, the man she murders resembles her husband in the photograph on the dresser. Jeanne solves
her problem, not by turning to the new, but by killing the old. Akerman insists:

> It's the logical end to what was going on before; it's neither positive nor
> negative, it just is. The murder is on the same level as all the other Freud-
> ian slips that happen after the visit of the second client.

Yet, as Seyrig points out, it's "the only time that Jeanne ever took a stand, or expressed revolt in any way." It is the only decisive action she takes.

The emotional impact of *Jeanne Dielman* is very powerful because we are forced to experience it phenomenologically in an unusual way. We must adapt to its unconventional style by going through several stages. At first, the routines and rhythms seem strange, frustrating, or even comical. We wait for something dramatic to happen; we wonder when the pace will quicken or when the camera will move. Some people in the audience grow impatient and walk out, particularly those like Jeanne who cannot tolerate the new. Those who remain begin to realize that the entire film will move at this slow pace, that it is establishing new conventions. We alter our expectations, relax, and gradually become absorbed by the images and physically attuned to the rhythm. In many of the long takes, we can let our eyes wander freely within the frame, observing details that we would never notice in a more conventional movie; we have time to think about what is happening or not happening. Our participation becomes more active; we begin to feel in control. Increasingly, we feel at home with the familiar shots and slow pace. Whereas earlier we welcomed any visitor or outdoor scene, eventually we come to resent them as intrusions. On the third day, we're glad to see the noisy baby leave and we're relieved when Jeanne shuts the door on the mother. We are vaguely upset by the acceleration of the pace and the minor deviations. We are very disturbed by the sex and violence, which many of us in the audience at first hoped for, but which we now experience as highly disruptive. Like Jeanne, we are relieved to return to the immobility of the final shot. Of course, when the film is over, unlike Jeanne, we are released from the trap; yet our own susceptibility to the routines and resistance to the new have been demonstrated. We have experienced the trap from the inside and, as a result, our own perception and consciousness have been expanded. The film makes us see our own daily routines in a new way; it leads us to re-examine the relationship between our identity and our actions. Most important, it makes us more receptive to what is new and liberating in our experience.

Family Portraits:

FILMMAKERS EXPLORE THEIR ROOTS

ELISABETH WEIS

"Mommy, how do you feel about Peter and my living together without being married?"

"That's a marvelous question. As long as your father's not here, I can answer it."

A microphone pokes into the corner of the frame and reminds us that this "home movie" is going public. The mother's wry response is her way of acknowledging that her remarks are meant for her husband, as well as her daughter and the eventual audience of her daughter's film, *Living With Peter*. The episode gives us an inkling of how filmmakers' public and private lives intersect when they choose to make films about themselves and their families.

Since the days when proud Papa Lumiere first fed Baby in front of the camera, home movies have thrived. Unscripted, unedited, and unloved by anyone except the dearest of friends, they have generally deserved the affectionate scorn heaped upon them. But now there is a trend among independent film makers to make documentaries about their own families, and they go beyond and deeper than anything in the typical home movie.

The urge behind the making of these films comes from the film makers' desire to understand themselves in relation to their origins—genetic and ethnic. There are variations within the form, but basically the films are the same. Most often the film maker is conducting an interview, perhaps with a Jewish mother or an estranged father or a grandmother from the old country. In films like Dick Rogers' *Elephants* and Miriam Weinstein's *Living With Peter*, the filmmakers themselves remain the central figures. In others, a low profile is kept, and what mainly emerges is a sympathetic portrait of an older relative, as in Mirra Bank's *Yudie* and Martha Coolidge's *Old-Fashioned Woman*.

Film teachers report that a surprising number of their students have recently turned to the family portrait for their main efforts. But we're talking here about 16 mm. films made by the established independents—the ones that win the grants and prizes. Typically, these films are made by women in their late twenties who have passed through the parent-hating phase of tossing out their entire heritage and are now trying to sort out those values they'd like to discard from those they intend to keep.

As Amalie Rothschild says, in *Nana, Mom, and Me*, "When you start to think about yourself as a mother you have to stop thinking of yourself as a child. I see my parents in a new way. I've begun to feel the continuity between the generations as well as the change."

That rediscovery of one's parents is vividly depicted in *Joyce at Thirty-four*, by Joyce Chopra and Claudia Weill. The film is essentially an autobiographical exploration of how Joyce Chopra comes to terms with both raising a child and having a career. But some of the most revealing insights have to do with the film maker's reevaluation of her roots after she has her baby. For the first time in years, she wants to go to her grandmother's house for Passover (partly to show off her new daughter, Sara). And she sees her mother and grandmother in a new light. Her epiphany is stunning: "If my mother loved me as much as I love Sara, she must have suffered a great deal."

If there has been one main impetus for the recent spate of family portraits, it is the women's movement, which has prompted many artists, like the rest of us, to reassess their ideas about family roles. So far more women than men have dealt with the subject, while men have tended to express their autobiographies in fictional forms, in the tradition of Fellini, Truffaut, *et al*. Martin Scorsese's documentary about his parents, *Italianamerican*, is one of the most charming of the family portraits. But it is in some ways less personal than his fiction feature, *Mean Streets*, in which he expressed the anguish and confusion involved in a Catholic upbringing in Little Italy.

Similarly, Phil Messina's *Mamma* does not convey its director's personal sense of urgency about his roots. In *Mamma* the film maker had interviewed his grandmother in order to understand what he considers to be the profound psychological influence of Sicilian emigrants' values on their descendants here.

Amalie Rothschild's *Nana, Mom, and Me* is virtually the prototype of films that explore personal identity through family roles. Rothschild started out to portray her relationship to her 86-year-old grandmother. But her Nana was about as willing to answer personal questions as John Ford was for Peter Bogdanovich. "I've got nothing more to say about that," she snaps, when asked about her past. And she keeps her word. So Amalie turns to her mother to learn more about Nana. At first resentful at being "sandwiched" between two generations, the mother soon warms up, and eventually the film switches its focus to the two younger women.

Amalie is constantly on camera, asking questions in areas that most of us would avoid. She asks her mother, an artist, whether she resents her daughter's greater success and whether her child-rearing duties interfered with her artistic life. Amalie questions with an uncomfortable persistence. She doesn't hide the less flattering aspects of herself (Nana accuses her of being "bold" and "brazen"). And if she sometimes tricks her grandmother into talking (she records a phone conversation), she doesn't hide her bag of dirty tricks. Rothschild's films are not neat, comfortable aesthetic packages. They are raw social documents dealing with touchy issues, and they provoke strong reactions from their viewers.

Her approach finds stronger justification in her film, *It Happens To Us*, in which she interviews women who, like her, have had abortions. The film is predicated on the valid notion that a stigma attaches to abortions so long as women don't come out of the closet and talk about them. As in *Nana, Mom, and Me* Rothschild also probes her private life in front of the camera on the assumption that doing so will free others to deal with uncomfortable issues.

Whether Rothschild's self-explorations alienate or attract varies with the audience. Certainly the most moving moments in *Nana, Mom, and Me* come in the portrayal of her mother as an articulate, wise, yet unidealized woman. In one sequence, the mother looks through the family's old 8 mm home movies and snapshots, and she connects her sense of identity to her appearance. Nana had prepared her for the conventional woman's role, trying with dresses, make-up and permanents to transform her hopelessly plain daughter. The mother's lovely straight red hair had been forcibly crimped and primped in the fashion of the day. Not until she reached a sense of herself, in her late twenties, did Amalie's mother settle on the more becoming straight hair style she would stick with; and that change is documented on film. *Nana, Mom and Me* ends with the mother giving her daughter a haircut—in the style that her daughter chooses—and a hug.

What Amalie Rothschild attempts through dialogue—to explore connections between generations—Dick Rogers attempts through images. He hardly appears on camera—but his presence in *Elephants* is felt even more than Amalie's in *Nana*. His film combines the willingness, rare among young men, to expose himself through film, with the more lyrical approach of the older avant-garde figures discussed below.

Rogers' method is to create a sense of how it *feels* to live with his particular heritage. He comes from a family of wealthy New York ers who are upset with his inelegant life-style. Rogers is not much interested in having his parents talk at the camera. In one sequence he plays simultaneously the separate comments of each parent, so that we can pick up only catchwords—"success," "security," "responsibility," "love,"—as they might ebb and flow through the son's consciousness. The dominant images are of elephants—caged and chained—and they work beautifully as a metaphor for the way his past weighs down on him. Rogers conveys his ideas through the subjective use of sounds and images. But he doesn't seem to trust his poetic method and throws in a closing monologue to make his ideas explicit: "I'm twenty-nine years old . . . .I wanted to make a film about the . . .forces that limit someone, that they have no control over, like their family and their past and their relationship to power and the society they live in."

Rogers' film acknowledges openly what many others do tacitly— they serve as therapeutic "rites of passage," as they have been called. Many film makers have to liberate themselves by dealing with their own past on film before they can turn to other work.

More typical of the young male independent film maker's approach is Martin Scorsese's family film. His *Italianamerican* is less a self-investigation than an affectionate portrait of his parents. Scorsese's method is to let his parents be themselves. He questions them about his origins, but there is little anguish involved on his part or theirs. Rather, his low-key presence serves more as a catalyst for his parents to play their long-established familial roles for the camera. What sticks in our memory is not what they say but how the parents and son interact.

With Scorsese's mother as the family's spokesperson, *Italianamerican* is the chicken soup school of family portraits on film. These are affectionate portraits of women who offer recipes for food and happiness. They have a strong sense of self and are always the same, off camera or on. In Ken Schneider's *Chicken Soup*, a Catskill grandmother teaches the camera the only proper way to make the Kosher panacea, and then proceeds to fish for compliments from her husband as the two eat it. In *Italianamerican* Scorsese pays tribute to his mother's traditional values by printing as part of the end titles the recipe for the spaghetti sauce she has been cooking during the filming.

Some filmmakers use their camera equipment to keep their distance on the far side of the lens. Others use the filming as a way of communicating with their subjects. One young woman made a film about the father she idolized partly to persuade him that she could be serious about something. And Miriam Weinstein shot *Living With Peter* as a way of getting across to her boyfriend that she'd really rather be married to him than just shacking up. (The sequel is *We Get Married Twice*.)

Some films may have been therapeutic for their makers, but don't communicate much to us. Others make us wonder if there shouldn't be a sub-category of the personal film called the "too-personal film." There is a very thin line between taking the emotional risks necessary for art and making a fool of yourself.

Special problems arise when a filmmaker expects his family to share those risks. The advantage of filming relatives is that the filmmaker can capture intimate, relaxed moments that no stranger could ever get. An outsider would have to obtain a legal "release form" to use anyone on film. A relative depends on mutual trust.

One filmmaker asked me not to mention in writing a certain sequence that she kept in her film, after a month's agonizing, because it made a crucial point. Her sensitive relative whose hearing is weak hasn't noticed it, but her eyesight is fine.

It is fascinating to watch the unspoken "contracts" between filmmaker and family in these films. Some filmmakers ask only "safe" questions that won't upset the family. They press harder, knowing that their relatives will stop them if necessary.

Martha Coolidge's fascinating film *David: Off and On* could have been made only by David's sister. Martha interviewed her 21-year-old brother, a drug addict who still was institutionalized after three yeers of psychiatric treatment. David is remarkably open with his sister, sensing rightly that she won't exploit him. He talks about his step-father, his impotence, his time in jail. But when she asks him to discuss his "craziness" he just very quietly says, no, he won't talk about it. "Not even a little bit, David?" "No, not even a little bit."

If anything, the filming experience was beneficial for David. He was released shortly afterwards, and now, several years later, he is married and a father—and still "clean."

All of Martha Coolidge's films are about persons very close to her, but though she appears in her films, she believes that her personal struggles should not appear on film: "Films are too expensive to make self-indulgent personal statements. I make films for other people."

In *Old-Fashioned Woman*, her portrait of her 86-year-old Yankee grandmother, Coolidge says that she wants to see the links between her own past and the future. The film begins and ends with shots of the family's annual Thanksgiving reunion at the grandmother's house, but what emerges most vividly is a portrait of someone living alone with incredible dignity and strength of character. Mabel Tilton Coolidge is her own woman, with surprising, unpredictable opinions, given her conservative background (she is an active member of the DAR and the descendant of a patrician New England family distantly related to Calvin Coolidge). She's all for birth control, even if the method she herself practiced was "abstinence." Her senses are failing, but her mind isn't, and she is too busy for self-pity. Her comment on her granddaughter's questioning: "I never got into this psychological investigation of our inner selves. We didn't bother; we just lived."

Coolidge has finally put herself at the center of her latest film *Not A Pretty Picture*. The story of her actual rape in 1962 at the age of sixteen, the film cuts back and forth between then, in which Martha is played by an actress, and the present, in which Martha plays herself as director of the film. Thus, Martha has managed to make her most personal film through the use of fiction.

The film recreates the impact of the rape on Martha by showing how its reenactment, shot as a rehearsal, affects those working on the film. The actress, herself raped when she was fifteen, says the reenactment was a "milestone" for her. The actor playing the rapist, finds in himself the possibility for violence and reveals that he did not have total control over his actions (much as Erland Josephson and Liv Ullmann discovered their unknown potential for violence when they were filming the fight sequence in *Scenes From a Marriage*). If in *Old-Fashioned Woman* Martha's presence seemed an egotistical intrusion, her presence is the best thing in *Not a Pretty Picture*. The documenting of her own reactions during the filming is strong stuff; whereas the fictional parts of the film are amateurish.

Mirra Bank doesn't appear in her film about her aunt, *Yudie*. We don't even hear her questions—only Yudie's responses. Though the film was very personal, Bank decided not to make that personal side explicit on film. The niece saw herself in her father's sister in terms of her temperament and Jewish heritage, and she got to understand herself better as she got to know Yudie. But when it came to editing *Yudie* she cut her own presence out of the film. She explains: "I had more intimacy and freedom by not having to deal with my reactions to myself on film."

Nevertheless, her privileged position as relative and filmmaker raised subtle problems about how to render her aunt honestly without infringing on her dignity—a problem she solved exquisitely. Bank had to be especially careful not to edit the film in terms of her own preconceptions about the aunt's decision ·not to get married again after a brief, unsatisfactory marriage.

Yudie, in the heart of New York's Lower East Side, is an intelligent, personable and attractive woman. Despite her simple existence (she has one hot-plate for a kitchen and works in her brother's yard goods store), she has the spunk for life of Ruth Gordon's character in *Harold and Maude*—though without the eccentricities and coyness that ring false in that movie. Mirra Bank might have turned the film into a brief for happy single-womanhood. But it was more honest to register Yudie's ambivalence.

Yudie was not prepared to marry the wrong man. ("I would ask, 'Are you prepared to spend the rest of your life with this man, with all the intimacies of marriage and so on?' and invariably I would hesitate and the answer would be, no.") Yet she also insists that if the right man had come along she would have said yes in two minutes. Then she reflects, "You begin to feel that you've done the wrong thing and that you didn't have a family of your own—and that's how I feel."

So far we have been talking about family portraits produced by the so-called independent filmmakers. However, certain artists within the American avant-garde movement have shown a parallel interest in exploring their roots on film. Curiously, these films have been made not by young women, but by several older men who might be called the "father figures" of the American avant-garde. In filming their family portraits, Jonas and Adolfas Mekas, Jerome Hill, and Robert Frank each eschewed the conventional interview format and worked in their own individual styles.

Jonas Mekas made *Reminiscences of a Journey to Lithuania* and Adolfas Mekas made *Going Home* in 1972, during and after their first trip to their homeland after a 27-year exile that began in a Nazi labor camp. In *Reminiscences* Jonas Mekas has movingly preserved the spontaneity of his joyful reunion with his family through the way he plays with his camera. *Film Portrait* is an autobiographical essay by Jerome Hill, the artist and patron of avant-garde films, who died in 1972. He made his film, which like the Mekas works is part philosophy, part poetry, by playing around with his old turn-of-the-century photographs, home movies, and experimental films. And in *Conversations in Vermont* Robert Frank, legendary photographer of the beat generation, examines his role as a father through cinema-verité style discussions with his teenaged children.

Frank's film, like the explorations of the younger independents, is searching but unresolved. With that exception, the film-meditations of the other avant-garde figures (Hill, the Mekas Brothers) are aes-

thetically superior to the self-examinations of the younger independents. The older artists are simply more interesting as subjects, and
they have found lyrical visual styles that are more expressive than the
"talking heads" that plague synchronized sound interviews. However, the more openly searching films of the younger artists often
have an immediate, polemical appeal that off-sets their formal limitations.

What will be the outcome of the family portrait trend? For one
thing, the exploration-cum-interview may become less of a woman's
genre. As the feminist movement provokes young men to challenge
their traditional roles, more of them will probably make films which
reassess their connections with their families. Conversely, as sexual
roles continue to loosen up, some women will move from such personal statements to more fictional forms. Martha Coolidge's experiments in the area where distinctions between documentary and fiction break down recall Truffaut's relationship with Léaud and
Bergman's with Ullman—especially the sequences in his *Passion of
Anna* where the actors talk about their roles to the camera. Given the
number of documentary filmmakers who nourish a secret ambition to
make fiction films, this inbetween area may be a new direction which
other independent women filmmakers will follow as well.

La Souriante Madame Beudet (1923), a silent film masterpiece made by Germaine Dulac, a feminist before her film career began. Germaine Duirnoz and Arquillière.

Madame de enacts the tragic conflict: the individual against society. Danielle Darrieux in *Madame de* (1953).

Filmographies of Women Directors

compiled by PATRICIA ERENS and TOM BRUEGGEMANN

The following filmographies are a selective listing of major international women directors. Efforts have been made to include most of the women who have directed feature length films.

In making choices, I have concentrated on those women who have made significant contributions to the history of world cinema and whose films are presently in distribution. Therefore, many early American directors and women currently working in Eastern Europe and the Far East have not been included.

In selecting from among the burgeoning number of independent filmmakers, most of whom are producing short works, I have based my choice on the following criteria: 1) women who have created a significant body of work, 2) filmmakers who have demonstrated a commitment to feminist concerns, and 3) directors whose films have been written about or shown at women's film festivals. In listing independent filmmakers, I have not cited individual credits for producing, scripting, editing, or camerawork as most filmmakers are responsible for all of these functions.

I have made every effort to make these filmographies as complete as possible. Accurate information on many of these directors is hard to come by. Some of the listings are knowingly incomplete (and have been so noted); others unintentionally so. I am extremely grateful to all of the filmmakers who responded to my letters of inquiry and provided me with up-to-date information. Birthdates of directors are included wherever available. ———P.E.

The following abbreviations have been used throughout: pr (producer); scr (screenplay); act (actress); doc (documentary); feature (any film 50 minutes or longer).

PERRY MILLER ADATO   *USA*

Dylan Thomas—The World I Breathe (1968)
The Film Generation and Dance (1969)
Gertrude Stein: When This You See, Remember Me (1970)
The Great Radio Comedians (1972)
Untitled (1972) (short)
Eames at Moma (1973) (short)
An Eames Celebration (1974)
Mary Cassatt—Impressionist Philadelphia (1975) (short)
Georgia O'Keeffe (1977)
Frankenthaler: Toward a New Climate (1978) (short)

CHANTAL AKERMAN *Belgium* (1950–   )

[all shorts except where noted]
Saute ma ville (Blow Up My City) (1969)
L'enfant aimé (The Loved Child) (1972)
Hôtel Monterey (1973)
Hanging Out (1973)
La chambre et Yonkers (1973)
Je, Tu, Il, Elle (I, You, He, She) (1974)
Jeanne Dielman, 23 quai du Commerce, 1080 Bruxelles (1975) (feature)
News From Home (1976) (feature)
Les rendezvous d'Anna (Meetings with Anna) (1978) (feature)

In addition to the above films, Adato has also produced numerous television documentaries.

ANN AMBROSE   *Great Britain*

[all shorts]
Record Time (1973)
Noodle Spinner
Up and Down

MADELINE ANDERSON   *USA*

[all shorts]
A Tribute to Malcolm X (1969)
I Am Somebody (1970)
Being Me (1975)
shorts for Sesame Street and Electric Company
Clementine Hunter, Artist (1976)

KAREN ARTHUR *USA* (1941–   )

[all shorts except where noted]
Legacy (1975) (feature)
Eileen
Her's
The Mafu Cage (1978) (feature)

GERI ASHUR *USA* (1946–   )

Janie's Janie (1971) (with Peter Barton) (short)

DOROTHY ARZNER *USA* (1900–   )

Fashions for Women (1927)
Ten Modern Commandments (1927)
Get Your Man (1927)
Manhattan Cocktail (1928)
The Wild Party (1929)
Sarah and Son (1930)
Anybody's Woman (1930)
Working Girls (1930)
Paramount on Parade (1930) (one section)
Honor Among Lovers (1931)
Merrily We Go to Hell (1932)
Christopher Strong (1933)
Nana (1934)
Craig's Wife (1936)
The Bride Wore Red (1937)
Dance, Girl, Dance (1940)
First Comes Courage (1943)

Arzner is reputed to have directed *Behind the Make-up* (1930), which is officially credited to Robert Milton. Previous to directing, she was one of the best-known Hollywood editors, with credits including *Blood and Sand* (1923) and *The Covered Wagon* (1923).

JACQUELINE AUDRY *France* (1908–   )

Les Chevaux du Vercors (The Horses of the Vercors) (1943) (short)
Les Malheurs du Sophie (1945)
Sombre Dimanche (Gloomy Sunday) (1948)
Gigi (1949)
Minne, l'ingenu libertine (1950)
Olivia (Pit of Loneliness) (1951)
La Caroque Blonde (1952)
Huis clos (No Exit) (1954)
La Garçonne (The Bachelor Girl) (1957)
L'Ecole des Cocottes (Six Easy Lessons) (1957)

Mitsou ou comment l'esprit vient aux filles (1958)
C'est la faute d'Adam (It's All Adam's Fault) (1958)
Le Secret du Chevalier d'Eon (The Secret of the Chevalier d'Eon) (1960)
Les Petits Matins (Girl on the Road) (1962)
Cadavres en Vacances (Corpses on Holiday) (1962)
Fruits Amers (Bitter Fruits) (1966)
Soledad (1966)
Le Lys de mer (The Sea Lily) (1970)

RUTH ANN BALDWIN *USA*

The Black Page (1915) (short)
The Double Deal in the Park (1915) also scr (short)
An Arrangement With Fate (1915) also scr (short)
The Recoiling Vengeance (1916) also scr
The Butterfly (1917) also scr
Is Money All (1917) also scr
It Makes a Difference (1917) also scr
The Black Mantilla (1917)
When Liz Lets Loose (1917)
The Woman Who Could Not Pat (1917) also scr
The Rented Man (1917) also scr
A Soldier of the Legion (1917) also scr
The Storm Women (1917) also scr
A Wife on Trial (1917)
Three Women of France (1917)
Twixt Love and Desire (1917) also scr (short)
49–17 (1917)
The Mother's Call (1918)
Broken Commandments (1919) also scr
The Devil's Ripple (1920) also scr
The Marriage of William Ashe (1921) also scr
Puppets of Fate (1921)

MIRRA BANK *USA*

[all documentary shorts]
Yudie (1974)
Becoming Tough Enough (1974)
Fighting Back (1975)
Pass Me that Club, Please (1975)
Kid's Clothes (in progress)
The Rag Trade (in progress)
Anonymous Was a Woman (1978)

Bank also worked as an editor on *Woodstock* (1970), *Gimme Shelter* (1971), and *The Men Who Made the Movies*.

AMANDA BARTON   *USA*

Midnight Desires (1976) also scr

MARIA BASAGLIA *Italy*

Sua Altezza Ha Detto, No! (1954) also scr
Sangue di Zingara (1956) also scr

JOY BATCHELOR *England* (1914–)

[all animated shorts co-directed with John Halas except where noted]
The Pocket Cartoon (1941)
Dustbin Parade (1942)
Abu (1943) (4-film series)
Six Little Jungle Boys (1944)
Old Wive's Tale (1946)
Heave Away, My Johnny (1947)
Charley (1948) (7-film series)
First Line Of Defense (1949)
As Old As The Hills (1950)
Magic Canvas (1951)
Poet and Painter (1951)
Submarine Control (1951)
The Figurehead (1952)
The Owl and the Pussycat (1953)
The Moving Spirit (1953)
Power to Fly (1954)
Animal Farm (1954) (feature)
Speed the Plow (1955)
The History of the Cinema (1956)
To Your Health (1956)
The Candlemaker (1956)
The World of Little IG (1956)
All Lit Up (1957)
The Christmas Visitor (1958)
The Cultured Ape (1959)
The Insolent Matador (1959)
The Widow and the Pig (1959)
Foo Foo (1959) (33-film series)
The History of Inventions (1960)
Snip and Snap (1960) (26-film series)
Dam the Delta (1960)
The Colombo Plan (1961)
For Better, For Worse (1961)
Hamilton, The Musical Elephant (1962)
Automania 2000 (1963)
Hoffnung (1964) (4-film series)
The Question (1966)
Flurina (1966)
Ruddigore (1967) (feature)
Fairy Tale (1969)
Children and Cars (1970)
What is a Computer? (1970)

Batchelor has worked on over 950 films; the above is a selective listing.

MARY BEAMS *USA* (1945–   )

[all animated shorts]
Tub Film (1972)
Seed Reel (1975)
Going Home Sketchbook (1975)
Piano Rub (1975)
Solo (1975)
Paul Revere is Here

CONSTANCE (CONI) BEESON *USA*

[all shorts]
Health on Wheels (1968)
Dione (1968)
Unfolding (1969)
Thenow (1970)
Ann, A Portrait (1971)
Holding (1971)
Stamen (1972)
Watercress (1973)
The Doll (1973)
Sir (1973)
High on Drag (1973)
Gypsy and Me (1973)
Women (1974)
Firefly (1974)
Taos (1974)
Freude (1975)
Sisyphus (1976)
The Letter (1976)
Freedom on the Inside (1976)
feature on Joaquin Murietta (in progress)

In addition, Beeson has made numerous video tapes.

YANNICK BELLON *France*

[all shorts except where noted]
Goémons (1948)
Colette (1951)
Varsovie quand même (Still Warsaw) (1954)
Les Hommes oubliés (Forgotten Men) (1957)
Quelque part, quelqu'un (Somewhere, Someone) (1972) (feature)
La femme de Jean (John's Wife) (1972) (feature)

Jamais plus toujours (Never Again Always) (1975) (feature)
Viol (Rape) (in progress) (feature)

MARGOT BENACERRAF   *Venezuela* (1926–   )

Reveron (1958) (short)
Araya (1960)

MURIEL BOX   *Great Britain* (1905–   )

The Happy Family (US: Mr. Lord Says No) (1952) also scr
Street Corner (US: Both Sides of the Law) (1953) also scr
A Prince for Cynthia (1953) (short)
To Dorothy a Son (US: Cash on Delivery) (1954)
The Beachcomber (1954)
Simon and Laura (1955)
Eyewitness (1956)
The Passionate Stranger (US: A Novel Affair) (1957) also scr
The Truth About Women (1958) also pr
Subway in the Sky (1959)
This Other Eden (1959)
Too Young to Love (1960)
The Piper's Tune (1962)
Rattle of a Simple Man (1964)

Box is the wife of Sydney Box, the writer-producer with whom she frequently collaborated, and the sister-in-law of Betty Box, another producer. Before directing, she co-wrote *The Seventh Veil, The Years Between, The Brothers* and *Dear Murderer*, among others.

LIANE BRANDON   *USA*

[all shorts]
R.P.T.P. . . . Developing (1967)
Gum (1968)
Le Sujet C'est Nous (1960)
Sometimes I Wonder Who I Am (1970)
Anything You Want to Be (1971)
Betty Tells Her Story (1972)
Not So Young Now As Then (1974)

ANJA BREIEN   *Norway* (1940–   )

[all shorts except where noted]
The Bird From the Joste Valley (1967)
17th May, A Film About Rituals (1969)
Faces (1971)
Voldtekt (Rape) (1971) (feature)
Murene rundt fengslet (The Walls Around the Prison) (1972)

Hobos (1973)
Brothers and Sisters, Good Morning (1974)
Herbergistene (Men from the Lodging House/The Old Ones) (1975)
Hustruer (Wives) (1975) (feature) also scr
Den Allvarsamma leken (Games of Love and Loneliness) (1977)

VALENTINA BRUMBERG   *USSR* (1899–   )
ZENAJEDA BRUMBERG   *USSR* (1900–   )

[All animation]
The Young Samoyed (1929)
Great Troubles (1961)
Three Fat Men (1963)
The Brave Little Tailor (1964)
An Hour Until the Meeting (1965)
Golden Stepmother (1966)
The Little Time Machine (1967)
Big Misadventures (1969)

The Brumbergs are sisters.

CAMBRIDGE DOCUMENTARY FILMS *USA*

Taking Our Bodies Back (1974)
Rape Culture (1975)

Cambridge Documentary Films is a cooperative working in Cambridge, Mass.

CHRISTINE BURRILL   *USA* (1946–   )

[all documentary shorts]
Summer 1970 (1970)
King Arthur (1970)
Victim (1971)
A Half Million Teenagers (1974)
Cuba and Fidel (1975 co-directed)
To Plan Your Family (1976)
The Fondas: Through the Generations (1976 co-directed)
The New Maid (in progress)

Burrill also co-edited *Brazil: A Report on Torture, Introduction to the Enemy* and *The Double Day.*

MARY ELLEN BUTE   *USA* (1909–   )

[All animated except where noted]
Synchronization (1934) (with Lewis Jacobs and Joseph Schillinger)

Rhythm in Light (1936)
Anitra's Dance (1936)
Synchrony No. 2 (1936)
Evening Star (1937)
Parabola (1938)
Escape (1940)
Toccata and Fugue (1940)
Tarantella (1941)
Sports Spools (1941) (with Norman McLaren)
Polka-Graph (1953)
Abstronics (1954)
Mood Contrasts (1954)
The Boy Who Saw Through (1956) (live-action)
Color Rhapsody (1958)
Passages from James Joyce's Finnegan's Wake (1965) (live-action feature) also
    scr, pr
Out of the Cradle (in progress)

Much of Bute's work was in collaboration with her husband, cinematographer Ted Nemeth. Most of her animated work was experimental and abstract.

MARIA CARBONELL   *Venezuela* (1927–   )

Punto Debil (Weak Point) (1975)
La Anastenaria (short)
The Salt (short)
The Image (in progress)

LILIANA CAVANI·   *Italy* (1936–   )

I Cannibali (The Year of the Cannibals) (1970 also scr)
The Night Porter (1974) also scr
Milarepa (1974) also scr
The People of Misar (in progress)
Oltre Il Bene e Il Male (Beyond Good and Evil) (1977)

Cavani's background is in Italian television, where beginning in 1960 she directed several documentaries—*The Women of the Resistance, History of the Third Reich, The House in Italy*. Later, she made three dramatic films for television—*Francesco d'Assisi* (1964), *The Guest* (1966) and *Galileo* (1968).

DORIS CHASE *USA*

[all shorts]
Circles I (1971)
Circles I Variation II (1972)
Circles II (1972)

Circles II Variation II (1973)
Squares (1973)
Tall Arches (1973)
Tall Arches II (1973)
Moon Gates I (1973)
Moon Gates II (1974)
Moon Gates III (1974)
Tall Arches III (1974)
Roching Orange II (1974)
Sculpture for Children (1974) (with Laurie Steig and Elizabeth Wood)
Dance Eleven (1975)
Philadelphia Quartet (1975)
Improvizatio (1977)

Chase is an artist and filmmaker.

ABIGAIL CHILD *USA*

[all shorts]
Mother Marries A Man of Mellow Mien (A Love Story) (1973)
Savage Streets (1973)
Working Mothers (1973)
Except the People (with Jonathan Child)
Game (with Child)

JOYCE CHOPRA (1936–   )

[all shorts except where noted]
A Happy Mother's Day (1963) (with Richard Leacock)
Wild Ones (1965) (feature)
Tyrone Guthrie (1966)
Eye-Opener (1966)
Room To Learn (1967)
Essays/I.M. Pei (1968)
Present Tense (1969) (with Tom Cole)
Water (for Sesame Street) (1970)
New Lease On Learning (1972)
Joyce at 34 (1973) (with Claudia Weill)
Matina Horner: Portrait of a Person (1974)
Portrait of a Person
Girls at 12 (1975)
Clorae and Albie (1975)
Sally Garcia and Family (1977)

JOAN CHURCHILL   *USA*

[all shorts]
Campaign (with James Kennedy)
Sylvia, Fran and Joy
Other Women, Other Work (with Kennedy)

VERA CHYTILOVA *Czechoslovakia* (1929–)

Three Men (1957) also scr (short)
Green Roads (1959) also scr (short)
Villa in the Suburbs (1959) also scr (short)
The Ceiling (1961) (short) also scr
Academy Newsreel (1961) (short)
A Bag of Fleas (1962) also scr (doc)
O necem jinem (Something Different) (1963) also scr
The World Cafeteria (1965) (episode in Pearls of the Deep) also scr
Sedmikrasky (Daisies) (1966) also scr
The Fruit of Paradise (1969) also scr
Ovoce stromu rajskych jime (The Fruit of Paradise) (1969) also scr
Uvadi hra o jablo (The Apple Game) (1977)

Chytilova, a leading figure of the Czech New Wave of the mid-1960's, is married to Jaroslav Kucera, who was the cinematographer for most of her films. During most of the seventies she was prohibited from working in her native Czechoslovakia.

MICHELE CITRON *USA* (1948–)

April 3, 1973 (1973)
Self Defense (1973)
Integration (1974)
Parthenogenesis (1976)
Daughter Rite (1978) (feature)

SHIRLEY CLARKE *USA* (1925–)

Dance in the Sun (1953) (short)
In Paris Parks (1954) (short)
Bullfight (1955) (short)
Moment in Love (1957) (short)
Brussels 'Loops' (1958) (15 shorts)
Bridges-Go-Round (1958) (short)
Skyscraper (1959) (with Willard Van Dyke) (short)
Scary Time (1960) (short)
The Connection (1960) also pr
The Cool World (1963)
Robert Frost (A Lover's Quarrel With the World (1964) (with Charlotte Zwerin
    and Robert Hughes)
Man in the Polar Regions (1967)
Portrait of Jason (1967) also scr

Clarke began as a dancer and her early films reflect this interest. Continuing her career-long effort to experiment with all aspects of visual media, in recent years Clarke has worked in video rather than film.

NINA COMPANEEZ *France*

Faustine ou le bel été (1972)
The Two Women (1976)
Comme sur des roulettes (As On Roller Skates) (1976)

JULEEN COMPTON *USA*

Stranded (1967)
The Plastic Dome of Norma Jean (1967)

MARTHA COOLIDGE   *USA* (1945–   )

[all shorts except where noted]
David: Off and On (1972)
More Than A School (1973) (feature)
Old-Fashioned Woman (1974)
Not A Pretty Picture (1975) (feature)
Boogie, Don't Boogie (in progress)

Coolidge has also served as director, editor, and soundwoman on 15 shorts and documentaries between 1965–1972.

SHARON COUZIN *USA*

[all shorts]
A Cutting Away (1971)
Some (1972)
Dance For Well Spaced Teeth (1972)
Year of the Mice (NIMBUSODILONGRADIVA) (1973)
True Flick (1973)
Fly Once Over Lightly (1975)
Roseblood (1975)

NELL COX *USA*

[all shorts except where noted]
A to B (1970) also actress
Cities and Technology
Fifty-Fifty (scr. only) (feature)
Five Portraits
French Lunch
Frontier Nurse
The Hand that Rocks the Ballot Box
It's All in a Day's Work
Liza's Wagon Train Diary (feature)
Operator
Reflections Made in Japan
Trial (feature)

SALLY CRUIKSHANK ·USA (1949–   )

[all animated shorts]
Ducky (1971)
Fun On Mars (1971)
Chow Fun (1972)
Quasi At The Quackadero (1975)

Cruikshank has also worked on assorted commercials between 1972–1975.

MIREILLE DANSEREAU   *Canada* (1944–   )

Moi, un jour (1967) (short)
Compromise (1968) (short)
Forum (1969) (originally shot on video)
Markets (1970) (short)
La Vie rêvée (Dream Life) (1972)
Je me marie, je me marie, pas (Marriage) (1973)

JOAN DARLING *USA*

First Love (1977)

Darling has been an actress and acting coach for the last fifteen years. She has also directed episodes for several television comedies, including the "Mary Hartman, Mary Hartman" pilots and the "Mary Tyler Moore Show."

STORM DE HIRSCH *USA*

[all shorts]
Journey Around a Zero (1963)
Goodbye in the Mirror (1964) (feature) (made in Italy)
Divinations (1964)
Peyote Queen (1965)
Hudson River Diary: Book I (1966)
Newsreel: Jonas in the Brig (1966)
Sing Lotus (1966)
Shaman, A Tapestry for Sorcerers (1967)
Cayuga Run (1967)
Third Eve Butterfly (1968)
Trap Dance (1968)
The Tatooed Man (1969)
An Experiment in Meditation (1971)
Lace of Summer (1973)
River-Ghost (1973)
Wintergarden Hudson River Diary: Book III (1973)
The Color of Ritual The Color of Thought
Cine Sonnets (1973)

DONNA DEITCH *USA* (1945–   )

[all shorts]
Berkeley 12 to 1 (1969)
P.P.I. (1969)
Memorabilia (1970)
She Was a Visitor (1970)
Portrait (1971)
Woman to Woman (1975)

LILIANE DE KERMADEC *France*

short on Emma Stern (1964)
Home, Sweet Home (1972) also scr
Aloise (1975) also scr
Amour, Amour (short)
Qui a donc rêvé (short)
Edith (project)

De Kermadec began her film career as an actress before turning to screenwriting and directing. She now has her own production company, Unité Trois, in association with Guy Cavagnac and Paul Vecchiali.

JOHANNA DEMETRAKAS *USA*

Celebration at Big Sur (1970–1971) (with Baird Bryant)
Cornbread (1971) (short)
Womanhouse (1973) (short)
The Naropa Family Movie (1974–75) (co-directed)
The Dinner Party (in progress)

Demetrakas has also edited several documentaries and features.

MAYA DEREN *USA* (1917–1961)

[All shorts]
Meshes of the Afternoon (1943) (with Alexander Hammid)
The Witch's Cradle (1943) (unfinished)
At Land (1944)
A Study in Choreography for Camera (1945)
Ritual in Transfigured Time (1946)
Meditations on Violence (1948)
The Very Eye of Night (1959)

Deren studied dance before turning to filmmaking. In addition to the films listed above, there exists unedited footage which Deren shot in Haiti in the mid-forties.

NIKKI DE ST. PHALLE *France*

Daddy (1973)
feature film (in progress)

MARIA DO ROSARIO *Brazil*

Wednesday (1973) (short)
I'm Brazilian (1974) (short)
Branded For Life (1975) also pr, scr, act

ARIEL DOUGHERTY *USA*

[all shorts]
Mother America (1970) (with Sheila Paige and Dolores Bargowski)
The Trials of Alice Crimmins (1971) (with Paige)
Sweet Bananas (1972)

The last film was produced by Women Make Movies, Inc., an organization devoted to feminist films.

LINDA DOVE *Great Britain*

miss/Mrs (1972)
Serve and Obey (1972) (with Sheila Malone)

LILIANE DREYFUS *France*

August 16
Femme au soleil (1974)
Schmates (project)

GERMAINE DULAC (Charlotte-Elisabeth-Germaine Saisset-Schneider) *France* (1882–1942)

Les Soeurs ennemies (Enemy Sisters) (1915)
Geo le mystérieux (Mysterious George) (1916)
Vénus victrix (Venus Victorious) (1916)
Dans l'ouragan de la vie (1916)
Le Bonheur des autres (1918)
Ames de fous (Souls of the Mad) (1917) also scr
La Fête espagnole (1919)
La Cigarette (1919)
Malencontre (1920)
La Belle dame sans merci (1920)
La Mort du soleil (1921)
Werther (1922) (unfinished)
La Souriante Madame Beudet (The Smiling Madame Beudet) (1923)
Le Diable dans la ville (The Devil in the City) (1924)

Ame d'artiste (1925)
La Folie des vaillants (The Madness of the Valiant) (1925)
Antoinette Sabrier (1926)
La Coquille et le clergyman (The Seashell and the Clergyman) (1927)
L'Invitation au voyage (1927)
Le Cinema au service de L'Histoire (1927) (compilation film)
La Princesse mandane (1928)
Mon Paris (1928) (supervisor only)
Disque 927 (1927)
Themes et variations (1928)
Etude cinegraphique sur une arabesque (1929)
Le Picador (1932) (supervisor only)
compiled by Joan Braderman

YOLANDE DU LUART *USA*

Angela Davis: Portrait of a Revolutionary (1971)

MARGUÉRITE DURAS   *France* (1914–   )

La Musica (1966) (with Paul Seban) also scr
Détruire dit-elle (Destroy, She Said) (1969) also scr
Jaune le soleil (1971)
Abahn Sabana David (1971) also scr
Nathalie Granger (1972) also scr
La femme du Gange (Woman of the Ganges) (1973) also scr
India Song (1975) also scr
Son nom de venise dans Calcutta Désert (1976)
Le camion (The Truck) (1977) also scr, act
Les rendezvous échoués (Unkept Appointments) (1978)

Duras is a leading French novelist. She first worked in film as author of Alain Resnais' *Hiroshima, Mon Amour* (1959). Many of her novels have been filmed by other directors.

JILL EATHERLEY *Great Britain*

[all shorts]
Deck (1971)
Heather in Circle Film (1973)
Land and Sea Film (1973)
Lens and Mirror Film (1973)
Tubes (1973)
Window in Circle Film (1973)
Table Film (1974)

NANCY EDELL *Great Britain*

[all shorts]
Black Pudding (1969)
Charlie Co. (1972)

JUDIT ELEK   *Hungary* (1937–   )

[all shorts except where noted]
Encounter (1963) also scr
Occupants of Manor House (1966) also scr
How Long Does Man Matter, Parts 1 and 2 (1967) also scr
The Lady from Constantinople (1968) (feature)
Island on the Continent (1969) (feature)

LINDA FEFERMAN *USA*

[all shorts]
Dirty Books (1971)
Menstruation (1974)
Happy Birthday, Nora
The Park Film
Elizabeth Swados: The Girl with the Incredible Feeling (1977)

MARY FIELD *Great Britain* (1896–1968)

[all shorts except where noted]
Secrets of Nature (1926) (series)
Strictly Business (1931) (feature)
This Was England (1934)
Secrets of Life (1934) (series)
King's English (1934)
The Changing Year (1934)
They Made the Land (1938)
Shadow of the Stream (1938)
Babes in the Wood (1938)
The Medieval Village (1940)
Winged Messengers (1941)
I Married a Stranger (1944)

Field spent her career specializing in children's films and documentaries, particularly at Gaumont-British. From 1944, she produced only for J. Arthur Rank, the Children's Film Foundation, and British television.

CINDA FIRESTONE *USA*

Attica (1973) (doc)

COLLEEN FITZGIBBON *USA*

[all shorts]
FFF (1973)
KII Print (1973)

Gymnastic Exercises (1973)
Test Print/Dogs (1973)
Calgary, Alberta (1973)
Springfield, Illinois (1973)
Pacific Christ Mission of Chicago (1973)
Stripper (1973)
Business Management (1973)
Chicago, Illinois (1973)
FM/TRCS (1974)
7222doubleXdoubleperf (1974)
7277 4Xreversal (1974)
23essex/C60/7277-4X/CM72A (1974)
Internal System (1974)
Bell & Howell (1974)
Black Infra-Red (1974)
Paros, Greece (1974)
Frame of Mind (1974)
Bathers (1974)
Exposed Film (1975)
Oral Art (1975)
Public Records (1976)
Restoring appearances to order in 1 min.

BERYL FOX   *Canada* (1931–   )

[all documentaries]
One More River (with Douglas Leiterman) (1963)
Balance of Terror (1963) (co-directed)
The Chief (1964) (co-directed)
The Single Woman and the Double Standard (1965)
Summer in Mississippi (1965)
The Mills of the Gods: Viet Nam (1965)
The Hon. Rene Levesque (1966)
Youth: In Search of Morality (1966)
This Hour Has 7 Days (1966)
Saigon (1967)
Last Reflections on a War: Bernard Fall (1968)
View From the 21st Century (1968)
Memorial to Martin Luther King (1969)
The Crew (1969) (associate director)
Spring Valley (1969) (associate director)
The Fabulous Sixties (1969)
North with the Spring (1970–72)
Here Come the 70's (1970–72)
Top Breed Dog Food (1970–72)
Toward the Year 2000 (1973)
Travel & Leisure (1973)
Target the Impossible (1974)
Wild Refuge (1974)
Take My Hand (1975)

How to Fight with Your Wife (1975)
The Visible Woman (1975)
Take 5 (1976) (co-director)
Creative Producer Programming (1976)
Surfacing (in progress) (fiction feature)

Fox has worked almost exclusively for television and is married to documentary filmmaker Douglas Leiterman.

BARBARA FRANK   *USA*

Rising Target (1976)

BONNIE FRIEDMAN   *USA* (1946–   )

[all documentary shorts]
Childcare: People's Liberation (1970) (with Karen Mitnick)
How About You? A Film On Birth Control and Sexuality (1972) (with Deborah
    Shaffer and Marilyn Mulford)
Chris and Bernie (1974) (with Shaffer)
Becoming Orgasmic: A Sexual Growth Program for Women (1975) (9 part
    series)

Friedman also worked as camerawoman and soundwoman on many documentaries.

FREUDE (BARTLETT) *USA*

[all shorts]
Folly (1972)
One and the Same (1972–1973) (with Gunvor Nelson)
My Life in Art (1968–1974)
Promise Her Anything But Give Her the Kitchen Sink (1968)
Stand up and Be Counted (1969) (with Scott Bartlett)
The Party (1969) (with Bartlett)

Sweet Dreams (1970)
Women and Children at Large (1972)
The Sacred Heart of Jesus
Shooting Star
A Trip to the Moon (with Bartlett)
Redheads on Parade (in progress)

LILLIAN GISH   *USA* (1896–   )

Remodeling Her Husband (1920) also scr

Gish's one attempt at direction was a critical and popular success, but she rejected all further offers.

ELINOR GLYN *Great Britain* (1864–1943)

Knowing Men (1930)
The Price of Things (1930)

Glyn was a romantic novelist whose brief fling at filmmaking was overshadowed by the numerous film adaptations of her work (the best known are *Three Weeks* and *It*). She also spent a few years in Hollywood as a scenarist during the 1920's.

ANNA GOBBI *Italy*

Tre e due (Three Plus Two) (1947) (short)
Lo Scandalo (The Scandal) (1967) also scr

In the years between her two films, Gobbi both wrote and designed costumes for Italian films. *Aida* (1954) is the only one of her writing credits to be shown internationally.

JILL GODMILOW *USA*

La Nueva Vida (1967)
Tales (1969) (co-directed) (documentary)
Antonia: A Portrait of the Woman (1973) (with Judy Collins)
Where Do All the Mentally Ill Go? (1974)
The Popovich Brothers (1978) (doc feature)
Nevelson in Process (1977) (with Susan Fanshel)

Godmilow was assistant editor on *The Godfather* (1972) and *The Candidate* (1972).

MILLIE GOLDSHOLL   *USA* (1920–   )

[all animated shorts co-directed with Morton Goldsholl]
Night Driving (1956)
Dissent Illusion (1963)
Reconstruction (1964)
Animation (1967)
Up Is Down (1969)
Acquarius (1971)
Rebellion of the Flowers (in progress)

The Goldsholls have also created numerous commercial shorts.

SILVIANNA GOLDSMITH *USA*

[all shorts]
Coney Island of the Mind (1973)

Orpheus Underground (1974)
Nightclub (1975)
Abstract
Destructive Relationships
Last Tango in Miami
Lil Piard: Art is a Party, the New Party is Art
Mexico On 5 and 10 Dollars A Day
Orpheus Underground II
The Transformation of Persephone

SARA GOMEZ *Cuba*

De Cierta Manera (In a Certain Fashion) (1974–77)

NANCY GRAVES *USA*

[all shorts]
200 Stills at 60 Frames (1970) (silent)
Goulimine (1970) (silent)
Izy Boukir (1971)
Aves: Magnificent Frigate Bird, Great Flamingo (1973)
Reflections on the Moon (1974) (co-d: Linda Leeds)

Graves is an artist and filmmaker.

HELEN GRAYSON *USA* (1903–1962)

[all documentaries]
The Cummington Story (1945)
Starting Line (1947)
A Nation Sets Its Course
The New World
To Freedom
also films for the U.S. Information Agency and private institutions

AMY GREENFIELD *USA*

Encounter (1967)
Dirt (1971)
Transport (1971)
Element (1973)
Image To Remind Me
Resoled
Shadow Play

Greenfield is a dancer/choreographer who appears in her own
dance films.

CLAUDINE GUILMAIN *France*

Veronique au l'ete de mes treize ans (Veronique, or the Summer of My 13th
    Year) (1975)

ALICE GUY BLACHÉ   *France* (1873–1968)

La Fée aux Choux (1897)
Les Fredaines de Pierrette (1897–1906)
J'ai un Hanneton dans mon Pantalon! (1897–1906)
La Fève Enchantée (1897–1906)
Charmant Frou-frou (1897–1906)
Démenagement à la Cloche de Bois (1897–1906)
Lui (1897–1906)
Le Fiancé Ensorcelé (1897–1906)
Minuit (1897–1906)
Le Noël de Pierrot (1897–1906)
La Legende de Saint-Nicolas (1897–1906)
Faust et Mephisto (1897–1906)
La Voiture Cellulaire (1897–1906)
Ballet de Singes (1897–1906)
Les Apaches pas Veinards (1903)
Rapt d'Enfants par les Romanichels (1904)
Les Petits Peintres (1904)
La Première Cigarette (1904)
Relubilitation (1904)
L'Assassinat du Courrier de Lyon (1904)
Le Baptême de la Poupée (1904)
Les Petits Coupeurs de Bois Vert (1904)
La Crinoline (1905)
Une Noce au Lac Saint-Fargeau (1905)
Esmeralda (1905)
La Vie du Christ (1906)
La Fée Printemps (1906)
Descente dans les Mines à Fumay (1906) (with Victorin Jasset)
Reves d'un Fumeur d'Opium (1906) (with Jasset)
Le Cake-walk de la Pendule (1906)
La Messe de Minuit (1906)
Mireille (1906) (with Louis Feuillade)
Carmen (1906–1907)
Manon (1906–1907)
Mignon (1906–1907)
Le Couteau (1906–1907)
Les Soeurs Mante Danseuses Mondaines (1906–1907)
Les Ballets de l'Opera (1906–1907)
Fanfan la Tulipe (1906–1907)
La Vivandière (1906–1907)
Les Dragons de Villars (1906–1907)
Madame Angot (1906–1907)
Les Cloches de Corneville (1906–1907)

A Child's Sacrifice (1910)
Falling Leaves (1910)
Mignon (1912)
Hotel Honeymoon (1912) (with Henri Menessier)
The Million Dollar Robbery (1912)
The Sewer (1912)
Mickey's Pal (1912) (with Edward Warren)
The Yellow Traffic (1912) (with Herbert Blaché)
The Rogues of Paris (1912)
The Beasts of the Jungle (1912)
Fra Diavolo (1912)
Kelly From the Emerald Isle (1913)
The Pit and the Pendulum (1913)
Dick Whittington and His Cat (1913)
The Shadows of the Moulin Rouge (1913)
Fortune Hunters (1913)
The Star of India (1913)
Matrimony Speed Limit (1913)
The Dream Woman (1914)
The Monster and the Girl (1914)
The Woman of Mystery (1914)
Fighting Death (1914)
Beneath the Czar (1914)
The Tigress (1914–1917)
Michael Strogoff (1914–1917)
The Ragged Earl (1914–1917)
House of Cards (1914–1917)
What Will People Say? (1914–1917)
My Madonna (1914–1917)
The Sea Wolf (1914–1917)
The Adventurer (1917)
The Empress (1917)
A Man and the Woman (1917)
The Great Adventure (1918)
Tarnished Reputations (1920)
A House Divided (1923)

Alice Guy Blaché was responsible for hundreds of films. The above is an incomplete listing of her work. Films dated after 1910 were made in the United States and produced by Alice and Herbert Blaché under various company names including Solax Company, Blaché Features Inc., and The U.S. Amusement Corporation. Several of the later works were made for other American companies.

DEE DEE HALLECK *USA*

[all shorts]
Mural on Our Street (1965) (with Kirk Smallman)
Minimoviemakers (1968) (co-directed)

Mr. Story (1972) (with Anita Thacher)
Jaraslawa (1974)
Meadows Green (1975) (co-directed)
Apple Tarte Aunte Jeanne (1975)
Portrait: Jean Dupuy (1975)
Song of Innocents (1975)
Bronx (in progress) (with Richard Serra)
Morag (in progress)

BIRGIT HEIN   *West Germany*

[all shorts co-directed with Wilhelm Hein]
S & W (1967)
Und sie (1967)
Grün (1968)
Bamberg (1968)
Rohfilm (1968)
Reproductions (1968)
625 (1969)
Square Dance (1969)
Auszüge aus einer Biographie (1970)
Madison/Wis (1970)
Portraits (1970–1972)
Replay (1970)
Fotofilm (1970)
Autobahn I & II (1971)
Home Movies I-IX (1971–1973)
Dobbelprojektion (1971–1972)
Zoom lange Fassung (1971)
Zoom kurze Fassung (1971)
Liebesgrüsse (1972)
Yes to Europe (1972)
Aufblenden/Abblenden (1972)
Doppelprojektion VI-VII (1972)
Handkurbel (1972)
Scharf/Unscharf (1972)
Dokumentation (1972)
Fussbal (1972)
Ausdatiertes Material (1973)
God bless America (1973)
Stills (1973)
London (1973)
Dreifachprojektion I (1974)
Strukturelle Studien (1974)
Ausdatiertes Material (revised version) (1974)
Home movies X-XVI (1973–1974)
Teil A (in progress)
Teil B (in progress)
Teil C (in progress)
Teil D (in progress)

ASTRID HENNING-JENSEN   *Denmark* (1914–   )

[Co-directed with Bjarne Henning-Jensen]
Paper (1940) (shorts)
Sugar (1941) (short)
The Foal (1942) (short)
When You Are Young (1943)
Ditte, Daughter of Man (1946)
Dansk Politi Sverige (The Danish Brigade in Sweden) (1946)
Stemming i April (Impressions of April) (1947)
Palle, Alone in the World (1949)
The Unknown (1952)
Directed alone:
Mr. Krane's Tearoom (1951)
Children of the Ballet (1954)
Hvor bjergene seljer (In the Country of Icebergs) (1956)
Infidelity (1966)

ANN M. HERSHEY   *USA* (1938–   )

[all shorts]
Mrs. Teabottle Meets Mr. Magic (1972)
Never Give Up-Imogen Cunningham (1973–1975)
We Are Ourselves (1976) (doc)
Back Home (in progress)
Mail Order Dyke (in progress)
Marie's Little Girl (in progress) (doc)

ISA HESSE   *Switzerland*

[all shorts]
Momumento Moritat (1969)
Spiegelei (Sunny Side Up) (1969)
Viele Grüsse aus . . . (Salutations from . . .) (1970)
Der rote Blau (The red Blue) (1971)
Über einen Teppich (About a Carpet) (1972)
Notizen über Annemie Fontanza (Notes on Annemie Fontana) (1973)
Spaetholz (feature) (project)

SANDRA HOCHMAN   *USA*

The Year of the Woman (1973)

Hochman is a novelist and poet who has thus far made only one film.

FAITH HUBLEY   *USA* (1924–   )

[all animated shorts co-directed with John Hubley]
Adventures of an * (1956)
Harlem Wednesday (1957)

Tender Game (1958)
Moonbird (1959)
Children of the Sun (1960)
Of Stars and Men (1962)
The Hole (1963)
The Hat (1964)
Urbanissimo (1966)
Tijuana Brass Double Feature (1966)
The Cruise (1967)
Windy Day (1968)
Zuckerkandl (1968)
Of Men and Demons (1969)
Eggs (1970)
Sesame Street Segments (1970–73)
Electric Company Segments (1970–73)
Dig (1972)
Upkeep (1973)
Cockaboody (1973)
Voyage to Next (1974)
People People People (1975)
W.O.W.-Women of the World (1975)
Everybody Rides the Carousel (1975)

DANIELE HUILLET   *West Germany*

[all with Jean-Marie Straub]
Othon (Les Yeux ne veulent pas en tout temps se fermer ou Peut-etre qu'un
     jour Rome se permettra de choisir a son tour) (1969) also scr
Geschichtsunterricht (History Lessons) (1972) also scr
Einleitung zy Arnold Schoenbergs Begleitmusik zu einer Lichtspielscene (Intro-
     duction to Arnold Schoenberg's Accompaniment to the Cinematographic
     Scene) (1972) also scr (short)
Moses und Aron (Moses and Aaron) (1975) also scr

Huillet is Straub's wife, and previously assisted him in various
functions. She has co-edited all of his films.

MARTHA HASLANGER   *USA* (1947–   )

[all shorts]
Focus (1972)
Your Home Is You (1973)
Outlines (1974)
June (1974)
Syntax (1974)
Joe (1976)
Frames And Cages and Speeches (1976)

LOUVA ELIZABETH IRVINE   *USA*

Dig We Must (1966) (short)
Ananda (1966) (short)

Landscapes (1966) (documentary)
Three Lives (1970) (with Kate Millett, Susan Kleckner and Robin Mide) (documentary)
Cowgirl Blue (1970) (with Mide) also actress (short)
Rain (1972) (short)
Circus (1972) (with J. D. Clegg)
Mirror Image (1972) (short)
Citywalk (1973) (short)
Aegean (1973)
Sophie Newman (1974) (short)
Murray Hill Morning (1974)
Blue Moment (1974)
Love (1975) (short)
European Journal (in progress)
Playground (in progress)
Portrait of Thomas Messer (in progress)

Irvine has also served as a consultant on several films.

BARBARA ISAACS *USA*

[all shorts]
Institute of Design (1963)
The Knowledge Box (1963)
Marie & Henry (1965)
Fifteen Women (1967)
Revolution for Two (1970)
Negative Earth (1973)
Ixtapa (1976) (in progress) (doc)

NORA IZQUE *Peru*

[all documentary shorts]
Encuentro (Encounter) (1967)
How They Filmed *The Green Wall* (1969)
Runan Cayu (I Am a Man) (1973)

SYLVIE JALLAUD *France*

[all shorts co-directed with Pierre Jallaud]
Des Maisons et des hommes (1953)
Donjere-Mondragon (1954)
Fleuve-Dieu (1955)
Spirales (1956)
L'Age des Cavavelles (1958)
Journal d'un certain David (1958)
47, rue Vielle-du-Temple (1960)
Comme un Reflet d'Oiseau (1961)
Les Six Jours de la Création (1962)

KAREN JOHNSON *USA*

[all shorts]
Orange (1969)
Lizard Mosaic (1971)
Hands

MARIA KANIEWSKA *Poland*

Not Far from Warsaw (1954)
Much Ado About Little Basia (1959) also scr
The Imp of the Seventh Grade (1960) also scr
On the Threshold of Art (1962)
Panienka z Okienka (1964)

NELLY KAPLAN   *Argentina* (1934–   )

Magirama (1956) (with Abel Gance)
Gustave Moreau (1961)
Rudolphe Bresdin (1961)
Dessins et merveilles (Drawings and Wonders) (1961)
A la Sorce, la femme aimée (At the Fountain of the Beloved) (1963)
Abel Gance, hier et demain (Abel Gance: Yesterday and Tomorrow) (1963)
Les Années 25 (1966)
La Nouvelle Orangerie (1966)
Le Regard Picasso (The Picasso Look) (1967)
André Masson (1968)
La Fiancée du pirate (US: A Very Curious Girl) (1960) also scr
Papa, les petits bateaux (1971)
Nea (1976)

Although Kaplan was born in Argentina, she has spent all of her adult life in France. Before directing her own films, she worked as an assistant to Abel Gance. In 1975, she co-wrote *Il faut vivre dangéreusement* with Claude Makovsky, who directed.

ANNA KARINA (Hanne Karin Blarke Beyer)   *Denmark* (1940–   )

Vivre ensemble (Living Together) (1973) also scr, act

Karina became a leading actress of the French New Wave, appearing prominently in the films of her husband, Jean-Luc Godard, until their divorce.

SUSAN KLECKNER *USA*

Three Lives (1971) (with Kate Millett, Louva Irvine and Robin Mide)
Birth (1972) (short)

BARBARA KOPPLE *USA*
Chrystal Lee (in progress)
Harlan County, USA (1976) (doc feature)

The film was produced by The Cabin Creek Center for Work and Environmental Studies.

ALEXIS RAFAEL KRASILOVSKY *USA*

[all shorts]
Audience (1970) (loops)
Bed and Grass (1971) (with Paul Nieto, Wade Aguiercia and John Ortinau)
The Divine Comedy (1971)
Charlie's Dream (1972)
Cows (1972)
End of the Art World (1972)
Her Way to Star (1972)
La Belle Dame Sans Merci (1973)
Charlie Dozes Off & The Dog Bothers Him (1973)
Guerrilla Commercial (1973)
Blood (1975)

BONNIE KREPS *Canada*

After the Vote (1969)
Portrait of My Mother (1974)
This Film is About Rape (1978)

ESTER KRUMBACHOVA *Czechoslovakia* (1923–   )

The Murder of Mr. Devil (1970) also scr
Valerie and Her Week of Wonders (1971) also scr

Krumbachova's major contribution to Czech cinema has been her scripts for other directors: Vera Chytilova (*Daisies* and *The Fruit of Paradise*) and Jan Nemec (*Report on the Party and the Guests*).

EVELYN LAMBART *Canada*

[all shorts]
Begone Dull Care (1949) (with Norman McLaren)
Family Tree (1950)
Rhythmetic (1956) (with McLaren)
Lines (Horizontal & Vertical) (1961) (with McLaren)
Mosaic (1965) (with McLaren)
Fine Feathers (1968)
The Hoarder (1969)
Paradise Lost (1970) (with McLaren)
Mr. Frog Went A-Courting (1974)
The Story of Christmas (1973)
The Impossible Map

KATHLEEN LAUGHLIN *USA* (1945–   )

[all animated shorts]
A Round Feeling (1970)
Opening/Closing (1972)
Disappearance of Sue (1972)
Susan Through Corn (1974)
Interview (1974)
Some Will Be Apples (1974)
Madsong (1976)
Sam E. (1976)
Gone By (1976)

CAROLINE LEAF   *USA* (1946–   )

[all animated shorts]
Sand, or Peter and the Wolf (1969)
Orfeo (1971)
How Beaver Stole Fire (1971)
The Owl Who Married The Goose (1975)
The Street (1976)
Metamorphosis (in progress)

CHRISTINE LEPINSKA *France*

Je suis Pierre Rivière (I am Pierre Rivière) (feature)

Lepinska has directed several shorts.

NAOMI LEVINE *USA*

[all shorts]
Yes, Jeremelu (1964)
From Zero to 16 (1967)
Optured Fraiken Chaitre Joe (1967)
Prismatic (1969)
Premoonptss (1969)
A Very Long Journey to Venus, Perhaps (1970)
I.A.I.a London Bridges Falling Down (1970)
Zen Plus the Art of Baseball (1971)
At My Mother's House (1971)

HELEN LEVITT *USA*

The Quiet One (1949) (with James Agee and Janice Loeb)
In the Street (1952) (edited version of The Quiet One) (short)
Another Light (short)

Levitt ·has also assisted in the making of several features and served as camerawoman on *The Savage Eye* (1960).

GUNNEL LINDBLOM *Sweden* (1931–   )

Summer Paradise (1978)

Lindblom is well known as an actress, especially for her work with Ingmar Bergman.

BARBARA LINKEVITCH *USA* (1950–   )

[all shorts]
Musical Chairs (1970)
Winter (1971)
Goodman (1972)
Thought Dreams (1972)
Traces (1973)
Silverpoint (1974)
Chinamoon (1975)

JOAN LITTLEWOOD *Great Britain* (1916–   )

Sparrows Can't Sing (1963) also scr

Littlewood, who created the Theatre Workshop in London, is one of Britain's leading stage directors.

BARBARA LODEN *USA* (1936–   )

Wanda (1971) also scr, act
The Boy Who Liked Deer (short)
The Frontier Experience (short)

Loden, the wife of director Elia Kazan, is also an actress, mainly in the theater.

JANICE LOEB *USA*

The Quiet One (1948) (with James Agee and Helen Levitt) also pr
In the Street (1952) (edited version of The Quiet One) (short)

LONDON WOMEN'S FILM GROUP *Great Britain*

[all shorts except where noted]
Serve and Obey (1972)
Bettshanger '72 (1972)
The Amazing Equal Pay Show (1973–1975) (feature)
Whose Choice? (1976)

MARIANNE LUEDCKE *West Germany*

Die Wollands (The Wollands) (with Ingo Kratisch) also co-scr
Familienglueck (A Happy Family Life) (1975) (with Kratisch) also co-scr

IDA LUPINO *USA* (1918–   )

Not Wanted (1949) (with Elmer Clifton) also pr, scr
Never Fear (1950) also scr
Outrage (1950) also scr
Hard, Fast and Beautiful (1951)
The Bigamist (1953) also act
The Hitchhiker (1953) also scr
The Trouble With Angels (1966)

Lupino became a director after a lengthy period as a Warner
Brothers' actress. Throughout the 1950's and 60's she directed many
television episodes including *Have Gun Will Travel; Mr. Novak;* and *The
Untouchables.* She also wrote *Private Hell 36*, which Don Siegel directed in
1953 for her production company. In addition, she produced *On The
Loose* and *Beware, My Lovely* in 1951.

SHIRLEY MacLAINE *USA* (1934–   )

The Other Half of the Sky: a China Memoir (1974) (with Claudia Weill) also pr

MacLaine is best known as an actress.

CLEO MADISON *USA* (1882–1964)

Liquid Dynamite (1915) also pr
King of Destiny (1915)
Her Defiance (1916)
Chalice of Sorrows (1916) (other sources say that Rex Ingram directed)

Madison was an actress at Universal during this period.

CECILIA MANGINI *Italy* (1927–   )

All'armi siam fascisti (1961)
Processo a Stalin (1963)
Essere donne (To Be Women) (1964) (short)
La scelta (The Choice)

SARAH MALDOROR (Sarah Ducados) *Guadeloupe*

Sambiganza (1972) also scr (made in Angola)
Saint-Danis sur avenir (short) (made in France)

Maldoror was a member of the African dance troupe in Paris and served as an assistant on Gillo Pontecorvo's *The Battle of Algiers* (1965).

BABETTE MANGOLTE

What Maisie Knew (1975)

Mangolte is primarily a camerawoman and was cinematographer for Yvonne Rainer's two features and for other independent filmmakers.

FRANCES MARION *USA* (1888–1973)

The Love Light (1921) also scr
Just Around the Corner (1922) also scr
The Song of Love (1924) (with Chester Franklin) also scr

Marion was one of the most prolific Hollywood screenwriters of the 1920's and 30's (*Stella Dallas, The Scarlet Letter, The Big House, The Champ, Dinner at Eight,* etc.).

AGNES MARTIN *USA*

Gabriel (1977)

Martin is an abstract painter.

ELAINE MAY *USA* (1932–   )

A New Leaf (1971) also scr, act
The Heartbreak Kid (1972)
Mikey and Nicky (1976)

May acted in *Luv* and *Enter Laughing,* and under a pseudonym adapted *Such Good Friends* for Otto Preminger.

MARGARET MEAD *USA* (1901–1979)

Childhood Rivalry in Bali and New Guinea (1952)
Trance and Dance in Bali (1952)

In addition to the two films listed above (originally shot in the 1930's, but not released until 1952), there exists hundreds of feet of unedited footage shot during Mead's anthropological expeditions.

MARIE MENKEN *USA* (1910–1970)

[all shorts]
Visual Variations on Noguchi (1945)
Hurry! Hurry! (1957)
Glimpse of the Garden (1957)
Dwightiana (1959)
Faucets (1960) (unfinished)
Eye Music in Red Major (1961)
Arabesque for Kenneth Anger (1961)
Bagatelle for Willard Maas (1961)
Zenscapes (1962) (unfinished)
Moonplay (1962) (unfinished)
Notebook (1963)
Mood Mondrian (1963)
Wrestling (1964)
Go Go Go (1964)
Drips in Strips (1961–1963) (unfinished)
Andy Warhol, Andy Warhol (1965)
Silent Version (1965)
Lights (1966) (unfinished)
Sidewalks (1961–1966) (unfinished)
Excursion (1968)
Watts With Eggs (1969)

Menken was married to filmmaker Willard Maas, some of whose films she worked on. During the Second World War, she served in the U.S. Signal Corps. Later, she also acted in several independent films.

MARTA MÉSZÁROS *Hungary* (1931–   )

They Smile Again (1954) (short)
A History of Albertfalva (1955) (short)
Beyond the Calvin Square (1955) (short)
It Also Depends on Us (1960) (short)
Heartbeat (1961) (short)
The Colors of Vasarhely (1961) (short)
Janos Tornyai (1962) (short)
Children-Books (1962) (short)
Saturday, July 27, 1963 (1963) (short)
Care and Affection (1963) (short)
Blow-ball (1964)
The Town of Painters (1964) (short)
Socialist Artists in Fine Arts 1933–1944 (1964)
Fifteen Minutes About 15 Years (1964)
The City of Bells (1966) (short)
Miklos Borsos (1966) (short)
The Girl (1968) also scr
Binding Sentiments (1969) also scr
Don't Cry, Pretty Girls (1970) also scr
Szabad (Good Riddance) (1973) also scr

Orokbefogadas (The Adoption) (1975) also scr
Kilenc Honap (Nine Months) (1976)
OK Ketten (The Two of Them) (1977).
Sidewalk in the Rain (1978)
Women (1978)

Mészáros was the wife of Hungarian director Miklos Jancso.

PILAR MIRO   *Spain*

La Petición (The Request) (1976)
Miro's previous work has been in video.

CLAUDE MISONNE   *Belgium*

Car je suis l'Empereur
Concerto
Dix petits nègres
El était un vieux savant
Formule X 24
Tintin et le crabe aux princes d'or

JEANNE MOREAU   *France* (1928–   )

Lumière (1976) also scr, act
new feature about the summer of 1939 in French Province (project)

Moreau has been a leading French actress of the last generation.

LAURA MULVEY   *Great Britain*

Penthesilea (1974) (with Peter Wollen) (made in USA)
Riddles of the Sphinx (with Wollen) (1977)

MUSIDORA (Jeanne Roques)   *France* (1889–1957)

Vicenta (1918) also scr, act
La Flamme Cachée (The Hidden Flame) (1920) also act
Pour Don Carlos (1921) also act
Soleil et ombre (Sun and Shadow) (1923) also act
La Terre des Taureaux (Land of the Bulls) (1924)
Le Berceau de Dieu (1926)
La Magique Image (Magic Image) (1951)

Musidora also acted in other director's films throughout her career.

ALLA NAZIMOVA   *Russia* (1879–1945)

Salome (1923) (uncredited) also act

Nazimova left her native Russia for Hollywood where she made films between 1915–1930.

DORE O. (NEKES)   *West Germany*

[all shorts]
Jüm Jüm (1967) (with Werner Nekes)
Alaska (1968)
Lawale (1969)
Kaldalon (1970–1971)
Blonde Barbarei (1972)
Kaskara (1974)

GUNVOR NELSON *Sweden* (1931–   )

[all shorts]
Schmeerguntz (1965) (with Dorothy Wiley)
Fog Pumas (1967) (with Wiley)
My Name is Oona (1969)
Kirsa Nicholina (1969)
Five Artists: Billbobbillbillbob (1971) (with Wiley)
Take-Off (1972)
Moon's Fool (1973)
One and the Same (1973) (with Freude)
Trollstenen (1976)

Nelson has made all of her films in the United States.

ANNABEL NICHOLSON *Great Britain*

[all shorts]
Abstract
Anju
Fez
Frames
Market
Mill Film
Scenes—Canada
Shapes
Slides (parts 1-4 & 5)
Slides
Spaced

GITTA NICKEL *East Germany*

[all documentaries]
We Understand Each Other (1965)
Then Spring My Heart (1966)
Siberia, My Home (1967)
Songs Make People (1968)
Here and There (1969)

She (1970)
Portrait of Walter Felsenstein (1971)
Portrait of Palucca (1971)
Portrait of Paul Dessau (1971)
The Peasant Women (1971)
Haying Weather (1972)
Tay-Ho, The Village in the Fourth Zone (1973)

MABEL NORMAND *USA* (1894–1930)

[all shorts made in 1914 in which she also acted]
Mabel's Strange Predicament
Love and Gasoline
Mabel at the Wheel
Caught in a Cabaret
Mabel's Busy Day
Mabel's Married Life
Won in a Closet
Mabel's Bare Escape

Normand was an early Vitagraph and Keystone comedy actress. Charles Chaplin, a frequent co-star, acted in several of the shorts she directed.

YOKO ONO *Japan* (1933–   )

[all shorts co-directed with John Lennon except where noted]
Film No. 4 (1964) (directed alone)
Apotheosis
Bottoms
Erection
Fly
Imagine
Rape II

JAN OXENBERG *USA*

[all shorts]
Home Movie (1973)
A Comedy in Six Unnatural Acts (1975)
Spilt Milk (in progress)

SHEILA PAGE *USA*

[all shorts except where noted]
Testing, Testing, How Do You Do? (1969)
Mother America (1970) (with Ariel Dougherty and Dolores Bargowski)
The Trials of Alice Crimmins (1971) (with Dougherty)
The Women's Happy Time Commune (1972) (feature)

The last film was produced by Women Make Movies, Inc., an organization devoted to feminist films.

IDA MAY PARK *USA*

Simple Pool (1913) (with Joseph de Grasse)
The Tangled Hearts (1916)
The Rescue (1917) also scr
The Fires of Rebellion (1917) (with de Grasse)
Bondage (1917) also scr
Broadway Love (1918) also scr
The Grand Passion (1918) also scr
Risky Road (1918) also scr
The Model's Confession (1918) also scr
Bread (1918) also scr
Amazing Wife (1919) also scr
Vanity Pool (1919) also scr
The Butterfly Man (1920) also scr
Bonnie May (1920) (with de Grasse)
The Midlanders (1920) (with de Grasse)
Penny of Top Hill Trail (1920) (with de Grasse)

CLAIRE PARKER *USA*

[all animated shorts co-directed with Alexandre Alexeieff]
Une Nuit Sur Le Mont Chauve (Night On Bald Mountain) (1934)
La Belle Aux Bois Dormant (Sleeping Beauty) (1935)
En Passant (In Passing) (1943)
Le Nez (The Nose) (1963)
Pictures At An Exhibition (1971)

With her husband Alexeieff, Parker created the pin screen and made animated films first in France and later in Canada. The couple gradually turned to making commercials, producing over thirty films between 1935–1960.

BARBARA PEETERS *USA*

The Dark Side of Tomorrow (1970)
Bury Me an Angel (1972) also scr

WA PING *China*

Story of Liupao Village (1957)
Constant Beam (1958)
Battle of Shanghai (1959)
Meng Lung Sha (1961)
Locust Tree Village (1962)
Sentinels Under the Neon Lights (1963) (with Ko Hsin)

Wa Ping is also a film actress.

SUZAN PITT-KRANING *USA* (1943–   )

[all animated shorts]
Walker Art Center (1968) (doc)
Cleaning, Giving Birth, Trying to Dance and Not Being Able To (1969)
Bowl, Theatre, Garden, Marble Game (1970)
Crocus (1971)
A City Trip (1972)
Cels (1972)
Whitney Commercial (1973)
Jefferson Circus Songs (1973)

ANNE-CLAIRE POIRIER *Canada* (1932–   )

Trente Minutes, M. Plummer (1962) (short)
La Fin des etes (1964) (short)
Les Ludions (1965) (shorts)
Impot et tout . . . en tout (1967) (short)
De Mere en fille (Mother To Be) (1968)
Le Savoir-faire s'impose (1971)
Le Temps de l'avant (1976)

Poirier's entire career has consisted of making films for the National Film Board of Canada and other Canadian agencies.

IRINA POPLAVSKAYA *USSR*

The Revenge (1959)
Jamilya (1970)

SALLY POTTER *Great Britain*

[all shorts]
Hors d'Oeuvres
Jerk
Play

Potter is also a dancer/choreographer in experimental theater.

OLGA PREOBRAZHENSKAYA *USSR* (1885–   )

Miss Peasant (1916) also scr
Kashtanka (1922)
Locksmith and Chancellor (1923) (with Vladimir Gardin)
The Village of Sin (1927)
The Peasant Women of Ryazan (1927)
The Last Attraction (1929)

The Quiet Don (1931) also scr
Paths of Enemies (1935) (with Ivan Pravov)
Grain (1936) (with Pravov)
Children of Taigo (1941) (with Pravov)

Preobrazhenskaya was an actress in pre-Revolution Russian films, and was an assistant to Vladimir Gardin before directing on her own.

TANIA QUARESMA   *Brazil*

Nordeste: Cordel, Repente, Cancao (Music and People of the Northwest) (1975) (doc)

YVONNE RAINER *USA*

Line (1969) (short)
Lives of Performers (1972)
Film About a Woman Who . . . (1974)
Kristina Talking Pictures (1976)

Rainer is also an avant-garde dancer and choreographer.

JACQUEE RAYNAL *France*

Deux fois (1970)

Raynal is an editor whose credits include Eric Rohmer's *La Collectioneuse* and *Paris vu par.* . . .

MRS. WALLACE REID (Dorothy Davenport) *USA* (1895–   )

Human Wreckage (1923)
Quicksands (1923)
Linda (1929)
Sucker Money (1933)
Road to Ruin (1933) (with Melville Shirer)
Woman Condemned (1934)

Reid's husband was a leading actor who died of drug addiction in 1923. His widow started making films to warn the public about the evil of drugs.

JULIA REICHERT *USA* (1946–   )

[all documentaries]
Growing Up Female: As Six Become One (1970) (with Jim Klein)
Methadone: An American Way of Dealing (1974) (with Klein)
Union Maids (1976) (with Klein and Miles Mogulescu)

LENI RIEFENSTAHL *Germany* (1902–   )

Das Blaue Licht (1932) also co-scr, act
Sieg des Glaubens (1933)
Tiefland (1934) (with Alfred Abel) also scr, act (unrealized)
Triumph des Willens (1935)
Tag der Freiheit-Wehrmacht (1935)
Olympia, Part I and II (1938)
Berchetesgarten uber Selzburg (1938)
Penthesilea (1939) also scr (unfinished)
Kriegswochenschauen (1939) (unfinished)
Van Gogh (1943) (unfinished)
Das Blaue Licht (1952) (unfinished)
Tiefland (1954) (with G.W. Pabst) also scr, act
Die Roten Teufel (1954) also scr (unfinished)
Ewige Gipfel (1954) (unfinished)
Friedrich and Voltaire (1955) (unfinished)
Drei Sterne am Mantel der Madonna (1955) (unfinished)
Schwartze Fracht (1956) also act (unfinished)
The Blue Licht (1960) also scr (unfinished)
Nuba (1973) (unfinished)

Riefenstahl turned to acting after working as a dancer. Her best known role was in *White Hell of Pitz Palu* (G.W. Pabst, 1928).

LOTTE REINIGER *Germany* (1899–   )

[all animated shorts except where noted]
Das Ornament des Verliebtet Herzens (Ornament of the Loving Hearts) (1919)
Amor und das Standhafte Liebespaar (Love and the Steadfast Sweethearts) (1920)
Der Fliegende Koffer (The Flying Coffer) (1921)
Der Stern von Bethlehem (The Star of Bethlehem) (1921)
Aschenputtel (Cinderella) (1922)
Dornroeschen (Sleeping Beauty) (1922)
Die Nibelungen (1923) (animated sequences) (dir: Fritz Lang)
Die Geschichte des Prinzen Achmed (The Adventures of Prince Achmed) (1923–1926) (feature)
Doktor Dolittle und Seine Tiere (Doctor Dolittle and His Animals) (1928) (three shorts)
Die Jagd Nach Dem Glueck (The Chase After Fortune) (1929–1930)
Zehn Minuten Mozart (1930) (animated sequences from) (dir: Gliese and Koch)
Harlekin (Harlequin) (1931)
Sissi (1932)
Don Quichote (Don Quixote) (1933) (animated sequence from) (dir: G. W. Pabst)
Carmen (1933)
Das Rollende Rad (The Rolling Wheel) (1934)
Der Graf von Carabas (Puss in Boots) (1934) (made in Switzerland)
Das Gestohlene Herz (The Stolen Heart) (1934)
Der Klein Schornsteinfeger (The Little Chimney Sweep) (1935) (made in Switzerland)

Galathea (1935) (made in Switzerland)
Papageno (1935) (made in Switzerland)
The King's Breakfast (1936)
Tocher (1937) (animated sequence from La Marseillaise) (dir: Jean Renoir)
    (made in Switzerland)
Dream Circus (1939)
L'Elisir D'Amore (1939)
Die Goldene Gans (The Golden Goose) (1944)
The Daughter (1949)
Mary's Birthday (1951)
Aladdin (1953)
The Magic Horse (1953)
Snow White and Rose Red (1953)
You've Asked for It (1953)
Caliph Storch (Caliph Stork) (1954)
Hansel and Gretel (1955)
Thumbelina (1955)
Jack and the Beanstalk (1955)
The Star of Bethlehem (1956)
La Belle Helene (1957)
The Seraglio (1958)
Aucassin and Nicolette (1975) (made in Canada)

MARTA RODRIQUEZ   *Colombia*

[all documentary shorts co-directed with Jorge Silva except where noted]
Chiricales (The Brickmakers) (1968–1972)
Planas: Testimonio de un Entocidio (Testimony on Ethnicide) (1973)
Campesinos (Peasants) (1976) (feature)

Rodriquez is married to Jorge Silva.

KATHY ROSE *USA*

[all animated shorts]
Portraits (1971)
Novers (1972)
The Mysterians (1973)
The Moon Show (1974)
Mirror People (1974)
The Arts Circus (1974)
The Doodlers (1975)
Rubber Cement (1976)
Pencil Booklings (in progress)

MICHELLE ROSIER   *France*

George qui? (George Who?) (1972)
Mon coeur est rouge (My Heart is Red) (1977)

STEPHANIE ROTHMAN *USA*

It's a Bikini World (1966) also co-scr
The Student Nurses (1970)
The Velvet Vampire (1971) also co-scr
Group Marriage (1972) also co-scr
Terminal Island (1973) also co-scr
The Working Girls (1974) also scr

For several years Rothman produced her own films under the name of Dimension Films which she ran with her husband Charles Swartz.

AMALIE ROTHSCHILD *USA* (1946–   )

[all documentary shorts]
Woo Who? May Wilson (1969)
The Center (1970)
Safari (1970)
It Happens To Us (1971)
Radioimmunoassay of Renin/Radioimmunoassay of Aldosterone (1973)
Nana, Mom and Me (1974)
Willard Van Dyke (in progress)

PAT RUSSELL *USA*

Reaching Out (1976)

LEONTINE SAGAN *Germany* (1889–1974)

Maedchen in Uniform (1931)
Men of Tomorrow (1932) (in Great Britain)

Sagan was an actress in Germany prior to becoming a director.

GABRIELA SAMPER *Colombia*

[all shorts made with Ray Witlan]
El Paramo de Cumanday (The Plain of Cumanday) (1965)
La Selva Vencida (The Selva Conquered) (1966)
El Hombre de la Sal (The Man of Salt) (1970)
Los Encontalados (1970)

Samper was married to Ray Witlan.

HELMA SANDERS *West Germany* (1940–   )

Angelika Urban Verkauferin Verlobt (1970)
Gewalt (Violence) (1971) (doc)
Die Industrielle Reserve-Armee (1971) (doc)

Der Angestellte (The Employee) (1972) (doc)
Die Maschine (The Machine) (1973)
Die Letzten Tage von Gomorrha (The Last Days of Gomorrha) (1974)
Erdbeben in Chili (Earthquake in Chile) (1974) (doc)
Unterm Pflaster Ist der Strand (Beach Under the Sidewalk) (1975)
Shirins Hochzeit (Shirin's Wedding) (1976)
Heinrich (1977)

CAROLEE SCHNEEMANN *USA*

[all shorts]
Carl Ruggles Christmas Breakfast (1963) (with James Tenney)
Meat Joy (1964)
Viet-Flakes (1965)
Body Collage (1966)
Water Light/Water Needle (1966)
Fuses (1964–1967)
Falling Bodies (1967) also actress
Plumb Line (1968–1972)
Illinois Central (1968)
Cooking With Apes or Subtle Gardening (1973)
Acts of Perception (1973)
Kitch's Last Meal (1973–1976)
Up To and Including Her Limits (1975) (mixed media)

Schneemann is a dancer as well as a filmmaker.

ESTHER SCHUB   *USSR* (1894–1959)

[all documentaries]
Padeniye Dinasti (The Fall of the Romanov Dynasty) (1927) also scr
The Great Road (1927) also scr
The Russia of Nikolai II and Lev Tolstoy (1928) also scr
Today (1930)
Komsomol (1932)
The Subway at Night (1934)
The Soviets' Land (1937)
Spain (1939)
Twenty Years of Soviet Cinema (1940) (with V.I. Pudovkin)
The Face of the Enemy (1941)
Sideways to Arax (1947)
Chilly Scenes of Winter (in progress)

As director of editing for the Soviet Cinema Archive, Schub is said
to have taught Eisenstein the art of editing. Later along with Dviga
Vertov she was the leading Russian newsreel maker.

LILLIAN SCHWARTZ   *USA*

[all shorts]
Pixillation (1970)

Mathoms (1970)
Olympiad (1971)
U.F.O.'s (1971)
Enigma (1972)
Googolplex (1972)
Apotheosis (1972)
Affinities (1972)
Mutations (1972)
Mis-Takes (1972)
Innocence (1973)
Papillons (1973)
Metamorphosis (1974)
Galaxies (1974)
Mirage (1974)
Metathesis (1974)
Kinesis (1975)
Collage (1975)
Alae (1975)
Pictures From A Gallery (1975)
Oberhausen (1976)
Cine Golden Eagle (1976)
The Artist and the Computer (1976)
La Saritata (1976)
Fantasies (1976)
Experiments (1976)
Bagatelles (1976)

ANNE SEVERSON *USA*

[all shorts except where noted]
I Change, I Am the Same (1969) (with Shelby Kennedy)
Riverbody (1970) (with Kennedy)
Introduction To Humanities (1971)
Near the Big Chakra (1972)
Animals Running
The Struggle of the Meat

DEBORAH SHAFFER   *USA* (1949–   )

[all shorts]
How About You? A Film On Birth Control and Sexuality (1972) (with Bonnie
    Friedman and Marilyn Mulford)
Chris and Bernie (1974) (with Friedman)
Make Out

KATHLEEN SHANNON *Canada* (1935–   )

[all shorts]
I Don't Think It's Meant For Us . . . (1971)
Like the Trees (1974)
Working Mothers (1974–1975) (10 part series)

. . . and they lived Happily Ever After (1975)
Goldwood (1975)

LARISSA SHEPITKO *USSR* (1939–   )

Znoy (Heat) (1963)
Krylya (Wings) (1966)
The Homeland of Electricity (1968)
Ty i ya (You and I) (1972)
Woschozdenie (The Ascent) (1977)

Shepitko is married to Soviet director Elem Klimov.

NELL SHIPMAN *Canada*

The Black Wolf (1917)
Baree, Son of Kazan (1918)
The Golden Yukon (1919)
The Girl from God's Country (1921) also scr, act
Neptune's Daughter (1922)
Back to God's Country (1927)

All of the films Shipman made in the United States reflected her attachment to her native Canada.

SHU SHUEN *Hong Kong*

The Arch (1969)

JOAN MICKLIN SILVER   *USA*

[all shorts except where noted]
The Immigrant Experience: The Long Long Journey (1972) (with Linda
   Gottlieb)
The Fur Coat Club (1973)
The Case of the Elevator Dock (1974)
Hester Street (1975) also scr (feature)
Bernice Bobs Her Hair (1976)
Between the Lines (1977)
Chilly Scenes of Winter (in progress)
Silver also wrote Limbo directed by Mark Robson (1973).

JUDY SMITH *USA*

The Woman's Film (1971) (with Louise Alaimo and Ellen Sorin) (short)

ANNA SOKOLOWSKA *Poland*

Beata (1965)

HELENA SOLBERG-LADD *Brazil* (1938–   )

The Interview (1966)
Noon (1970)
The Emerging Woman (1974)
The Double Day (1976) (feature)
Simplemente Geni (1977)

Solberg-Ladd's third and fourth films have been produced by the Women's Film Project and the International Women's Film Project, respectively.

YULIA SOLNTSEVA *USSR* (1901–   )

Shchors (1939) (with Alexander Dovzhenko)
Liberation (1940) (with Dovzhenko)
The Fight for the Soviet Ukraine (1943) (with Y. Avdeyenko and Dovzhenko)
Victory in the Ukraine (1945) (with Dovzhenko)
Life in Bloom (1974) (with Dovzhenko)
Life in Bloom (1947) (with Alexander Dovzhenko)
Igor Bulichov (1952)
Unwilling Inspectors (1954)
Poem of the Sea (1958)
Years of Fear (1960)
The Enchanted Desna (1964)
Unforgettable (1969)

Solntseva was originally an actress who became Alexander Dovzhenko's collaborator after their marriage.

SUSAN SONTAG *USA* (1933–   )

Duet for Cannibals (1969) also scr
Brother Karl (1971) also scr
Promised Lands (1974)

PENELOPE SPHEERIS *USA*

[all shorts]
National Rehabilitation Center (1968)
I Don't Know (1969)
Hats Off to Hollywood (1971)

SYLVIA SPRING *Canada*

Madeleine (1969) (short)
Madeleine Is (1970)

KIRSTEN STENBAEK *Denmark*

Miss Julie (1969) (short)
The Mad Dane
Lenin, You Rascal, You (1972)
The Dreamers

JANET STERNBURG *USA*

El Teatro Campesino (1970)
Virginia Woolf: The Moment Whole (1972) (short)

VIRGINIA STONE *USA*

Evil in the Deep (1976)

MILDRED (CHICK) STRAND *USA*

[all shorts]
Eric and the Monsters (1963)
Angel Blue Sweet Wings (1966)
Anselmo (1967)
Waterfall (1968)
Mosori Monika (1970)
Cosas de Mi Vida (1976)
Elasticity
Guacamole
Mujer de los Milfuegos

VERA STROYEVA *USSR* (1903–   )

The Rights of Fathers (1931)
Petersburg Nights (1934) (with Grigori Roshal)
Generation of Conquerors (1936) (with Roshal)
    (1940–45)
Marite (1947)
The Grand Concert (1951)
Boris Godunov (1955)
Khovanshchina (The Heart of Russia) (1959) also scr
Heart of Russia (1971)

Before directing, Stroyeva worked on the scripts of several films directed by her husband, Grigory Roshal. She also directed numerous shorts between 1940–1945.

MARIANNE SZEMES *Hungary* (1924–   )

I Shall Be a Seaman (1957) also scr
Travel Notes on Egypt (1957) also scr

(newsreels 1960–62)
Three Clouds of White Smoke (1964)
Divorce in Budapest (1964)
Exams and Confessions (1964)
Pilgrimage (1965)
Women Will Do Everything (1966)
It's So Simple (1967) also scr
I Am Angry for Your Sake (1968) also scr
I Do What I Like (1969) also scr

Szemes is married to Mihaly Szemes, a director with whom she wrote a number of scripts before turning to directing. Most of her own films have been documentaries.

KINOYU TANAKA   *Japan* (1910–1977)

Love Letter (1953)
The Moon Rises (1955)
Love Under the Crucifix (1966)

Tanaka was a prominent Japanese screen actress who appeared in Kenji Mizoguchi's *Ugetsu*. She directed several features including the two listed above.

ANITA THACHER *USA*

[all shorts]
Permanent Wave (1967)
Back Track (1969)
Mr. Story (1972) (with Dee Dee Halleck)
Hommage to Magritte (1974)
By Heart (in progress)

WENDY TOYE *Great Britain*

The Stranger Left No Card (1952) (short)
The Teckman Mystery (1954)
Three Cases of Murder (1954) (in the picture episode)
Raising A Riot (1955)
All For Mary (1955)
On the Twelfth Day (1955) (short)
True As a Turtle (1956)
We Joined the Navy (1962)
The King's Breakfast (1963) (short)

ANNIE TRESGOT *France*

Les Enfants de Néant (1967) (with Marcel Brault)
El Ghorba (The Passengers) (1971)
Visages de l'emigration

NADINE TRINTIGNANT *France* (1934–   )

Fragilité, ton nom est femme (Fragility, Thy Name is Woman) (1966) (short)
Mon amour, mon amour (1967) also scr
Le Voleur de crimes (The Crime Thief) (1969) also scr
Ca n'arrive qu'aux autres (It Only Happens to Others) (1971) also scr
Défense de savoir (1973) also scr
Le Voyages de. noces (The Honeymoon Trip) (1975) also scr

Trintignant, wife of actor Jean-Louis Trintignant, went from script girl to editor before directing.

LAILA TUHUS *Norway*

Oss (Us)

AGNES VARDA *France* (1928–   )

La Pointe courté (1954) (short)
O saisons, o chateaux (1957) (short)
L'Opera Mouffe (1958) (short)
Du coté de la côté (1958) (short)
Cleo de 5 a 7 (1961)
Salut les Cubains (1963) (doc short)
Le Bonheur (1965)
Elsa (1966)
Les Créatures (1966)
Loin du Vietnam (Far from Vietnam) (1967) (one section)
Uncle Yanco (1967) (short)
Black Panthers (1968) (doc)
Lions Love (1969)
Nausicaa (1970)
Mon Corps est à moi (1972)
Daguerreotypes (1975) (doc)
Response de femmes (1975) (short)
L'une chante, l'autre pas (One Sings, the Other Doesn't) (1977)

Varda lives with director Jacques Demy. Varda's career has included both documentary and fictional features.

JUDIT VAS *Hungary* (1932–   )

All educational films:
Polarised Light (1960)
Who Can Carry On Any Longer? (1962)
Circadian Rhythms (1965)
Bobe (1965)
Where Are You Going? (1966)
Who Is Your Friend? (1967)
Trio (1967)

NICOLE VEDRÈS *France* (1911–1965)

Paris 1900–1948) also scr
La Vie commence demain (Life Begins Tomorrow) (1950)
Amazone (1951) (short)
Aux frontières de l'homme (The Limits of Man) (1953) (with Jean Rostand)
   (short)

JACQUELINE VEUVE *France*

Les lettres de Stalingrad (Letters from Stalingrad) (documentary)
Mais, vous les filles
No More Fun and No More Games
Susan
Swiss Graffiti (1976) (short)

THEA VON HARBOU *Germany* (1888–1954)

Elisabeth und der Narr (1933)
Hanneles Himmelfarht (1934) also scr

Von Harbou was married to German film director Fritz Lang for whom she wrote all his scripts from 1921 to 1933. She remained in Germany after Lang's departure in 1933.

MARGARETHE VON TROTTA *West Germany*

Die Verlorene Ehre der Katharina Blum (The Lost Honor of Katharina Blum)
   (1975) (with Volker Schlondorff) also co-scr, act
Zweite Erwachen (The Second Awakening of Christa Klages (1978)

Von Trotta is married to Volker Schlondorff with whom she has co-authored several screenplays. She also acted in his film *A Free Woman* (1972).

ALIDA WALSH *USA*

[all shorts]
Wake Dream (1968)
The Martyrdom of Marilyn Monroe (1973)
Happy Birthday I'm Forty (1974)
Abstractions
Destruct Action
Prelude to HB

PATRICIA WATSON *Canada*

[all shorts]
Every Second Car (1964)

The Summer We Moved To Elm Street (1966)
The Purse (1966)
The Invention of the Adolescent (1967)
The Admittance (1968)
Death and Mourning (1969) (feature)

LOIS WEBER *USA* (1882–1939)

The Eyes of God (1913)
The Jew's Christmas (1913) (with Phillips Smalley) also scr
A Fool and His Money (1914) also act
The Merchant of Venice (1914) (with Smalley) also act
False Colors (1914) also act
Like Most Wives (1914) also scr
Hop, the Devil's Brew (1915) (with Smalley) also act
Sunshine Molly (1915) also act
A Cigarette, That's All (1915)
Scandal (1915) (with Smalley) also scr, act
Hypocrites (1915) (with Smalley) also scr
It's No Laughing Matter (1915)
The Dumb Girl of Portici (1916) (with Smalley) also scr
Saving the Family Name (1916) (with Smalley) also scr
The People vs. John Doe (1916) also act
Idle Wives (1916) (with Smalley)
Where Are My Children (1916) (with Smalley)
The Flirt (1916) (with Smalley)
Discontent (1916) also scr
The French Downstairs (1916)
Alone in the World (1916) (with Smalley) also scr
The Rock of Riches (1916) (with Smalley) also scr
John Needham's Double (1916)
Shoes (1916) also scr
The Price of a Good Time (1917)
Even As You and I (1917)
The Hand That Rocks the Cradle (1917) (with Smalley) also pr, act
The Mysterious Mrs. Musslewhite (1917)
The Man Who Dared God (1917)
There's No Place Like Home (1917)
For Husbands Only (1918)
The Doctor and the Woman (1918) also scr
Borrowed Clothes (1918)
Mary Regan (1919) also scr
A Midnight Romance (1919) also scr
When a Girl Loves (1919) also scr
Home (1919) also scr
Forbidden (1919) also scr
To Please One Woman (1920)
Too Wise Wives (1921) also scr
What's Worthwhile (1921) also pr, scr
The Blot (1921) also pr, scr
What Do Men Want? (1921) also pr, scr
A Chapter in Her Life (1923) also scr
The Marriage Clause (1926) also scr

The Sensation Seekers (1927) also scr
The Angel of Broadway (1927)
White Heat (1934)

Most of Weber's work has disappeared. The above is an incomplete list of films which she directed. Beginning as an actress, she turned to directing, at times working with her husband, actor Phillips Smalley. During the teens she ran her own production studio, first under the auspices of Universal Studios and later, known as Lois Weber Productions, for Famous Players-Lasky.

CLAUDIA WEILL *USA* (1946–   )

[all shorts except where noted]
Metropole (1968)
Radcliffe Blues: Fran (1968)
Putney School (1969) (with Eliot Noyes, Jr.)
This is the Home of Mrs. Levant Graham (1970) (with Noyes)
IDCA (1970) (with Noyes)
Sesame Street (1971–1972) (15 live action and 2 animated segments)
Commuters, Yoga-Great Neck, Roaches, Marriage Bureau, Subway Lost and
    Found, Belly Dancing, Bad Dog (1972–1973) (with Noyes)
Not So Young Now As Then (1971–1973) (with Liane Brandon) (photog. only)
Joyce at 34 (1972) (with Joyce Chopra)
Year of the Woman (1972) (dir: Sandra Hochman) (photog. only)
The Other Half of the Sky: A China Memoir (1974) (with Shirley MacLaine)
    (feature documentary)
Girlfriends (1978)

RACHEL WEINBERG *France*

Pic et pic et colegram (Hocus Pocus) (1972)
L'ampélopède (The Amonolopede) (1973)

MIRIAM WEINSTEIN *USA*

[all shorts except where noted]
Liberate the Ladies (1969)
Not Me Alone: Preparation for Childbirth (1971) (co-directed)
Talking About Breastfeeding (1971) (co-directed)
How To Make A Woman (1972) (feature)
My Father the Doctor (1972)
Day Care Today (1973)
Living with Peter (1973)
I Am Mrs. Malcolm Peabody (1973) (co-directed)
We Get Married Twice (1973)
Not Together Now; End of a Marriage (1975)
When a Child Enters the Hospital (1975)

LINA WERTMÜLLER (Arcangela Wertmüller von Elgg)   *Italy*
(1932–   )

I Basilischi (The Lizards) (1963) also scr
Questa volta parliamo di uomini (Let's Talk About Men) (1965) also scr
Non stuzzicate la zanzara (Don't Tease the Mosquito) (1967) (short) also scr
Rita la zanzara (Rita the Mosquito) (1966) (short) also scr
Mimi mettalurgico ferito nell'onore (US: The Seduction of Mimi) (1971) also
    scr
Film d'amore e d'anarchia (Love and Anarchy) 1972) also scr
Tutto a posto e niente in ordine (US: All Screwed Up) (1973) also scr
Travolti da un insolito destino nell' azzurro mare d'agosto (Swept Away by
    an Unusual Destiny in the Blue Sea of August) (1974) also scr
Pasqualino Settebellezze (Seven Beauties) (1975) also scr
The End of the World in Our Usual Bed in a Night Full of Rain (1977)

After a theatrical background, Wertmüller became an assistant to
Fellini on $8^1/_2$. She has worked on film scripts for other directors in
cluding *Brother Sun, Sister Moon* (Franco Zefferelli, 1972).

JOYCE WIELAND *Canada*

[all shorts except where noted]
Larry's Recent Behavior (1963)
Peggy's Blue Skylight (1964)
Patriotism, Parts I & II (1964)
Water Sark (1965)
Barbara's Blindness (1965) (with Betty Ferguson)
Sailboat (1967)
1933 (1967)
Hand-Tinting (1967)
Catfood (1968)
Rat Life and Diet in North America (1968)
La Raison Avant la Passion (Reason Over Passion) (1969) (feature)
Dripping Water (1969) (with Michael Snow)
Pierre Vollieres (1972)
Solidarity (1973)
The Far Shore (1976) (feature)
True Patriot Love (in progress)

Wieland is married to experimental filmmaker Michael Snow.

DOROTHY WILEY *USA*

[all shorts]
Schmeerguntz (1965) (with Gunvor Nelson)
Fog Pumas (1967) (with Nelson)

Five Artists Billbobbillbillbob (1971) (with Nelson)
Cabbage
Coffee and Cobwebs
Helping Frogs Avoid Their Death
Letters
Miss Jesus Fries On Grill
The Weenie Worm or the Fat Innkeeper
Zame Forbidden

FRANCINE WINHAM *Great Britain*

[all shorts]
Put Yourself in My Place (1973)
Hell Girl House (1974)
Careless Love (1975)

LINDA YELLEN *USA*

Looking Up (1977)

MAI ZETTERLING *Sweden* (1925–   )

[all films with only English titles are documentaries made in Great Britain,
     with the exception of Visions of Eight]
The Polite Invasion (1960)
Lords of Little Egypt (1961)
The Prosperity Race (1962)
The War Game (1963) (short)
The Do-It-Yourself Democracy (1963)
Alskande par (Loving Couples) (1964)
Langtan (Night Games) (1966)
Doktor Glas (Doctor Glas) (1968)
Flickorna (The Girls) (1968)
Van Gogh (Vincent the Dutchman) (1971)
Visions of Eight (1973) (segment on weight lifting) (made in Japan)

An actress in Swedish films since the 1940's, Zetterling went to
Britain in the late 1950's where she and her husband David Hughes
collaborated on a series of documentaries.

BINKA ZHELJAZKOVA *Bulgaria*

We Were Young (1961)
The Attached Balloon (1967)
The Last Word (1974)

Bibliography

The following bibliography constitutes a lengthy but not exhaustive listing of books and articles on the image of women in film and on individual female directors. In compiling this list, efforts were made to include a wide variety of journals, a cross-section of film genres, and as many directresses as possible. Where magazine titles have not clearly indicated the subject of an article, I have inserted the director's name in parenthesis. I have also included some articles going back to the beginning of the century which deal with individual directors and the position of women in the industry.

In selecting material, I was able to include only a small number of film reviews. Therefore, I chose those reviews which dealt specifically with feminist concerns. Lastly, as space limitations precluded any treatment of women screenwriters, editors, and producers within the main text of this anthology, I have tried to cover these women in the bibliography.

Books

Atkins, Thomas (ed.). *Sexuality in the Movies*. Bloomington: Indiana University Press, 1975. Selected essays dealing with sex in the cinema, several of which touch on the treatment of women in films with a strong male bias.

Barsam, Richard Meran. *Filmguide to Triumph of the Will*. Bloomington: Indiana University Press, 1975. A thorough-going analysis with background information on Leni Riefenstahl's documentary masterpiece.

Betancourt, Jeanne. *Women in Focus*. Dayton, Ohio: Pflaum Publishing, 1974. A reference guide to over 70 films by and about women with suggestions for classroom use. Also includes a reading list.

Billard, Pierre. *Vamps*. Levallois, Société d'Editions. A picture book dealing with famous *femme fatales* of the screen.

Box, Muriel. *Odd Woman Out*. London: Frewin, 1974. An autobiography of a British writer/director/producer of the 1940's and 1950's.

Bruno, Michael. *Venus in Hollywood: The Continental Enchantress From Garbo to Loren*. New York: Lyle Stuart, Inc., 1970. Deals with European glamor stars on the American screen.

Cameron, Ian and Elisabeth. *Broads*. New York: Praeger, 1969. English title: *Dames*, London: Studio Vista, 1969. A collection of pictures and biographies of the tough women who peopled the underworld films post-1939.

Dawson, Bonnie. *800 16mm Films By Women*. San Francisco: Booklegger Press, 1975.

Deren, Maya. *An Anagram of Ideas on Ideas on Art, Form and Film*. Yonkers, New York: The Alicat Book Shop Press, 1946. Reprinted in *Film Culture*, no. 39. A theoretical text setting forth Deren's notions on art and filmmaking.

Durgnat, Raymond. *Sexual Alienation in the Cinema: The Dynamics of Sexual Freedom*. London: Studio Vista, 1972. A loose meandering book which touches upon women's roles in films dealing with sexual themes.

Duvillars, Pierre. *Pin-up, femme fatales et ingenues libertines*. Paris: Editions du XXe siecle, 1951. Devoted to stars and their images in the movies.

Ferlita, Ernest and John R. May. *The Parables of Lina Wertmüller*. New York: Paulist Press, 1977. Essays on Wertmüller's life and works with specific attention to her concepts of myth-making, politics, and the relationship between women and men in society. Good bibliography.

Ford, Charles. *Femmes cinéastes, ou, le triomphe de la volonté*. Paris: Denoël, 1972. Biographical essays on world famous women directors.

Ford, Charles. *Germaine Dulac, 1882–1942*. Paris: Anthologie du cinéma, 1968. A long essay on the life and the work of a French pioneer filmmaker.

French, Brandon. *On the Verge of Revolt: Women in American Films of the Fifties*. New York: Frederick Ungar Publishing Co., 1978. Analyses of thirteen popular films of the 1950s which support French's contention that the era was not as tranquil as critics had supposed, but rather a period of ambiguity and schizophrenia which prepared the ground for the feminist outburst in the 1960s.

Glyn, Anthony. *Elinor Glyn: A Biography*. Garden City, New York: Doubleday & Co., 1955. A biography of the British writer/producer who had an impressive career in Hollywood during the 1920's.

Haskell, Molly. *From Reverence to Rape: The Treatment of Women in the Movies*. New York: Holt, Rinehart and Winston, 1973. A history of the representation of women in American cinema from 1920 through the early 1970's. Includes a chapter on the European scene. Special emphasis on the work of individual directors.

Kay, Karyn and Gerald Peary (ed.). *Women and the Cinema: A Critical Anthology*. New York: E. P. Dutton, 1977. A collection of articles dealing with all phases of women and film: images, actresses, women in production, and feminist politics and theory. Includes good bibliographies.

Loos, Anita. *A Girl Like I*. New York: Viking Press, 1966. An autobiography of the prolific Hollywood screenwriter whose career dates back to 1912.

Loos, Anita. *Kiss Hollywood Good-By*. New York: Viking Press, 1975. Second installment of the above.

MacLaine, Shirley. *You Can Get There From Here*. New York: W. W. Norton & Company, Inc., 1975. An autobiography which includes description of the filming of *The Other Half of the Sky: A China Memoir*.

Marion, Frances. *Off With Their Heads!* New York: Macmillan Company, 1972. An autobiography of Hollywood screenwriter active in the 1920's and 1930's.

Mekas, Jonas. *Movie Journal: The Rise of a New American Cinema, 1959–1971*. New York: Collier Books, 1972. Reviews of underground films of the 1950's and 1960's. Includes works by several women filmmakers.

Mellen, Joan. *The Waves at Genji's Door: Japan Through Its Cinema.* New York: Pantheon Books, 1976. A critical text which illucidates the treatment of women in Japanese society and on the screen.

Mellen, Joan. *Women and Their Sexuality in the New Film.* New York: Horizon Press, 1973. Critical essays on contemporary American and European films, which dissect the roles of women. Strong political emphasis.

Morin, Edgar. *The Stars.* Translated by Richard Howard. New York: Grove Press, 1960. An analysis of the star phenomenon in our culture.

Rosen, Marjorie. *Popcorn Venus: Women, Movies and the American Dream.* New York: Coward, McCann & Geoghegan, 1973. A history of women's roles in the American cinema, especially as they relate to the social and cultural pressures within the society. Covers period from 1900 to 1970. Brief chapter on women directors.

Russett, Robert and Cecile Starr. *Experimental Animation: An Illustrated Anthology.* New York: Van Nostrand Reinhold Company, 1976. Essays on film animators, including several women filmmakers.

Siclier, Jacques. *La femme à l'écran.* Brussels: Club du Livre de Cinema, 1957. Deals with the image of women in the movies.

Siclier, Jacques. *La femme dans le cinéma français.* Paris: Editions du Cerf, 1957. Deals with the representation of women in French cinema.

Siclier, Jacques. *Le mythe de la femme dans le cinéma américain de "La Divine" à Blanche Dubois.* Paris: Editions du Cerf, 1956. Deals with the presentation of women in American films from Greta Garbo to Vivien Leigh.

Slide, Anthony. *Early Women Directors: Their Role in the Development of the Silent Cinema.* South Brunswick, New Jersey: A. S. Barnes and Company, 1977. A collection of essays on Alice Guy Blaché, Lois Weber, Margery Wilson, Mrs. Wallace Reid, Frances Marion, Dorothy Arzner, and other early women directors.

Smith, Sharon. *Women Who Make Movies.* New York: Hopkinson and Blake, 1975. Reference book devoted exclusively to women directors throughout the world. Long listing of contemporary American women filmmakers.

Tyler, Parker. *Screening the Sexes: Homosexuality in the Movies.* New York: Holt, Rinehart, and Winston, 1972. Devoted to male homosexuality, which periodically sheds light on sexual portrayal of women as well.

Zierold, Norman. *Sex Goddesses of the Silent Screen.* Chicago: Henry Regnery Company, 1973. Deals with lives and films of stars like Theda Bara, Pola Negri, and Clara Bow.

Pamphlets, Programs, and Special Magazine Editions

"Le Donne del cinema contro questo cinema." *Biance e nero,* no. 1-2, January-February, 1972.

"Femmes." *Ecran,* no. 28, August-September, 1974.

"Les Femmes et le cinema." *Le Revue du cinéma/Image et son,* no. 283, April, 1974.

Festival of Women's Films. The Second International Festival of Women's Films. New York, 1976.

Films By Women/Chicago '74. The Film Center of the Art Institute of Chicago, 1974.

"Hungarian Women Directors." *Hungarofilm,* no. 3, 1969.

Johnston, Claire (ed.). *Notes on Women's Cinema.* London, Society for Education in Film and Television, 1973.

Johnston, Claire (ed.). *The Work of Dorothy Arzner: Towards a Feminist Cinema.* London, The British Film Institute, 1975.
"La Femme au cinéma." *Image et son,* no. 167–168, November-December, 1963.
"La Femme et le cinéma." *Cahiers du cinéma,* vol. 5, no. 30, Christmas, 1953.
The Legend of Maya Deren. Film Culture. 3 vols. in progress.
"1965—Comback for Leni Riefenstahl." *Film Comment,* vol. III, no. 1, Winter, 1965.
"Sexual Politics and the Film." *The Velvet Light Trap,* no. 6 Fall, 1972.
"Special Issue: Women in Film," *Journal of the University Film Association,* vol. XXVI, no. 1-2, 1974.
"Tribute to Leni Riefenstahl." *Film Culture,* no. 56-57, Spring, 1973.
Women & Film, vol. I, no. 1, 1972—vol. II, no. 7, 1975.
"Women and Film." *Cinema,* no. 35, 1976.
"Women and Film." *Film Heritage,* vol. II, no. 2, Winter 1975–1976.
Women and Film—La Femme et le Film 1896–1973. Toronto International Festival, 1973.
"Women in Film." *Film Library Quarterly,* vol. 5, no. 1 Winter, 1971–1972.
"Women in Film." *Take One,* vol. 3, no. 2, February, 1972.
Women's Films—A Critical Guide. Indiana University Audio-Visual Center, 1975.
"Writings of Maya Deren." *Film Culture,* no. 39, Winter, 1965.

Achtenberg, Ben. "Helen van Dongen: An Interview." *Film Quarterly,* vol. XXX, no. 2, Winter, 1976–1977.
"Background: Female Directors." *Film,* no. 1, April, 1973.
Barkhausen, Hans. "Footnote to the History of Riefenstahl's *Olympia.*" *Film Quarterly,* vol. XXVIII, no. 1, Fall, 1974.
Barnouw, Erik. "Leni Riefenstahl" in *Documentary: A History of the Non-Fiction Film,* London, Oxford University Press, 1974.
Barsam, Richard Meran. "Leni Riefenstahl: Artifice and Truth in a World Apart." *Film Comment,* vol. IX, no. 6, November–December, 1973.
Barsam, Richard Meran. "Leni Riefenstahl" in *Nonfiction Film: A Critical History,* New York, E. P. Dutton & Co., Inc., 1973.
Berg, Gretchen. "Shirley Clarke" (Interview). *Dance Perspectives,* no. 30, Summer, 1967.
Bettelheim, Bruno. "Reflections (Concentration-Camp Survival)," *New Yorker,* August 2, 1976.
Biskind, Peter. "Lina Wertmüller: The Politics of Private Life," *Film Quarterly,* vol. XXVIII, no. 2, Winter, 1974–75.
Biskind, Peter. "Tightass and Cocksucker: Sexual Politics in *Thunderbolt and Lightfoot,*" *Jump Cut,* no. 4. November–December, 1974.
Blumenfeld, Gina. "The (next to) Last Word on Lina Wertmuller." *Cinéaste,* vol. VII, no. 2, Spring, 1976.
Blumer, Ronald H. "The Camera as Snowball: France 1918–1927" (Germaine Dulac). *Cinema Journal,* vol. IX, no. 2, Spring, 1970.
Bosworth, Patricia. "Women Assistant Directors." *Action,* vol. 9, no. 1, January–February, 1974.
Bourget, Jean-Loup. "Romantic Dramas of the Forties; An Analysis." *Film Comment,* vol. X, no. 1, January–February, 1974.
Brackett, Leigh. "A Comment on the Hawksian Woman." *Take One,* vol. III, no. 6, July–August, 1971. Published October, 1972.

Brackett, Leigh. "From *The Big Sleep* to *The Long Goodbye* and More or Less How We Got There." *Take One*, vol. IV, no. 1, September–October, 1972. Published January, 1974.

Braderman, Joan. "Report: The First Festival of Women's Films." *Artforum*, vol. XI, no. 1, September, 1972.

Brandy, Susan. "Joan Tewkesbury: The Woman Behind *Nashville, Ms.*, vol. IV, no. 1, 1975.

Brenner, Marie. "Is Sue Mengers Too Pushy for Hollywood." *New York*, vol. VIII, no. 11, March 17, 1975.

Brownlow, Kevin. "Leni Riefenstahl." *Film*, no. 47, Winter, 1966.

Brownlow, Kevin. "Margaret Booth." *The Parade's Gone By*. . . . New York, Alfred A. Knopf, 1969.

Campbell, Gregg M. "Beethoven, Chopin and Tammy Wynette: Heroines and Archetypes in *Five Easy Pieces*." *Literature/Film Quarterly*, vol. II, no. 3, 1974.

Canby, Vincent. "Two Formidable Female Stars." *The New York Times*, July 21, 1974.

Changas, Estelle. "Slut, Bitch, Virgin, Mother: The Role of Women in Some Recent Films," *Cinema* (Los Angeles), vol. VI, no. 3, Spring, 1971.

Childs, James. "Penelope Gilliatt" (Interview). *The Hollywood Screenwriters*, edited by Richard Corliss. New York, Avon Books, 1972.

Clarens, Carlos. "*India Song* and Marguerite Duras" (Interview). *Sight and Sound*, vol. 45, no. 1, Winter, 1975–76.

Clarke, Shirley, and Storm De Hirsch. " 'Female' Film-Making." *Arts Magazine*, vol. XLI, no. 23–24, April, 1967.

"A Conversation: Storm de Hirsch and Shirley Clarke." *Film Culture*, no. 46, Autumn, 1967.

Cook, Pam. "Exploitation Films and Feminism." *Screen*, vol. 17, no. 2, Summer, 1976.

Cook, Pam and Claire Johnston. "The Place of Women in the Films of Raoul Walsh," *Raoul Walsh* edited by Phil Hardy. Edinburgh Film Festival, 1974.

Coolidge, Martha. "You Mean People Get *Paid* To Do That." *American Film*, vol. I, no. 8, 1976.

Cooper, Karen. "Kate Millett's *Three Lives*: Interviews with Kate Millett, Louva Irvine, and Susan Kleckner." *Film-makers Newsletter*, vol. V, no. 3, January, 1972.

Cooper, Karen. "Shirley Clarke." *Filmmakers Newsletter*, vol. V, no. 8, June, 1972.

Corliss, Richard. "Leni Riefenstahl." *Film Heritage*, vol. V, no. 1, Fall, 1969.

Cornwell, Regina. "*True Patriot Love*: The Films of Joyce Wieland." *Artforum*, vol. X, no. 1, September, 1971.

Cowie, Peter. "Mai Zetterling." *Sweden II*, New York, A.S. Barnes and Co., 1970.

Davidon, Ann Morrissett. "A Great Man Who Humiliates Women?" *The Village Voice*, February 1, 1973.

Davis, Russell E. "*Alice Doesn't Live Here Anymore*: Under the Comic Frosting." *Jump Cut*, no. 7, May–July, 1975.

Dawson, Jan. "*India Song*: A Chant of Love and Death." (Interview). *Film Comment*, vol. II, no. 6, November–December, 1975.

De Lauretis, Teresa. "The Case of *The Night Porter*: A Woman's Film?" Film Quarterly, vol. XXX, no. 2, Winter, 1976–1977.

de Laurot, Yves. "The Public As Vanguard of the People: A Woman's Liberation and the Avatars of Madame Prometheus." *Cinéaste*, vol. IV, no. 4, Spring, 1971.

Denby, David, "Men Without Women, Women Without Men." *Harper's*, vol. 247, September, 1973.

Des Pres, Terrence. "Bleak Comedies: Lina Wertmuller's Artful Method." *Harper's*, vol. 252, no. 1513, June, 1976.

"Dialogue on Film" (Interview with François Truffaut and Jeanne Moreau)." *American Film*, vol. I, no. 7, May, 1976.

"Dialogue on Film" (Interview with Verna Fields). *American Film*, vol. I, no. 8, June, 1976.

Dove, Linda and the London Women's Film Group. "London Letter: Feminist and Left Independent Filmmaking in England." *Jump Cut*, no. 10–11, 1976.

Dowd, Nancy Ellen. "The Woman Director Through the Years." *Action*, vol. 8, July–August, 1973.

Durgnat, Raymond. "Mth Marilyn Monroe." *Film Comment*, vol. X, no. 2, March–April, 1974.

Edwards, Susan. "*The Other Half of the Sky: A China Memoir:* Women Hold Up Half the Sky." *Jump Cut*, no. 10–11, 1976.

Elley, Derek. "Larissa Shepitko: Age and Dust." *Films and Filming*, vol. XX, no. 6, March, 1974

Elley, Derek. "Marta Mészáros: Breaking Free." *Films and Filming*, vol. XX, no. 5, February, 1974.

Elley, Derek. "Nelly Kaplan: First Make 'em Laugh." *Films and Filming*, vol. XX, no. 4, January, 1974.

Emmens, Carol. "In Search of Alternative Film Distributors." *Media & Methods*, vol. XI, October, 1974.

Emmens, Carol A. *"Janie's Janie."* *Film Library Quarterly*, vol. VI, no. 2, 1973.

Emmens, Carol A. "Who's Who in Filmmaking: Amalie Rothschild, feminist Filmmaker." *Sightlines*, vol. VII, no. 4, 1974.

Erens, Patricia. "*Love and Anarchy:* Passion and Pity." *Jump Cut*, no. 2, July–August, 1974.

Erens, Patricia. "Making and Distributing *Nana, Mom, and Me*" (Interview). *The Feminist Art Journal*, vol. IV, no. 2, Summer, 1975.

Erens, Patricia and Virginia Wexman. "Writer for Altman" (Joan Tewkesbury). *Sight and Sound*, vol. 45, no. 2, Spring, 1976.

Farber, Stephen. "Violence and Bitch Goddess." *Film Comment*, vol. X, no. 6, November–December, 1974.

Finkle, David. "Random Thoughts on a First Viewing of *The Women.*" *Filmograph*, vol. III, no. 4, 1973.

Fox, Terry Curtis. "Stephanie Rothman: Feminist on Poverty Row." *Film Comment*, November–December, 1976.

Froug, William. "Fay Kanin." *The Screenwriter Looks at the Screenwriter*, New York, Dell Publishing Co., 1972.

Garson, Barbara. "Upfront with Lina Wertmüller." *Ms.*, vol. III, no. 11, May, 1975.

Garson, Barbara. "The Wertmüller Ethic," *Ms.*, vol. IV, no. 11, May, 1976.

Gelder, P. "Lotte Reiniger: Figures in Silhouette." *Film*, no. 59, Summer, 1970.

Geraghty, Christine. *"Alice Doesn't Live Here Anymore."* *Movie*, no. 22, Spring, 1976.

Gerard, Lillian. "The Ascendance of Lina Wertmüller: Reviving the 'Foreign

Film'." *American Film,* vol. I, no. 7, May, 1976.

Giroux, Henry. *"Night Porter:* The Challenge of Neo-Fascist Culture." *Cinéaste,* vol. VI, no. 4, n.d.

Glaessner, Verina. "Women's Films at Knokke." *Jump Cut,* no. 8, August–September, 1975.

Gough-Yates, Kevin. "The Heroine." *Films and Filming,* vol. XII, nos. 8–11, May–August, 1966.

Gould, Lois. "Pornography For Women." *The New York Times Magazine,* March 2, 1975.

Gow, Gordon. "The Underground River" (Agnès Varda). *Films and Filming,* vol. XVI, no. 6, March, 1970.

Greenberg, Caren. *"Carnal Knowledge:* A Woman is Missing." *Diacritics,* vol. V, no. 4, Winter, 1975.

Greene, Linda. *"A Very Curious Girl:* Politics of a Feminist Fantasy." *Jump Cut,* no. 6, March–April, 1975.

Greenfield, Amy. "Dance As Film." *Filmmakers Newsletter,* vol. IV, no. 1, November, 1970.

Greene, Linda. *"Woman to Woman."* *Jump Cut,* no. 12–13, December, 1976.

Greenstone, Rosa. "A Week to Remember." *New York,* January 3, 1977.

Grossvogel, D. I. "Heads or Tails: Women in American Movies and Society." *Diacritics,* vol. V, no. 3, Fall, 1975.

"Halas and Batchelor." *International Film Guide,* no. 2, 1965.

Halberstadt, Ira. *"Hester Street"* (Interview). *Filmmakers Newsletter,* vol. IX, no. 3, January, 1976.

Halberstadt, Ira. "Independent Distribution: New Day Films," Filmmakers Newsletter, vol. 10, no. 1, November, 1976.

Harmetz, Aljean. "Rape an Ugly Movie Trend." *The New York Times,* September, 1973.

Harmetz, Aljean. "Two Dolls Play House." *Ms.,* vol. II, no. 7, January, 1974.

Hartt, Laurinda. "Kathleen Shannon: Working Mothers Series" (Interview). *Cinema Canada,* vol. II, no. 15, August–September, 1974.

Haskell, Molly. weekly columns in *The Village Voice,* especially 20, October 1, October 22, 1970; February 25, March 25, April 22, May 13, July 15, August 26, September 30, October 21, October 28, November 11, 1971, January 20, April 13, April 27, June 29, November 9, November 23, November 30, December 21, December 28, 1972; January 4, February 22, March 1, May 10, June 21, August 2, October 25, 1973; January 31, September 19, November 21, 1974; January 6, February 3, April 28, May 19, September 22, October 20, December 29, 1975; and January 26, April 26, June 21, June 28, July 12, 1976.

Haskell, Molly. "Here Come the Killer Dames." *New York,* May 19, 1975.

Haskell, Molly. "Howard Hawks: Masculine Feminine." *Film Comment,* vol. X, no. 2, March–April, 1974.

Haskell, Molly. "Women Directors: On Toppling the Male Mystique." *American Film,* vol. I, no. 8, June, 1976.

Henshaw, Richard. "A Festival of One's Own: Review of Women Directors." *The Velvet Light Trap,* no. 6, Fall, 1972.

Henshaw, Richard. "Women Directors." *Film Comment,* vol. VIII, no. 4, November–December, 1972.

Husserl-Kapit. "An Interview with Marguerite Duras." *Signs,* vol. I, no. 2, Winter, 1975.

Ibranyi-Kiss, Augie. "Bonnie Kreps: Feminist Filmmaker." *Cinema Canada,*

June–July, 1974.

Ibranyi-Kiss, Augie. "Carol on Camera." *Cinema Canada*, no. 16, October–November, 1974.

Ibranyi-Kiss, Augie. "Women in Canadian Films" (Interview with Mireille Dansereau)." *Cinema Canada*, no. 5, December–January, 1972–73.

"Interview with Shirley Clarke." *Film Culture*, Spring, 1967.

Israel, Lee. "Saving an Endangered Species: Women and Film." *Ms.*, vol. III, No. 8, February, 1975.

Jacobs, Diane. "Lina Wertmüller: The Italian Aristophanes." *Film Comment*, vol. XII, no. 2, March–April, 1976.

Jacobson, Mark. "Sex Goddess of the Seventies?" *New York*, May 19, 1975.

Jarvie, I. C. "Recent Films About Marriage." *The Journal of Popular Film*, vol. II, no. 3, 1973.

Jebb, Julian. "Truffaut: The Educated Heart." *Sight and Sound*, vol. XLIV, no. 3, Summer, 1972.

Johnston, Claire. "Femininity and the Masquerade: *Anne of the Indies*." *Jacques Tourneur* edited by Claire Johnston and Paul Willemen, Edinburgh Film Festival, 1975.

Johnston, Claire. "Feminist Politics and Film History." *Screen*, vol. XVI, no. 3, Autumn, 1975.

Johnston, Claire. "Towards a Feminist Film Practice: Some Theses." *Edinburgh '76 Magazine*, no. 1, 1976.

Kane, John. "Beauties, Beasts and Male Chauvinist Monsters." *Take One*, vol. IV, no. 4, July, 1974.

Kaplan, Abraham. "The Feminist Perspective in Film Studies." *University Film Association Journal*, vol. XXVI, no. 1–2, 1974.

Kaplan, Ann E. "Aspects of British Feminist Film Theory: A Critical Evaluation of Texts by Claire Johnston and Pam Cook." *Jump Cut*, no. 12–13, December, 1976.

Kaplan, Ann E. "The Importance and Ultimate Failure of *Last Tango in Paris*." • *Jump Cut*, no. 4, November–December, 1974.

Kaplan, Ann E. "*Women's Happytime Commune*: New Departures in Women's Films." *Jump Cut*, no. 9, October–December, 1975.

Kay, Karyn. "*The Beguiled*: Gothic Misogyny." *The Velvet Light Trap*, no. 16, Fall, 1976.

Kay, Karyn and Gerald Peary. "Dorothy Arzner's *Dance, Girl Dance*," *The Velvet Light Trap*, no. 10, Fall, 1973.

Kay, Karyn. "Part-Time Work of a Domestic Slave." *Film Quarterly*, vol. XXIV, no. 1, Fall, 1975.

Kay, Karyn. "You Can Get a Man with a Gun: Or the True Story of Annie Oakley." *The Velvet Light Trap*, no. 8, 1973.

Kent, Leticia. "What Makes Susan Make Movies." (Susan Sontag). *The New York Times*, October 11, 1970.

Kinder, Marsha. "*Scenes From a Marriage*." *Film Quarterly*, vol. XXVIII, no. 2, Winter 1974–1975.

Kinder, Marsha. "The Return of the Outlaw Couple." *Film Quarterly*, vol. XXVII, no. 4, Summer, 1974.

Kinder, Marsha and Beverle Houston. "Truffaut's Gorgeous Killers." *Film Quarterly*, vol. XVII, no. 2, Winter, 1973–74.

Klein, Michael. "*Day For Night*: A Truffaut Retrospective on Women and the Rhetoric of Film." *Film Heritage*, vol. IX, no. 3, Spring, 1974.

Klein, Michael. "*The Story of Adele H*." *Jump Cut*, no. 10–11, 1976.

Kleinhans, Chuck. "*Chris and Bernie:* The Virtues of Modesty." *Jump Cut,* no. 8, August–September, 1975.

Kleinhans, Chuck. "Julia Reichert and Jim Klein: 'Our First Priority is Reaching People' " (Interview). *Jump Cut,* no. 5, January–February, 1975.

Kleinhans, Chuck. "*Wanda, Marilyn Times Five:* Seeing Through Cinema Verité." *Jump Cut,* no. 1, May–June 1974.

Klemesrud, Judy. *The New York Times,* February 9, April 7, and October 13, 1974.

Kosinski, Jerzy. "Seven Beauties—A Cartoon Trying to Be a Tragedy." *The New York Times,* March 7, 1976.

Koszarski, Richard. "The Years Have Not Been Kind to Lois Weber." *The Village Voice,* November 10, 1975.

Kuhn, Annette. "Women's Cinema and Feminist Film Criticism." *Screen,* vol. 16, no. 3, Autumn, 1975.

Lennard, Elizabeth and Nicole Lise Bernheim. "European Directors—By the Dozen." *Ms.,* vol. V, no. 7, January, 1977.

Lennon, John and Yoko Ono. "John Lennon Yoko Ono: Our Films." *Filmmakers Newsletter,* vol. VI, no. 8, June, 1973.

Lesage, Julia. "The Human Subject—You, He, or Me? (Or, the Case of the Missing Penis)." *Jump Cut,* no. 4, November–December, 1974. Reprinted with comments in *Screen,* vol. XVI, no. 2, Summer, 1975.

Lesage, Julia, Barbara Halpern Martineau, and Chuck Kleinhans. "Julia Reichert and Jim Klein: New Day's Way" (Interview). *Jump Cut,* no. 9, October–December, 1975.

Lichtenstein, G. "In Liliana Cavani's Love Story, Love Means Always Having to Say Ouch" (Interview). *The New York Times,* October 13, 1974.

Lippard, Lucy R. "Distancing: The Films of Nancy Graves." *Art in America,* vol. LXIII, no. 6, November–December, 1975.

Lippard, Lucy R. "Yvonne Rainer on Feminism and Her Film." *The Feminist Art Journal,* vol. IV, no. 2, Summer, 1975.

Loveland, Kay and Estelle Changas. "Eleanor Perry: One Woman in Film" (Interview). *Film Comment,* vol. VII, no. 1, Spring, 1971.

Lupino, Ida. "Me, Mother Directress." *Action,* vol. II, no. 3, May–June, 1967.

McBride, Joseph and Michael Wilmington. "*Seven Women.*" *Film New York,* vol. VII, August, 1973.

McCormick, Ruth. "*Night Porter:* Fascism *a la mode* or Radical Chic?" *Cinéaste,* vol. VI, no. 4, n.d.

McCormick, Ruth. "Women's Liberation Cinema." *Cinéaste,* vol. 5, no. 2, Spring, 1972.

McGregor, Craig. "Mai is Behind the Camera Now." *The New York Times,* April 30, 1972.

McNally, Judith. "*India Song:* An Interview with Marguerite Duras." *Filmmakers Newsletter,* vol. IX, no. 3, January, 1976.

McNally, Judith. "The Making of Antonia" (Interview). *Filmmakers Newsletter,* vol. VIII, no. 6, April, 1975.

McVay, Douglas. "The Goddesses." *Films and Filming,* vol. II, no. 11, no. 12, August, September, 1965.

McWilliams, Dean. "The Novelist as Filmmaker: Marguerite Duras' *Destroy, She Said.*" *Literature/Film Quarterly,* vol. 3, no. 3, Summer, 1975.

Mapp, Edward. "Black Women in Film: A Mixed Bag." *Black Films and Film-Makers* edited by Lindsay Patterson. New York, Dodd, Mead & Co., 1975.

Martineau, Barbara Halpern. "*The Far Shore:* A Film About Violence. A Peaceful Film About Violence." *Cinema Canada*, no. 27, April, 1976.

Martineau, Barbara H. *"La Femme du Gange:* Or, as the French Say, Who is Marguerite Duras?" *Jump Cut*, no. 5, January–February, 1975.

Martineau, Barbara Halpern. "Women vs. Cannes." *Cinema Canada*, no. 9, August–September, 1973.

"Meeting with Mai Zetterling." *Cahiers du cinéma* (English), no. 6, December, 1966.

Mekas, Jonas. "Movie Journal." *The Village Voice*, February 15, 1973.

Melton, Ruby. "Barbara Loden on *Wanda.*" *The Film Journal*, vol. 1, no. 2, Summer, 1971.

Merritt, Mharlyn. "A Giant Step Sideways From 'Sapphire' to 'Billie'." *The Village Voice*, February 1, 1973.

Michelson, Annette. "Marguerite Duras." *The Village Voice*, June 27, 1974.

Michelson, Annette. "Yvonne Rainer, Part Two: *Lives of Performers.*" *Artforum*, vol. XXII, no. 6, February, 1974.

Modleski, Tania. "Wertmuller's Women: Swept Away By the Usual Destiny." *Jump Cut*, no. 10–11, 1976.

Mulvey, Laura. "Visual Pleasure and Narrative Cinema." *Screen*, vol. XVI, no. 3, Autumn, 1975.

Murphy, Kathleen. "Films & Feminism." *Movietone News*, no. 36, October, 1974.

Myers, John Bernard. "Marie Menken Herself." *Film Culture*, no. 45, Summer, 1967.

Nolan, Jack Edmond. "Ida Lupino." *Film Fan Monthly*, no. 89, November, 1968.

Nolan, Jack Edmond. "Ida Lupino." *Films In Review*, vol. XVI, no. 1, January, 1965.

Olshan, Mike. *Millimeter*, vol. II, February, May, and September, 1974.

Oppenheimer, Joel. "Lina Wertmuller Is a Realist!" *The Village Voice*, September 29, 1975.

Orth, Maureen. "How to Succeed: Fail, Lose, Die." *Newsweek*, vol. LXXXIII, March 4, 1974.

Parker, Francine. "Approaching the Art of Arzner." *Action*, vol. 8, July–August, 1973.

Parker, F. "Discovering Ida Lupino." *Action*, vol. VIII, July–August, 1973.

Peary, Gerald. "Dorothy Arzner." *Cinema* (Los Angeles), no. 34, 1974.

Peary, Gerald and Karyn Kaye. "Dorothy Arzner Interview." *Cinema* (Los Angeles), no. 34, 1974.

Perry, Eleanor. "A Femme Behind the Scenes in Movies by Men." *Variety*, January 9, 1974.

Perry, Eleanor. "Women Still Get a Raw Deal in the Movies." *Vogue*, vol. 162, no. 1, July, 1973.

Petersen, Roberta. "Women and Myths." *Film Library Quarterly*, vol. VII, no. 2, 1974.

Place, Janey and Julianne Burton. "Feminist Film Criticism," *Movie*, no. 22, Spring, 1976.

Putterman, Barry. "Black-oriented Action Films: Wasting Women's Talent." *Audience*, vol. VII, December, 1974.

Putterman, Barry. "One Good Girl in a Deplorable Genre." *Audience*, October, 1973.

Quacinella, Lucy. "How Left is Lina?" *Cinéaste*, vol. VII, no. 3 Fall, 1976.

Ravitiz, Myrna W. and Others. "Confronting the Film Industry: A Dialogue with Women." *Millimeter*, vol. II, September–October, 1974.

Reiniger, Lotte. "*The Adventures of Prince Achmed.*" *The Silent Picture,* no. 8, Autumn, 1970.

Rheusen, Joyce. "Joseph von Sternberg: The Scientist and the Vamp." *Sight and Sound,* vol. 42, no. 1, Winter, 1972–73.

Richards, Jeffrey. "Leni Riefenstahl: The Documentary and Myth." *Visions of Yesterday.* London, Routledge, 1973.

Richardson, Brenda. "Women, Wives, Filmmakers: An Interview with Gunvor Nelson and Dorothy Wiley." *Film Quarterly,* vol. XXV, no. 1, Fall, 1971.

Riley, Brooks. "Lina Wertmüller: The Sophists' Norman Lear." *Film Comment,* vol. XII, no. 2, March–April, 1976.

Rivers, Caryl. "Why Can't Hollywood See That 35 is Beautiful, Too?" *The New York Times,* April 1, 1973.

Rock, Gail. "Sandra Hochman's Poetic Polemic Political Tour." *Ms.,* vol. I, no. 8, February, 1973.

Rosen, Marjorie. columns in *Ms.,* especially June, 1974; December, 1974; February, 1975; April, 1975; June, 1976, and July, 1976.

Rosen, Marjorie. "Is *A Free Woman* the Woman We've Been Waiting For?" *The New York Times,* July 7, 1974.

Rosen, Marjorie. "Isn't it About Time to Bring on The Girls?" *The New York Times,* December 15, 1974.

Rosen, Marjorie. "Movies, Mommies, and the American Dream." *American Film,* vol. I, no. 4, January–February, 1976.

Russell, Michele. "*A Woman Under the Influence.*" *Cinéaste,* vol. VII, no. I, Fall, 1975.

Sarachild, Kathie. "Women's Films—The Artistic is Political." *The Feminist Art Journal,* Winter, 1973.

Sarris, Andrew. "Barbara Loden's Wanda." *The Primal Screen,* New York, Simon and Schuster, 1973.

Schrank, Lee H. "Films for Feminist Conscious-raising." *Media & Methods,* vol. X, December 1973.

Schutzer, Anne and Perry Miller Adato. "*Gertrude Stein: When This You See, Remember Me.*" *Filmmakers Newsletter,* vol. V, no. 5, March, 1972.

Schwartz, Nancy. "Coming of Age: A Masculine Myth?" *The Velvet Light Trap,* no. 6, Fall, 1972.

Shevey, Sandra. "A Critique of Women's Roles in U.S. and European Pies." *Variety,* May 8, 1974.

Silver, Joan and Raphael. "*On Hester Street.*" *American Film,* vol. I, no. 1, October, 1975.

Simon, John. "Wertmüller's *Seven Beauties*—Call It a Masterpiece." *New York,* February 2, 1976.

Sitney, P. Adams. "Maya Deren" in *Visionary Film: The American Avant-Garde,* New York, Oxford University Press, 1974.

"Sketch" (Vera Chytilova). *Film,* vol. LI, Spring, 1968.

Slide, Anthony. "Forgotten Early Women Directors." *Films in Review,* vol. XXV, no. 3, March, 1974.

Slide, Anthony. "Lost and Found: *The Blot.*" *American Film,* vol. I, no. 1, October, 1975.

Slide, Anthony. "Talkies: First Women Directors." *Films In Review,* vol. XXVII, no. 4, April, 1976.

Sloan, Margaret. "Keeping the Black Woman in Her Place." *Ms.,* vol. II, no. 4, January, 1974.

Sobchack, Vivian C. "*The Leech Woman's* Revenge, or a Case of Equal Misrepresentation." *The Journal of Popular Film,* vol. IV, no. 3, 1975.

Sontag, Susan. "Leni Riefenstahl and Fascism." *The New York Review of Books,* February 6, 1975.

Sontag, Susan. "Susan Sontag Tells How it Feels to Make a Movie." *Vogue,* vol. 164, July, 1974.

"Special Report: The Woman Director." *Action,* vol. VIII, no. 4, July–August, 1973.

Sternburg, Janet. "Movies That Remember Mama." *Ms.,* vol. III, no. 9, March, 1975.

Strand, Chick. "Woman As Ethnographic FilmMaker." *Journal of Visual Anthropology,* Spring, 1974.

"Susan Sontag: A Diners' Club Card and the Need to Communicate." *Millimeter,* vol. II, November, 1974.

"Talks on Her Movie: It Only Happens To Others" (Nadine Trintignant). *Show,* vol. II, no. 10, December, 1971.

Teitelbaum, Irving. "Let the Women Speak . . . and Speak . . . and Speak." *Film and Television Technician,* June, 1973.

Tom, Lily. "Swashbuckling Swordswomen." *Ms.,* vol. I, no. 10, April, 1973.

Trecker, Janice Law. "Sex, Marriage and the Movies." *Take One,* vol. III, no. 5, May–June, 1971.

Trémège, Bernard. "L'experience americaine d'Agnès Varda." *Jeune cinéma,* no. 52, February, 1971.

Trojan, Judith. "An Interview with Martha Coolidge," *The Feminist Art Journal,* Summer, 1976.

Trojan, Judith. "Who's Who in Filmmaking: Beginnings . . . Martha Coolidge." *Sightlines,* vol. 6, May–June, 1973.

Turim, Maureen. "Gentlemen Consume Blondes," *Wide Angle,* Spring, 1976.

Ursini, James and Alain Silver. "The Female Vampire." *The Vampire Film.* South Brunswick, A.S. Barnes & Co., 1975.

Van Wert, William. "Love, Anarchy, and the Whole Damned Thing." *Jump Cut,* no. 3, November–December, 1974.

Varda, Agnès. "Notes on Toronto." *Revue du cinéma/Image et son,* no. 283, April, 1974.

Waldman, Diane. "*A Very Curious Girl:* The Eternal Return of Circe." *The Velvet Light Trap,* no. 9, Summer, 1973.

Wallace, Peggy. "The Most Important Factor Was the 'Spirit': Leni Riefenstahl During the Filming of *The Blue Light.*" *Image,* vol. XVII, no. 1, 1974.

Warhol, Andy. "Interview with Anna Karina." *Interview,* vol. IV, March, 1974.

Warren, Madeline and Robert Levine. "Gloria Katz and Willard Huyck: *Graffity* Kids Get Lucky" (Interview). *Film Comment,* vol. II, no. 2, March–April, 1975.

Webb, Teena and Betsy Martens. "*Alice Doesn't Live Here Anymore:* A Hollywood Liberation." *Jump Cut,* no. 7, May–July, 1975.

Weinberg, Gretchen. "Interview with Mary Ellen Bute." *Film Culture,* no. 35, 1964–65.

Weiner, P. "New American Cinema." (Marie Menken). *Film,* no. 58, Spring, 1970.

Weiss, Marion. "Have We Really Come a Long Way, Baby?" *University Film Association Journal,* vol. XXVI, no. 1, 1974.

Wexman, Virginia Wright and Patricia Erens. "Clothes-Wise: Edith Head." *Take One,* vol. V, no. 4, October, 1976.

"Where, Oh Where, Is the Liberated Female?" *Show* (USA), vol. II, no. 6, August, 1971.

Whitehall, Richard. "The Face of the Vampire" and "The Flapper." *Cinema* (Los Angeles), vol. III, no. 3, no. 4, July–August, 1966.

Wikarska, Carol. "The Making of *Attica*" (Interview). *Film-makers Newsletter*, vol. VIII, no. 5, March, 1975.

Willis, Ellen. *"Deep Throat:* Hard to *Swallow."* *Sexuality in the Movies* edited by Thomas R. Atkins. Bloomington, Indiana University Press, 1975.

Wise, Naomi. "The Hawksian Woman." *Take One*, vol. III, no. 6, July–August, 1971, published October, 1972.

Wood, Michael. "Lina Wertmuller: All Mixed Up." *The New York Review of Books*, March 18, 1976.

Yates, John. "Why There Are No Women in the Movies." *The Journal of Popular Film*, vol. IV, no. 3, 1975.

"You Cannot Make the Revolution on Film: An Interview with Linda Wertmuller." *Cinéaste*, vol. VII, no. 2, Spring, 1976.

Yvonne. "The Importance of Cicely Tyson." *Ms.*, vol. III, no. 2, August, 1974.

Acknowledgements

For permission to reprint all works in this volume by each of the following authors, grateful acknowledgement is made to the holders of copyright and publishers named below:

Cook, Pam. "Approaching the Work of Dorothy Arzner." *The Work of Dorothy Arzner: Towards a Feminist Cinema*, edited by Claire Johnston. The British Film Institute, 1975. Pamphlet available upon request. © 1975 British Film Institute.

Cornwell, Regina. "Maya Deren and Germaine Dulac: Activists of the Avant-Garde." *Film Library Quarterly*, Volume 5, Number 1, Winter, 1972. Reprinted by permission of *Film Library Quarterly*, © 1972.

Elley, Derek. "Mai Zetterling: Free Fall." *Films and Filming*, Volume 20, Number 7, April, 1974. © 1974 Derek Elley.

Erens, Patricia. "Towards a Feminist Aesthetic: Reflection-Revolution-Ritual." *Oyez Review*, Volume 9, Number 1, 1975. © 1975 *Oyez Review*.

Haskell, Molly. "Swept Away on a Wave of Sexism." *The Village Voice*, September 29, 1975. © 1975 *The Village Voice*.

Haskell, Molly. "*Madame de*: A Musical Passage." *Favorite Movies: Critics' Choice*, edited by Philip Nobile. Macmillan, 1973. © 1973 Molly Haskell.

Kleinhans, Chuck. "*Two or Three Things I Know About Her*." *Women & Film*, Volume 2, Numbers 3-4, 1974. © 1974 *Women & Film*. Revised especially for this edition.

Kay, Karyn. "*A Very Curious Girl*: The Revenge of Pirate Jenny." *The Velvet Light Trap*, Number 9, Summer, 1973. © 1973 *The Velvet Light Trap*.

Kinder, Marsha. "Reflections on *Jeanne Dielman*." *Film Quarterly*, Volume 30, Number 4, Summer, 1977. ©1977 by The Regents of the University of California. Reprinted from *Film Quarterly*, Vol. 30, No. 4, pp. 2-8 by permission of The Regents.

Johnston, Claire. "Women's Cinema as Counter-Cinema." *Notes on Women's Cinema*, edited by Claire Johnston. *Screen*, Pamphlet 2, Society for Education in Film and Television, 1973. © 1973 Claire Johnston.

Lesage, Julia. "Feminist Film Criticism: Theory and Practice." *Women & Film*, Volume 1, Numbers 5-6, 1974.

© 1974 *Women & Film*. Especially revised for this edition.

Lenne, Gérard, "Le proie et le monstre," *Ecran*, Number 28, August-September, 1974. © 1974 *Ecran*. Translated for this edition by Elayne Donenberg and Thomas Agabiti.

Lacassin, Francis. "Out of Oblivion: Alice Guy Blaché." *Sight and Sound*, Volume 40, Number 3, Summer, 1971. © 1971 The British Film Institute.

Leyda, Jay. *Films Beget Films*, George Allen & Unwin Ltd., 1964. © 1964 George Allen & Unwin Ltd.

Rich, B. Ruby. "Leni Riefenstahl: The Deceptive Myth" is here published for the first time by arrangement with the author. All rights reserved.

Rosen, Marjorie. "Popcorn Venus or How the Movies Have Made Women Smaller Than Life." *Ms.*, April, 1974. © 1974 Marjorie Rosen. Miss Rosen is the author of *Popcorn Venus: Women, Movies and the American Dream*, (Avon Books).

Scholar, Nancy. "Maedchen in Uniform." *Women & Film*, Volume 2, Number 7, Summer, 1975. © 1975 *Women & Film*.

Serceau, Daniel. "Japonaises opprimées." *Ecran*, Number 28, August-September, 1974. © 1974 *Ecran*. Translated for this edition by Leah Maneaty.

Steene, Birgitta. "Bergman's Portrait of Women: Sexism or Subjective Metaphor?" Originally delivered at the annual meeting of The Society for Cinema Studies under the title "Are Bergman's Women Obsolete?" Revised for this edition. Printed by permission of the author. All rights reserved.

Weis, Elisabeth. "Family Portraits: Filmmakers Explore Their Roots." *American Film*, Volume I, Number 2, November, 1975. © 1975 The American Film Institute. Reprinted by permission of *American Film*. Revised especially for this edition.

Fischer, Lucy. "The Image of Woman As Image: The Optical Politics of *Dames*." *Film Quarterly*, Volume 25, Number 1, Fall, 1976. © 1976 by The Regents of the University of California. Reprinted from *Film Quarterly* by permission of The Regents.

Taylor, Anna Marie. "*Lucia*." *Film Quarterly*, Volume 28, Number 2, Winter, 1974-75. © 1974 by The Regents of the University of California. Reprinted from *Film Quarterly*, Vol. 28, No. 2, pp. 53-59, by permission of The Regents.

I wish to thank the following people for providing photographs and stills: Victor Aronovich, Cinemabilia, Martha Coolidge, Mary Corliss and Valorie Hart (The Museum of Modern Art-Film Stills Archive), Henry Guettel (Cinema 5 Ltd), Armelle Maala (l'Ambassade de France), Michie Mitchell (National Film Archives), (Canada-Stills Library), Amalie Rothschild (New Day Films), Anthony Slide (The Academy of Motion Picture Arts and Sciences-Special Projects), and Sally Wrigley (John Springer Associates, Inc.).

A special thanks goes to Luz Campos for her help in the preparation of this manuscript, to Tom Brueggemann for his work on the filmographies and to Stephanie Goldberg. Also, I would like to express my gratitude to Gene Siskel and The Chicago *Tribune* and to The Film Center of The School of the Art Institute who made possible Films By Women/Chicago '74.